Stolen Dreams

Stolen Dreams

The 1955 CANNON STREET ALL-STARS and LITTLE LEAGUE BASEBALL'S CIVIL WAR

CHRIS LAMB

UNIVERSITY OF NEBRASKA PRESS • LINCOLN

The University of Nebraska Press is part of a land-grant
institution with campuses and programs on the past,
present, and future homelands of the Pawnee, Ponca,
Otoe-Missouria, Omaha, Dakota, Lakota, Kaw, Cheyenne,
and Arapaho Peoples, as well as those of the relocated Ho-
Chunk, Sac and Fox, and Iowa Peoples.

Library of Congress Control Number: 2021030586

Set in Minion Pro by Laura Buis.

This book is dedicated to Augustus Holt, 1946–2020
And to the Cannon Street YMCA All-Stars
And to my parents,
Robert Lamb, 1923–2020
Jean Lamb, 1925–2016

It was a long time ago.
I have almost forgotten my dream.
But it was there then,
In front of me,
Bright like a sun—
My dream.
And then the wall rose,
Rose slowly,
Slowly,
Between me and my dream.
Rose until it touched the sky—
The wall.
Shadow.
I am black.
I lie down in the shadow.
No longer the light of my dream before me,
Above me.
Only the thick wall.
Only the shadow.
My hands!
My dark hands!
Break through the wall!
Find my dream!
Help me to shatter this darkness,
To smash this night,
To break this shadow
Into a thousand lights of sun,
Into a thousand whirling dreams
Of sun!

—LANGSTON HUGHES, "As I Grew Older" (1925)

CONTENTS

ACKNOWLEDGMENTS

I met Gus Holt in Charleston, South Carolina, in 2012, when I was teaching journalism at the College of Charleston.

Historian Steve Hoffius, a mutual friend, told me about the 1955 Cannon Street All-Stars and suggested I write their story. I had never heard of the team. Steve introduced me to Gus. Gus and I then met at the college's library. He came to our meeting with several folders full of research. Gus and I probably met a dozen times over the years and he almost always brought research with him.

I received my PhD more than twenty-five years ago, and I've been a college professor longer than that. Gus, who had a high school diploma, was a better researcher than a lot of people with PhDs. He was intrepid—as a researcher and as a man, whether he was challenging bigotry in the East Cooper Recreation Department, organizing reunions for the Cannon Street All-Stars, urging reporters to tell the team's story, reviving Little League Baseball in Charleston, or struggling with the overwhelming health issues of loved ones or the health issues that eventually took his own life.

This is the story of the 1955 Cannon Street All-Stars. But it is really Gus's story, even though he didn't live to see the publication of the book. Gus brought the story back to life and willed it into something that transcended the saga of eleven- and twelve-year-olds being denied the chance to play baseball because of the color of their skin. Gus understood what I finally understood myself: The Cannon Street All-Stars are part of a much larger story of how racial bigotry poisoned the people of Charleston and so many others since the arrival of the first slave ship. People continue to suffer and die every hour of the poison of bigotry because much of white America denies the existence of this virulent virus. This virus is particularly toxic among children because it takes away their dreams, as Langston Hughes wrote about in his poem "Harlem—A Dream Deferred."

I initially told Gus I wasn't interested in writing the book. I was working on other books. I would be leaving Charleston soon to take a job at Indiana University–Purdue University at Indianapolis. There would be so many other things gnawing at my time.

But when I got to Indianapolis, I couldn't get the story out of my head.

Trey Strecker, then the editor of *Nine: A Journal of Baseball History and Culture*, asked me to give the keynote speech at *Nine's* spring-training conference. I talked about the Cannon Street team. I kept getting deeper into the story. I met Mike Lennox, the executive director of Play Ball Indiana, an affiliate of RBI, Reviving Baseball in the Inner Cities, which gives boys and girls the opportunity to participate in baseball and softball. Mike asked me to talk about the Cannon Street All-Stars during a fundraising for the organization.

Whenever my wife, Lesly, son, David, and I went to see my in-laws, Dan and Eleanor Jacobs, in Charleston, I went to the Avery Research Center, which includes archives of the Black experience in Charleston, and to the South Carolina room of the Charleston County Public Library, where I looked at 1955 newspaper articles about the Cannon Street All-Stars. I often met with Gus, who kept asking me questions. If I didn't know the answer or if I answered incorrectly, he would stare at me in disbelief. I finally got to the point when I could answer his questions, and his stare turned to a smile as he said, "You got it."

Gus knew more about the Cannon Street story than anyone else—even though he didn't play for the team. When I first asked him how he became involved with the story, he said, "Through divine inspiration." He ran into racism when he coached a team in a league run by the City of Charleston Recreation Department. As he investigated the history of the recreation department, he learned about the Cannon Street All-Stars and began unearthing the story, buried under forty years of neglect. Gus became an honorable member of the team. He put me in contact with John Rivers, the team's shortstop, who became a successful architect in Georgia. This book could not have been written without John's memories of growing up in Charleston, playing for the Cannon Street Little League, making the All-Star team, and then being denied playing in games because white teams refused to play a Black team, even though the Cannon Street team was every bit as deserving to play in the tournament as any of the white teams. I am grateful to John for sharing his story. John, who now lives in Ecuador, was generous with his time and his photographs.

I would like to acknowledge the people I interviewed: Gus Holt, John Rivers, and other Cannon Street players, including Vermort Brown and Leroy Major. Lamar Holt told me about his older brother Gus. Lee Drago, a friend and a retired history professor at the College of Charleston, shared his knowledge of South Carolina history, including Wade Hampton and the reign of terrorism perpetrated by white supremacist Ben Tillman. I depended on Drago's knowledge of the Avery Normal Institute, which was once one of the best Black schools in the South, in chronicling the story of Robert Morrison. Morrison graduated from Avery Institute and became one of the most important Black people in Charleston during the mid-1900s. Morrison, as president of the Cannon Street YMCA, created the Cannon Street Little League to challenge segregation in Charleston. This act, in the aftermath of *Brown v. Board of Education*, put the Cannon Street YMCA All-Stars in the middle of a collision course between white segregationists in the South Carolina Little League Baseball organization and the national Little League Baseball organization, whose rules prohibited racial discrimination.

Morrison transformed the Y into the safe place where Black kids could escape the bigotry of the streets and schools of Charleston. It became a meeting place for Black adults who had become radicalized after World War II, as Blacks demanded racial equality. I appreciate the insight of Paul Stoney, executive president and CEO of the Greater Charleston YMCA, for sharing his knowledge of Morrison and the past and present of the organization.

I interviewed the incomparable Sam Lacy a quarter century

ago for another book I wrote, *Conspiracy of Silence: Sportswriters and the Long Campaign to Desegregate Baseball*. Lacy was one of a handful of Black sportswriters, including Wendell Smith, who crusaded for the integration of Major League Baseball. He was recognized for his contributions with the J. G. Taylor Spink Award from the Baseball Writers' Association of America. In 1955 Lacy was the most important sportswriter working for a Black newspaper. He understood the Cannon Street team's significance and why it was important to tell their story. He wrote several stories about the team during the summer of 1955 and then mentioned the team again in his autobiography in 1999.

When Morrison registered his Cannon Street All-Stars in a Little League tournament, it put Danny Jones, the popular director of the East Cooper Recreation Department, in the middle of a conflict over racial equality that divided the country. I could not have told Danny Jones's story without three of his children, Charles "Bubba" Jones, Sallie Frenkel, and Tesa Livingston, whom I interviewed in North Charleston, South Carolina. I appreciate the contributions of Lance Van Auken, vice president of Little League Baseball, who is also the author of *Play Ball: The Story of Little League Baseball*. I interviewed Van Auken at the Little League Museum in South Williamsport, Pennsylvania. He shared with me newspaper articles about the 1955 Little League World Series and letters written by Peter McGovern, president of Little League Baseball, which I had not seen, and photographs of the Cannon Street team at the World Series, which are included in this book. Thank you Adam Thompson for tracking down those photos for me.

In addition, I interviewed Ron Menchaca, a former student and award-winning reporter at the *Charleston Post and Courier*, who told me about how the *Post and Courier* transformed itself from a mediocre newspaper that defended segregation into a high-quality newspaper as most of the newspaper industry was struggling and some newspapers had even quit publishing. While I was in Charleston, I also discussed the *Post and Courier* with Brian Hicks, a terrific and prolific reporter and columnist with the newspaper. Hicks has probably written more newspaper articles and columns about Charleston's racially fraught history than anyone else. Hicks's books on Charleston mayor Joe Riley and federal judge J. Waties Waring each tell the story of racially progressive white men who dragged the city of Charleston and the state of South Carolina into the modern era as other white citizens howled in protest. Both books proved valuable in understanding the racial history of Charleston and South Carolina. Jack Bass, another South Carolina historian who has written a biography of U.S. senator Strom Thurmond and a book about the Orangeburg Massacre, also gave me his time and insights. I also would like to acknowledge the work of Gene Sapakoff, the supremely talented sports columnist with the *Post and Courier*, who gave the team national exposure with a piece he wrote for *Sports Illustrated* twenty-five years ago. He has written about the team and its players many times since. I owe a debt of gratitude to the fine research of Ramon Jackson, who wrote his master's thesis on the Cannon Street team, and Milicent Brown and Stephen O'Neill, who wrote dissertations on civil rights in Charleston, South Carolina. Their work was invaluable to understanding Charleston during the mid-1950s.

I thank Ted Haddock, executive director of the Edward E. Haddock Jr. Family Foundation and an accomplished filmmaker, who wrote the screenplay and produced the documentary *A Long Time Coming*, about a Black Little League team from Pensacola, Florida, that played a white team in the Florida state tournament in 1955. The film aired at festivals throughout the country and then appeared on Netflix. Its story is of course similar to the one of the Cannon Street YMCA. White teams refused to play a Black team. The stories of the Cannon Street team and the Pensacola Jaycees have different endings. A white team from Orlando agreed to play the Pensacola team in the state Little League tournament. Ted allowed me to use the script of his documentary so I could include a chapter in the book on the Pensacola team. He also allowed me to use photographs from the film. I thank him for his kindness and generosity.

I would like to acknowledge my appreciation for an Indiana University New Frontier Grant from the Office of the Vice Provost for Research that awarded me funds so I could travel several times to Charleston and to South Williamsport, Pennsylvania. I would like to express my appreciation to Fraya Fox, Jeffrey Wilson, and particularly Eric Hamilton for their contributions in securing the grant and then assuring that I correctly filled out the right forms. I also would like to thank Jonas Bjork, then the chair of the Department of Journalism and Public Relations at Indiana University–Purdue University at Indianapolis, for writing a letter of recommendation for the grant. Patrick Washburn, professor emeritus of journalism at Ohio University, and Steve Hoffius also wrote letters on my behalf. I also would like to thank Paul Ashdown, professor emeritus at the University of Tennessee, who inspired me to become a journalist, and the history professors I had while earning my undergraduate and graduate degrees at the University of Tennessee and Bowling Green State University.

This book would not have turned out as well as it did without Steve Hoffius, who helped me in so many ways. First, he suggested that I write the book and put me in contact with Gus Holt. Secondly, he listened patiently as I expressed my frustrations with the book's progress—and sometimes lack of progress. Thirdly, his knowledge of the history of Charleston and South Carolina was invaluable. Fourthly, he read drafts of parts of the book. Steve is a skilled editor who not only corrected errors but made suggestions on what to add or delete from the manuscript. He also is a good friend and a terrific historian.

I also would like to thank my literary agent Emily Williamson, who also looked at an early draft. This is the second book I've worked on with Emily.

Then there are the contributions of people who probably are unaware of their contributions. I would like to thank my friends who listened patiently as I told them about the progress of the book: Vince Benigni, Jonas Bjork, Marc Bona, John Bruns, Mike Cline, my brother Larry Lamb, Larry Lester, Mark Long, Harold Miller, the late Will Moredock, Randy Norris, Bob White, and David Wiggins. Will Moredock was a good friend who captured the racial tensions in Charleston with his weekly columns in the alternative newspaper the *Charleston City Paper*. He had such wit and integrity. John Bruns read over some of the manuscript and gave me his thoughtful criticism, which I then used to strengthen the book.

In addition, I owe my thanks to Mark Armour, president of the board of directors of the Society of American Baseball Research (SABR) and the author of a number of terrific baseball books. Mark looked at the manuscript and offered insights that served me well as I revised the book into the final form. I also thank Andy Brack, publisher of the *Charleston City Paper*, who helped me find a photo of the removal of the John C. Calhoun statue from downtown Charleston. And thank you Rob Byko for giving me permission to use the photo.

I also want to acknowledge those who replied to my questions and inquiries: Phil Anastasia, Cyrus Buffum, Joseph Tucker Edmonds, Virginia Ellison, Harlan Greene, Ethan Kytle, Georgette Mayo, Belinda Swindler, John Willman, and Amy Woelburn. I organized a panel on book writing at the Association for Journalism and Mass Communications conference in Washington DC in 2018. The panel included Kathy Roberts Forde, a journalism professor at the University of Massachusetts; Joseph Campbell, a communication professor at American University; Andrew Billings, the Ronald Reagan Chair of Broadcasting in the Department of Journalism and Creative Media at the University of Alabama; and Rob Taylor, senior acquisitions editor at the University of Nebraska Press. The insights they expressed during the panel discussion made me a better author. In addition, Luis Ulloa, one of my master's students, wrote his term paper for our class on the Monterrey, Mexico, team that became the first all-minority team to win the Little League World Series in 1957. The team won again in 1958. I refer to the team in the book. I am happy to use Luis's work.

I would like to acknowledge the staffs at archives and research institutions that assisted me in my research. This includes particularly the South Carolina room of the main Charleston County Public Library in Charleston, South Carolina; the South Carolina Historical Society reading room at Addlestone Library on the campus of the College of Charleston; the interlibrary loan department of the University Library at Indiana University–Purdue University at Indianapolis (IUPUI); the Avery Center in Charleston, South Carolina; and the reading room of the National Archives in Washington DC. This book could probably not have been written—or at least it could not have been written the way I wanted to write it—without the website newspapers.com and the electronic archives of the *Charleston News and Courier* and *Charleston Evening Post*, the predecessor of the *Post and Courier*.

I expressed my appreciation to Rob Taylor previously, but I will do so again here. This is the fifth book of mine published by the University of Nebraska Press. Rob has been the editor on the last four: *Conspiracy of Silence: Sportswriters and the Long Campaign to Desegregate Baseball* (2012); *From Jack Johnson to LeBron James: Sports, Media, and the Color Line* (2016); *Sports Journalism: A History of Glory, Fame, and Technology* (2020); and this one. I want to acknowledge the terrific work of Karen H. Brown, who copyedited the manuscript. Others at the press who contributed to the publication of the manuscript include Courtney Ochsner, Joeth Zucco, and Sara Springsteen.

When I began working on this book, my parents, Bob and Jean Lamb, were both living. They each passed away during the time I wrote the book. My mom died in March 2016 and my father in August 2020. My father passed on his love of baseball to me and coached my Little League team one year. I miss both parents and think of them every day. I am fortunate to have a second pair of parents, my in-laws, Dan and Eleanor Jacobs, who have given me their love and kindness since I met them more than twenty years ago. They also contributed to the writing of this book in a way I want to acknowledge here. Whenever I went back to Charleston, I had a spare room in which to sleep, good meals to eat, and their wonderful company after a day of doing research.

Lastly, I could not have written this book without my son, David, and my wife, Lesly. Lesly and I have been married during the publication of all twelve of my books. This book required far more of my time, and this meant less time for the two of us. She demonstrated patience as I worked hour after hour after hour in my upstairs office. She listened as I told her about the joys and pitfalls of the project. She read over drafts of chapters and provided honest feedback that improved what I had written. But more than any of this, she has given me her love, and I love her for that. In addition, I am thankful for my son, David, who has grown from a boy into a college student, who, as Henry David Thoreau instructed, is moving confidently in the direction of his dreams.

Stolen Dreams

"THE TEAM NOBODY WOULD PLAY"

The Cannon Street YMCA All-Stars did not know when they left Charleston, South Carolina, on August 24, 1955, to go to the Little League World Series in Williamsport, Pennsylvania, that they were riding into something that was ripping the country apart and confronting how Americans saw themselves and each other. The civil rights movement, as it became known, brought change in ways that were unprecedented, unpredictable, and often violent. It would not be clear to those eleven- and twelve-year-old African American boys for years, perhaps decades, that they were part of the struggle for civil rights in the United States.

John Rivers, the team's shortstop who became a successful architect, was asked when he was in his seventies to describe the team's significance. "It's part of American history. It's part of the civil rights movement," he said. "If you strip away baseball, it's part of the 1950s movement. It's tied to *Brown v. Board of Education*."[1]

Douglas Abrams said that the story of the Cannon Street All-Star team belongs in the larger story of *Brown v. Board of Education*. But so far, Abrams said, "the story has evidently gone untold in extended stories on the Court's landmark decision."[2] The U.S. Supreme Court's decision in *Brown* shook the foundations of the Deep South like no earthquake could. Southern politicians, newspaper editors, and others understood that their way of life was being threatened and it would collapse if they did not confront any attempt to end segregation. If African American boys were allowed to take the field against white boys in a baseball tournament, the South would turn to dust and blow away like so many other civilizations. The response to the Cannon Street All-Star team reflected the campaign of massive resistance that had developed in Charleston and elsewhere in the South as a result of demands by African Americans for racial equality in the 1940s and 1950s.[3]

This is the story of an African American Little League Baseball team that entered a baseball tournament in the summer of 1955 and all hell broke loose. White Little League teams refused to play the Black team and the boys on that team were denied their dream of playing for a chance of going to the Little League World Series. It is the story of how racial discrimination "scarred the souls of black children," as historian Lee Drago put it. "How much harm did it do to the little kids' souls. It caused them to doubt their self-worth, to diminish their pride. They took on a bad image of themselves. It got in their soul."[4] John Rivers said the pain of that summer never went away. "You carry it with you your whole life," he said. "Some people overcome it. As I get older, I think about this more. You can achieve a lot. But you're still scarred for the rest of your life."[5]

The former All-Stars spent much of their lives trying to forget what happened to them that summer and the rest of their lives telling people why their story must be remembered. William "Buck" Godfrey, a member of the team, called his memoir about the Cannon Street All-Stars "The Team Nobody Would Play."[6] Creighton Hale, who was once chief executive officer of Little League Baseball, described the Cannon Street YMCA All-Stars as "the most significant amateur team in baseball history."[7] Gus Holt, who revived the story long after it had been forgotten, said the story of the team is a twist on an old story. "Man's inhumanity to man has been a constant through history," Holt said. "This is about man's inhumanity to kids."[8]

The story of the Cannon Street YMCA All-Stars is part of the story of racial bigotry in Charleston, South Carolina, where Africans were whipped, lynched, and raped, where their lives were devalued, dehumanized, and forgotten, and how all of this shaped the city and its people, from the arrival of enslaved people to the present. No city in America is more connected to its past. No city is more connected to slavery and no city prospered more because of the exploitation of enslaved people. When Northern politicians called for abolishing the slave economy, South Carolinians met in Charleston and seceded from the United States in 1860. The Civil War began in the Charleston harbor, and African Americans celebrated when Union troops victoriously marched into the city toward the end of the war. Reconstruction brought the promise of racial equality, but such promises proved no more sustainable to the winds and tides than a child's sandcastle on the beaches of Sullivan's Island.

Enslaved people built Charleston's mansions, plantations, churches, and cobblestone streets, and hundreds of years later, the city's economy depends on tourists who come to visit those mansions, plantations, and churches, walk on those cobblestone streets, and go to the Atlantic Ocean and splash in the water where hundreds of thousands of enslaved people were brought to America. "For all its appeal," Ron Stodghill wrote in the *New York Times*, "Charleston also evokes a brutal chapter of American life, a city built on and sustained by slave labor, for nearly two centuries. Beneath the stately façade of this prosperous city is a savage narrative of Jim Crow . . . right through the Civil Rights movement."[9]

White supremacy runs through the history of Charleston. But so, too, does Black resistance. There were slave rebellions and race riots in Charleston. Blacks stood their ground during and after the Civil War. African Americans confronted racial discrimination during and after World War I and World War II and during the civil rights movement, and they continue to do so today in response to unrelenting bigotry and unspeakable tragedies such as the murder of nine African American parishioners at the historic Emanuel African Methodist Episcopal (AME) Church in 2015.

The story of the Cannon Street All-Stars is inextricably linked to postwar Charleston and a white federal judge, J. Waties Waring, who broke with his aristocratic family and decided in one ruling after another that racial discrimination was unconstitutional. Waties's nephew, Thomas, the editor of the *Charleston News and Courier*, became the voice of segregation and white supremacy.

Danny Jones, the director of the parks and recreation department and the state's director of Little League Baseball, found himself torn between the rules of Little League Baseball that prohibited racial discrimination and the laws and customs of South Carolina that prohibited integration, but then sided with the segregationists. Jones's primary antagonist was Robert Morrison, an African American businessman, who had been a racial accommodationist most of his life; but in the last decades of his life he became a race man. It also is the story of Augustus Holt, who brought the story back to life and redeemed the Cannon Street All-Stars nearly forty years later as he struggled with his own personal tragedy.

ROBERT MORRISON, THE PRESIDENT of the Cannon Street YMCA in downtown Charleston, was in his seventies when Little League Baseball approved his application for a league. His tired eyes saw beyond the white lines of a baseball field. He knew there were no Black teams in any of the Little Leagues in Charleston or anywhere else in the state. If youth baseball could be integrated in Charleston, he thought, so could municipal parks, swimming pools, and schools. If there could be equal opportunities for Black kids, there could be equal opportunities for Black adults. Morrison wanted Blacks to have the same opportunities as whites. He intended to use the Cannon Street team and Little League Baseball to further that agenda.

The news of a league for Black boys meant one thing to Morrison but something else to the nine-, ten-, eleven-, and twelve-year-olds who lived on the peninsula, some of whom had been playing baseball with broomsticks and rubber balls that were cut in half. To those boys, it meant wearing uniforms and playing with bats and baseballs on a diamond with bases and chalked basepaths and an outfield fence for home runs and having your family cheer you from the bleachers.

During the early spring of 1954, dozens of boys tried out for one of the league's four teams. When the season ended, the best players from every Little League team were selected for an All-Star team that played against other All-Star teams in district tournaments throughout the state. The winner of the tournament advanced to the state tournament. If you won that tournament you went to one of eight regional tournaments. If you won one of the regionals, you played in the Little League World Series in Williamsport, Pennsylvania. The Cannon Street YMCA league did not have a team in that year's Charleston tournament because first-year leagues were not eligible.

When Morrison registered the Cannon Street All-Stars for the district tournament the following summer, it put Morrison, the All-Stars, and the forces of integration on a collision course with Danny Jones, Thomas Waring, Senator Strom Thurmond, and the state's political establishment. The *Brown* decision prompted Waring and Thurmond to call for massive resistance against any attempt to end segregation. "Segregationists believed that any crack in white solidarity constituted an existential threat to white supremacy," Richard Gergel, a federal judge in Charleston, said.[10]

Jones did not object when Morrison told him he wanted to start a Black Little League because he probably thought its players would stay on their own diamonds and white players would stay on theirs. Jones supported baseball for African American children, but he drew the line at Blacks and whites playing on the same field. Jones had no reason to think that Morrison would register his team in the district tournament. Morrison's "dastardly act," as Jones called it, was an act of belligerence.[11]

All the white teams withdrew from the district tournament. The Cannon Street team won by forfeit and advanced to the state tournament. Jones, who was responsible for organizing the state tournament, petitioned Little League Baseball's president, Peter McGovern, to have a segregated state tournament. McGovern rejected the request because it violated the organization's rules prohibiting racial discrimination. Jones then organized his own tournament. He resigned as state director of Little League Baseball. All the white teams withdrew from the state tournament, leaving only the Cannon Street YMCA team.

Having won the state tournament by forfeit, the Cannon Street team advanced—or at least should have advanced—to the regional tournament in Rome, Georgia. If they won there, they would have played in the Little League World Series. This did not happen. Rome's director disqualified the Cannon Street team because it had advanced by forfeit. Little League Baseball's rules said that a team had to play and win at least one game in each qualifying tournament. Morrison appealed the decision. In his response, McGovern expressed his regret for excluding the Cannon Street team but maintained that the organization had to follow its own rules.

This was the end of the team's season and the end of their dream of playing in the Little League World Series, and, although nobody knew it at the time, the end of Little League Baseball in South Carolina and in much of the South. Having segregated boys' baseball in South Carolina, Jones sought to segregate baseball in the rest of the South. He created the Little Boys League. The league's charter excluded Blacks.[12] The Little Boys eventually changed their name to the Dixie Youth Baseball, which is still being played throughout the South.[13]

Thomas Waring defended Jones's decision to resign from Little League Baseball and the white teams for refusing to play the Cannon Street All-Stars. He said it was not their fault that the tournament had been canceled. It was the fault of northern agitators who were compelled to destroy all that was good and decent in the state. "The Northern do-gooders who have needled the Southern race agitators into action may have to answer for their consequences," Waring wrote. The editorial did not identify the "Northern do-gooders."[14] It did not have to. Waring's readers knew, because he was regularly criticizing the communists and agitators in the North, including the U.S. Supreme Court, who interfered with the rights of southerners to live as they chose.

The U.S. Supreme Court issued its decision in *Brown v. Board of Education* shortly after the Cannon Street Y Little League began its first season. In its unanimous ruling, the court cited the impact that segregation had on children. "Segregation of white and colored children in public schools has a detrimental effect upon the colored children," the court said. "The impact is greater when it has the sanction of the law, for the policy of separating the races is usually interpreted as denoting the inferiority of the negro group. A sense of inferiority affects the motivation of a child to learn. Segregation with the sanction of law, therefore, has a tendency to [retard] the educational and mental development of negro children and to deprive them of some of the benefits they would receive in a racial[ly] integrated school system."[15]

A year later, on May 31, 1955, the court returned to *Brown*, in what became known as *Brown II*, restating the "fundamental principle that racial discrimination in public education is unconstitutional" and "all provisions of federal, state or local law requiring or permitting such discrimination must yield to this principle." The court, however, appeared less willing to tell lower courts and school boards how and when schools must be integrated and what, if anything, would happen if they did not. The court's ambiguous language, "with all deliberate speed," gave southern obstructionists the legal authority to delay integration as long as possible.[16] Strom Thurmond expressed his contempt for the Supreme Court in speech after speech in the U.S. Senate. He called for southern states "to resist integration by any lawful means."[17] Thomas Waring used his newspaper to condemn the *Brown* decisions. Southern tradition and God Almighty had called for Blacks and whites to be separate, and how could nine justices on the Supreme Court rule otherwise?

Douglas Abrams wrote that the court's decisions in *Brown v. Board of Education* and in *Brown II* may have elated those who supported racial equality, but it incensed those who were committed to doing anything, legal or otherwise, to preserve segregation. Abrams said that the image of African American boys sharing the same baseball field with white boys was no less acceptable than Black children attending schools with white children. "The prospect of integrated Little League tournaments struck a raw nerve among white parents enraged by *Brown*'s threat to the existing legal and social order," Abrams said. "Images of black schoolchildren such as the Cannon Street All-Stars playing organized baseball against whites evoked reactions similar to images of black schoolchildren sitting side by side with classmates."[18]

McGovern could have made an exception to the organization's rules and allowed the Cannon Street team to play in Rome. But he did not. Rules were rules. This deprived the boys of the dream of going to Williamsport. The boys were left with an open-ended question that has haunted them the rest of their lives. What if they had played in Rome? "We will never know how far we could've gone," John Bailey, one of the Cannon Street All-Stars, said.[19]

Peter McGovern knew that Little League Baseball had played a part, however unwillingly, in this injustice. He invited the team to be guests of Little League Baseball at the World Series in Williamsport. Robert Morrison accepted. Morrison borrowed a bus from Esau Jenkins, a Charleston civil rights activist who had used it to drive African Americans to register to vote—an act so brazen that it could get a person killed. Morrison's act of taking a busload of ballplayers and coaches through the rural South to Williamsport was brazen enough. Ku Klux Klan membership had been on the increase since the *Brown* decision and with it came a rise in the anxiety of southern African Americans. Fifteen hundred Klansmen and their families attended a speech by E. L. Edwards of Atlanta, the KKK's imperial wizard, in a pasture outside Conway, South Carolina, a hundred miles north of Charleston.[20]

The Cannon Street bus would take the team close enough to Conway that the players and coaches could practically smell a burning cross if they had left a few days earlier. The adults decided to leave at nightfall and drive north through the night to avoid raising suspicion. "They didn't want us traveling through Klan country at night," Rivers said.[21] Many of the boys' parents were worried about the dangers involved in sending their sons hundreds of miles—most of them on country roads that ran through rural towns, where the boys and their coaches would not be allowed to eat in restaurants or use public bathrooms.

The bus broke down outside of Williamsport and the team was towed into town. After breakfast with the other All-Stars the next morning, they went to the stadium to watch the championship game between Morrisville, Pennsylvania, and Delaware Township, New Jersey. The Cannon Street players and coaches were each introduced to the standing-room-only crowd. There was heartfelt applause from the crowd—many of whom had read about the team in newspaper articles. After all the players and coaches were introduced, the Cannon Street players remembered, there was more applause, and then came a voice from the bleachers.

"Let them play!" it said.

Someone else repeated the words.

Others began chanting the words.

The words became louder and louder.

"Let them play!"

"Let them play!"[22]

The response gave the Cannon Street team chills. The players on the team have repeated those words over and over. They say they can still hear them several decades later.

"I remember it as if it were this morning," John Rivers said.[23]

The Cannon Street team and coaches watched the game from their seats. What is it like to get so close to your dream and see someone else living it? "It remains one of baseball's cruelest moments," *Boston Globe* columnist Stan Grossfeld wrote in 2002.[24]

The team got back on Esau Jenkins's repaired school bus on the morning of Sunday August 28, several hours after Emmett Till, not much older than the Cannon Street players, was snatched from his uncle's house in Money, Mississippi, and was tortured, murdered, and dumped into the Tallahatchie River. On December 1, a little more than three months after the Cannon Street boys went to Williamsport on a bus, Rosa Parks was arrested in Montgomery, Alabama, for refusing to give up her seat to a white man on a municipal bus. This began a year-long boycott of Montgomery buses. The U.S. Supreme Court ruled that segregation on public buses was unconstitutional. Martin Luther King Jr., a Baptist minister in Montgomery, emerged as the leader of the American civil rights movement.

The stories of Emmett Till, Rosa Parks, and the Montgomery bus boycott remain defining events of the civil rights movement. The Cannon Street All-Stars faded into history.

The team was a national story for a few weeks and then it disappeared. But the Cannon Street All-Stars never forgot. It remained a source of pain and rejection and sorrow. They returned from Williamsport forever changed. For all they achieved—or did not achieve—in life, the Cannon Street All-Stars remembered the heartbreak of 1955, even as everyone else forgot about them.

This story would have remained buried if it were not for Augustus Holt, who unearthed the story decades after it happened. In 1993 Holt's son Lawrence made the All-Star team in the Dixie Youth Baseball League, which had long since been integrated.[25] When Lawrence put on his uniform, his father glared at the patch of the Confederate flag on the sleeve. Gus's anger turned to curiosity. He investigated how the Confederate flag—the symbol of white supremacy—had ended up on his son's uniform. He learned about the Cannon Street All-Stars and how the Dixie Leagues had been created. "Dixie Youth came out of the resistance of white leaders not wanting their children playing with Blacks," Holt said.[26]

Holt began contacting the former All-Stars, who were then in their fifties. He organized a reunion. He brought Little League Baseball back to Charleston. In 2002 the Cannon Street All-Stars returned to Williamsport to the field where they had not been allowed to play and the disappointment of the day long ago washed over them with their tears. They were finally awarded the state title they had won in 1955. They were then recognized at the Little League World Series. In the coming years, they would return to Little League World Series. They were recognized at a Major League ballpark in Washington DC and annually at a Minor League ballpark in Charleston. There would be stories about them in newspapers and on radio and on television. "There's no sex or violence or murders," John Bailey said. "But [ours] is a great story."[27]

2.

AMERICA'S ORIGINAL SIN

Historian Ira Berlin has described the transatlantic slave trade and slavery as "ground zero" in the saga of race relations in the United States.[1] "Simply put," Berlin said, "American history cannot be understood without slavery. Slavery shaped the American economy, its politics, its culture, and its fundamental principles. For most of American history the society of the mainland colonies and then the United States was one of slaveholders and slaves." Slavery was replaced by Jim Crowism, a different yet equally crippling and suffocating manifestation of bigotry. Civil rights activist W. E. B. Du Bois said that the great problem in America in the twentieth century was that racism—what has been called "America's original sin"—was founded on the institution of slavery.[2]

Charleston, South Carolina, was the capital of the slave trade in the American colonies. Nearly one thousand cargoes of enslaved people entered the port of Charleston between 1670 and when the transatlantic slave trade was abolished in 1808.[3] A few hundred thousand African Americans—or perhaps half of all enslaved people who came to America—came through Charleston harbor.[4] "Any history of slavery in America begins in Charleston," *Charleston Post and Courier* columnist Brian Hicks wrote.[5]

For this reason, Charleston has been called the "Ellis Island for African Americans."[6] Such a designation, however, is inherently perverse. European immigrants came to America by their own free will. African Americans came in shackles and chains. European immigrants came to seek the American dream. African

Americans were someone else's property to do what whatever his or her master ordered. Many of the African Americans who came aground in Charleston remained in the Lowcountry to work on plantations, cultivating rice out of swamps that were full of alligators, snakes, and malaria-carrying mosquitoes. Planters became rich by exploiting the labor of enslaved people, who lived at the mercy of their masters and mistresses, dreading any mistake—or perception of one—because it could result in being deprived of food for lesser offenses to being whipped, beaten, castrated, tortured, burned, raped, or killed for more egregious ones.[7]

Enslaved people were subjected to the urges of their masters. Female slaves—particularly those in their early twenties, in their teens, or younger—who worked inside homes lived in fear of sexual assaults; some young girls were bought with this in mind. Harriet Jacobs, who escaped from slavery in North Carolina, wrote, "If God has bestowed beauty upon a slave woman, it will prove her greatest curse." Jacobs wrote of being raped by her master. "He peopled my young mind with unclean images, such as only a vile monster could think of. I turned from him with disgust and hatred. But he was my master. I was compelled to live under the same roof with him—where I saw a man forty years my senior violating the most sacred commandments of nature."[8]

Things were no better in South Carolina, which earned the distinction of being the most repressive of Southern states. "From my earliest recollections, the name of South Carolina had been little less terrible to me than that of the bottomless pit," a Maryland slave, Charles Ball, said in 1837. "In Maryland, it had always been the practice of masters and mistresses, who wished to terrify their slaves, to threaten to sell them to South Carolina," he said, "where, it was represented, that their condition would be a hundred times worse than it was in Maryland."[9] One South Carolina slave, Thomas Brown, remembered what happened to him after he was returned to his plantation after trying to escape. "I was severely punished by a board cut full of holes to raise the blisters, then I was whipped with a strap to burst the blisters, which were then salted and peppered," Thomas Brown said. "This burned me very badly."[10]

AMERICA'S ORIGINAL SIN

W. E. B. Du Bois traced lynchings and other brutal, racist acts of white authoritarianism in the twentieth century to the plantations of the eighteenth and nineteenth centuries. "The mere fact that a man could be, under the law, the actual master of the mind and body of human beings had to have disastrous effects," Du Bois said. "It tended to inflate the ego of most planters beyond all reason; they became arrogant, strutting, quarrelsome kinglets; they issued commands; they made laws; they shouted their orders; they expected deference, and self-abasement."[11]

Du Bois recognized the dark heart that lay inside Charleston's beautiful exterior. "Here [in Charleston] is a subtle flavor of Old World things, a little hush in the whirl of American doing. Between her guardian rivers and looking across the sea toward Africa sits this little lady (her cheek teasingly tinged to every tantalizing shade of the darker blood) and her shoulder ever toward the street and her little laced and rusty fan beside her cheek, while long verandas of her soul stretch down the backyard into slavery."[12]

CHARLESTON WAS ESTABLISHED IN 1670 as Charles Town, named for King Charles II of England, and quickly expanded in size, wealth, and influence because of the slave trade.

By the mid-1700s enslaved people accounted for more than 70 percent of Charleston's population.[13] Slave-owning whites used force to control their enslaved people. Yet such brutality did not bring slave owners peace because so many enslaved people were brought to America that there were more slaves than whites in and around Charleston. This was a problem of the slave owners' creation. Walter Edgar wrote in his history of South Carolina that the lust for money was more powerful than the fear of rebellious slaves. "Money, of course, was at the root of slavery in South Carolina," Edgar said. "Fear may have been present from time to time, but if whites were so afraid of the black majority, why did they keep importing thousands of Africans? The answer was that greed was a more powerful stimulant than fear."[14]

South Carolina politicians argued that the enslaved people were better off in bondage in America than living free in their own country. But if this was so, why did so many slaves try to escape, knowing that they had long odds of making it to freedom and knowing the severity of the punishment if they were captured? The Charleston Lowcountry was, as one writer observed, a human prison camp, protected by a natural fortress. Any possibility of freedom meant traveling hundreds of miles through swamps, marsh grass, and oppressive heat, filled with dangerous wildlife, while outrunning bounty hunters.[15]

The abundance of so many free and enslaved African Americans created a network of determined souls in and around Charleston, and contributed, in part, to slave rebellions and other acts of resistance. On September 9, 1739, a number of enslaved people met on the Stono River, twenty miles southwest of Charleston, where they broke into a store near Stono Bridge, murdered the owners, stole guns and ammunition, and continued on the main road, killing whites and burning houses and barns. They wanted to get to Florida, then a Spanish colony, where they hoped to find freedom. Word of the rebellious slaves moved faster than they did. A militia overpowered the rebels, killing many of them and then capturing and executing those who survived. Their heads were decapitated and hung on mileposts to remind other African Americans that this fate awaited them if they attempted such treachery.[16]

The Commons House of Assembly, the governmental body in South Carolina, instituted a slave code that put severe restrictions on enslaved people and required them to carry passes from their masters if they traveled outside their plantation. Slaves were prohibited from learning how to read or write or carry an "offensive weapon." The code limited worship services for African Americans to daylight hours and required that the majority of parishioners in any church be white. Walter Edgar called the slave code "one of the most far-reaching pieces of legislation" in the state's history.[17]

Religious persecution against African Americans was not restricted to the South. In 1816 Richard Allen created the Bethel African Methodist Episcopal (AME) Church in Philadelphia in response to racial discrimination he experienced at his church. Allen's successes encouraged other Blacks to create their own churches. African American Methodists in Charleston, facing discrimination of their own, sent two of their leaders, Morris Brown and Henry Drayton, to Philadelphia to become ordained as ministers of the AME Church.[18] Upon Brown's return to Charleston, he created a branch of the AME Church. Thousands of African Americans left white Methodist churches and joined the church on Reid and Hanover Streets in the Hampstead neighborhood.[19]

Denmark Vesey, a charismatic free African American who had been born a slave but had bought his freedom with the winnings of a lottery, joined the church with his wife, Susan. Vesey went to the pulpit exhorting parishioners about freedom by preaching from the Book of Exodus, which describes how Israelites escaped from slavery in Egypt. Vesey quoted Exodus 21:16, which says: "And he that stealeth a man, and selleth him . . . shall surely be put to death."[20]

Whites became suspicious of the church's growing congregation and began monitoring the church and harassing members.[21] In 1818 Richard Allen, while visiting from Philadelphia, delivered a sermon at the church. Police raided the church and arrested 140 parishioners and charged them with violating the slave code. Such raids continued over the next few years.[22] In 1822 Charleston officials closed the local AME church and parishioners began meeting in private homes, including the Vesey's.[23]

Vesey was suspected of planning a rebellion in hopes of duplicating what had happened in the Caribbean thirty years earlier, when enslaved people and freed slaves overthrew the government and created the independent country of Haiti. Vesey and his conspirators reportedly planned a rebellion for July 14, Bastille Day, when they would conduct a violent offensive against whites and escape to Haiti. Vesey and his confidants learned that Charleston officials had heard of the plot and reportedly moved up the date of the insurrection to June 16. James Hamilton, the city's ambitious mayor and the son of a wealthy Charleston planter, ordered a purge of anyone thought connected to the plot.[24]

More than 130 Black men—almost of whom were free—were charged with conspiracy over the next five weeks, and about half of them were convicted and dozens executed with little regard to constitutional safeguards such as the right to a public trial and the right to face your accuser.[25] Vesey was hanged on July 2, vowing his innocence. Having quelled the insurrection, authorities destroyed the Hampstead church and ransacked the homes of its leaders. Morris Brown was imprisoned for several weeks before escaping to Philadelphia. White Charlestonians blamed the rebellion on freed slaves, the African Methodist Episcopal Church, Haiti, and Northern abolitionists. The city of Charleston subsequently outlawed African American churches in response to Nat Turner's slave rebellion in Virginia in 1831. The Hampstead congregation met in secret until after the Civil War.[26]

William Johnson of Charleston, a justice who served on the U.S. Supreme Court, expressed doubt about the existence of a conspiracy. Johnson wrote that the Vesey plot was contrived by whites to quash any thoughts of a rebellion. He said that innocent slaves had been hanged years earlier in the Edgefield District in the western part of South Carolina after hysteria swept through the white community concerning rumors of a plot by enslaved people. Johnson's criticism appalled Charleston whites and he was excoriated in newspapers. Johnson, who left Charleston and never returned, offered a tepid apology. Bernard Powers, professor emeritus of history from the College of Charleston, said that Vesey was indeed trying to do what the Charleston authorities feared. "He was very unusual in that one typically would not have found a free black who had something to lose—a lot to lose—risking what he already had to organize an insurrection among slaves," says Powers. "He was obviously a self-sacrificing man and pledged it all to the freedom of other people."[27]

Johnson was neither the first nor last white Charlestonian to leave the city after daring to question the official line on apartheid. Sisters Sarah and Angelina Grimke were born into a slave-holding family in Charleston but became repulsed by the practice of slavery. They left Charleston and moved north, becoming abolitionists, writing and lecturing about the evils of slavery.[28] They never returned to Charleston, partly by choice and partly because their notoriety had made them so many enemies. Police told the sis-

AMERICA'S ORIGINAL SIN

ters' mother that they would be arrested if ever they returned.[29] A century later, J. Waties Waring, a federal judge, and his wife, Elizabeth, left Charleston after enduring years of intimidation because of their own criticisms of segregation.

CHARLESTONIANS TURNED TO THEIR legislators in Washington DC and in Columbia, the state capital, in the aftermath of the Vesey incident to protect them against further slave insurrections, real or imagined. Authorities asked Secretary of War John C. Calhoun to send federal troops to calm fears of another rebellion. Calhoun, a Charlestonian by marriage, obliged, and an artillery brigade sailed from St. Augustine. In addition, the South Carolina Legislature passed an "Act to Establish a Competent Force to Act as a Municipal Guard for the Protection of the City of Charleston and its vicinity" to construct a federal arsenal in downtown Charleston.[30] In 1842 the state legislature converted the arsenal into the Citadel military academy, and the parade ground on the north side of the Citadel grounds became known as the Citadel Green.[31]

John C. Calhoun was born in 1782 in the Abbeville District in western South Carolina. After Calhoun's father died, John, then fourteen, took over the family's plantation and studied on his own until he left to attend Yale University, where he distinguished himself with his keen mind and intellect. He was chastised, however, by one of his professors for loving sophistry more than principles.[32] Calhoun's love of sophistry would be the one true love of his life. He was elected to the U.S. House of Representatives in 1810 and was then married to the daughter of John E. Colhoun, a U.S. senator from Charleston. John Calhoun left Congress in 1817 to become secretary of war in the James Monroe presidential administration and then served as vice president in the administrations of John Quincy Adams and Andrew Jackson.

While serving as vice president in the late 1820s, Calhoun believed that the South was being weakened by tariffs instituted by the Northern majority in Congress and advanced the theory of nullification, which said that states could ignore federal laws they considered unconstitutional. This put him at odds with President

Andrew Jackson, who reportedly once told him: "John Calhoun, if you secede from my nation, I will secede your head from the rest of your body." Calhoun resigned as vice president in 1832 to become a U.S. senator; he continued to be an influential and divisive figure because of his support for slavery. He defended slavery in a speech in the Senate by saying that "slavery was a positive good" because it improved the lives of slaves and slave owners. "I appeal to facts," he said. "Never before has the black race of Central Africa, from the dawn of history to the present day, attained a condition so civilized and so improved, not only physically, but morally and intellectually."[33]

Calhoun, who was dying of pneumonia, opposed the Compromise of 1850, which allowed slavery in some states and territories but not in others. In his speech, Calhoun endorsed secession because one region of the country should not be subordinate to another. This particular reasoning, one would think, would support the argument that no one group of people should be subordinate to another—and yet this bit of sophistry was lost on or purposely ignored by Calhoun. He died a few weeks after his speech was read in the Senate. A parade following Calhoun's death is believed to be one of the largest in Charleston's history. He was laid to rest in St. Philip's Cemetery in downtown Charleston.[34] Whites celebrated Calhoun's life. Blacks celebrated his death. Boundary Street, one of the main streets in downtown Charleston, was renamed Calhoun Street.[35] A statue of Calhoun was completed in April 1887 on the grounds of the Citadel Green. Calhoun's face looked out over the antebellum mansions and the business district in downtown Charleston and his back was turned to the neighborhoods where Blacks lived. The statue was one of hundreds of memorials constructed in the decades after Reconstruction to celebrate white supremacy.[36]

Calhoun was a fanatic defender of slavery but he was not a fanatic himself—at least to the degree of the so-called fire-eaters he inspired, who were given their name because of their maniacal support for slavery.[37] One of the fire-eaters was Robert Barnwell Rhett, a plantation owner who published the *Charleston Mercury*, a newspaper he used to spread his racist ideologies and to advance his political ambitions.[38] Rhett was elected the state's attorney general and then to Congress before being appointed to finish Calhoun's term in the U.S. Senate. In Rhett's absence, his son, Robert Jr., edited the *Mercury*, which continued to represent the attitudes of his father, who called African Americans "an ignorant, semibarbarous race, urged to madness by the licentious teachings of our northern brethren."[39] The Rhetts and other "fire-eaters" argued that secession was necessary to preserve the Southern economy. If slavery was illegal in the free states that joined the Union, it was only a matter of time before the South was reduced "to the condition of Haiti," said James Henry Hammond, who served prominently in South Carolina politics during the mid-1800s.[40]

Hammond enhanced his social status by marrying into the Wade Hampton family, one of the wealthiest planters and largest slaveholders in the country. Hammond married Catherine Fitzsimmons, who was, Joseph Kelly wrote in *America's Longest Siege*, "so unattractive and awkward that no one but the bride believed he was moved by a genuine passion."[41] With the Hampton political connections, Hammond was elected to the U.S. House of Representatives in the 1830s and then governor. Hammond proclaimed that slavery was not just good for slave owners like himself, it was good for slaves, who were so inferior as a race that they would not exist if left to their own capabilities. Hammond sexually assaulted his female slaves, including a woman, a seamstress, who produced several of his children, and then when one of the daughters—his biological daughter—was old enough, he had his way with her. He then passed on his knowledge of sexual conquest to his son. "In the end," Kelly said, "he did not know which offspring were his children and which were his grandchildren."[42]

Other whites did not care how Hammond treated his slaves. That was his business, and because other slave owners raped their slaves, they could hardly criticize Hammond. What did, however, trouble white society and, in particular, his extended family was that Hammond, who was then governor, also sexually abused his teenage nieces, Wade Hampton II's daughters, one of whom was twelve. Hammond blamed his nieces—none of whom ever married. Hampton and his son, Wade III, the brother of the girls, spread word of the behavior of Hammond, who was then governor, driving him out of politics temporarily but not for good.[43]

Hammond returned to politics in the years preceding the Civil War to become a U.S. senator and one of the state's leading advocates for secession. He warned the North not to interfere with slavery or the Southern economy. The American economy would collapse without cotton and the institution of slavery, he said. "You dare not to make war on cotton," Hammond proclaimed. "No power on the earth dares to make war upon it. Cotton is king." If America and the world depended on the cheap price of cotton, the South could demand that slavery be preserved, Hammond said.[44] Hammond's argument for slavery was no more stable than he was.

ABRAHAM LINCOLN'S ELECTION TO the presidency in 1860 sounded an alarm in the Southern states. There were four million enslaved people in the United States, and four hundred thousand of them—10 percent—lived in South Carolina, where about 60 percent of the population was either free or enslaved African Americans. Most of the largest slave owners in the country lived in and around Charleston.[45] If slavery was abolished, plantation owners stood to lose their source of labor and with it their wealth and privilege.

On December 20, six weeks after the presidential election, 170 South Carolinians met at Institute Hall, 134 Meeting Street, in Charleston and unanimously voted to secede from the Union, making it the first state to do so.[46] Delegates adopted the "Declaration of the Immediate Causes Which Induce and Justify the Secession of South Carolina from the Federal Union." The declaration stated that the reason for secession was the "increasing hostility on the part of the non-slaveholding States to the Institution of Slavery."[47] The *Charleston Mercury* responded to news of secession with an enthusiasm bordering on delirium. "The high, burning, bursting heart alone can realize it," it reported. "A mighty voice of great thoughts and great emotions spoke from the mighty throat of one people as a unit."[48]

Shortly after South Carolina seceded, U.S. Army major Robert Anderson abandoned his vulnerable position at Fort Moultrie on Sullivan's Island and moved to Fort Sumter, an unfinished sea fort in the middle of Charleston harbor, where his troops were better protected from the increasingly hostile rebels. In April 1861, a month after Lincoln's inauguration, Confederate brigadier general P. G. T. Beauregard ordered Anderson to surrender. When Anderson refused, Beauregard instructed his troops to begin shelling Fort Sumter, firing the first shots of the Civil War.

Charleston harbor saw witness to acts of defiance against the Confederacy in the next few years—one involving Robert Smalls, an enslaved man who piloted the CC *Planter*, an armed transport ship, and sailed out of the harbor with a crew of enslaved African Americans and their families. When the *Planter* approached the Union ships, Smalls surrendered the ship and its cargo, including maps of mines in the harbor. Small's heroism helped convince the Lincoln administration to enlist Blacks in the fight against the Confederacy.[49] Lincoln authorized the recruitment of African American troops and this resulted indirectly in another act of defiance in Charleston harbor when the all-Black Fifty-Fourth Massachusetts Infantry Regiment charged the heavily fortified Fort Wagner on July 18, 1863. Nearly half of the regiment was killed, wounded, or captured.[50]

On January 31, 1865, Congress passed the Thirteenth Amendment, formally abolishing slavery. By this time the Civil War was nearly over, and the Confederacy had nearly been defeated. Union troops captured Charleston on February 18. The first Northern soldiers into the city were African American troops singing "the truth goes marching on" from the abolitionist song "John Brown's Body." Whites stayed inside their homes while African Americans ran through the downtown streets with tears flowing to cheer their liberators. On March 29 African Americans took part in a parade that began on the Citadel Green, where a mule-drawn cart carried two women to a mock slave auction. The cart was followed by a slave coffin of sixty men in chains. The coffin was draped in a banner that said, "Slavery is dead."[51]

Lincoln believed that the war should end in Charleston because that is where it began. A rededication ceremony was scheduled for Fort Sumter for April 14, the fourth anniversary of the Union's surrender of the fort. Invitations were sent to abolitionists William Lloyd Garrison, Wendell Phillips, and Henry Ward Beecher. The invitations also included Major Martin R. Delany, the Union's first African American field officer; Lieutenant Robert Smalls, who had commandeered the *Planter*; and Robert Vesey, the son of Denmark Vesey. The *Planter* and other ships entered the harbor for the celebration the next day, passing Sullivan's Island and Morris Island and what remained of Battery Wagner. Fireworks lit the sky. In his speech, Garrison, who had often criticized Lincoln for not acting aggressively enough to end slavery, praised the president, saying that his "brave heart beats for human freedom everywhere." Lincoln was assassinated that evening in Washington DC.[52]

The Union victory meant the end of slavery and of slave codes and other laws that had restricted African Americans from worshiping in their own churches. On September 25 thousands of African Americans observed the laying of the cornerstone for the new AME church on Calhoun Street, between Elizabeth and Meeting Streets. Robert Vesey was the church's architect.[53] Reverend Richard H. "Daddy" Cain became the first pastor of the AME congregations, which included the church he called Emanuel—or "God is with us"—and a nearby church, Morris Brown AME, which was named for Charleston's first AME minister.[54] The church remains at 110 Calhoun Street.

3.

THE CHARLESTON BASEBALL RIOT

On July 26, 1869, the Savannah Base Ball Club played the Carolina Club on the grounds of the Citadel Green, a square in downtown Charleston that was occupied by The Citadel Military Academy.[1] Savannah won the afternoon game, 35–17, before a crowd of about two thousand spectators and the all-Black Washington Cornet Band, which had accompanied the Savannah team. The teams decided to continue their competition with a throwing contest. This required police to move the crowd that had spilled onto the field. When spectators, the majority of whom were African American, didn't move quickly enough, the police became aggressive.[2]

One African American man, Rafe Izzard, who was reported to be drunk, cursed a police officer. Izzard, depending on the account, either struck the officer or the officer struck him. Izzard was arrested. The *Charleston Daily News* reported that Izzard was then detained in a guardhouse with several Irish soldiers who had been arrested for violating regulations. "Rafe had hardly been thrust inside of the prison before the soldiers set upon him and commenced to beat him most unmercifully," the newspaper reported, "and most probably would have killed him had he not been taken out."[3]

Izzard's screams of protest after he was arrested and then dragged to the guardhouse got the attention of other African American spectators. Word quickly spread to the surrounding mixed-race neighborhood of Hampstead. The *Charleston Courier* reported that "three thousand negroes" descended on the Citadel Green.[4] A half dozen soldiers grabbed baseball bats to assist the police in trying to control the crowd. The *Charleston Daily News* reported the African Americans would have overpowered the police and soldiers had it not been the arrival of a squad of armed soldiers with fixed bayonets. The crowd retreated to the corner of Calhoun and Meeting Streets when the group of African Americans began throwing bricks at the soldiers.[5]

The Civil War, which had ended four years earlier, was still fresh in the minds of African Americans in Charleston, many of whom were former slaves. President Abraham Lincoln emancipated slaves in the months preceding the end of the Civil War. But it took the Union victory to end slavery. To African Americans, the Republican Party—the party of Lincoln—was responsible for Reconstruction reforms aimed at creating racial equality. The Democratic Party represented white supremacy. The federal government stationed soldiers in Charleston to preserve the peace as the city transitioned from the Confederacy back into the United States.[6]

The Union victory and the abolition of slavery gave hope for a better day for African Americans, who let it be known they would resist any attempt to take away their freedom. Benjamin Mills, who was arrested in the melee, said, "We are strong enough to rule this city and there is no damn person to put us down! Stand and fight and die here if necessary."[7] Charleston police and federal troops confronted what the *Charleston Courier* called "a mob of infuriated black-skinned hell hounds," who became more infuriated when the Washington band began playing "Dixie" as the police and troops suppressed the riot. African Americans screamed and hissed at the Black musicians for playing the anthem of Confederate pride, called them "damned" Democrats, and then began throwing rocks and bricks when the musicians kept playing. Several musicians were injured and their instruments were damaged. The *Daily News* reported that one of the musicians "seized his trombone by the small end with both hands and swung it around, knocking down several assailants."[8]

The Savannah team went to its hotel, changed into street clothes, and collected their belongings before going to the Vigilant Engine House restaurant on State Street, where the two teams joined politicians and other dignitaries for dinner. Mayor Gilbert Pillsbury expressed regret for the disturbance. He pledged that the Savannah team would receive protection for the rest of their stay in Charleston. Soldiers, with loaded rifles and fixed bayonets, escorted the baseball team and musicians to the wharf, where they boarded a steamer for their return to Savannah.[9]

A number of musicians were among the injured and several men were arrested, including whites and African Americans. The *Courier* praised the quick response of the federal troops and the local police, including African American officers who were hired to keep the peace in the adjacent neighborhoods. The *Courier* said the Black rioters deserved far worse than being injured or arrested. "It was rumored," it said, "that one of the mob was shot, but unfortunately that rumor turned out to be incorrect." The newspaper warned the city it must be prepared or the next time things would be worse. "The result points plainly to one fact. That there is in our city a number of idle, vagabond, lawless negroes, who must be put down," the newspaper said, "and if the mayor of the city, elected partly by them, and the police force, composed of men of their own color, cannot make them behave in a decent, respectable manner, the citizens of the community must prepare themselves to keep the public peace."[10]

Charleston had an urban population of about fifty thousand, split evenly among whites and African Americans. But whites ran the newspapers—as they did in most, if not all, cities—so the press was dominated by a racially biased perspective that skewed news coverage.[11] In the days following the incident, the story became known as "the Charleston race riot." Newspapers throughout the country, including the *New York Times* and the *Baltimore Sun*, reprinted the *Courier*'s account that the riot caused "intense indignation among the whites."[12] The *Nashville (TN) Republican Banner* published the *Courier*'s account with the headline "Three Thousand Infuriated Darkies on the Rampage."[13] Other white newspapers reported the story with headlines such as "Riot in Charleston," "The Base Ball

Riot," and "Another of Those Southern 'Negro Riots,'" which put the fault on African Americans.[14] *Wilkes' Spirit of the Times*, one of the earliest sports publications, had this comment: "The blacks thereupon raised a fight, which, if it did not end in bloodshed, was a disgrace to the city."[15]

Charlestonians, hoping to repair the city's tarnished image, raised $160 to replace the damaged equipment of the Washington band and asked the Savannah team for a rematch. The Savannah team agreed to return to Charleston.[16] The *Charleston Daily News* warned readers that whites must protect the Savannah team and its band against "certain turbulent negroes among us." By contrast, the Reverend Richard H. "Daddy" Cain, minister of the Emanuel AME Church on Calhoun Street, called for peace in his sermon on the day of the game, Sunday, August 16.[17] Two companies of federal troops were joined by the Charleston police force and stood prepared with Winchester rifles and bayonets to maintain order if African Americans tried to interfere with the game. "The negroes generally kept within doors and very few were to be seen on the streets," the *New York Times* reported.[18]

The "Charleston race riot" served as a cautionary tale to a country becoming increasingly wary of Reconstruction reforms that many believed sacrificed social control for racial equality, prompting newspapers and magazines to question the wisdom of racial equality. "When Southern white baseball players were threatened by African American fans, there were no questions about what might have been done to illicit a strong response," Swanson said. "Instead rifles and bayonets appeared in support of white Southern baseball competition." *The Nation* wondered if the Charleston riot would affect Reconstruction: "It was a base ball club; the throng was immense; the riot ensued; and thus, did a little game of ball affect the great game of Reconstruction."[19] Other former abolitionist publications—such as *Harper's Weekly* and the *Atlantic Monthly*—began to question Black Americans' capability to participate equally in the white man's world. "Such expressions doubtless did much to add to the reconciliation of North and South, but they did so at the expense of the Negro," C. Vann Woodward wrote in *The Strange Career of Jim Crow.* "Just as the Negro gained his emancipation and new rights through a falling out between white men, he now stood to lose his rights through the reconciliation of white men."[20]

The *Charleston News and Courier* returned to the story of the baseball riot in May 1887. The article blamed a white soldier for starting the disturbance.[21] When the police and soldiers tried to move the spectators off the field, one of the spectators, presumably Rafe Izzard, said something to a soldier, who then "planted a 'wunner' [*sic*] on the left optic of the sassy n——." Rumors quickly spread that a soldier had killed the man. This, the article said, incited the growing crowd that had gathered on Calhoun, King, and Meeting Streets. Tempers were further intensified by the music of the Washington band. Many of the rioters began screaming at the Washington band and charged at the musicians, who used their instruments to defend themselves. "As unexpected and as violent as was the attack it was gallantly met," the article said, "and as queer a battle ensued as has ever been witnessed."[22]

The story said that a cornet "was smashed into a hundred pieces over the thick skull of burly ruffian armed with a fence rail; the tenor horn was flattened across the forehead of another, and the altos, B-flat cornets and E-flat horns flew in every direction." The writer of the article singled out the heroics of the tuba player, in particular. "But who can describe the wonderful deeds of the tuba?" the writer continued. "Grasping the instrument in both hands, the butt end towards the enemy, the player rushed to the charge, and everything fled before him or was left hors de combat on the field. Wherever the tuba went it mowed down the ranks of the enemy. The band was reinforced by the police and soldiers and order was restored."[23]

THE CHARLESTON RIOT, WHICH served as another example of Black resistance to white might in the long history of what is called the "Holy City," happened as the city was adjusting to the carnage of the war and as baseball was establishing itself as the "national game." Baseball had largely been limited to the north-eastern part of the United States before the Civil War. But the sport spread south and west as soldiers played it during breaks in the fighting. The *Charleston (SC) Mercury* reported that heavy rains had left conditions for Confederate troops near Centreville, Virginia, so soggy they could not play baseball. Confederate soldiers played the game in Union prisoner-of-war camps and people in the South watched games played by Northern troops in Union-controlled areas. Abraham Mills, a future president of the National League, wrote that forty thousand spectators attended a game between two teams of federal soldiers on Christmas 1862 in Northern-controlled Hilton Head, South Carolina.[24] The *Charleston Sunday News* reported that Northern troops brought the game to Charleston when it took the city in early 1865 "and it speedily acclimated itself here."[25]

Albert G. Spalding, a baseball player turned sporting goods magnate turned baseball executive, used hyperbole, whether intended or not, by writing that baseball served as a diversion for soldiers during the war and then united bitter foes and served as a "balm" for a wounded country after the war. "It healed the wounds of war and was balm to stinging memories of sword thrust and saber stroke. It served to fill the enforced leisure hours of countless thousands of men suddenly thrown out of employment," Spalding said. "It calmed the restless spirit of men who, after four years of bitter strife, found themselves all at once in the midst of a monotonous era, with nothing at all to do."[26]

Baseball helped establish a sense of normalcy after the war in Southern cities such as Charleston, Richmond, Atlanta, and New Orleans that had suffered the most damage. "Never had a completer ruin fallen upon any city than fell upon Charleston," one observer said.[27] Charleston newspapers ran accounts of white and African American teams playing baseball on the Citadel Green. The *New York Times* noted that the popularity of the game in the cradle of the Confederacy signaled an easing of regional tensions. "One of the best evidences that the last spark of rebellion's feelings has died out among the people here may be found in the marked revival of sporting tastes," The *Times* reported. "The base ball fever has attacked the rising generation of Charlestonians, and there are nearly a dozen clubs, white and black."[28]

African Americans and whites may have shared in the national mania over baseball in the years after the Civil War, but segregation prevailed when Blacks tried to join white baseball associations or even when they attempted to play white teams in those associations.[29] "While black players gained respect from some members of the ball-playing fraternity," George Kirsch wrote, "racist stereotypes, discrimination and segregation barred them from achieving equality on America's diamonds."[30]

Baseball came to represent a means by which African Americans tried to achieve racial equality. Charles Douglass, the son of abolitionist Frederick Douglass, was one of the first Black soldiers to enlist in the Union Army during the Civil War and served in the esteemed Fifty-Fourth Massachusetts Regiment that fought so gallantly and lost so many men in their attack on Battery Wagner in Charleston harbor in 1863. Douglass then served as one of the first clerks in the Freedmen's Bureau after the war.[31] Douglass organized all-Black teams in Washington DC and challenged white authorities when they were denied public spaces or restricted from joining white baseball associations. Douglass organized the Alert baseball team but had left the team before it played in what was called the first game between a Black team and a "major" white team, the Washington Olympics of the National Association of Base Ball Players, which had denied African American teams. The Olympics won 56–4. The Olympics then accepted a challenge from Douglass's team, the Mutuals. The Olympics won that game, 24–15. Other challenges were rejected.[32]

The Philadelphia Pythians found success playing other African American teams in and around Philadelphia but also in cities such as Baltimore and Washington DC. The Pythians' best player and captain was Octavius Catto, who had been born in Charleston in 1839, but whose father, a Presbyterian minister, had moved his family to Philadelphia, hoping his children would have opportunities that were denied in the Deep South. Catto grew up with an education and with other privileges uncommon among Blacks in

Philadelphia or anywhere else. "Catto's credentials as a 'preacher's kid,'" Swanson wrote, "prepared him for leadership."[33]

The Pythians applied to join the Pennsylvania Association of Base Ball Players, a white professional league, but their application was narrowly rejected in a vote of the league's owners. In challenging segregation, the charismatic Catto won the respect of the African American community. He was hired to reform Black schools in Washington DC. He subsequently returned to Philadelphia and resumed playing for the Pythians while teaching and working as a political organizer, registering African Americans to vote in the Black Fifth Ward. The Fifteenth Amendment had been ratified in 1869, but many whites refused to accept it. White mobs turned to violence to stop African Americans from voting on Election Day in 1871.[34]

When Catto went to vote, he was roughed up by a number of whites but not seriously hurt and proceeded to his polling precinct. When someone yelled angrily at Catto, he turned around and was shot multiple times, dying at the scene. The thirty-year-old was praised as a martyr in the Black newspaper the *New National Era*, published in Washington DC. Another newspaper, the *Washington (DC) Chronicle*, a white newspaper, reported that Catto had been assassinated "because he was one of the fearless champions of his race."[35] The *New National Era* also praised Catto as a martyr. "His death will not have been in vain if it rouses the people of this city and country of a more earnest determination to protect citizens of every class and color in the exercise of a citizen's most sacred right—the right to vote as his conscience directs him."[36]

The white-owned *Philadelphia Sunday Mercury* called Catto a victim of his own politics. "What American," the newspaper said, "could witness the scenes exhibited in parts of our city last Thursday, without feeling disgusted at the attempt to foist political equality between the descendants of Europeans and Africans?" Had Catto and other Blacks stayed in their place, the newspaper said, the violence would not have happened.[37] In 2017 a statue of Catto was unveiled outside city hall in Philadelphia.[38]

FOR A BRIEF TIME after the Civil War, there was reason to believe that baseball—like America—could achieve its promise of equality for all. Baseball became part of America's flirtation with racial equality after the war only to see the promise of "all men are created equal" destroyed by the impulses of nationalism, segregation, and Jim Crowism. Baseball's first professional team, the Cincinnati Red Stockings, played its first game in 1869, and other towns and cities began their own teams and joined leagues and associations. During the 1870s and 1880s, dozens of Blacks played in what was called "organized baseball," including John W. "Bud" Fowler, who has been credited with being the first African American professional ballplayer.[39] Fowler learned the game on the baseball fields of Cooperstown, New York, where, according to myth, Abner Doubleday invented it. African American players in professional baseball were tolerated for a time but were never accepted. Teammates shunned them; spectators vilified them; and opponents brutalized them. Fowler, who played second base, has been credited with the invention of shin guards to protect himself from baserunners digging their metal spikes into his leg. Moses Fleetwood Walker, a catcher, played for Toledo in the American Association, which was briefly considered one of the Major Leagues, but was released after a season of unceasing bigotry. The *Sporting News* expressed sympathy for the circumstances of African American ballplayers. "What fame they may have won has been made in the face of very disheartening circumstance," it said. "Race prejudice exists in professional base ball ranks to a marked degree, and the unfortunate son of Africa who makes his living as a member of a team of white professionals has a rocky road to travel."[40]

In mid-July of 1887, the International League, a top Minor League, decided that there would be more contracts for African American players. So-called gentlemen's agreements like these kept African Americans out of the Major Leagues and the rest of organized baseball for the next six decades. Segregation in baseball coincided with the implementation of segregation in American society.[41] The Fultons, a semiprofessional Black team in Charleston, was organized in the 1870s and joined the all-Black Southern League in 1886. The

News and Courier included a number of articles about the Fultons, which the newspaper called "the much talked about Fultons [with] their showy uniforms, which consisted of dark blue shirts, white belts, light blue pants, red stockings and white caps with a double horizontal red bar." Financial difficulties forced the team to dissolve in July and the collapse of the league soon followed.[42]

The *News and Courier* reported stories about amateur African American teams—though it often emphasized the unruliness associated with them more than it did the talent of the players. The newspapers reported that an African American man was shot and mortally injured during a game between Black teams in Darlington, South Carolina.[43] The newspaper published multiple stories about the rowdiness involved with boys—both Black and white—playing baseball in vacant lots or on city streets. Another story quoted the Charleston police chief who warned boys that they would be arrested if they were caught playing baseball in vacant lots. On May 29 the newspaper reported that police chased after "a very small and very black boy, begrimed with baseball dust and perspiration" for playing baseball on King Street. When police approached him, he ran off and was chased into a milliner's shop, where he was apprehended hiding in a "ladies' sitting room."[44]

On June 3, 1886, the *News and Courier* reported that a judge had decided to make an example of twelve African American boys, between the ages of five and fifteen, who were arrested by undercover police officers and charged with playing ball in the street. The boys' mothers pleaded for mercy and the boys sobbed, promising, as the newspaper reported, "they would never play base ball again." The judge had no mercy. "This was a case in which the claims of justice overbalanced the feelings of mercy," the article said. The judge announced that the boys between the ages of five and nine were to be fined $2 or must serve a sentence of five days in jail; the ten-year-olds were fined $3 and must serve ten days in jail; and all the boys "over 10 years old were sentenced to be hanged." The newspaper expressed little sympathy for the severity of such a sentence. "It's a rather serious matter, being hanged, but baseball playing in the streets has to be stopped, and the only way to stop it, in the opinion of the courts, is to do a little hanging," it said. The story ended with this note of moderation: "As a special mark of mercy the execution of all the malefactors will be postponed until after the close of the regular base ball season in September."[45]

There was no additional story about the incident, which raises the distinct likelihood that while the incident may have been real, the newspaper's reporter was having fun at the boys' expense. If so, this raises serious issues about the reporter's sense of humor. The incident did not bring an end to ballplaying in the street. The newspaper reported at least twenty instances of police arresting white and African American boys for playing baseball on city streets in the late 1880s and early 1890s. The punishments of $2 or $3 or serving ten or fifteen days in jail were comparable to the punishment meted out to adults for simple assault or being drunk and disorderly. The City of Charleston was not opposed to the playing of baseball—as long as it was played on a baseball field or on a sandlot and not on a street. On June 4, 1886, the *News and Courier* reported that "a greatly annoyed citizen" had complained about the noise caused by young African American boys who were playing baseball every afternoon on a vacant lot near Tradd Street. "The owner of the lot has made every effort to abate the nuisance," the newspaper said, "but is informed he will have to build a fence around it as he cannot otherwise interfere with the invaluable right of every boy to play ball whenever he can get a chance."[46]

THE EMERGENCE OF LEGAL segregation coincided with an increasing sense of nationalism in the decades before and after the turn of the century as Americans sought to define the values of Americanism. Those living in the United States with European, particularly Western European, roots were determined to be more American followed by those with light skin from other countries. Those with dark skin were deemed inferior to other Americans and excluded from voting, running for office, attending school, working in certain professions, or living in certain neighborhoods. In doing so, white Americans defined what was or was not uniquely American.

Sportswriter Henry Chadwick questioned whether baseball was a purely American game, as other sportswriters and journalists had claimed for generations, or whether it was, as Chadwick suggested, derived from the British children's game of rounders, which he had played as a boy in England. Albert Spalding disagreed and appointed a commission, headed by National League president Abraham Mills, to investigate the origins of baseball for the sole purpose of validating that the sport was uniquely American.[47] This proved difficult—or even impossible—because baseball was not uniquely American. In 1905 the Mills Commission accepted the opinion of a huckster named Abner Graves, who said he had been present at the creation when his childhood friend Abner Doubleday explained the rules to Graves and other boys in 1839. In 1839 Graves was five years old and Doubleday was twenty and a cadet at West Point Academy. Graves later died in an insane asylum after murdering his wife.[48]

The myth of Doubleday and the creation of baseball intersects in Charleston Harbor with so many other myths. Confederate brigadier general P. G. T. Beauregard ordered the shelling of Fort Sumter, a Union sea fort in Charleston Harbor, on April 12, 1861, that began the Civil War. U.S. Army captain Abner Doubleday, the fort's second in command, fired the first Union shot of the war. He was later promoted to brigadier general. Doubleday died in 1893 not knowing that he had invented baseball. His obituary does not mention his discovery or even the word *baseball*. It did mention his notoriety during the Civil War.[49] For this, Doubleday learned from a newspaper reporter that Charlestonians wanted his head. "Fortunately, I was not there to gratify them," Doubleday responded. A century after the war, the *News and Courier* ran a story that said that Doubleday had taught his troops and perhaps other Charlestonians to play baseball when he was stationed at Fort Moultrie at Sullivan's Island before the Union troops moved to Fort Sumter. "Thus, it is clear," the article said, "that Charleston is the mother city of Southern baseball."[50]

Baseball's creation myth was every bit as illusory, though far less benign than the game's democratic myth, which claimed that everyone was equal on the playing field. Segregation revealed the fraudulence of such a claim. According to the white baseball writers and the baseball establishment, any boy could grow up to be a big leaguer if only he had the requisite ability and character. Sam Lacy, a sportswriter who spent his professional career working for Black newspapers, said that the history of baseball demonstrated that one's character had rarely been a requirement for a white player if he had the ability, but no Black player was accepted in organized baseball, regardless of whether he had the highest ability or character.[51]

The best white professional ballplayers were paid a good salary, traveled by train, stayed in hotels, and played according to a schedule in front of ticket-paying spectators in well-kept ballparks. Newspapers included summaries of games and bestowed hero status on the best players.[52] African Americans had their own brand of ball, disorganized and vaguely professional. They made a fraction of what white players did and received little, if any, recognition. They played wherever they could, whenever they could, and were often prohibited from staying in whites-only hotels or eating in whites-only restaurants. The first generation of African American players, Donn Rogosin wrote in *Invisible Men: Life in the Negro Leagues*, "passed their lives in obscurity, absent from the sports pages of white newspapers, obliterated from American sports history."[53]

Conditions improved marginally for African American players after the creation of the Negro Leagues in 1920. But to survive, as Jules Tygiel wrote in *Baseball's Great Experiment*, "a team had to travel," and because most of the country's Black population lived in the South, the teams had to go there, where segregation and racism were particularly oppressive and accommodations were miserable. Teams sometimes had to play multiple games in different cities, sleeping in buses or in cars or outside ballparks or in infested rooming houses where the players stayed up all night fending off bed bugs.[54]

The best Negro League teams—such as the Kansas City Monarchs, which was fronted by pitcher Satchell Paige—could demand better transportation and accommodations. They often played in front of good crowds in stadiums in towns and cities, but the white owners of the stadiums exploited the players by taking most of the game's receipts.[55] African American teams came to Charleston and began playing at College Park on the western part of the peninsula after it opened in 1940.

John "Buck" O'Neil, who played first base for the Monarchs, remembered coming to Charleston. The team arrived in town before their boarding rooms were available.

"Satchel" Paige, the team's star pitcher, signaled to O'Neil.

"Come with me," Paige said.

Paige and O'Neil drove to where slaves had been auctioned.

The two men stood there, as O'Neil remembered, "maybe ten minutes, not saying a word, just thinking."

"You know what?" Paige asked O'Neil.

"What, Satchel?" O'Neil said.

"Seems like I've been here before," Paige said.

"Me, too," O'Neil said. "I know that my great grandfather could have been there. My great grandmother could have been auctioned off on that block."[56]

4.

THE LOST CAUSE

T he Republican Party triumphantly emerged from the Civil
War; and the Democratic Party, which had clung to states'
rights and slavery, was left, like much of the South, in ruins. Having won a war based, in part, on the issue of racial egalitarianism,
Republicans included African Americans in their Reconstruction
reforms. The U.S. Congress approved the Thirteenth Amendment,
which abolished slavery; the Fourteenth Amendment, which guaranteed Blacks citizenship rights and "equal protection under the
law"; and the Fifteenth Amendment, which said that voting could
not be denied on "race, color or previous condition of servitude."
Congress also established the Freedmen's Bureau, which, among
other things, educated former enslaved persons and other African
Americans.[1] African Americans, who outnumbered whites, won
a majority in the South Carolina Legislature and revised the state
constitution in 1868 to guarantee them the same rights as whites.[2]
What happened in South Carolina was repeated throughout the
Deep South. "There was cause to hope that a new day had dawned
in their country," Douglas Egerton wrote in *The Wars of Reconstruction*, "and that most Americans were finally ready to live up
to the promise that all men were created equal."[3]

But such hopes never materialized. White lawmakers in South
Carolina refused to accept the constitution.[4] Rural whites joined
the newly created Ku Klux Klan and other racist organizations
to resist what they considered the abomination of racial equality.
Klansmen murdered hundreds of African Americans through-

out the South, often leaving their corpses hanging from trees. The Klan was at its most brutal away from cities where federal troops were scarce, such as the Upcountry of South Carolina, the westernmost part of the state. Between November 1870 and September 1871, the Klan in York County "established a level of brutality seldom seen in the United States: eleven black Carolinians were murdered, six hundred whipped, and black schools and churches were burned," Walter Edgar wrote.[5]

WADE HAMPTON III, WHO was born at 54 Hasell Street in Charleston, was a former slave owner and Confederate general who became the leader of "the Lost Cause" movement, which perpetuated the myth that the people of the defeated South did not fight the Civil War to defend slavery but for reasons honorable and just, to defend the southern way.[6] Hampton said that white southerners must "dedicate themselves to the redemption of the South." In 1876 Hampton ran for governor to oust the Republican incumbent Daniel Henry Chamberlain with the support of the so-called Red Shirts, members of gun clubs so named because of their distinctive uniforms. The "Red Shirts" became the paramilitary—or terrorist—wing of the Democratic Party in much of the South, marching in parades during the political campaigns, disrupting Republican rallies, and suppressing African American voters through intimidation and violence. Hampton supported the Red Shirts but discouraged the outright murder of Blacks, pledging what he called "force without violence."[7]

Ben Tillman—or "Pitchfork Ben" Tillman, as he was later known—of the Edgefield District made no attempt to negotiate the difference between intimidation and violence.[8] In July 1876, Tillman and the Red Shirts attacked a federal militia of Blacks in the town of Hamburg in Aiken County. The Hamburg Massacre, as it became known, elevated Tillman's reputation among whites. Six Blacks were killed and dozens injured. None of the perpetrators were brought to justice. Two months later, in nearby Ellenton, a white woman claimed a Black man attacked her. A few days later, hundreds of whites went on a murderous rampage, killing dozens of Blacks.[9]

Tillman and the Red Shirts then intimidated Republican voters at the polls. When one Black Republican, who had been driven off his land several weeks earlier, showed up to vote, he was met by a "whooping and holloing" mob, which included Tillman, who drew pistols and told the man that if he came any closer to the ballot box, he would have to "come through blood."[10] The campaign of terror against African Americans and their white Republican supporters helped Democrats achieve their desired outcome on Election Day. Hampton became governor and the Democrats took control of the legislature. Stephen Budiansky wrote that the promises of Reconstruction were defeated not by democracy but by terrorism in what he called "a well-orchestrated campaign of violence, fraud, and intimidation—thereby putting an end to Reconstruction, erasing the freedman's newly won political rights, and securing conservative home rule to the South for a hundred years."[11] Tillman did not deny he did these things to seize power; in fact, he bragged about how he had. "We have scratched our heads to find out how we could eliminate the last one of them. We stuffed ballot boxes. We shot them. We are not ashamed of it," he said.[12]

Samuel Tilden, the Democratic candidate for president, won the majority of votes in the presidential election, but he did not win enough electoral votes to secure the presidency against his Republican opponent, Rutherford B. Hayes. The electoral votes were disputed in three states—South Carolina, Florida, and Louisiana, all of whom still had federal troops to protect Reconstruction reforms. Hayes won the support of those states by promising he would withdraw the troops if elected. After his inauguration, Hayes ordered troops out of the South, which left African Americans and their white sympathizers at the mercy of mobs, signaling the end of Reconstruction.

Tillman and his Red Shirts were not satisfied by seizing control of the state. They used violence as a means of social control and used lynching, in particular, to control the libidos of Black men who, as another myth went, could not control their carnal desires around white women. Tillman said he would lead a lynch mob against any Black man accused of raping a white woman.[13]

The *News and Courier* said lynching was necessary to protect the virtue of white women.[14] Tillman was elected governor in 1890. Hampton's relative moderation toward African Americans succumbed to Tillmanism.[15] "The triumph of Tillmanism did not satisfy white supremacists; it empowered them," C. Vann Woodward wrote. "Indeed, the more defenseless, disenfranchised, and intimidated the Negro became the more prone he was to ruthless aggression of mobs."[16]

After one term as governor, Tillman was elected to the U.S. Senate but continued to exert his influence in South Carolina, demanding a constitutional convention to replace the 1868 state constitution. The state's legislature revised the constitution in 1895 to deprive African Americans of the rights they had secured during Reconstruction. The constitution disenfranchised African American voters, preventing them from holding office or serving on juries. Legislators created impediments to voting, including poll taxes and literacy tests. The revised constitution allowed only whites to vote in the Democratic primary, which, for the next several decades, remained the only meaningful election in South Carolina because the party remained the only legitimate political party in the state.[17]

A century after Tillman's death, he remains a revered figure in South Carolina—in part because of his contributions to agriculture and the establishment of Clemson University and in part because he returned political power to whites after Reconstruction. A larger-than-life monument of Tillman stands outside the state capitol in Columbia. There is a statue of Tillman at Clemson University and buildings bear his name at Clemson University and at Winthrop University. It did not matter to a lot of whites then—and it apparently does not matter to a lot of whites now—that Tillman was a sociopath who seized the state government by violent means and kept control of the government by murdering and disenfranchising African Americans. "Tillman's true legacy lives on whenever Americans continue to shore up the battered foundations of white supremacy. It lives on whenever dissent is met with violence; wherever white men are the only first-class citizens, wherever 'populism' is reduced to what one contemporary called Tillman's 'gospel of discontent,'" Stephen Kantrowitz wrote in *Ben Tillman and the Reconstruction of White Supremacy*.[18]

Tillman inspired generations of similar-thinking South Carolina politicians. Coleman Blease, who became South Carolina governor in 1911 and later served a term in the U.S. Senate, endorsed lynching as "necessary and good" to protect the virtue of white women.[19] Blease, after watching a lynching, would sometimes celebrate the murder "with a bizarre death dance" one observer noted.[20] Blease's tenure in the Senate overlapped with that of Ellison D. "Cotton Ed" Smith, who was born in the appropriately named town of Lynchburg, South Carolina. Smith served in the U.S. House of Representatives from 1896 to 1900 and then in the U.S. Senate from 1909 to 1944, and who blocked all federal antilynching legislation.

WHEN REPUBLICAN WILLIAM MCKINLEY became president in March 1897, he appointed hundreds of GOP loyalists to federal patronage jobs, including dozens of African Americans such as Frazier B. Baker, a forty-year-old schoolteacher from Florence, South Carolina, as postmaster of nearby Lake City, a hundred or so miles northwest of Charleston. Southern whites opposed the appointment of African American postmasters because white women using the post office were forced to interact with an African American man on an equal basis. Senator Ben Tillman and other South Carolina politicians called on McKinley and Postmaster General James Gray to rescind Baker's appointment. When neither McKinley nor Gray intervened, whites in Lake City tried to intimidate Baker into resigning. They fired gunshots near him as he walked home after work and then burned the post office to the ground. Baker moved the post office into his home.[21]

Shortly after midnight on February 22, 1898, a mob of three hundred whites surrounded Baker's house and set it on fire. As Baker, his wife, and children tried to escape through the door, they were met with gunfire. One bullet mortally injured Baker, who fell back into the house. Baker's wife, Lavinia, who was carrying her infant daughter, was shot in the forearm; the daughter was hit in the head and died instantly. Lavinia and her two other children survived their wounds. Investigators found the charred bodies of Baker and his daughter the next day. More than a hundred bullets were found in what remained of the house.[22]

Local law enforcement officials did not investigate the murders of Baker and his daughter. But the particular savageness of the murders prompted progressives to pressure McKinley to investigate the murder of a postmaster—and his daughter—as a federal crime. The trial took place in April 1899 in the U.S. Circuit Court in Charleston.[23] It was called the first of anyone suspected of lynching since Reconstruction. The *Sumter Watchman and Southron* called the murder of Baker and his daughter "probably the most brutal crime in the history of the state."[24] Two of the suspects testified that the lynch mob had organized with the intent to kill Baker because they could not accept having an African American postmaster. The all-white jury said there was not enough evidence for a conviction and the suspects were exonerated after a hung jury.[25]

The *Charleston News and Courier* blamed postmaster general Gray for the murders. "Authorities in Washington had been notified of their mistake and error in appointing this man, they knew of his incompetency," the newspaper said. "And the people of the whole United States ought to be acquainted with the fact that the postal authorities in Washington are largely responsible for the death of Frazier B. Baker."[26] More than a half century after the murderers of Baker and his daughter were exonerated in a Charleston federal courtroom, history would be made in another Charleston courtroom when a white judge, J. Waties Waring, rejected the constitutionality of segregated schools in *Plessy v. Ferguson* in a minority opinion in *Briggs v. Elliott*.[27]

In 1896, a year after South Carolina revised the state's constitution to segregate the races, the U.S. Supreme Court upheld the constitutionality of segregation on Louisiana train cars by creating the doctrine of "separate but equal" in *Plessy v. Ferguson*, ruling that "legislation is powerless to eradicate racial instincts."[28] States, particularly in the South, passed what C. Vann Woodward called a "mushroom cloud of discriminatory and segregation laws." The *Charleston News and Courier* opposed Jim Crow legislation by saying that Blacks and whites had coexisted since the Civil War without the need to segregate the races. It warned that segregation could result in absurd measures if left in the hands of extremists. The newspaper sarcastically asked if railroad cars could be segregated, why not everything else?[29]

Within a decade, much of the state had become segregated and the *News and Courier* had accepted segregation. Segregation meant that whites lived in one part of a town and African Americans in another. This was not so in Charleston, however, where Blacks and whites lived near or even next to one another. There was, however, rarely an attempt to apply laws equally. Southern cities passed vagrancy laws that restricted African Americans during the day and curfew laws that restricted them during the night. What was not segregated by law was segregated by custom. For instance, an African American woman could push a white baby around Colonial Lake on the Charleston peninsula, but she was prohibited from sitting on any of the benches. Only on the Fourth of July were Blacks allowed on the battery. African Americans were expected to go to the back doors of white homes and to address whites as "Master," "Miss," "Massa," or "Boss" but not "Mr." or "Mrs." And whites, regardless of age, used first names when referring to Blacks. If a courtesy title was necessary, a white would not refer to the Black man or woman as "Mr." or "Mrs." but rather as "uncle, daddy, aunty, or mama." White children were taught never to use the terms "lady" and "gentlemen" when referring to a Black person.[30] Blacks learned not to question Jim Crow laws. "For whites," Walter Edgar said, "a misstep could be socially embarrassing. For Blacks, it could be fatal."

SUCH WAS THE FRAGILITY of African American lives—and particularly those of Black men, when the most routine of circumstances could result in arrest or death. Whenever there was a crime, or the rumor of one, police often arrested the nearest African American person they could find, threw him or her in jail, and justice—or a poor excuse for it—was exacted by an all-white jury and a white judge unless a mob bypassed due process and put a rope around the Black man's or woman's neck. In June 1910, Max Lubelsky, a tailor, was found murdered in his King Street store. Police arrested Daniel Duncan, a twenty-three-year-old African American. He was tried and quickly sentenced to be hanged— even though there were serious questions about his guilt. On the day of the execution, Duncan handed a note to his minister that said, "Tell them I am at rest because I am innocent and the Lord knows that I am today." The gallows malfunctioned. Duncan spent nearly forty minutes swaying at the end of the rope before he was dead.[31] A century after his death, a pardon was sought for Duncan. "I think it will be good for all of us to look back on history and not be ashamed of it, to see a wrong be righted," said the Reverend Clementa Pinckney, pastor at the Mother Emanuel AME Church on Calhoun Street. The state's board of paroles and pardons rejected the request. Duncan was reportedly the last African American executed in South Carolina by hanging after a trial.[32]

About five thousand African Americans were lynched in the United States between 1880 and 1968. None of the recorded lynchings in South Carolina came in Charleston County.[33] But one did not have to go far outside of Charleston to hear about or witness a lynching. Dorchester County, which lies adjacent to Charleston County, reported its first in early December 1902 when a Black man, John Fogle, was suspected of assaulting a white woman near the town of Georges. Three hundred men from the town and nearby towns, using blood hounds from Charleston, caught him. After the woman identified Fogle, he was hanged, his body was "left dangling from the limb of one of the trees of the forest as a silent warning," the *Orangeburg (SC) Times and Democrat* reported. The newspaper article ended with the following warning: "Dorchester County has had its first lynching, but it won't be the last unless the black brutes down there keep their hands off of white women."[34]

A month later, another Black man, General Lee, with the incongruous name of a Confederate icon, was lynched after being suspected of repeatedly knocking on the door of "Mrs. Wimberly," a widow living in Rivesville and then running away. A warrant was sworn out for Lee in nearby Georges and a magistrate put him under arrest. The magistrate's buggy was then surrounded by fifty white men who seized the prisoner. Lee's mutilated body was found tied to a tree. The mob first "sprinkled the body with small shot" and then moved closer and "then advanced to within a few feet and discharged their shotguns into the dying man's face and belly." The newspaper account reported that Mrs. Wimberly said the man who knocked on her door was not General Lee.[35]

THE NATIONAL ASSOCIATION FOR the Advancement of Colored People (the NAACP) was created in 1909 by dozens of whites and several African Americans, including W. E. B. Du Bois, journalist Ida B. Wells-Barnett, and a handful of other African Americans, in response to the violence against—and particularly the lynching of—African Americans.[36] Two of the early members of the NAACP were Archibald Grimke and Francis Grimke, the sons of Henry Grimke who was the brother of abolitionists Sarah and Angelina Grimke.[37]

The NAACP's creation coincided with the beginning of the Great Migration, when millions of African Americans left the South during the first half of the twentieth century to escape segregation, low wages, lynchings, rape, and other violence. It also coincided with the start of World War I.[38] Du Bois encouraged African Americans to enlist in the military in his "closed-ranks" editorial in *The Crisis*. He expressed optimism that if Black soldiers were to fight to "make the world safe for democracy" in Europe, they would be allowed to participate in a democracy in their own country.[39] This did not happen. If African Americans "were determined to secure a larger share of democracy for themselves," John Hope Franklin wrote, "there were many white citizens who were as determined to see that there should be no wholesale distribution of the blessings of liberty."[40] This period saw the second iteration of the Ku Klux Klan. Dozens of African American war veterans were lynched in the South—many in their army uniforms.[41] Race riots erupted in twenty-five or so cities, including Charleston, during the bloody summer—or Red Summer—of 1919 in what Franklin called "the greatest period of interracial strife that nation had ever witnessed."[42]

WHEN THE UNITED STATES entered World War I in April 1917, thousands of rural whites and African Americans migrated to Charleston to find jobs, but only whites were hired. A clothing factory on the Navy Yard advertised six hundred openings for women but refused to hire Blacks. Edwin A. Harleston, head of the Charleston NAACP, contacted Du Bois and Archibald Grimke, who was president of the Washington DC chapter of the NAACP, and protested to the secretary of the navy. The factory hired 250 African Americans in the next six months.[43] The factory protest emboldened African Americans in Charleston, resulting in a dramatic increase in membership in the chapter of the NAACP from twenty-nine members in early 1917 to more than two hundred by the time the war ended in November 1918.[44]

A half century after the baseball riot, downtown Charleston again became the scene of another race riot when African Americans refused to cede their ground to hostile whites. On May 10, 1919, several drunken, white, navy sailors began attacking African American men in downtown Charleston that began after a sidewalk incident at the corner of Beaufain and Archdale Streets when, according to one account, a Black man, Isaiah Doctor, did not give way to two white sailors. Words were exchanged. Doctor reportedly threw rocks at the sailors and the growing crowd of white civilians. The white men then stole rifles, pistols, and boxes of ammunition from an indoor shooting gallery at 310 King Street and returned to seek vengeance on Doctor. Two of the sailors chased Doctor into an open yard and each fired two bullets at him, killing the African American man. The sailors claimed they shot Doctor in self-defense because he had a gun. No gun was found on Doctor. The two white men were arrested.[45]

White men continued their violence against African Americans on King Street. Septima Poinsette Clark, a teacher and NAACP member, remembered seeing sailors jumping on street cars near Citadel Square and "beating every black they could find." African Americans responded with force of their own. "Armed men came running through the streets with knives, hammers, hatchets, guns, razors, and sticks, and wholeheartedly joined the fight," one witness remembered. "On every street in that section [of town], blood was shed. Negroes and white boys who were eager for excitement entered and fought until they were beaten and exhausted."[46]

The riot resulted in the deaths of two Blacks and injuries to twenty-seven others, including several sailors.[47] Fridie's, at 305 King Street, an African American barber shop that was a meeting place for the Black YMCA, was among the Black-owned buildings destroyed.[48] Charleston's mayor, Tristian Hyde, reportedly acted swiftly and asked the U.S. Marines to work with local police to restore order. Hyde met with a delegation of Black community leaders, including Edwin Harleston, who owned a funeral home, and who demanded that the city compensate African Americans who lost property, punish the sailors who were responsible for the violence, and hire Black police officers. The city compensated African American business owners. The sailors who killed Doctor were arrested, found guilty of the crime, and imprisoned. The city of Charleston did not hire its first African American police officer for another thirty years.[49]

In 1919 the NAACP, behind the leadership of Harleston and Septima Clark, called for African Americans to teach in African American schools. The school board agreed. Charleston's white school superintendent, A. B. Rhett, however, objected. He said that the city did not have the racial problems as elsewhere in the state because African American children had white teachers. "I have always been of the opinion that the reason why there has been so little race friction in Charleston," he said, "was that the colored children from a very early age were under the control and influence of white principals and teachers and were taught to look up to and respect white people."[50]

Rhett's words demonstrated yet another enduring myth among Charleston's white establishment: that African Americans depended on their white masters and they would continue to suffer until they accepted that. Membership in the Charleston NAACP increased to more than eight hundred after African Americans won the right to teach in schools. But soon after, membership began to decline amid the perception that it had become an elitist organization that represented light-skinned elites and not the rest of the African American community. African American leaders—like Robert Morrison—became less interested in confronting racial discrimination than in working with the white establishment. By the 1930s, the secretary of the Charleston chapter reported to national NAACP officials that most of the two hundred members were "dilatory, lethargic and noncommittal," interested more in creating relationships with white Charleston than in working to better conditions of their own people.[51]

5.

THE ACCOMMODATIONIST

R obert Morrison was born July 26, 1883, into an established African American family in downtown Charleston. His maternal grandfather was Francis L. Wilkinson, a butcher who was president of the Friendly Moralist Society, a benevolent society of free mixed-race and Black people that had been organized in Charleston in 1838. His paternal grandfather and namesake was a free carpenter. Morrison's parents, Robert and Susan, who lived at 177 Coming Street, put their faith and money in their son by sending him to the nearby Avery Normal Institute, one of the most influential African American schools in the South.[1] This decision shaped the trajectory of Morrison's life.[2]

The Avery Institute was created after the Civil War by the American Missionary Association as part of the federal government's efforts to educate Blacks and poor whites through the Freedmen's Bureaus.[3] White administrators and teachers ran Avery with a strong sense of northern paternalism, instilling in students and their parents a sense of elitism. Educated African Americans saw themselves as superior to uneducated Blacks and light-skinned Blacks saw themselves as superior to darker-skinned Blacks.[4] Intellectuals like E. Franklin Frazier criticized northern missionaries for creating divisions between the Black elite and the Black masses. To Frazier, such schools rejected "the Negro and his traditional culture" to be identified "with the white America which continues to reject them."[5]

African American parents in Charleston rejected such criticism because they understood the significance of an Avery education. Most parents struggled financially to send their children to the school. One graduate remembered how his father "gave him the socks off his feet" so the boy could attend a spelling bee at the school.[6] Morrison's education and light skin put him among Charleston's African American elite and it made him acceptable to Charleston's whites as long as he obeyed the teachings of the missionaries who taught him how to adapt to—and not confront—the way of the world. "His education with the missionaries taught him well. He learned the sense of service, proper English and manners," Edmund Lee Drago said. "He was taught an emphasis on acting a certain way to get the respect of whites."[7]

Morrison and other Avery students were taught to accept the reality of racial discrimination and to do the best they could given their circumstances. This sense of "social uplift" echoed the philosophy of Booker T. Washington, who told African Americans not to challenge segregation or racial discrimination but to improve themselves through hard work, education, and economic independence. "In all things that are purely social we [Black and white] can be as separate as the fingers," Washington said in his Atlanta Compromise of 1895. "Yet one as the hand in all things essential to mutual progress."[8]

Washington ingratiated himself to white America by saying, among other things, that "the men who are lynched are invariably vagrants, men without property or standing." Two years later, when a reporter asked Washington if lynching was moving Blacks toward insurrection, he answered no. "God did not put much combativeness into our race," he said.[9] Washington's philosophy of accommodation made him popular among whites and conservative Blacks, but it was despised by progressive Blacks, including W. E. B. Du Bois. "Mr. Washington represents in Negro thought the old attitude of adjustment and submission," Du Bois said. "[His] program practically accepts the alleged inferiority of the Negro races."[10]

Avery students were taught to accept accommodation but to reject white superiority. The school's teachers taught their students the words of John C. Calhoun, who said, "If I could find a Negro who could master the Greek syntax, I would believe that the Negro has a soul and is capable of receiving an education." Students used Calhoun's contempt for them—and their contempt for him—to motivate them to work to improve their lives. When Kelly Miller, dean of the College of Arts and Sciences at Howard University, delivered the commencement address to the Avery class of 1906, he said he hoped that Calhoun, "buried as he is in Charleston," could "return to see how blacks were being educated at the school."[11]

Charleston's African Americans could not escape Calhoun's presence, whether it was walking on Calhoun Street or seeing his statue on Citadel Green.[12] When the Calhoun Memorial was erected in 1887, it was accompanied by a separate statue of Lady Justice, which many African Americans mistook for Calhoun's wife. "The impression prevails generally among the non-reading colored population that the statue of Justice is that of Mrs. Calhoun," the *News and Courier* reported. African Americans expressed their contempt for the Calhoun statue by vandalizing it. In February 1888, the figure of Justice looked as "if it had been on a spree," one observer noted. A tin kettle had been put in her hand and a cigar hung from her mouth. Another time the face of Justice was painted white. An African American boy was arrested for shooting a white boy with a tiny pistol. The boy told police he had been aiming at the statue of Justice. "I nebber shoot the chile," he said. "I shoot at Mr. Calhoun's wife, and when I hit 'um he sound like gong."[13]

The Calhoun Monument was later replaced and put on an eighty-foot podium to prevent further destruction, "so we couldn't get to him," said Mamie Garvin Fields, who grew up in Charleston and later became a teacher and activist. Fields believed whites gave the Calhoun statue such a prominent spot to make a statement to African Americans. "As you passed by, here was Calhoun looking you in the face and saying, 'N——, you may not be a slave, but I am here to see that you stay in your place,'" Fields said. "White people were talking to us about Jim Crow through that statue."[14]

AVERY GRADUATES BECAME CHARLESTON'S Black elite and their influence extended far beyond Charleston and the state. They became the founders of the Charleston chapter of the NAACP; they secured jobs and fought for higher salaries for African American teachers in the public schools and confronted segregation at the state's colleges; and they were at the front lines in the fight for civil rights in the South. The school's alumni included Edwin Harleston, artist and funeral home director who organized the Charleston branch of the NAACP; journalist John McCray, who edited the state's most vocal African American newspaper and created the Progressive Democratic Party to give Blacks a voice in South Carolina politics; Septima Poinsette Clark, an activist with the NAACP and the Southern Christian Leadership Council who was called "the queen mother of the civil rights movement"; Arthur J. H. Clement Jr., who became the first African American Democrat in South Carolina to run for Congress; John H. Wrighten III, who was denied admission into the segregated College of Charleston, attended the all-Black South Carolina State University as an undergraduate, and then sued the University of South Carolina when he was denied admission into its law school; and J. Arthur Brown, who served as president of the state's NAACP and confronted segregated schools, parks, and golf courses. Brown's daughter, Millicent, was one of the first African American children to integrate schools in Charleston. She later became a college professor.[15]

After graduating from Avery, Morrison attended Fisk University in Nashville, Tennessee, where he worked as a Pullman porter to pay tuition and other expenses. After he graduated from Fisk, he briefly worked for a drying plant for a knitting mill in Nashville before securing a teaching position in Alabama. He then became principal of a school in Florence, South Carolina. He left that job because of the poor salary and conditions in African American schools. He then returned to Charleston after finding a job with the Railway Mail Service, where he worked for more than thirty years.[16]

Morrison was fortunate to have a federal job because this meant he did not have to rely for employment on local whites who could fire him if he said or did anything they considered objectionable. "He could say what he wanted to say," his daughter Constance

Morrison-Thompson said. "No one could threaten to fire him."[17] For much of his life, however, Morrison did little to antagonize the white establishment, remaining a disciple of Booker T. Washington's philosophy that African Americans should accept segregation and find success in their own community by getting an education and working hard. When Morrison and other African American leaders asked the city for something, they did not question "separate but equal." In fact, they did not question anything and were satisfied with whatever they might receive.[18]

The industrious Morrison achieved success rare for an African American. He owned an Esso service station, a drug store, an apartment building, and a number of rental properties.[19] He never forgot what the missionaries told him. With financial success came the expectation that he would contribute to the school that had educated him. Morrison, who had been captain of Fisk University's basketball team, recognized how sports could instill pride in young African American men. He used sports to recruit students to Avery and then to keep them in school. In 1915 he organized a basketball team for boys and, a year later, one for girls. Morrison later established a football team for the school. Benjamin Cox, the school's principal, wrote a letter to the American Missionary Association that said: "Our athletic program has been one of the means of encouraging young men to enter school and of keeping them in school."[20]

The Avery Institute often struggled to pay its expenses, and the American Missionary Association frequently told the school it needed to shoulder more of the financial burden. Morrison, who was president of the school's alumni association, played a significant role in keeping the school open, raising money, and improving Black education in Charleston. "The ensuing crisis revealed how Avery alumni and many other residents perceived the school as a Charleston institution pertinent to upgrading Black education in the Low Country," Lee Drago wrote, while the AMA considered the school as just another school it ran. Morrison continued to raise money for the school until it closed in 1954.[21]

He would later be called upon to save the city's struggling YMCA.

"MR. BOB," AS MORRISON was known, became the unofficial spokesperson for African Americans in and around Charleston.[22] Morrison and others in the Black establishment, such as pharmacist John McFall, did not challenge segregation because they were aware of the consequences of defying white authoritarianism, which included jeopardizing donations from white benefactors.[23] Morrison's conciliatory approach made him acceptable to whites and moderate African Americans but eventually put him in conflict with a younger generation of Blacks, including John Henry McCray, Osceola F. McKaine, Modjeska Monteith Simkins, Septima Clark, Esau Jenkins, and John Wrighten.

McCray was born in Youngstown, Florida, but raised in the all-Black community of Lincolnville, near Charleston. He graduated as class valedictorian from Avery in 1931.[24] He continued his education at Talladega College, graduating with a degree in chemistry, before returning to Charleston in 1935 to work for North Carolina Mutual Life Company while working part time for the *Charleston Messenger*, where his reporting on race won the respect of the African American community.[25] He was selected president of the Charleston chapter of the NAACP. In 1937, however, McCray wrote an ill-advised letter to the *News and Courier* that criticized the aggressive posture of the national organization and expressed his opposition to a federal lynching law because, he said, lynching would fade away on its own. "We are content to wait," McCray said.[26]

NAACP executive director Walter White sharply responded to McCray in his own letter in the *News and Courier*. He said that McCray had embarrassed intelligent Blacks in the South. McCray was ousted as president and his reputation as a civil rights activist was damaged. Louise Purvis Bell, who belonged to the executive committee of the Charleston NAACP, called McCray an "Uncle Tom and a traitor."[27] McCray's letter delighted the *News and Courier's* editor, W. W. Ball, a hardline segregationist who accused the national NAACP of being responsible for the racial unrest in the state because of the organization's criticism of racial bigotry.[28] Morrison, who had been one of the original members of the African American Y, was among the many who dropped out after its reputation had been tarnished as an Uncle Tom organization.[29]

McCray, who lost credibility after the letter, moved to Columbia where he reemerged as one of the South's leading civil rights activists, creating the newspaper, the *Lighthouse and Informer*. His editorials demanded Black political participation for African Americans, racial equity, and social justice. He joined with an increasingly militant NAACP to urge the organization to confront segregation in the courts.[30] In 1944 McCray organized the Progressive Democratic Party to increase voter participation and to pressure the state's Democratic Party to open its primaries to Black voters.[31]

McCray and the *Lighthouse and Informer* became the NAACP's chief propagandist, informing readers of the triumphs of NAACP attorney Thurgood Marshall in a series of court decisions in the 1940s and 1950s that included ending the whites-only primaries and ordering white colleges to either accept African Americans, to allocate money to improve Black colleges and universities, or to provide scholarships for students to attended African American colleges and universities.[32] McCray and the more militant Columbia NAACP stood in sharp contrast to the passive chapter in the more populous Charleston. By 1942 membership in the Charleston NAACP had dwindled to 67, compared with 964 members in Columbia.[33]

Younger African Americans, frustrated with the seeming indifference of the NAACP chapter, took it upon themselves to confront segregation. In 1944 John H. Wrighten applied to the all-white College of Charleston. The NAACP leadership criticized Wrighten. John A. McFall wrote to the college's board of trustees that his chapter was "entirely without knowledge of the movement" and attributed the application to Wrighten's "exaggerated ego." To the NAACP and other African American leaders in Charleston, "racial advancement could only come by working within guidelines established by the white power structure," Stephen O'Neill wrote, "and actions like Wrighten's, which challenged the very system of segregation, could only have a harmful effect on race relations."[34]

Four years later, Wrighten sued the University of South Carolina after being denied admission into its all-white law school. *News and Courier* editor William Watts Ball raged about the lawsuit for weeks in the *News and Courier*. If Wrighten won admission to the law school, the people of South Carolina "would insist upon the closing of the institution to white students [and] withdrawing public support from it."[35] Federal judge J. Waties Waring, applying the *Plessy* standard, ruled that the university had to either integrate its law school for Wrighten and two other African American applicants, close its law school, or build a law school on the campus of the state's African American college, South Carolina State College. The state took the least practical and far and away the costliest of the options—approving the construction of a law school on the campus of South Carolina State College in Orangeburg. The cost was projected to be $700,000 for the first year of the school. Waring called it an "absurdity to start a new law school" when it could simply purchase a few more chairs for the qualified African American applicants at the white law school.[36]

Morrison endorsed a compromise whereby African Americans would drop demands to integrate white colleges and universities if the state designated money for scholarships for South Carolina State University. Morrison told Wrighten that "the time was not right for such a move" because he feared that if there was too much pressure it could jeopardize efforts in the African American community to raise money for the Avery school. Morrison's response infuriated Wrighten and many other Blacks, who saw the actions of Morrison and other traditionalists as acts of bad faith.[37]

Many returning war veterans, who found jobs working at the naval shipyard in north Charleston, began to question why racial discrimination persisted in America after the country had stopped the spread of racism in Europe. Albert Brooks and other war veterans created the Veterans Civic Organization (vco) in 1946, which grew to several hundred members over the next five years. "What were we fighting for?" the veterans asked. The organization raised the expectations of race-conscious men and women. The organization challenged the prohibition that banned African Americans from walking through Hampton Park or using County Hall for events. There was no resistance when the members met one day at the park. They won access to County Hall after challenging the prohibition at a city commission meeting. John McCray and Modjeska Simkins were among the speakers at the first mass meeting at County Hall that drew a crowd of three thousand. The VCO's activism made Morrison uncomfortable. When Morrison and others urged calm, Brooks responded, "You have tried it your way. Now give us a try."[38]

The VCO pressured Charleston city officials in ways that Morrison had not, and in doing so, won the admiration of younger African Americans. The VCO supported John Wrighten III's effort to challenge the College of Charleston to admit African Americans.[39] The VCO also succeeded in enclosing Harmon Field with a ten-foot cinder-block fence and improving the drainage for the segregated athletic field, which was built in 1927 with money donated by a white philanthropist, William Harmon. Harmon wanted African American children to have a healthy space to play sports. The field stood on a former landfill where the waste from the housing projects was dumped.[40] It became the playing field for the Cannon Street YMCA Little League, described by one writer as "an inner-city clay patch located on a landfill overrun by crabgrass and littered with rocks." The African Americans boys were prohibited from playing on the well-kept fields where white boys played.[41] "The VCO helped to raise the expectations of race-conscious men such as Morrison in postwar Charleston," Millicent Brown wrote in her dissertation, "Civil Rights Activism in Charleston." The organization disbanded in 1953 and donated the funds in its treasury to the Cannon Street YMCA. A few of its members, including Lee Bennett and Rufus Dilligard, were active in the Y's Little League.[42]

Brown's dissertation chronicles the renewal of African American activism in postwar Charleston, which was led in part by Septima Clark, who, as a young woman, was involved in the early years of the Charleston chapter of the NAACP in its fight for African American teachers in Black schools. Clark remained an educator and civil rights activist for the next several decades. She was prohibited from teaching in Charleston public schools because of her skin color and instead taught in rural Johns Island. She joined the NAACP and went door-to-door collecting signatures for a petition demanding that African Americans teach in Black schools. She became involved in the NAACP lawsuit *Duvall v. Seignous*, which argued that it was discriminatory to pay white teachers more than African American teachers. She led workshops at the Highlander School in Monteagle, Tennessee, where she taught African Americans voting rights and worked with activists, including Martin Luther King Jr. and Rosa Parks, to discuss strategies for confronting racial discrimination. The South Carolina Legislature passed a law that said teachers could not belong to the NAACP. She refused to resign from the NAACP and was fired from her job and stripped of her pension.[43]

Clark also worked at the Highlander School with Esau Jenkins, who grew up on Johns Island in the 1910s and attended a one-room school with fifty other children, some of whom had to walk an hour or more each way because there were no buses for African American schoolchildren. Jenkins quit school in the fourth grade to help his father on the farm. When Jenkins was old enough, he moved to Charleston where he worked on a fishing boat. He later returned to Johns Island to farm for himself—first cotton and then fruits and vegetables. Upon learning that most of the produce stores were owned by Greeks, he thought he could make more money for his crops if he learned rudimentary Greek. So he did. He made enough money to start a trucking business and then he bought a fruit store and motel in downtown Charleston.[44]

Jenkins bought a bus and began driving workers to their downtown jobs, children to school, and families to downtown Charleston to shop, or to Atlantic Beach. As Jenkins matured into his forties, he began to confront the indisputable inequalities of life for African Americans on Johns Island, where families lived in shacks and suffered from malnutrition and diseases associated with poverty and isolation. They lived lives of squalor with little or no chance of advancement, deprived of an education, decent housing and jobs, and disenfranchised from the political process.[45]

South Carolina law required Black voters to pay a poll tax and pass a test on the Constitution before they could vote. Such restrictions effectively prevented Blacks from voting or serving on juries. Jenkins taught himself the Constitution so he could pass the exam and he began to vote. This small act of defiance transformed Jenkins. "I asked myself the question," he later said, "Am I my brother's keeper? And the answer was, 'You are.' So I decided to myself, since I'm no better than anybody, I don't feel like I'm worse than anybody. So I decided to do everything I can to help people in order to help myself." In 1948 he started the Progressive Club of Johns Island, where Jenkins and Clark developed citizenship schools, promoting adult literacy, and teaching adults the Constitution so they could pass the literacy tests required to vote. Clark urged Jenkins to attend the Highlander School. Through contacts there, Jenkins raised money to open additional citizenship schools in the Charleston Lowcountry, which resulted in the voting registration of perhaps two thousand African Americans.[46]

ROBERT MORRISON CONTINUED TO work with the white Charleston establishment. The *News and Courier* published a story about him as part of what the newspaper called its series of African Americans "who had made a success in business." The article identified Morrison as a retired mail-service employee who owned a gas station at 170 Coming Street, which was in the middle of the Black business district. "It caters largely to Negro customers but several steady white customers attest to a friendly inter-racial situation," the article said. Morrison, it said, worked toward improving schools for African American children and to provide lights for the Harmon Field. "The 65-year-old businessman is certain that one of the great needs of his people is better educational and recreational opportunities," the article said.[47]

In the last decades of his life, Morrison went from being a nonthreatening figure to the white establishment to an adversarial one, evolving from an accommodationist as a young and middle-aged man, when being anything else in the South would have been dangerous, to a race man in the last decades of his life, when being anything else would have been an act of betrayal. Morrison, who was too old to serve in the military, did not come to his activism as did veterans, who recognized that accommodation was a sham and Jim Crowism was a suffocating, brutal, and inhumane relic of slavery that offered African Americans nothing but continued suffocation, brutality, and inhumanity.

Morrison accepted "separate but equal" until he realized that there was no "equal" to "separate but equal." He then separated himself from accommodationism. His activism was something as simple as an aging man who had seen too much, had had enough, and decided to do something about it. Or maybe Morrison decided he had to either jump aboard the freedom train or he would hear the derisive jeers from those aboard while he chased after it. Morrison did not change overnight. But that change transformed him into a race man. In the last decades of his life, Morrison rejected segregation and became an agitator, who took his fight to city hall and the board of education and the pages of the local newspapers. He refused to accept what he had long accepted. Other African American activists would confront Jim Crowism in court. Morrison would do so on a baseball field.

6.

THE BLINDING OF ISAAC WOODARD

S gt. Isaac Woodard, a twenty-six-year-old African American army veteran, boarded a Greyhound bus in Atlanta, Georgia, on the evening of February 12, 1946, to go to Winnsboro, South Carolina, to see his wife, and then the two of them would go to see his parents in New York City. A few hours earlier, Woodard had been honorably discharged at Camp Gordon in Atlanta after serving with distinction in the Pacific Theater, where he worked as a longshoreman in a labor battalion. He was promoted to sergeant, where he earned a battle star for unloading ships under enemy fire in New Guinea. He received a number of other medals during his more than three years in the army.[1]

Woodard sat on the bus with other soldiers who were passing around a bottle of whiskey in celebration of the fact they had survived the war and were finally going home. Woodard had put his life on the line for his country. He had his life ahead of him and if he wanted to have a drink or two of liquor on the bus, he had earned it.[2]

The bus had been on the road for an hour or so when the driver, A. C. Blackwell, stopped at a drugstore, Woodard said.[3]

Woodard walked to the front of the bus and asked if he had time to "take a piss."

"Boy," Blackwell told Woodard, "go back and sit down and keep quiet and don't be talking so loud."

"Damn it," Woodard snapped, responding to being called "boy."

"Talk to me like I talking to you. I am a man just like you," Woodard later testified.[4]

Blackwell then told Woodard he could use the restroom.

"Go ahead," the bus driver snapped, "and get off and hurry back."[5]

Woodard left the bus, went to the restroom, and returned. Nothing else was said between the two men until they got to Batesburg.[6]

Batesburg, which is now called Batesburg-Leesville, sits in parts of Lexington and Saluda Counties, just north of Aiken County, site of the Hamburg and Ellenton Massacres in July 1876. John C. Calhoun, "Pitchfork Ben" Tillman, and Strom Thurmond all came from this part of the state. And so, too, did a brutal, heavy-set sheriff named Lynwood Shull.

When the bus stopped in Batesburg, Blackwell left for several minutes and when he returned, he told Woodard there was someone outside the bus who wanted to talk to him.[7] When Woodard got off the bus, two law enforcement officers, Shull and officer Eliot Long, were waiting. Blackwell told the police officers that Woodard was drunk and had made a disturbance on the bus. Woodard later testified he had said "piss," but it's a matter of dispute whether he was drunk.[8] Other passengers, including a soldier, said that Woodard had been drinking but was not drunk and had not caused a disturbance.[9] White law enforcement officers often accused African Americans of being drunk when there was no other cause to arrest them. If he or she protested, the officer would then have the justification to use force—though a lot of white cops needed little reason to use their blackjack or pistol to subdue African American men and women.

When Woodard tried to respond to Blackwell, one of the police officers—it not clear whom—hit him on the head with a nightstick. Shull then grabbed Woodard by the arm and walked him around a street corner out of the sight of the bus's passengers. Long followed. Shull began asking Woodard questions and became angry when Woodard answered "yes" and not "yes, sir." Shull repeatedly hit Woodard with his nightstick until Woodard grabbed it and did not let go. Officer Long then pulled his gun and aimed it at Woodard.[10]

Shull escorted Woodard to the jail where the sheriff repeatedly hit the former soldier in the face with his nightstick, Woodard later testified.[11] It is not known how many times Shull hit Woodard. Woodard said that Shull repeatedly jabbed Woodard in the eyes with the blunt end of his nightstick, gouging the eyes out of their sockets. Shull admitted striking Woodard but denied using the blunt end of the nightstick on Woodard's eyes.[12]

When Woodard awoke in the morning, he could not see and could not remember anything. Shull told him that he would be okay after he washed his face. He then took Woodard to the courthouse, where a judge repeated Shull's testimony that he had been disorderly the night before. When Woodard protested, "No, sir," the judge replied, "We don't have that kind of stuff down here."[13] After Woodard told the judge that he had been beaten by an officer, Shull said, "He wring my billy out of my hand, and I told him if he did not drop it, I would drop him." Woodard then realized that the officer who had walked him to the courthouse was the one who had blinded him.[14]

The judge charged Woodard with disorderly conduct for drinking in the back of the bus and fined him $50. Woodard had his discharge check from the army for $695 but did not have enough cash in his pocket to pay the fine. The judge sent him back to jail before he was taken to a veterans' hospital in Columbia.[15] Woodard's memory began to recover under the care of doctors and nurses. But his sight did not. Doctors told him his eyes were irreparably damaged. Woodard stayed in the hospital for two months before his sisters took him to New York City, where he lived with his family.[16] His wife stayed in South Carolina and filed for legal separation because Woodard's blindness left him unable to make a living.[17]

THE BEATING OF WOODARD was one of many attacks on African American soldiers in the months preceding and following the end of World War II.

On November 17, 1945, St. Claire Pressley, a war veteran, got off a bus in Johnsonville, South Carolina. Pressley was immediately arrested for a minor disturbance that had occurred before he had arrived in town. As Pressley walked down the street toward the jail, the police officer shot and killed him. In December a police officer in Union Springs, Alabama, overheard Black men discussing racial equality. The police officer then unloaded his pistol, killing two of the men and injuring the third. On February 8 a decorated marine named Timothy Hood was shot five times by a street conductor after taking down a Jim Crow sign in Bessemer, Alabama. The town's white police chief followed the dying Hood as he staggered home and emptied his pistol into the man's head. On February 25 three police officers beat war veteran Kenny Long, his brother, and a cousin outside a filling station near El Campo, Texas. One of the officers, a deputy sheriff, shot the unarmed Long, saying, "Don't you know I hate a goddamn n——."[18]

The first race riot in postwar America began the same day in Columbia, Tennessee, after an African American woman, Gladys Stevenson, went to a department store to complain that her radio had not been repaired. Gladys's son, James, who had recently been discharged from the navy, accompanied his mother. When Mrs. Stephenson told the store's owner, Billy Fleming, that the radio had not been fixed, Fleming slapped her across the face. James Stevenson interceded on his mother's behalf. In the scuffle that followed, James shoved Fleming through the store's plate-glass window. The Stevensons were arrested and taken to jail. The sheriff then smuggled them out of town to avoid a lynching.[19]

Whites in Columbia let it be known they would seek retribution against Mink Slide, the adjacent African American community. Black citizens, including many war veterans, suspecting their lives were in danger, armed themselves. "We fought for freedom overseas," one of the veterans shouted, "and we'll fight for it here." White police officers tried to enter Mink Slide. Shots were exchanged and the police officers were wounded.[20] State police arrived in Columbia early the next day. Law enforcement officers and local townspeople entered homes in Mink Slide and seized whatever weapons they found. They broke into businesses, emptying cash registers, and taking anything of value and destroying everything else. Over the next two or three days, dozens of African Americans were arrested and charged with inciting a riot and attempted murder. No whites were arrested. On February 28 two unarmed suspects were shot to death in the jail.[21]

Charges were dropped against all but two of the suspects. NAACP attorneys Thurgood Marshall, Alexander Looby, and Maurice Weaver represented the defendants. One was convicted, the other exonerated. When the trial ended, Marshall and the other attorneys knew it was not safe for them to remain in Columbia at night and decided to drive to Nashville. Marshall drove the car that included Looby, Weaver, and a white journalist from New York City. Shortly after leaving Columbia, the men were pulled over by three state highway patrol cars. The state troopers arrested Marshall for drunken driving—even though he had had nothing to drink—handcuffed him, and put him in one of the cars and said they were taking him back to Columbia. Looby, Weaver, and the journalist were ordered to continue to Nashville.

They ignored the order and followed the police cars as they turned down a dirt road to a secluded river where a group of white men awaited. Upon seeing Marshall's friends, the police knew that they could not continue with the lynching with such witnesses, including a reporter, who could put them at the scene. Marshall was then taken back to Columbia to face charges of drunken driving. The police officer walked Marshall to the judge's chamber and said, "We got this n—— for drunken driving." The elderly judge demanded that Marshall breathe into his face. Marshall obliged. The judge then turned toward officer and snapped: "This man hasn't had a drink in twenty-four hours. What the hell are you talking about?"

Marshall was free to leave town but clearly worried about what would happen to him once he got back on the same road where he had been pulled over. Local African Americans escorted Marshall and the others out of town, hiding in different cars to escape a second lynching attempt. The experience made an impression with Marshall. "He had a newly found fear of white mobs and violent policemen," his biographer Juan Williams wrote.[22]

ISAAC WOODARD—UNLIKE MANY OTHER African American veterans—survived to tell the story about his assault at the hands of law enforcement officers. By moving to New York City, Woodard could speak directly with people who were sympathetic, including the NAACP, which had influence with white political progressives who were aggressively confronting racial injustices in New York City and in the state of New York. In March 1945, the New York Legislature passed the Ives-Quinn Act, which banned discrimination and created a commission to investigate complaints.[23]

When Walter White, executive secretary of the national NAACP, learned what had happened to Woodard, he wrote Secretary of War Robert Patterson and included a copy of a deposition signed by Woodard, which was widely printed in newspapers.[24] The NAACP asked John McCray, editor of the newspaper *Lighthouse and Informer*, to investigate the Woodard incident. The *Lighthouse and Informer* was the first newspaper to report the assault. Other Black newspapers expressed their anger at the irony of a soldier who had survived three years in the Pacific only to be blinded by another American, "for whom he faced death to preserve the American way of life, liberty, and pursuit of happiness," *New York Age* editor Ludlow Werner wrote.[25] The *Chicago Defender* referred to the incident as an "atrocity" carried out by a "hate-crazed Dixie police officer." The *Amsterdam News* said that Woodard's eyes "were gouged and torn out by the blunt end of a cracker policeman's billy."[26]

White newspapers, including the *New York Times* and *New York Post*, wire services, and radio stations also reported the incident. The *Post* accompanied the story with a photograph of Woodard and his mother.[27] Woodard and his dark sunglasses became the face of police brutality against Black war veterans. Walter White contacted Orson Welles, the writer, director, and star of the movie *Citizen Kane*. Welles wrote a syndicated newspaper column and broadcast a weekly political commentary program on radio. Welles delivered a series of radio commentaries about Woodard in July and August 1946.[28] On July 28 Welles read Woodard's deposition. Welles said he would fight for Woodard because he had fought for his country. "The blind soldier fought for me in this war, the least I can do is fight for him. I have eyes. He hasn't. I have a voice on the radio. He hasn't," Welles said. "I was born a white man, and until a colored man is a full citizen, like me, I haven't the leisure to enjoy the freedom that a colored man risked his life to maintain for me. Until somebody beats me and blinds me I am in his debt."[29]

Woodard's deposition mistakenly said he had been beaten in Aiken. Welles criticized Aiken for its part in the incident and the state of South Carolina for failing to take action against Linwood Shull. The city of Aiken, which had been wrongly charged with being the scene of the crime, demanded an apology from Welles. The city banned Welles's films from any of its theaters and threatened to sue the actor for libel.[30] Aiken did not follow up on the lawsuit—in part, perhaps, because any additional stories might have mentioned a sign on a road at the city limits that said, "N——, don't let the sun go down on you in Aiken County."[31] Welles acknowledged his error in a subsequent commentary and the mistake was corrected in news stories. The Associated Press quoted Shull as saying that Woodard's account of the beating "was a lie from start to finish."[32]

Yet when a reporter asked Shull if he had hit Woodard with his blackjack, he admitted he had. "I hit him across the front of the head," he told the Associated Press. "He attempted to take away the blackjack. I grabbed it away and cracked him across the head."[33] This did not explain how a single blow across the head could have gouged out the sockets in both eyes. An army veteran who had been on the bus with Woodard confirmed the soldier's account. He said he had not come forth sooner in fear of retaliation.[34]

The publicity of the Woodard story brought attention to other incidents of violence against Black war veterans that summer. On July 14 a mob of whites in Monroe, Georgia, shot and killed George Dorsey, a sharecropper who had returned nine months earlier after serving in the Pacific, his pregnant wife, Mae, Dorsey's brother-in-law, Roger Malcom, and his wife Dorothy. Malcom was accused of stabbing a white man. The mob fired sixty rounds into the four victims and cut out the fetus from Mae's stomach. There were no arrests.[35] Walter White said the murders were the result of the Ku Klux Klan's intimidation and the racist rhetoric of southern politicians, including Georgia governor-elect Eugene Talmadge.[36]

On August 8 John C. Jones, a former army corporal who had fought in the Battle of the Bulge, was released from jail in Minden, Louisiana, after being suspected of breaking into the home of a white family. When Jones left the jail, a mob was waiting for him. The mob took Jones several miles deep into the woods, stripped him of his clothes, and beat him to force a confession. When Jones did not confess, he was tortured slowly with a meat cleaver and a blow torch until he died.[37] The *Pittsburgh Courier* called it "the most gruesome lynching of the year."[38] The NAACP appealed to President Truman to do something to address the violence against Black veterans. John Egerton wrote in *Speak Now Against the Day*: "The blinding of Isaac Woodard in South Carolina, the 'race riot' in Columbia, Tennessee, the quadruple lynching in Walton County, Georgia, the torching and dismemberment of John C. Jones in Minden, Louisiana," including other assaults on Black men who had served in the military, made an impression on Truman.[39]

THE NAACP ORGANIZED A benefit concert for Woodard on August 16, 1946, at Lewisohn Stadium at the City College of New York City.[40] Mayor William O'Dwyer read a speech by Welles, who was directing a film in Los Angeles: "Woodard is on the conscience of America. The sin which was committed against him is the sin committed every day against his race, which is the human race. We cannot give him back his eyes. But we can make tough new laws—laws to drive the concentration camps out of our country," the speech said. "If Woodard had to lose his sight to show us that we need those laws, the least we can do for him is to make these laws and make them now and make them stick. If we don't, we're more blind than he."[41]

Other public figures attending the benefit included heavyweight boxing champion Joe Louis, actor and civil rights activist and singer Paul Robeson; and entertainers, including Woody Guthrie,

Cab Calloway, Billie Holiday, and Milton Berle. Guthrie sang "The Blinding of Isaac Woodard," which he adapted from the deposition. Guthrie later recalled singing the song in front of the crowd of more than twenty thousand spectators. "I thought I fought on the islands to get rid of their kind," the song concludes. "But I can see the fight lots plainer now that I am blind."[42] The New York City benefit raised money for Woodard that supported the small monthly pension he received from the Veterans Administration. It also brought attention to the violence against Black veterans. But it did nothing to address Woodard's assault. South Carolina did not prosecute Shull.

On September 19, 1946, Walter White met with Truman in the Oval Office to discuss Woodard. Truman then wrote a letter to Attorney General Tom Clark ordering the U.S. Justice Department to prosecute Woodard's perpetrators if the state of South Carolina would not.[43] On October 2 federal prosecutors indicted Shull because Woodard had been in his army uniform when he was attacked. Federal judge George Bell Timmerman, who would normally have been assigned to the case because it fell within his jurisdiction, recused himself because of a personal relationship with Shull. Timmerman asked J. Waties Waring of Charleston to preside over the case. Waring agreed.[44] U.S. attorney Claud Sapp and Justice Department special counsel Fred S. Rogers were assigned to the case. As the November 5 trial approached, neither attorney "seemed to be familiar with the detailed facts of the case," an NAACP attorney observed.[45] Prosecutors presented a weak case against Shull. Sapp mispronounced Woodard's name in his opening argument and asked few questions during the trial, including how Shull had knocked eyes out of their sockets with one blow to the head. Sapp then ended his summation by telling the jury— many of whom he probably knew—that the prosecution of Shull was just part of his job.[46]

Shull's attorneys, Jefferson Davis Griffith and Jack D. Hall, appealed to the racist instincts of the jury. If Shull was convicted, Hall said, police could no longer protect their wives and children. He then said that if deciding against the federal government "means

South Carolina'll have to secede again, then let's secede." The defense argued that Woodard belonged to "an inferior race that the South has always protected and that the language the soldier used on the bus was proof he was intoxicated. That's not the talk of a sober n—— in South Carolina."[47] The jury quickly exonerated Shull. The courtroom broke into applause after the verdict was read.[48]

Orson Welles revived the Woodard story during a BBC television broadcast on May 7, 1955, where he addressed how power and authority could corrupt good police officers before pivoting to Shull. "That sort of policeman is the exception," Welles said. "That sort of policeman is a criminal."[49] Alfred Duckett, who would later co-write one of Jackie Robinson's autobiographies, condemned the verdict in an editorial in the *New York Age*. "Congratulations to the South Carolina justice which found the hick sheriff not guilty because allegedly Isaac Woodard was drunk and didn't know 'a Negro's place.'"[50]

President Truman may have held little sway over the South Carolina courts. But he was not without influence. Isaac Woodard "made an everlasting impression on Truman," David McCullough said in his biography of the president, "moving him in a way no statistics ever would have." Truman created the President's Committee on Civil Rights—the first national civil rights commission—by executive order in December 1946 to investigate civil rights and make recommendations to guarantee that the civil rights of all Americans were protected.[51]

On June 29, 1947, Truman became the first standing president to address the NAACP, calling civil rights a moral priority in a speech that was broadcast on radio.[52] The speech was inspired in part by the violence against Black soldiers, including Woodard, but also by the lynching a few months earlier of Willie Earle, a twenty-four-year-old Black South Carolinian. Earle was arrested in Pickens, South Carolina, for the attempted murder and robbery of a white cab driver, who subsequently died from the wounds. No evidence connected Earle to the crime. A mob of whites—some of them driving cabs—took Earle from his jail cell and drove him out of town. The white men took turns beating Earle, then stabbed him repeatedly in the stomach, and then shot him numerous times in the head. Strom Thurmond, the state's governor, called for an investigation. Thirty-one men were charged in the Earle lynching. This made it the biggest lynching trial in U.S. history. The defense attorneys said the charges were politically motivated by the Truman administration and that the lynching never would have happened if Blacks knew their place. The trial ended on May 21 with the acquittal of all defendants.[53]

Truman's Committee on Civil Rights released its report, *To Secure These Rights*, on October 29, 1947, which documented examples of civil rights violations and urged the federal government to take a more aggressive position in protecting the civil rights of those whose constitutional rights were being violated. The recommendations included the creation of antilynching legislation, anti–poll tax legislation, fair employment practices legislation, and the desegregation of the armed forces. He submitted civil rights legislation to Congress on February 2, 1948, which incorporated many of the commission's recommendations. "If we wish to resolve hope to those who have already lost their civil liberties, if we wish to fulfill the promise that is ours, we must correct the remaining imperfections in our practice of democracy," Truman said. "We know the way. We need only the will."[54]

On July 26, 1948, Truman further angered southern conservatives by issuing Executive Orders 9980 and 9981 that ordered the desegregation of the armed forces and the federal government. When the Democratic Party adapted a civil rights plank in its platform during the 1948 presidential campaign, the Deep South saw this as yet another affront to its sovereignty. Delegates from South Carolina, Mississippi, and Alabama, nominated Strom Thurmond and Mississippi governor Fielding Wright as the presidential and vice presidential candidates of the States' Rights Democrats, or Dixiecrats. "I want to tell you," Thurmond said in his acceptance speech, "there's not enough troops in the army to force the southern people to break down segregation and admit the Negro race into our theaters, into our swimming pools, into our homes, and into our churches."[55]

Truman won the election.

Woodard faded into obscurity, dying at the age of seventy-three, in the Veterans Administration Hospital in the Bronx on September 23, 1992. He was buried at the Calverton National Cemetery in Calverton, New York.[56] Lynwood Shull died in Batesburg on December 27, 1997, at the age of ninety-two and was remembered "as a kindly and faithful elderly usher at the local Methodist church."[57] In 2019 the city of Batesburg, which changed its name to Batesburg-Leesville, unveiled an historic marker to remember Woodard and the attack that blinded him.[58]

Woodard's blinding left a lasting impression on both Truman, who formed the first presidential civil rights commission and desegregated the armed services, and the judge in the trial, Waties Waring. Richard Gergel, who wrote a biography of Waring, said the judge was deeply affected by the trial and verdict and later issued several decisions that overturned segregation laws. "By all accounts," Gergel said, "Isaac Woodard was never aware of the impact of his blinding on President Truman and Judge Waring."[59]

7.

"IT'S TIME FOR SOUTH CAROLINA
TO REJOIN THE UNION"

J udge Waties Waring watched from his bench during the trial of
Lynwood Shull for beating Isaac Woodard but could do little to
intervene. Waring knew the jury would give little or no thought to
whether Shull should be punished for savagely blinding the former
soldier. Waring couldn't change the verdict. But he could delay it.
After addressing the jury, he retreated to the judge's chambers. He
put on his hat, walked out of the office, and told a deputy marshal
he was going for a walk and would not return for twenty minutes.

"But judge," the deputy marshal said, "the jury ain't going to
stay out for twenty minutes."

Waring responded that the jury would indeed stay out for twenty
minutes because he wouldn't let them back in the courtroom until
he returned

"I'm not going to be back here for twenty minutes," he said.[1]

As Waring walked, he became angry, thinking that there had
been no justice for Woodard. Shull was acquitted, as Waring
knew he would be. The state's white-owned newspapers praised
the verdict. Woodard got what he deserved, the *Columbia State*
editorialized.[2]

It had not been a fair trial, Waring thought; it had been a lynching, and Shull, his defense attorneys, and the prosecuting attorneys had all been part of it. Waring did not criticize the jury. "I
couldn't ask them to find [Shull] guilty on the slimness of that
case," he said. Waring said he was "shocked at the hypocrisy of my
government" for "submitting that disgraceful case before a jury. I

also was hurt that I was made a party to it, because I had to be a party to it, however unwilling I was."[3]

Waring had thought relatively little about racial bigotry until that day. "This case laid bare the injustice that black Americans faced every day," Brian Hicks wrote in his biography of Waring, *In Darkest South Carolina: J. Waties Waring and His Secret Plan That Sparked a Civil Rights Movement*, "and he would never forget it."[4]

When Waring returned to his hotel room, he found his wife, Elizabeth, who had witnessed the trial, sobbing. He later said the Woodard case was his wife's "baptism in racial prejudice." When Elizabeth returned to Charleston she saw a woman she knew casually and told her what she had witnessed during the Woodard trial. "Mrs. Waring," the woman said, "that sort of thing happens all the time. It's dreadful, but what are we going to do about it?"[5] The Woodard trial may also have been Waties Waring's "baptism in racial prejudice," Brian Hicks wrote. Waring was haunted by the trial and haunted by the response of the woman to his wife. "What are we going to do about it?" Waties Waring was a federal judge. There were things he could do.[6]

Waring, like Robert Morrison, would undergo a political transformation. The Shull trial transformed Waring from someone who had been relatively indifferent on racial issues to someone who spent the rest of his life using whatever influence he had to ending racial inequality. When the Warings returned to Charleston, Elizabeth began reading about southern culture, politics, and racism. She read W. J. Cash's *The Mind of the South*, where the South Carolina writer examined racial prejudices. She also read Gunnar Myrdal's *An American Dilemma: The Negro Problem and Modern Democracy*. In his detailed study, Myrdal, a Swedish sociologist, wrote that African Americans lagged behind whites because of an unending cycle of racial prejudice.[7]

The Warings had created a scandal in Charleston's elite social circle because they had engaged in an affair with one another while married to other spouses. They were married after their divorces. The Warings escaped from the city on weekends by driving to the nearby sea islands, where they passed by the dilapidated homes of African American families. Elizabeth convinced the judge to stop at the home of a family she had met. They began stopping by the home regularly and making friends with other African Americans in Charleston, including Septima Clark.[8] Waring's evolving progressiveness on race relations influenced his decisions on racial issues. His marriage to Elizabeth had made him a pariah in the aristocratic class in Charleston, but his judicial rulings and opinions made him an enemy to white South Carolinians. Politicians tried to impeach him for his decisions. Whites crossed the street when they saw him coming their way. Waties and Elizabeth received death threats. Crosses were burned outside their house and bricks were thrown through the windows.

THERE WAS LITTLE IN Waties Waring's family history to foreshadow he would become the most progressive southern judge on civil rights in the 1940s and 1950s.

Waring, the son of a Confederate soldier, was born the youngest of four children on July 27, 1880. He was an eighth-generation Charlestonian whose ancestors came from England to Charles Town in 1683, thirteen years after it was settled, and the family became part of the city's aristocratic social class.[9] By the time Waties was born, the Warings and Charleston had each seen better days. The Civil War had left the Warings with little beyond their name and their aristocratic past. Most of the Waring family, like much of the South, lived in the past. "Waring didn't worship old Charleston," Hicks said, "He said, 'I grew up on rice and recollections.'"[10]

Waties admired his only brother, Thomas, who was nine years older. Thomas attended Hobart College in upstate New York on a full scholarship. When Thomas graduated, he returned to Charleston and eventually became editor of the *Evening Post*. Waties, lacking scholarships or money, attended the College of Charleston, where he graduated second in his class, passed the bar, and went into private practice.[11] In 1913 he married the socially prominent Annie Gammell, moved into her home at 61 Meeting Street, and the couple socialized with other prominent families.[12]

Waring's social connections became political connections. He became a U.S. attorney and worked as Charleston County campaign chair for U.S. senator "Cotton Ed" Smith. Waring liked Smith but recognized him as a racist demagogue. "His racial talks were to get the boys in the backwoods to vote for him, and they did," Waring said. "He was a nice chap in a great many ways and very amusing and could make a wonderful speech to a half-literate group of voters."[13] Waring also worked for Charleston mayor Burnet Maybank's campaign during his successful campaign to be governor. Waring's connections served him well. President Franklin D. Roosevelt nominated Waring to be a federal judge and he was confirmed in January 1942.[14]

Waring was sixty-one. His political transformation did not happen immediately but gradually, profoundly, and permanently.

VIOLA LOUISE DUVALL, a Black teacher at Burke Industrial high school, Charleston's only public Black high school, sought equal pay with white teachers, who were paid more than a third more than Black teachers. Duvall and the NAACP sued the school district and its superintendent. NAACP attorney Thurgood Marshall represented Duvall in *Duvall v. Seignous* when the trial began on February 10, 1944. Four years earlier, Marshall had won a court judgment in *Alston v. School Board of the City of Norfolk*, when the Fourth Circuit Court of Appeals in Richmond, Virginia, declared a discriminatory pay system unconstitutional.[15]

Marshall had not expected the same verdict in *Duvall v. Seignous*. He did not think it was possible to get a fair trial this deep in the Deep South. He did not know that Waring had immersed himself in civil rights law. Marshall, who had already argued and won cases before the U.S. Supreme Court, did not know that Waring knew more about him than he knew about Waring. Waring drilled the school board's attorneys on case law, leaving them flustered. He then sided with Duvall, ruling that the state must equalize pay between African American and white teachers within two years. Marshall later described the case as "the only [one] I ever tried with my mouth hanging open half the time" because the judge "was so fair."[16] Waring was impressed with Marshall, who would appear again and again before the Charleston jurist. The two would become friends and then conspirators in trying to overturn *Plessy v. Ferguson*.

By this time, Waring's public opinions were not yet raising eyebrows on Broad Street—but his private life was. In early 1945, Waring told Annie, his wife of thirty years, that he was divorcing her to marry Elizabeth, the divorced wife of a wealthy Connecticut textile manufacturer. Waties and Elizabeth Waring were ostracized from Charleston high society.[17] Charlestonians loathed the second Mrs. Waring initially because the divorce had caused so much pain for the first Mrs. Waring, but then as they learned more about Elizabeth, they loathed her for who she was and because she was everything they were not: a liberal northerner who was critical of Charleston conservatism and dismissive of the Charleston social elite and, perhaps worst of all, she believed in equality between the races. The Warings began inviting their new friends—African American and white activists—to their Meeting Street home for dinner and conversation. If Waties Waring could have done anything to displease his former social circle more than leaving his wife to marry a Yankee woman, it was having African Americans to his Meeting Street house. This was enough to turn blue blood red.

Judge Waring's decision in *Elmore v. Rice* sent Charleston whites into fits of purple rage. As Waring did in *Duvall*, he did not make law; he merely followed it. In 1944 the U.S. Supreme Court ruled in *Smith v. Allwright* that Democrats in Texas had to open their primaries to African American voters, who had been excluded by the party's primaries since the end of the nineteenth century.[18] Marshall called *Smith v. Allwright* his most important court victory to that point because, he said, it argued that the Texas law violated the Fourteenth Amendment and therefore established the basis for civil rights.[19]

South Carolina governor Olin Johnson ordered the legislature to delete any reference to the Democratic Party from state law or the state would find itself in court as Texas had. If African Americans, who composed a third of all residents of voting age, were allowed to vote, they would have enough power to end white rule. "White supremacy will be maintained in our primaries," Johnson said.[20]

Waring saw through the Democrats' subterfuge. On July 12, 1947, he ruled in *Elmore v. Rice* that it was unconstitutional for the state's Democratic Party to exclude African Americans from the state's primary.[21] "The Constitution," Waring said, "gave all men the right to vote in whatever primary they chose." Waring was following the Supreme Court's precedent. In his decision, he used language that was intended to agitate the state's white ruling class.

"It's time for South Carolina to rejoin the Union," he said.[22]

The *Evening Post* responded sharply to Waring's remark about the state's secession from the Union. "It would have been edifying to the citizens of his state," it said, "had Judge Waring informed them how long South Carolina has been out of the Union." The editorial urged the state to appeal the decision.[23]

Waring's decision—and particularly the tone of his opinion—infuriated W. W. Ball, the editor of the *Charleston News and Courier*. Ball called the ruling "un-American." If *Elmore* was upheld on appeal, it said, "there is nothing left for South Carolinians but to abandon completely the name of the Democratic Party, divorcing themselves from national affiliation, and re-establishing an exclusive white man's club under a new title."[24] In making its case for a white aristocratic rule, Ball said "white primaries" were exclusive because "they exclude the negroes, which we approve," and because they exclude people without money to pay a poll tax.[25]

Waring released his opinion in *Wrighten v. Board of Trustees of the University of South Carolina* the same day as the *Elmore* decision.

The *News and Courier* ran a front-page article next to the story about Waring's *Elmore* decision that reported a vicious attack upon three African American Boy Scouts attending a local conference at Camp Pinckney, a Black campground, when white men, ages nineteen and twenty, fired dozens of rounds of buckshot into the Boy Scouts' tent in the middle of the night. The boys were taken to Roper Hospital.[26] The white men said it was meant as "a prank" to scare the African American boys. No charges were brought.[27]

There was no direct connection between the shooting of the

three boys and Waring's decisions in *Elmore* and *Wrighten*. But there may have been an indirect one because of the Charleston newspapers' constant criticism of Black activists, particularly the NAACP, which had become more vocal in demanding equality. The newspaper argued that the *Elmore* decision was a threat to the white rule that had long dominated politics in South Carolina.

U.S. representative L. Mendel Rivers, who represented Charleston, went on the floor of Congress and called for Waring's impeachment. If Waring was not removed from office, Rivers said, "I prophesize bloodshed because he is now in the process of exacting a pound of flesh from the white people of South Carolina."[28] Nothing came of Rivers's demands because he lacked any constitutional grounds.[29] Waring's decision in *Elmore* made the judge an enemy in his own state, as he himself said. Waring was now, Richard Gergel said, a traitor to his family and his class and to whites throughout the state and the South.[30] One magazine described him as the "lonesomest" man in town.[31] The Warings had grown accustomed to their phone not ringing. That changed, however, after the *Elmore* decision. The Warings received threatening phone calls on a nightly basis—some of them threatening the judge's life and a few threatening the life of Elizabeth, who was a formidable woman in her right.

Elizabeth Waring had agreed to speak at the Black YWCA on Coming Street but the Y was pressured by influential white women in Charleston to rescind the invitation. When Elizabeth was asked to cancel the speech, she refused. A crowd of a hundred and fifty attended the speech. "It was brave of you to invite me to speak here and brave of you to come to hear me, for the white 'powers that be' have done everything in their power to keep me from speaking to you," she said. "But we only feel sorry for them, for their stupidity, as it will hurt them, and not us." Whites, she said, were afraid of her husband and her because they wanted to destroy the "white supremacy way of life."[32]

Elizabeth Waring's speech brought praise in some northern newspapers but near universal condemnation by southern editors and politicians. W. W. Ball, however, took a surprisingly moderate position. He said anyone had the right to express their opinion in public. "Whoever shall abuse or annoy a person exercising that right is not only an enemy of free government but a fool," Ball said. Ball's temperance was perhaps a consequence of the fact that he was related by marriage to Waties Waring. To other whites in Charleston, Elizabeth was "the witch of Meeting Street."[33]

Elizabeth—at least publicly—said she was not afraid of the Ku Klux Klan or anyone else who made harassing phone calls or wrote death threats. "I'm about ten times as scared of a mouse as I am of the whole Ku Klux Klan," she said.[34] The Warings had every reason to think the Klan might attack them.[35] The Warings were in New York on March 11 when they learned that a cross had been burned in their backyard. The initials "KKK" were etched into the charred remains of the cross. The *News and Courier* referred to the incident as a "prank." Waties Waring, however said there were four to five hundred Klan members working out of Charleston.[36] "This was no work of pranksters," he said.[37]

The Warings were playing canasta in their living room on the evening of October 9, 1950, when a brick crashed through the window and another brick hit the front door. Waring, who was then seventy, crawled on the floor to the phone and called police. "You can expect this sort of thing in South Carolina," he told reporters. "It's a state dominated by the Klan—a crime-committing Klan that has gone unpunished. We do not live in darkest Africa. We live in darkest South Carolina." The *News and Courier* responded to the attack on the home of a federal judge as it did the burning of a cross outside the judge's home. The newspaper said it was the work of "pranksters." Waties Waring again disagreed. The Warings were scared and with good reason.[38]

ONE MONTH AFTER THE Waring home was attacked, Waring held a pretrial conference on a challenge to a school segregation case in Clarendon County, northwest of Charleston County, where Richard Kluger, author of the book *Simple Justice*, said life had barely changed "since the end of slavery."[39] In 1944 fourteen-year-old George Stinney Jr., who lived in the town of Alcolu in Clarendon County, became the youngest person executed in South Carolina less than three months after his arrest for bludgeoning two white girls to death. An all-white jury decided his fate in less than ten minutes, without considering whether he was innocent. Seventy years later, a judge vacated Stinney's conviction because he had been denied a fair trial. The judge also found that the execution of the boy constituted "cruel and unusual punishment."[40]

In 1947 Joseph DeLaine, a school principal and minister of an African Methodist Episcopal (AME) church in the town of Summerton in Clarendon County heard from parents about the obstacles their children faced in trying to attend school. Harry Briggs, a gas station attendant and war veteran, told DeLaine his son and other children had to row across a flooded creek and then walk for several miles to a one-room school. There were no buses for Black children—even though Black children outnumbered white children more than three to one. Some Black children had to walk nine miles each way to their schools. DeLaine petitioned the Summerton School District for a bus. "We ain't got no money to buy a bus for your n—— children," R. W. Elliott, the school board's chairman, responded.[41]

The Summerton School District was run by an all-white board, even though the community was mostly Black. The white schools had running water and indoor restrooms. The Black schools had neither electricity nor running water. "The black schools were ramshackle structures with outdoor privies and a community well for water," Richard Gergel wrote in the book *Unexampled Courage*. "A credible claim of equality of facilities simply could not be made."[42] DeLaine and his supporters were not asking for the end of segregation; they just wanted a school bus to transport their children to their inferior school. Even so, the request was met with intimidation. Twenty parents, Briggs, and his wife, Eliza, a motel maid, filed suit against Elliott and the Summerton School District.[43] Thurgood Marshall, the NAACP's chief counsel, represented the parents. *Briggs v. Elliott* was scheduled to begin on Monday, November 20, 1950.[44]

Waring scheduled a pretrial conference for Friday, November

17. When Marshall arrived in the Charleston federal court, he was told Waring wanted to see him in private quarters. Waring told Marshall he didn't want another "separate but equal" case—he wanted a "frontal attack on segregation." Marshall disagreed. This is not the case, this is not the time, Marshall responded. Waring answered, "This is the case and this is the time."[45] Waring told Marshall, "You've got to do this."[46]

Marshall said he might win in Waring's court but would lose on appeal. Waring told Marshall to argue in federal court. Waring told Marshall he would lose 2–1 in the three-judge federal court. The judge said he would vote with the plaintiffs, Briggs, but the other two judges, John Parker and George Bell Timmerman, voted with the defendant, Elliott. If Marshall lost in federal court, Waring told him, the verdict would automatically be appealed to the Supreme Court. "That's where you want to be," Waring told Marshall.[47] Marshall filed suit in federal court on December 22, 1950, demanding an end to segregated schools.[48] It would be the first lawsuit to directly challenge school segregation since the Supreme Court's decision in *Plessy v. Ferguson*.[49]

South Carolina politicians saw *Briggs v. Elliott* as yet another attempt by the NAACP to weaken segregation. James Byrnes, who had been elected governor in November 1950, had already tried to foil the NAACP's ambitions to end segregation in schools by promising that the state would spend more money on improving African American schools if courts would give them the time. If courts did not do so, or if the NAACP or Black activists interfered, the state would end public education, Byrnes warned.[50]

Byrnes said that the majority of African Americans supported "separate but equal" schools.[51] He included no evidence to support this. The state's politicians and newspapers, like the *News and Courier*, perpetuated this falsehood without seeking out the NAACP or other African Americans. The *News and Courier* and other newspapers perpetuated yet another myth by quoting Byrnes as saying that African Americans and whites would have good relations if it were not for agitators in the Ku Klux Klan and the NAACP, who, he said, were equally at fault for stirring up racial discord. "I do not need the assistance of the Ku Klux Klan nor do I want interference by the National Association for the Advancement of Colored People," Byrnes said.[52]

Byrnes grew up in Charleston and became one of the most influential politicians in the country, serving at one point or another as congressman, senator, secretary of state, U.S. Supreme Court justice, and governor. Byrnes was a close adviser to President Franklin Roosevelt, who appointed him secretary of state and then to the Supreme Court. Byrnes thought FDR would select him as his running mate in 1944. But FDR bypassed Byrnes because he was an unapologetic white supremacist. He selected Harry Truman instead. FDR understood that the Democratic Party and American society were becoming more progressive on racial issues.[53] If Byrnes had become vice president, he would have become president when FDR died in April 1945; the federal government—in all likelihood—would not have prosecuted Isaac Woodard's blinding, and Truman's executive orders never would have been issued.

Byrnes's comparison between the KKK and NAACP, which probably angered both organizations, was as duplicitous as it was problematic. Byrnes may have been uncomfortable with the methods used by the KKK, but he had far more in common with the Klan than the NAACP did. Byrnes's comparison was a cynical ploy to marginalize the NAACP. Walter White, executive director of the NAACP, responded to Byrnes's criticism of the organization by accusing him of suffering from "senility" and the "bile of bitterness." James Hinton, South Carolina's director of the NAACP, wondered how a former Supreme Court justice could believe that the NAACP was "interfering," as Byrnes stated, by seeking "relief through due process of law."[54]

John McCray reported in the *Lighthouse and Informer* that Hinton's response to Byrnes did not appear in any of the white newspapers in the state. McCray questioned why the state's white newspapers published Byrnes's criticism of the NAACP but said nothing about Hinton's response to him. McCray wondered if Byrnes and the mainstream press were afraid of "letting white citizens know the truth" in South Carolina. Byrnes called on African

American teachers to reject the NAACP lawsuit in *Briggs v. Elliott*. Newspapers such as the *News and Courier* called on school boards to fire teachers who belonged to the NAACP and school boards did as they were told. Byrnes blamed the NAACP and African American journalists like McCray with "arousing the prejudices" of the Klan and stirring up racial violence.[55]

The Reverend DeLaine, Harry Briggs, and other plaintiffs in the *Briggs* case faced what Richard Gergel called "a merciless and methodical campaign of retaliation and intimidation." The school district fired DeLaine and his wife, two sisters, and a niece from teaching positions. DeLaine's house was burned down.[56] The intimidation did not achieve its objective. Not one of the plaintiffs asked that their names be withdrawn from the lawsuit. McCray praised the plaintiffs in his newspaper for their courage in standing up to the Klan. "Under the skins of these plaintiffs beat the kind of heart not easily stopped, one moved only by God's right," he said.[57]

The trial of *Briggs v. Elliott* began on May 28, 1951, in the federal courthouse in downtown Charleston. As the sun rose in Charleston on the first day of the trial, African Americans arrived by the carload from Summerton and across the state, and hundreds lined up outside the historic courthouse and down Broad Street as far as the eye could see. When Thurgood Marshall saw this, he told his co-counsel Robert Carter, "It's over." Carter then asked Marshall what he meant by that. "They're not scared anymore," Marshall said.[58] Waring, too, remembered how moved he was to see the huge turnout among Blacks for the oral arguments. "They'd come there on a pilgrimage. They'd never known before that anybody would stand up for them, and they came there because they believed the United States District Court was a free court," Waring said. "It was like watching a breath of freedom."[59]

Marshall's questioning of witnesses revealed the vast disparity between the white and Black schools in Clarendon County. Marshall asked a state education official, E. R. Crow, if integration in school would lead to violence. Crow said whites and Blacks had told him this would happen. Marshall asked Crow if he could remember the names of any Blacks who told him this. No, Crow said, he could not remember. Marshall questioned psychologists who told him that the Black children of Clarendon County who "have been subjected to an obviously inferior status have been definitely harmed, with the kind of injury that will endure as long as the situation endures."[60]

The three judges on the federal court released their decision on June 23, 1951, after a month of testimony. The three-judge panel ruled as Waring expected. Timmerman and Parker affirmed the constitutionality of school segregation. Waring rejected it. In his dissent, Waring said the 14th Amendment to the Constitution was meant to confer upon Blacks full rights as citizens and that segregation was an "unreasonable, unscientific and unadulterated prejudice." He added: "Segregation in education can never produce equality. . . . Segregation is per se inequality."[61]

Tom Waring, who had become editor of the *News and Courier* upon Ball's retirement, criticized his uncle Waties's dissent by saying that mixing whites and African Americans would lead to the "extermination of the white race in the United States."[62] He said he was relieved that the reasoned judgment of Timmerman and Parker had won the day. Tom Waring called the court's decision a "victory for American rights." He could not foresee how it could be overruled.[63] In three years, however, *Briggs v. Elliott* would be joined with four other cases that would find their way to the Supreme Court. They would be known as *Brown v. Board of Education*. Waring's dissent, "segregation is per se inequality," would form the legal foundation for the U.S. Supreme Court's ruling in *Brown v. Board of Education*.

8

THE STORY OF LITTLE LEAGUE BASEBALL

W hen Carl Stotz was growing up in Williamsport, Pennsylvania, in the late 1910s and early 1920s, he and his friends would play baseball on an abandoned lot with worn-out balls that were covered with friction tape and adult bats that were held together with nails or tape. The bats were so big that the boys had to choke up on them. "And when you choked up" on the bat, Stotz remembered, "the end of it was in your stomach."[1] The games were not so different from those being played on sandlots across the country, where games were interrupted while the boys argued whether a baserunner was safe or out or a ball was fair or foul. Some of the boys' minds wandered as the game was interrupted again and again because there was another argument, the ball had come apart and needed more tape, the bat had broken, or a ball had landed in a fenced-in yard patrolled by a menacing dog.

Stotz, at some point, quit playing baseball, as most boys eventually do. He got married, had a daughter, and found work as a clerk at the Pure Oil Company in Williamsport. He renewed his interest in baseball with his young nephews—Jimmy and his older brother, Harold "Major" Gehron—who lived nearby. The boys sat on their uncle's porch and listened to Sol Wolf broadcast the home games of the Williamsport Grays, a Class A Eastern League team who played their home games at Bowman Field, where bands would play before games and between innings. After listening to the game, the boys would go to their backyard and play catch and complain about the lack of organized baseball for boys like them.[2]

During an August day in 1938, Stotz was playing catch with the boys when "Major" threw a ball over his uncle's head. Stotz ran after the ball and as he reached down to retrieve it, he stepped on a lilac bush that scraped his ankle. Stotz sat down in pain. All of sudden, wincing from the sharp stems of the lilac bush, an image came to him like the one he had daydreamed about as a boy. "Now this thing is hard to explain unless you have experienced it yourself sometime in your life, where all at once something comes to you in what they call a 'flashback,'" Stotz said. "There it is in one scene. And that's what happened."[3]

In that instant, as Stotz repeated in the years to come, Little League Baseball was created. Stotz saw a scaled-down field with the boys wearing baseball uniforms. He shared his revelation with the Gehron brothers and asked them how they would like to play on a team, where they would wear uniforms and adults would coach and umpire. Would there be a band, they asked? Stotz promised the boys he would create such a league. He began organizing pickup games for the Gehron boys and their friends at Memorial Park—a field just west of Williamsport, on the banks of the Susquehanna River, adjacent to Bowman Field. They regularly returned to that field during the summer. Stotz made the distance between bases sixty feet—or two-thirds of the distance between bases in the big leagues. He set the distance between home plate and the pitcher's rubber at thirty-eight feet, or about two-thirds of the distance between home plate and the pitcher's rubber in the big leagues. The games would be six innings instead of nine.[4]

Pure Oil Company closed its plant in Williamsport and Stotz lost his job. This temporarily forced him to shift his priorities. Stotz then found a job with Lundy Lumber Company, where he collected unpaid bills, worked at the sales counter, and helped with the bookkeeping. He continued to adapt baseball's rules to a boys' league, allowing baserunners to leave base only when the ball had passed the plate. He created a system of drafting players so that no team had all the best players. He needed sponsors to pay for expenses such as uniforms, baseballs, bats, and catcher's equipment. Stotz contacted dozens of companies and all but one turned him down—Lycoming Dairy Farms. "Although I had only one sponsor and one manager, me," he said, "I saw no turning back. It was time to begin calling boys together for team tryouts."[5] "Tuck" Frazier, who played during the first year, remembered Stotz coming to his Sunday school class. "You fellows want to play in an organized league with uniforms and scheduled games and umpires?" he asked the boys. "And we all jumped at the thing!" Frazier remembered.[6]

Enough boys showed up for the tryout on May 8, 1939, to have three teams. Stotz recruited two more sponsors, the Jumbo Pretzel Company and Lundy Construction, a family-run business that owned Lundy Lumber Company. He found volunteers to manage the teams, bought equipment, uniforms, and baseballs, and then tried to find a field to practice and play games. The city of Williamsport did not allow Stotz to play at Memorial Field because it was already used for so many other recreational leagues. The city told him he could use nearby Point Park. Stotz now had a field and a league, but the league did not have a name. He thought about calling it the Junior League but that name already belonged to a women's organization. Stotz came up with Little League.[7]

Lundy's Lumber defeated Lycoming Dairy, 23–8, in Little League Baseball's first game on June 6. Halfway through the game, Stotz went to the pitcher's mound and appealed to the crowd for donations to defray costs. The *Williamsport Sun* provided a summary of the game that included a box score and a note that said the next game would be played between Jumbo Pretzel and Lycoming Dairy.[8]

Stotz created the guiding principles of Little League Baseball, which established that the organization had authority over the teams composing the league; the distance between the bases and the distance between the pitcher's mound and home plate; that players for a team or league must come from a well-defined geographic area; that a given number of players be placed on each team; that all funds contributed by sponsors were put in a common treasury for the benefit of all teams; that exploitation by commercial interests was not permitted; and that players were selected "without regard to race, color, or creed, or sex."[9]

The league's principles have not changed since they were written in 1939. African American boys were playing in the league long before Black men were playing in the Major Leagues. Lance Van Auken, vice president and executive director of Little League Baseball, said there is no record of the first African American boy to play in the organization because Blacks were playing from the point of creation.[10]

AS CARL STOTZ DROVE to and from Point Park the summer of 1939, he passed by an overgrown lot at the corner of Memorial Avenue and Demorest Street. Where other people saw an abandoned lot of weeds and rocks—if they saw anything it at all—Stotz saw a baseball field with raked dirt, a grassy outfield, bleachers, and a scoreboard. During the offseason, he recruited volunteers to clear tree stumps, haul away trash, and lay dirt for the infield and grass seed for the outfield. John Lindemuth, Stotz's boyhood friend who managed a team in the league during the second year, was one of those who spent hour after hour constructing the baseball field. "When I came on board that 1940 season," Lindemuth said, "fathers pitched in and energetically cleared two hundred trees to create a new playing field."[11]

Stotz's dedication to the league absorbed much of his free time and encroached on his job responsibilities at Lundy Lumber. Stotz's boss, Jack Lundy, remembered Stotz regularly coming to him and asking if he could leave early. Stotz said he would do the work he did not finish on evenings and weekends. "I've really got to get with the boys at the ballfield," Stotz told Lundy. Lundy said that Stotz would always do as he promised. Lundy recognized what Little League Baseball meant to Stotz and what Stotz meant to Little League Baseball. Stotz's commitment was obvious to the boys and their parents. Art Kline brought a first baseman's glove to his first tryout at age ten. One of the other boys told him he needed a fielder's glove. "Well, this is all I have," Kline said. "It's all my family can afford." Embarrassed, the boy began walking off the field when Stotz stopped him. "I don't want you to leave. I have a fielder's mitt right here that I don't use," Stotz said. "I want you to have it."[12]

During World War II, Stotz added a second league in Williamsport, and soon after, other leagues were added in nearby towns and cities. The war meant shortages for civilians as America transformed into a wartime economy. The military needed material for uniforms and sporting goods for the recreation of soldiers. "One thing I can't forget is the trouble we had getting uniforms," Jack Sargent, who coached a team, remembered about the 1946 season. "But we were suited up by opening day," he said. "The uniforms were flannel; leather belts held up baggy pants. The boys wore ankle-high canvas sneakers with rubber soles."[13]

Stotz traveled to other cities and towns recruiting new leagues. Sometimes he brought enough boys who would play a game in their uniforms. "I think we should remember always that Little League Baseball belongs to the boys," he would say. "You know, we can't do too much for our boys because we're only young once."[14] Art Kline described Stotz as an evangelist who preached the virtues of youth baseball. "Carl was, in a sense, if I can use this term, an evangelist," Kline said. "He was so sincere. He could get up in front of a group and convince you that there was nothing better than Little League Baseball."[15]

The city of Williamsport allowed Little League to play their games at Memorial Park once the organization became more and more popular.[16] Stotz decided to have a tournament for all interested teams at the end of the 1947 season. The Williamsport community lent their support to what Stotz called the National Little League Tournament and then the Little League World Series. The Williamsport Grays opened their locker rooms at nearby Bowman Field to the ballplayers. The Calvary Methodist Church provided meals for the ballplayers. Local businesses and organizations, including the YMCA, Confair Bottling, Capitol Bakers, and Grit Publishing, acted as sponsors. Stotz assigned volunteers to each team to act as what were called "team uncles"—or chaperones, a custom that continues to the present. Twelve teams registered for the 1947 tournament, including an integrated team from Hammonton, New Jersey.[17] The integrated Hammonton team returned in 1949 and won the tournament.[18] In 1950 the integrated Bridgeport,

Connecticut, team lost 2–1 in the championship game. Its pitcher was John Lewis, an African American.[19]

Stotz invited Major League greats, including Cy Young, the winningest pitcher in Major League history, who came to the tournament every year until his death in late 1955.[20] The Associated Press covered the tournament.[21] "Bud" Berndt, who worked for a Williamsport radio station, broadcast the championship game for several years until NBC took over the broadcast; he then worked with Ted Husing, one of the most recognized voices in sports.[22] The *Saturday Evening Post* published a story on Little League Baseball in May 1949 with the headline, "Small Boy's Dream Come True." Shortly thereafter, an article on the Little Leagues appeared in *Reader's Digest*.[23] Connie Mack, the owner-manager of the Philadelphia Athletics, praised Little League Baseball on its tenth anniversary. "It is one of the finest enterprises of which I know and I extend my congratulations to the men of the original Little League and to all those who, in the interest of boys, have started leagues in their communities," he said. "The boys of the nation will be happier and its future citizens better if this program continues to grow."[24] In May 1955 North Dakota became the last of then forty-eight states to add a Little League. It was estimated that a half million boys participated in the organization.[25]

Nothing had a grip on American boys like Little League Baseball. Baseball was the most popular sport in America and Little League Baseball was far and away the most popular youth baseball organization. Playing Little League Baseball made an impression on boys that lasted far into adulthood. "That's one thing we hear from a lot of people," Van Auken said. "They tell us that when they were kids they went to bed wearing their uniforms and slept with their gloves."[26]

STOTZ'S PROMISE TO HIS nephews had grown far beyond anything he—or anyone else—could have imagined. But he had not yet addressed one of the complaints he had when he played baseball as a boy. When kids choked up on the adult bats, the end of the bat often poked them in the stomach when they swung. In addition, nobody made athletic shoes for children, who used metal spikes that led to bloody feet or legs for infielders tagging a sliding baserunner. In December 1947 Stotz talked to Charles Durban, assistant advertising director of United States Rubber Company, which had a factory in Williamsport, to see if the New York–based company could design an athletic shoe for boys. A year later, U.S. Rubber marketed the first rubber-cleated athletic shoe. Stotz contacted Hillerich and Bradsby, which manufactured bats for boys. The Spalding sports equipment company produced baseballs for Little League Baseball.[27]

Little League Baseball had become too big for Stotz to run by himself. U.S. Rubber, which became the organization's first corporate sponsor, contributed $5,000 to fund the National Tournament in 1948. The company paid for the transportation for out-of-town teams, hotel accommodations, and trophies. A year later, the company assumed all expenses for a national headquarters for the organization. In 1950 a nonprofit corporation, known as Little League Baseball Incorporated, was created. Durban selected the organization's board of directors, which included, among others, Major League Baseball Commissioner Ford Frick. The board elected Durban as chair of the board of Little League Baseball, Inc. Stotz became commissioner of Little League Baseball. Stotz's friend John Lindemuth became the assistant commissioner.[28]

Stotz and Durban—at least in the short term—understood that Little League Baseball needed to be run like an organization. But the conflict came in the details on how this would be accomplished. Stotz thought the board had too many outsiders who did not share his vision that Little League Baseball remain unaffected by commercial interests. Durban wanted Little League Baseball to have a strong centralized control, including owning the fields. Stotz disagreed. "In retrospect," Stotz later said, "I can see it was the beginning of a deep philosophical conflict. At the time, I didn't dwell on it, but sadly, such honest differences continued."[29]

For the most part, Stotz did what he wanted to do without any interference from Durban, who lived in New York and rarely came to Williamsport.[30] That changed after Durban resigned in 1951.

Peter J. McGovern, who was director of public relations for U.S. Rubber, succeeded Durban and moved to Williamsport. McGovern and Stotz took an immediate dislike to one another. The tall and athletic McGovern was soft-spoken but had a domineering presence. McGovern was an autocrat who was used to having things his way. But, when it came to Little League Baseball, the much smaller Stotz was used to having his way.[31] "Carl and Peter McGovern had different personalities," Van Auken said. "Anything McGovern wanted, Carl was against it."[32]

McGovern, however, had the support of the board of directors, which consisted of outsiders. Stotz wanted more local representation on the board and asked to add a representative from the *Williamsport Sun-Gazette*. The board voted him down. He was the only dissenting vote.[33] McGovern's corporate vision for Little League clashed with Stotz's bucolic one. Relations deteriorated between the two men. "Little League had to decide whether it should remain a somewhat disorganized, romantic, altruistic venture or whether it should be run as a corporation," Gary Fine wrote in his book *With the Boys: Little League Baseball and Preadolescent Culture*. "Was it to be a small-town crusader's dream or an efficient, streamlined business?"[34]

McGovern and Stotz each wanted as many boys to play as possible and they were both opposed to racial discrimination. Both men believed that Little League could became a means to spread American values such as hard work, teamwork, and democracy. They were, as Van Auken put it, "staunch capitalists, pro-America, pro-military."[35] Leagues were started in Japan and South Korea, which had only a few years earlier been a part of a unified Korea. But after World War II, Korea split into separate countries, North and South Korea, one democratic, the other communist. When Little League Baseball was introduced to South Korea, the country was embroiled in a war with communist-controlled North Korea. U.S. Army soldiers tutored Korean boys on the fundamentals of baseball and created makeshift baseball fields. Little League Baseball sent bats, gloves, and baseballs. One American soldier said that baseball gave the war-torn country a bit of normalcy. "What

Little League Baseball did was to help those Korean boys forget for a time the war and the death," the soldier said.[36]

The spread of communism throughout Asia and in Eastern Europe produced widespread uneasiness that communism would spread to the United States. Conservative politicians like U.S. senator Joseph McCarthy exploited this sense of fear, which morphed into hysteria—or the Red Scare—in the United States, and anyone who could not "prove" their patriotism was susceptible to charges of being a communist. "McCarthyism" meant that Americans had to sign loyalty oaths to prove they were real Americans. The anticommunist hysteria of the times infiltrated Little League Baseball. Little League Baseball Inc. began publishing a newsletter, *Little League Hits*, which was edited by retired army colonel A. H. "Cappy" Wells and sent to every Little League president. Wells told readers that Little League Baseball was good for America and that the boys and adults who were involved with the organization were good Americans. Wells questioned the Americanism of adults who rejected the Little Leagues for their own baseball league. Such independence was contradictory to the values of Americanism, Wells said. Such a league, he added, "does not promote Americanism. It tends to nourish clashiness in every walk of life."[37]

To Wells, Little League Baseball was a deterrent to stopping the spread of communism. U.S. attorney general Herbert Brownell Jr. agreed. "The young Americans who compose the Little Leagues will prove a hitless target for the peddlers of godless ideology," Brownell said in an issue of *Little League Hits*. In another issue, FBI director J. Edgar Hoover, who served as a member of the Little League Board of Trustees, praised Little Leagues for instilling American virtues. "Little League Baseball is providing a splendid way for young people to fit themselves for the rigorous competition of life," Hoover said in 1950. "A clean, healthy body begets a clean, healthy mind, and the two are absolute essentials to good Americanism."[38]

Little League Baseball came to represent the zeitgeist of post–World War II America. Millions of servicemen and servicewomen returned from the war and found good jobs, went to college on the GI Bill, got married, had children, and moved to the suburbs. The U.S. economy expanded. The middle class increased. Americans had free time and disposable income. "Never had so many people had so much time on their hands—with pay—as today in the United States," *Business Week* said in 1953.[39] Many of those Americans spent that time on organized sports—and, in particular, Little League Baseball. "Summertime for the children of the late 1940s and early 1950s, became a ceremony of ice cream and sunshine and Little League Baseball," Harvey Frommer wrote.[40]

To historian Michael Carriere, Little League Baseball helped define a point in time for a country moving from the cities to the suburbs. "The story of Little League Baseball is essentially the story of the exploding postwar suburb and the increasing awareness of the societal and economic importance of perhaps suburbia's most important dweller, the pre-adolescent child," Carriere said. "Little League Baseball helped adults and children alike come to terms with the growing predominance of the American suburbs." Little League Baseball brought families closer together—particularly fathers and sons, who played catch on their suburban lawns, and through the ritual of throwing a ball back and forth developed something deeper. "In baseball," one Little League father explained, "a father and son meet on a common ground from which blooms companionship, respect, and real love."[41]

Men and boys had once joined together for the community good to raise barns or to farm. Now they put their hands in the soil and built Little League Baseball fields. In Naugatuck, Connecticut, more than three thousand cubic yards of earth were dug to create a playing field. One resident, Frank Shea, a former Major League pitcher, donated trucks from his construction company to create a baseball field. In Sherwood, Ohio, hundreds of volunteers dug out massive amounts of dirt to fill in a ravine to create a baseball field. When it was learned that many of the boys in the farming community were too busy with their chores to play baseball during the day, adults contributed their time and money to construct lights for night baseball.[42]

In postwar America, children increasingly grew up away from

the farms and into the suburbs, where they had more time on their hands. This by itself was little cause to worry. But what children were doing in their free time became the cause of handwringing. "Nowhere was this sense of anxiety more noticeable than when the nation discussed the place of children in this changing world," Carriere said. "In this period of uncertainty and apprehension, children came to represent a hope for stability in the future, yet these same young people seemed particularly susceptible to the 'troubles, anxieties, and sacrifice' that plagued adults. As intense fears of rising rates of juvenile delinquency gripped America, postwar citizens searched for ways to acclimate children to this new cultural climate."[43]

If Little League Baseball could stop the spread of communism, perhaps it could stop the spread of juvenile delinquency. J. Edgar Hoover called Little League Baseball "a common sense counter agency against delinquency."[44] Hoover said Little League Baseball was the greatest deterrent to juveniles who otherwise might turn to committing crime. The Williamsport Police Department found that the expansion of the Little Leagues occurred simultaneously with a drop in crime. One father wrote a letter to Little League Baseball that said his son had become far more obedient since playing in the Little Leagues. "In the anxious years when juvenile delinquency affords heartaches to many families," Peter McGovern said, "the existence of the Little League program is one of the best guarantees we have, in a large part of America, to hold the family together in common interest."[45]

U.S. representative William Cahill of New Jersey told Congress that Little League Baseball could reduce prejudice: "What better medium for improving race relations in the United States and developing better international relationships through the world, than this great sport of baseball played as it is under the conditions prescribed by Little League Baseball."[46] Wanaque Indian boys and white boys on the Maine–New Brunswick border played Little League. Harlingen, Texas, like everywhere else in the state, was segregated along racial lines. In 1953 an African American youngster appeared at a Little League practice wanting to play on the First Methodist Church team. The church was not willing to make this decision on its own and took the issue to the league office, which ruled that the Black youngster could practice with the league. Despite a few protests from parents, the boy was chosen for a team and played without incident.[47]

In 1955 white men in South Carolina refused to allow their sons to play an African American team. Little League Baseball quit being a game for the boys, as Carl Stotz intended. Adults coopted it for their own self-interests and used the baseball field to exchange their differences of opinion on the biggest issue of the day—whether whites and Blacks should go to the same schools or the same parks or sit in the same section of buses.

DANNY JONES WAS BORN in downtown Charleston on March 13, 1910, three weeks after Carl Stotz was born in Williamsport, Pennsylvania. Both men lived most of their lives in their respective hometowns, and yet the good they did was remembered far away from where they lived and long after they died. They are each remembered for their contributions to youth baseball.

One created the integrated Little League Baseball, the other the segregated Dixie Youth Baseball.

The two men each grew up loving sports and remained around sports the rest of their lives. When Jones was twelve he was the mascot for a Minor League baseball team, the Charleston Pals of the South Atlantic League. Jones was the athlete that Stotz was not. He excelled in track, football, and basketball at Charleston High School. He went to the College of Charleston, where he played basketball well enough to earn all-state honors. He also was a talented swimmer who once set a national YMCA record in the forty-yard backstroke and won mid-Atlantic titles in the fifty-yard backstroke and one-hundred-yard freestyle.[48] He established a Charleston record by swimming the annual five-mile race around the city in less than two hours.[49]

While attending college, Jones began working for the city's playground department at Marion Square Playground on the Citadel Green. In 1932 he was promoted to assistant director of the city's parks and playgrounds, where he worked until he enlisted in the navy. During World War II, Jones, who rose to the rank of lieutenant commander, was in charge of physical fitness programs at the Charleston Naval Yard. When he was transferred to the Midway Islands, he created a rest-and-recuperation center for the U.S. submarine forces in the Pacific.

When the war ended, Jones returned to Charleston, where he was hired as director of the Cooper River Parks and Playgrounds Commission. He had no employees, an annual budget of $11,000, and a single building, the Park Circle Community Center, which was described as "a tumbledown office and a weedy lot," in the unincorporated area in what is now the city of North Charleston.[50] Jones saw something in the dirt and weeds that few others saw. "He had a vision," his daughter Sallie Frenkel said. "He wanted to start a recreation department where there was nothing."[51]

Jones worked tirelessly to raise interest and money by talking to politicians, civic groups, businesses, and organizations. He negotiated with the federal government for the sale of a former USO building.[52] Under Jones's leadership, the Cooper River Recreation Department added baseball fields, playgrounds, swimming pools, and community centers. By 1958 the annual budget had increased to $73,031. He had a staff and scores of volunteers. There were sixty-four baseball teams and forty-two basketball teams.[53] In May 1959 more than a thousand people attended "Danny Jones Appreciation Day."[54] The Park Circle Pool and Recreation Center were renamed for him. State senator T. Allen Legare presented Jones with a new Plymouth sedan as a gift from the community. "No man has ever made more of a success of his life than Danny Jones," Legare said. "He has not amassed great wealth, nor has he accumulated great political power. Yet he is one of the most successful people in the world."[55]

Jones passed on his love of swimming to his children, who helped their father give lessons.[56] For decades, people told one or more of the Jones children that their father had taught them how to swim. "You don't know how many times I heard, 'Your daddy taught me how to swim,'" Bubba Jones said.[57] All the Jones children taught swimming lessons when they became old enough. Their father organized swim meets, where he did the public address announcing and his children wrote down the names and times of the different swimmers.[58] The Park Circle Community Center became a popular hangout for boys to engage in competitive sport but also for bands and teenage dances. "It was the place to be," Tesa Livingston, another daughter of Danny Jones, said.[59]

Jones became a local hero, whether it was building baseball fields or baseball leagues or organizing swim meets. He recognized how sports could give boys something to do so they did not end up doing something they should not be doing. He directed recalcitrant boys toward boxing and other sports. As Jones's seven children got older and grew into adulthood, they heard from many people what their father had meant to them. "My daddy told them, 'You have a choice between staying with the wrong crowd and doing something with your life,'" Sallie Frenkel said. Charles "Bubba" Jones said one man told him that his father told him, "'You need to come with me,' and he got him into boxing," Bubba Jones said. "He told me he saved his life."[60]

Jones's children remembered their father leaving home on Churchill Avenue in the morning—wearing a tie every day, Bubba said. It was usually "a bow tie," Tesa Livingston added. He then walked a few blocks to his office, which had room for little else except a desk and a couple chairs.[61] Like Carl Stotz, Jones understood the need for publicity. His children remember seeing him type press releases and box scores and schedules in his small office to send to the *News and Courier*, *Evening Post*, and other newspapers. "He would wear out typewriters," Bubba said. "Every time you walked in he was typing."[62]

If Jones was not at his spartan office, he would be watching a baseball game at the Park Circle or one of the other baseball diamonds. "When two obscure kids' teams played baseball—and maybe it was just one of thirty games or so being played that afternoon in North Charleston—that man over there in the corner of the dugout was Danny Jones. He dropped by to see how things were going, saying little and not advertising his presence. He just enjoyed," *Evening Post* sports editor Warren Koon wrote, "the sight of noisy kids playing a game. Any game."[63]

LITTLE LEAGUE BASEBALL SUCCEEDED because of Carl Stotz but that success also required men like Danny Jones, who organized the first Little League in South Carolina in 1949 and became the state's director of the organization.[64] Jones and Stotz no doubt knew one another through letters or phone calls. They may have met when Jones accompanied the North Charleston team to Williamsport when it played in the 1949 Little League World Series.[65] The team lost in the first round to a team from Corning, New York.

Jones and Stotz had a lot in common and probably agreed on far more than they disagreed. They each believed that all boys, whether they were African American or white, should be able to play baseball. Stotz created Little League Baseball because he wanted boys to play with and against each other without regard to race. Jones wanted "separate but equal" in youth baseball.[66] Jones resigned from Little League Baseball because the organization told him that he could not have a segregated league.

Jones—at least initially—had no objections to the Cannon Street team in the district tournament. On June 22, 1955, he told the *News and Courier* that the All-Stars had met all requirements for the tournament and he had been instructed to include them. The newspaper ran the headline "Negro Little League Team Will Compete."[67] Bubba Jones says the board of directors of the Cooper River Parks and Playgrounds Commission voted to keep the tournament segregated. It was not his father's decision, Bubba Jones said. It was the decision of the commission's board of directors. Jones's children and others say there was political pressure put on Jones and the board. "There had to be some sort of political influence behind it because segregation was political," Sallie Frenkel said.[68]

Every story needs a villain, and Danny Jones—the local hero—became the villain in this story because he was the director of the parks department that prevented the district tournament from being integrated.

Jones found himself in the middle of something bigger than he was.

"It was the times," his son Bubba said, "and he wasn't ready for it."

"It was the times," Sallie Frenkel agreed. "It was a hard decision."[69]

Frenkel said she never heard a bad word said about his father until the Cannon Street story. "Daddy was personally blamed for everything," Livingston said.[70]

9

THE YMCA

On August 2, 1941, Robert Morrison and two dozen other men—including Frank DeCosta Jr., principal of the Avery Institute; Arthur Clement Jr., who worked for North Carolina Mutual and would become president of the Charleston chapter of the NAACP; and pharmacist John McFall—created the Charleston YMCA board of directors and put African Americans in control of the Y for the first time in its decades-long history.[1] The certificate of incorporation served as a declaration of independence. The Cannon Street Y had long been a part of the African American community on the peninsula. But the organization became something a lot more once it became independent and had its own building at 61 Cannon Street. "The Cannon Street Y served as the central nervous system in the African American community" on the peninsula, said Paul Stoney, the current president and chief executive officer of the YMCA of Greater Charleston.[2]

To adults, the Cannon Street Y was a place where they could escape the suffocating pressure of white supremacy and talk about what could be done to confront discrimination without the steadfast gaze of whites watching them. The local NAACP met there. It became a community center for children, and especially boys, who were at the Y when they were not at church or at home. "The Cannon Street Y was on the middle of the peninsula. It was accessible by bicycle for everyone. If you were an African American, the Cannon Street YMCA had an impact on you or your family,"

Stoney said. "Not a day goes by when someone doesn't remind me of how it impacted their lives. It was the only place they could go."[3]

African American YMCAs were created because white-run YMCAs excluded Blacks since the first organization was created in 1852.[4] By the late 1940s, an increasing number of African Americans were confronting Jim Crowism, wherever and however it existed. Carl Murphy, publisher of the *Baltimore Afro-American* newspaper, complained to the National Council of Young Men's Christian Associations that he could not "get a cup of coffee or a piece of pie" in the cafeteria of the city's Central YMCA. Murphy said the YMCA should either remove the Christian from their name or practice Christianity.[5] "The history of African Americans in the YMCA is the story of the struggle for racial advancement," Nina Mjagkij wrote in *Light in the Darkness*. "It is the story of black communities overcoming class, gender, religious, and personal differences and uniting to raise funds for the creation of public spaces not controlled by whites. It is the story of the educated elite who created safe havens where African American men could build true manhood," Mjagkij continued. "Although separate black YMCAs were the product of discrimination and segregation, for many African Americans they represented 'a light in the darkness' of racism."[6]

ANTHONY BOWEN, A FORMER slave, established the first African American YMCA in Washington DC a decade after the first YMCA opened in London, England. In the years following the Civil War, other Black Y's were opened in a few other cities, including Charleston, where Henry Thomas established the Charleston Negro Christian Association in 1866.[7] The Charleston Y aimed to serve the African American community by promoting "growth in Christian character" among its male population.[8]

The Charleston YMCA refers to itself as the oldest, continuously operating Black YMCA in America.[9] But the words the "oldest, continuously operating" suggest a stability that does not accurately reflect the history of the Y. For the first several decades of its existence, the Y existed out of vacant offices, churches, and private homes. Like other Black Y's, the Charleston organization remained under the control of whites and depended on white benefactors for its survival. By the end of the century, it was on the verge of going out of business. In the early 1900s, the Y hired its first paid executive, Nathaniel M. Martin. In 1916 the Y, relying on donations from white and Black benefactors, acquired a house and a lot at 61 and 63 Cannon Street, where the organization evolved from a strictly religious organization to an organization that offered recreational, educational, and social activities for the African American youth on the peninsula. It called itself the "Cannon Street Branch YMCA."[10]

The Y, like the Avery school and the NAACP, served elite African Americans in Charleston, preferring light-skinned Blacks over darker-skinned Blacks. This created resentment among those who did not have the right skin color.[11] The Y began to shed its elitism when Arthur J. H. Clement Sr., the grandson of slaves who had dark skin, became its president. The YMCA, Lee Drago wrote, became "more responsive to the needs of a wider black community in Charleston."[12] Bernard Powers, professor emeritus of history at the College of Charleston, said that the Cannon Street Y became one of the few organizations in the city to survive Black elitism and white prejudice.[13]

The Y, however, struggled financially and the building was closed during the Depression. Morrison opened his home to Y meetings, used the tennis courts on his property for recreation, and worked to return the building to the organization.[14] In the 1940s the Y became independent and its board of directors asked Morrison to be executive director of the organization. There was no money for a salary. There was no money for a staff or for athletic equipment. There was no building. He was put in charge of fundraising for the Y as he had been put in charge of fundraising for Avery Institute.[15] The News and Courier praised Morrison for giving the organization "new life" by raising money from the local charitable organizations, the white chapters of the YMCA, and from the national YMCA organization.[16]

In 1943 the Y began operating out of a single room at 177 Coming Street. This gave members a small space for meetings but did little to address the need for a gymnasium and other demands to accommodate the needs of its members, which had increased to 325.[17] The Y's board of directors purchased the deed to its former property and in December 1949 began constructing what would become the Cannon Street YMCA.[18] White residents signed a petition opposing the construction of the building because it was "in a white residential area and we desire to keep it as such." The petition drive failed.[19]

On March 26, 1950, the Y at 61 Cannon Street opened. It included a snack bar, offices, a dressing room, showers, a gymnasium, and an auditorium. A newspaper article projected that membership was expected to increase to a thousand members when the building was completed.[20] The *News and Courier* acknowledged that the Cannon Street "YMCA in Charleston was one of the few organizations in the country operated solely by a negro board of directors and is the only community agency in the city working under its own negro board."[21]

Morrison knew from his experience coaching at Avery that sports could give young African American boys something positive to do with their idle time. The Y became a hangout for boys after school and on weekends, where they found adults who became their coaches and father figures, who taught them the fundamentals of sports and of life. If the boys stayed busy playing baseball on the vacant lot next to the building or playing basketball—or learning how to box—they would be more likely to stay in school and out of trouble, and more likely to do something productive with their lives—especially if they had encouragement from men who had learned to negotiate the treacherous pathways of racial discrimination.

Decades later, many of those boys, now well into middle age or beyond, remembered the importance the Y had in their lives. Nathaniel Washington, who later became the principal of James Simons Elementary School on King Street, said his friends who did not go to the Y ended up in trouble. "I stayed on the straight and narrow because of the Y," Washington said. "I saw a lot of my friends who weren't members of the Y go wrong."[22]

MORRISON, AS PRESIDENT OF the African American YMCA, became the unofficial spokesman for the African American community because he worked as a liaison between African Americans and whites. Morrison used what little he had—his typewriter—to write letters to the *News and Courier* to advance racial equality by appealing to the words "separate but equal" in *Plessy v. Ferguson.* He asked why there were no state parks for Blacks when there were many for whites. African Americans paid taxes, he said, why then did they not receive equal facilities in return? "What has become of the 'separate but equal' laws of this State? There is no separate but equal," he said.[23] In another letter, he asked why the city provided playgrounds for white children but not for African American children. He urged the city to maintain Harmon Field as it did baseball fields for white children.[24]

In 1945 Morrison, who continued to support "separate but equal," led an effort for the accreditation of Burke High School. State law required that all students be served by an accredited high school. Without accreditation, African American students could not attend a college or university. The state and local school boards initially rejected the attempts made by Morrison and others for accreditation. When Burke was finally accredited, the school board refused to update buildings or other facilities or build a gymnasium like the white high schools had. Whenever Morrison asked for such upgrades, he was told, "The time is not ripe" or "We have no money."[25]

Morrison's frustration with Charleston's refusal to heed the words "separate but equal" moved him toward activism. He became more aggressive and, in doing so, got the attention of Dan Henderson, a *News and Courier* reporter, who wrote a memo to the newspaper's editor, Thomas Waring, after hearing a speech by Morrison at a meeting of African Americans at a Baptist church on Meeting Street. Henderson said that Morrison had engaged in "rabble-rousing" by criticizing the city for collecting taxes from African Americans but not using any of that tax money to improve schools and other facilities. "I thought he was enjoying the immunity of the building," Henderson wrote. "I understand now he has made similar demands in public on several occasions."[26]

Morrison's political awareness continued to evolve. In 1955 Morrison wrote a letter to the *News and Courier* that called for the integration of Charleston County schools because this was the only way African Americans could rid themselves of the seventy-ton cotton gin that white America had used to shackle them. Morrison said the Supreme Court's ruling of "separate but equal" in *Plessy v. Ferguson* had failed because whites had made no attempt to give African American children the same equality of education as the court dictated. Morrison then chronicled how the Charleston County School Board had systematically constructed one standard of education for whites and a far inferior one for African Americans. White students attended accredited high schools, but there were no accredited high schools for African Americans until Burke High School in 1949.

White schools received more money so they had more schools and fewer students in their classrooms and better resources so students could learn something beyond a trade. Burke students had to go to school in shifts because there were too many students in school. White schools had their own gymnasium. Burke did not. When African American parents complained, they were told there was "no money" for a gymnasium. Things had not changed that much since the Supreme Court had ruled that Blacks should have "separate but equal" schools. Morrison said whites had had decades to give African Americans an equal education to whites but had failed. "We feel that the only way for the future Negro children to get a chance equal to whites in the atomic age is for us to go to the same schools that teach the things we want," Morrison said.[27]

To Thomas Waring and the *News and Courier*, Morrison was no longer an accommodationist. He was acting like one of the African American veterans—like Albert Brooks and Lee Bennett and others in the Veterans Civic Organization (vco)—who returned from the war and thought they deserved racial equality. When Bennett was discharged from the navy, he began working at the naval shipyard and he, too, began questioning why he had gone to fight against the white supremacy of Hitler's Germany and had returned to the white supremacy of the South. vco members also included Rufus

Dilligard, who played semiprofessional football for the Charleston Bears and served as a mentor for boys on the peninsula. Bennett helped create the Charleston Boys Club on Mary Street, which served as a community center on the east side of the peninsula and coached a team in a segregated youth baseball league.[28]

Morrison understood how sports could not only give African American boys something positive to do with their time, but it could also enhance their self-esteem. He also knew that sports could serve as an equal playing field between whites and Blacks. There was nothing manifestly political about sports as there was with integrating schools or expanding voting rights for African Americans. It is not known whether Morrison wanted to start a Little League because he wanted boys on the peninsula to be part of a national organization or whether he wanted to start a Little League to confront racial discrimination in Charleston.

If Morrison and the Cannon Street Y were going to create a chapter of Little League Baseball, they needed men like Bennett and Dilligard, who knew baseball and were committed to improving the lives of younger African Americans, but also shared Morrison's notion that baseball could be a vehicle for keeping boys involved in something good so they did not get caught up in something bad. Morrison knew these men because the circle of men in any city or town who want to save the world is not particularly large. Bennett went to the YMCA to coach and mentor boys but he also went because that is where men like him met to talk about the things that matter in a community. Dilligard remembered a meeting at the Y when Morrison proposed a baseball league. "I remember Mr. Morrison and the rest of us meeting right here. We said, 'Why not start a baseball league?'"[29]

In doing so, Morrison and the Y opened another front in their fight for racial equality in Charleston. Paul Stoney says the Little League became one of the reasons the Cannon Street Y became so important to the story of civil rights in Charleston. "This is where it all began," Paul Stoney said of the Y Little League, where volunteers were recruited to coach and where boys were recruited to play. "This is why the Cannon Street Y is so important."[30]

The Cannon Street League played informally in 1953. They wore t-shirts and jeans and there was no affiliation with Little League Baseball. That changed in 1954. If Morrison tried to integrate Little League Baseball in Charleston, it would complicate life for Danny Jones. Jones had never had to worry about the contrasting rules between Little League Baseball and the laws and customs in South Carolina because there had never been an African American Little League in South Carolina. Jones believed in segregation, as did most white adults in South Carolina and in the South. If the Cannon Street Y League joined Little League Baseball, Jones would be subject to the rules of Little League Baseball, which prohibited racial discrimination. Morrison met Jones before he applied for a charter with Little League Baseball. Jones, Morrison said, expressed no objections to a Black Little League. Morrison said that Jones told him that there were Black teams playing with white teams in North Carolina. "Danny Jones told us that North Carolina had a full colored team and a mixed team," Morrison said.[31]

The Cannon Street YMCA Little League began its first season in 1954. The four teams—Harleston Funeral Home, the Fielding Funeral Home, the Pan Hellenic Council, and Police Athletic League—played all their games against one another during the 1954 season. The Cannon Street League would be eligible to register a team in the district tournament the next year.

Morrison hoped to use the Cannon Street Y League to challenge segregation in Charleston. But the justices on the U.S. Supreme Court got ahead of him.

10

EVEN THE OCEAN WAS SEGREGATED

William "Buck" Godfrey remembered growing up in Charleston in the 1940s and 1950s where African Americans were born in the segregated wing of a hospital, raised in substandard houses on dirt streets, and attended schools that often lacked electricity or indoor plumbing. Students used textbooks—if they had textbooks—that had been discarded by white students. The textbooks had pages that were either ripped or torn out and said nothing about Black doctors, artists, athletes, inventors, poets, musicians, or businessmen or businesswomen. "We grew up in a society that had silently, meticulously and sardonically crafted the blueprint for our ultimate failure," Godfrey wrote in his memoir. "The process began early. African American babies were delivered into the world at black Roper Hospital. When they arrived at a certain age, they were educated at supposedly inferior black schools, thereby stunting their education."[1]

When Godfrey and other boys who would become the Cannon Street Y All-Stars were born, fewer than half of African American homeowners in Charleston had indoor toilets, compared with 96 percent of white homeowners. The Charleston Welfare Council, an interracial committee that included Robert Morrison, said that 80 percent of the more than 1,600 public housing units occupied by African Americans were substandard. Homes in the public housing projects—such as Gadsden Green near Hampton Park and The Citadel—often lacked sanitary safeguards, which exposed residents to diseases and sicknesses. Living conditions in public housing units were described as being "dangerous to life and limb."[2] Carl Johnson, one of the Cannon Street All-Stars, said that gangs of teenage boys menaced his neighborhood. Whenever you left home or returned to it, he said, "you had to duck and dodge."[3]

African American families had little chance of improving their lives because Jim Crow laws and customs denied them the education and other opportunities to do so. Most African American women worked as domestics and most African American men worked as laborers, if they worked at all. A lot of families depended on donations of food or clothing from churches and social service agencies. It was futile to complain because whites did not care about the living conditions of African Americans unless they protested, and, if they did that, they were deemed troublemakers and their insolence could cost them what little freedom they had after police found cause to arrest them and throw them in jail. African Americans had little or no chance to improve social conditions because whites controlled the political power in Charleston.

A lot of African Americans accepted racial inferiority because they knew the dangers of confronting racism or because they accepted institutionalized racism because they knew nothing else. While growing up, John Rivers said he did not think about racial discrimination because he had nothing to compare it with. "We didn't think about it this way. It was so ingrained in society. You got up. You had your routines, you went to school, you stayed in your neighborhood," Rivers said. "There were two societies—white and Black—and they operated in the same space but they didn't interact with one another."[4]

By the time Gus Holt got to a certain age, he knew he would have to leave Charleston. "I knew growing up in Jim Crow, it wasn't going to work for me," he said. "In your formative years, you're pounded by racism. It does irrevocable damage to you. You're damaged goods."[5] Holt said he began and ended every day burdened by racism. "I went to bed with this shit every night," he said.[6]

In his landmark study of race relations in the United States, *An American Dilemma*, Swedish sociologist Gunnar Myrdal wrote that segregation was so complete in the South "that the white Southerner practically never sees a Negro except as his servant and in other standardized and formalized caste situations."[7] But this was not the case on the Charleston peninsula, which was, according to one study, the least segregated of the more than a hundred major cities in the United States. But this reflected neither inclusiveness nor progressiveness. It instead served as a relic of the days of slavery when slaves lived near their master's house. The slave of the 1800s was the domestic of the 1900s.[8]

African American families may have lived near white families and their sons may have played ball with one another but any socializing ended there. "We never went to their houses" Leroy Major said.[9] John Rivers lived on unpaved Islington Court next to an apartment building where whites lived. But, Rivers said, the white parents wouldn't let their children play with the African American kids. He remembered a white boy named Sonny who watched Rivers and his friends from behind a fence, wishing he could play with them. "We'd be in the court playing stickball and he'd be watching us from behind a wire fence. And he would stand at the fence and look at us playing. There was such sadness on his face," Rivers said. "One ball got hit into his yard and he was so happy to get the ball and throw it back. If it were up to him, he would've played with us. He didn't care. If it were up to us, he'd have played with us. To this day, I can see the image of him watching us."[10]

Buck Godfrey remembers playing sandlot baseball games with white boys or pickup basketball games at Bishop England High School or at the Jewish Community Center. During the games, the basketball court was a meritocracy where each boy was judged by his ability. It was only when they took a break to take a drink of water that they would again be separated. When this happened, the African American boys drank from a water fountain with the word "colored" written above it and the white boys drank from a fountain with the words "whites only." As the boys aged, they drifted apart because laws and customs kept them apart. "The separation became habitual," Godfrey said, "and eventually they would resent each other without knowing why."[11]

African American children were warned by their parents and other older relatives not to question the way things were. They were told to walk directly to the back of a bus even if there were empty seats elsewhere on the bus. They were told to drink from their own drinking fountains, to stay in their own neighborhoods, and to "know their place," wherever that place happened to be. They were to be deferential in the presence of white adults and tolerant in the presence of white boys and girls, regardless of what the white adult or white child said or did to them. "We knew the existence of segregation, but not the vicious brutality of it," Godfrey said. "Our parents had insulated us from its sting."[12]

African Americans parents knew the cruelty around them and knew there was only so much they could do to protect their sons and daughters. "Black parents learned to fear more for some sons than for others: those who were surly, rebellious, careless, who had not learned the art of appearing to know one's place, were in far greater danger," Philip Dray wrote in his book *At the Hands of Persons Unknown*. "And, tragically, parents had no choice but to actively suppress those very qualities in their children—self-confidence, curiosity, ambitiousness—that might be misconstrued as insolence or arrogance by whites."[13]

JIM CROW LAWS KEPT African Americans and whites from attending the same schools in Charleston, sitting in the same theaters, eating in the same restaurants, or swimming in the same pools—or even being on same beaches of the Atlantic Ocean.

Even the ocean was segregated.

African Americans were prohibited from most beaches in and around Charleston and most coastal cities. A hundred miles north of Charleston was Atlantic Beach, a popular destination for African Americans, who were denied access to beaches from Virginia to Florida. An African American laundromat owner founded Atlantic Beach in the 1930s as a refuge from the harshly segregated world. "The Black Pearl," as it was called, flourished throughout the 1940s and 1950s. The beach's salty air filled with the joyful laughter and the banter of domestics who worked in area hotels and homes.

Families came by car and bus and farmworkers came by truck-load from local tobacco fields.[14] Musicians and singers—including Count Basie, Ray Charles, Billie Holiday, James Brown, and Bo Diddley—who worked at the white nightclubs near Myrtle Beach could not stay in the nearby hotels, so after performing before all-white crowds, they went to Atlantic Beach, often followed by white revelers, where they put on late-night shows at the Cotton Club, the Black Magic Club, or the Hawk's Nest.[15]

If you lived on the Charleston peninsula and wanted to go to Atlantic Beach, this meant waking up before sunrise, packing a picnic, and driving, if you had a car, or paying a few dollars to have someone like Esau Jenkins drive you there in one of his buses. "This was the highlight of the summer," Rivers said.[16] Families knew it was a long drive and they would not be allowed to use the restrooms at roadside white-owned gas stations and restaurants. "Our rest area was in the bushes," Leroy Major remembered. "We couldn't stop to use the facilities."[17]

African Americans, in Charleston and elsewhere, separated from the rest of society, carved out their own lives apart and inde-pendent from whites. They found relative comfort and security in their own neighborhoods, where they knew the people around them and they knew you, and if you were doing something you were not supposed to be doing, your mother would find out before you had finished doing what you were not supposed to do. Your grandparents and other members of your extended family may have lived near—or perhaps—with you. Your doctor and dentist might live within walking distance. If you needed extra help in school, you could walk or ride your bicycle to your teacher's house, and if "you needed grits and you didn't have any, you'd take your cup next door and get a cup of grits," Leroy Major remembered, "and everybody in the neighborhood looked out for each other."[18]

There were African American–owned drug stores, grocery stores, and service stations. Mrs. Taylor's bakery shop on Spring Street was famous for her butterfly buns and cinnamon rolls. Kids would buy them and sneak them into the Lincoln, the segregated movie house on King Street. After swimming in the pool behind

Harmon Field, children bought a link bologna sausage at Scotty's Soda Shop that popped when you bit into it. The Brooks brothers, Albert and Harvey, owned a number of businesses on Morris Street—a motel, a pool hall, a real estate office, and a few restaurants, including one that served what the restaurant called "the best lima bean dinner in America."[19]

WHITES IN CHARLESTON MAY have seen African Americans on the streets during the daytime hours or in the back of a bus or mowing the lawn or clipping the hedges of a white person's home, but they were, as Ralph Ellison said, largely invisible. Ellison's 1953 novel *Invisible Man*, which won the National Book Award, told whites something they probably didn't know and it told Blacks something most of them knew too well: Blacks were largely invisible to whites—unless whites saw them doing something they didn't like. "I am invisible, understand, simply because people refuse to see me. Like the bodiless heads you see sometimes in circus sideshows, it is as though I have been surrounded by mirrors of hard, distorting glass," Ellison wrote. "When they approach me they see only my surroundings, themselves, or figments of their imagination—indeed, everything and anything except me."[20]

If you read either of the Charleston newspapers, the *News and Courier* or *Evening Post*, you couldn't possibly know that tens of thousands of African Americans lived in and around the city. If either of the newspapers published a photo of a Black person, it was usually a mug shot. Nothing newsworthy, or at least newsworthy and legal, happened in Black communities. No African Americans served in public office or ran for public office. There were no photos of politicians, business leaders, or doctors. There were no African American civic leaders and no grip-and-grin photos of Black community leaders. The newspapers published countless photos of beauty pageant contestants. "If a positive article appeared," Buck Godfrey said, "one needed a Sherlock Holmes–type magnifying glass to read it."[21]

In 1947 William Brower of the *Toledo Blade*, who was one of the relatively few African American journalists working for a white newspaper, wrote Thomas Waring, managing editor of the *News and Courier*, inquiring about the newspaper's policy toward coverage of African Americans. Waring responded that the newspaper rarely published news about Blacks because most of the subscribers were white. "We try not to be offensive, but it does seem that negroes get into the news most frequently in crime stories since we are not developing and cultivating personal news about them as we do about whites," he said.

Waring added that the newspaper did not call Blacks "Mr.," "Mrs.," or "Miss" and referred to Blacks as "negroes," but only if the reporter was certain of his or her race. "To call a white person a negro is libel per se in South Carolina," Waring said, "and we cannot afford to make an error." Waring said the newspaper advocated segregation and justice for whites and African Americans. African Americans could vote in the general election but not in the primaries because that decision was left to the Democratic Party "We contend the Democratic Party is a private group of white persons in this state who have the privilege of excluding negroes, or any other group they see fit."[22] This was before Waties Waring ruled that such primaries were unconstitutional.

Charleston newspapers reinforced perceptions that African Americans were either criminals or, as newspapers and politicians pointed out, dependent on whites for public assistance. Whites, whether in Charleston or throughout the South and much of the country, knew little or nothing about the African American doctors, educators, musicians, or businessmen or women who were as essential to their own communities as talented whites were to their communities. Whites knew about athletes like Olympic track-and-field star Jesse Owens, heavyweight champion Joe Louis, or college football stars like Kenny Washington and Jackie Robinson, and Negro Leaguers like Satchel Paige and Josh Gibson, who traveled through the South in barnstorming exhibits and sometimes played in Charleston.

This changed when Robinson signed a contract with the Brooklyn Dodgers organization on October 23, 1945. Civil rights activist Roy Wilkins, who would later become executive director of the NAACP, said that the signing of Robinson meant that Blacks "should have their own rights, should have jobs, decent homes and education, freedom from insult, and equality of opportunity to achieve."[23] *New York Age* editor Ludlow Werner wrote that a lot of white Americans were hoping Robinson would fail. Robinson "would be haunted by the expectations of his race," he said. "Unlike white players, he can never afford an off day or off night. His private life will be watched, too, because white America will judge the Negro race by everything he does. And Lord help him with his fellow Negroes if he should fail them."[24]

Eighteen months after Robinson signed his contract, he played his first game for the Brooklyn Dodgers on April 15, 1947, forever changing baseball and society. The integration of baseball became the most important civil rights story in the years following World War II. And nothing in those years had a more pronounced impact on how white America saw Blacks and how Black America—particularly the generation of young African Americans that came of age during this time—saw themselves. Roger Wilkins, Roy Wilkins's nephew, was fifteen in 1947. He said that young Blacks like himself saw in Robinson that things that were once impossible were suddenly possible. "This man, in a very personal sense," Wilkins said of Robinson, "became a permanent part of my spirit and the spirit of a generation of black kids like me because of the way he faced his ordeal."[25] Poet Langston Hughes, who lived in New York City, marveled at what happened during Robinson's first season. "Anyway, this summer of our Lord 1947, the Dodgers are doing right with Jackie Robinson at first," Hughes said. "If Robinson and the Dodgers succeeded," he added, "a hundred years from now history will still be grinning."[26]

Nobody had to wait that long.

African Americans discussed with one another what Robinson did that day and in every game after that. Pastors delivered sermons about him and asked their parishioners to pray for him. People talked about Robinson in barbershops, taverns, and on the streets, in small towns and in big cities. In the years before Major League teams used chartered jets, teams traveled by train and often arrived late in the evening before a road game. When the Dodgers disembarked, they would invariably be met, no matter the hour, by crowds—usually fathers, most of them Black, with their young sons.[27] Fathers and sons—and mothers and daughters—listened to the Brooklyn games on the radio or on a short wave radio, read about Robinson in the newspaper, and called friends and relatives, if they had them, in New York City to query them for any additional information about Robinson and the Dodgers.[28]

Buck Godfrey, John Bailey, Leroy Major, John Rivers, and the other boys who would become the Cannon Street All-Stars grew up among the first generation of Blacks in America after the integration of baseball. The promise of baseball was that any boy could grow up to play in the Major Leagues. For the first time, these words meant something. "We would dream of playing in the big leagues," Godfrey said, "but for the moment there was the happiness and sanctity of our neighborhoods. It was there we learned the game."[29] African American boys pretended to be Jackie Robinson or Roy Campanella or Don Newcombe or other Black Major Leaguers like Larry Doby or Willie Mays when they played sandlot baseball. And when they played catch with their fathers, their fathers told them they could be Major League ballplayers just like their heroes. "All the fathers must have gone to some kind of convention," John Bailey says, "because they were all telling us we could be the next Jackie Robinson, Roy Campanella, or Don Newcombe."[30]

Until Jackie Robinson, African American children were taught—or learned on their own—to cling to their dreams because that was all they had. But Robinson gave wings to the dreams of Black boys—and those dreams gave wings to their hopes that could transport them out of poverty and away from bigotry. "Everybody wanted to be Jackie," John Rivers said. "He was our inspiration."[31] Vermort Brown and the other boys in his Gadsden Green neighborhood could not afford a baseball or a bat so they pretended to be Robinson or "Campy" or "Newk" while using a rubber ball and swinging a mop. The small yards and dirt streets and courts were no match for either their dreams or the force of a broomstick making full contact against a rubber ball, which would end up lost, or worse, in a yard with a hostile dog who dared any of the boys to take the ball from it. Their parents, who barely had—or often did not have—money for essentials, had no money for rubber balls. The boys would fish for crabs, casting their wire nets in the Ashley River, and sell what they caught to merchants so they could buy rubber balls and the game could go on.[32]

Any rubber ball they bought had a short life span. This forced them to improvise. The boys learned to play "half-rubber," as Vermort Brown called it, which required slicing a rubber ball in half and playing with that. They practiced throwing the half-rubber ball until they could make it curve, dip, or flutter. A half-rubber ball was hard to throw but far harder to hit. "Imagine trying to hit a drunken lightning bug in the dark with the cue end of a black pool stick," Godfrey said. "That was how difficult it was hit to hit a ball that, when thrown, defied all laws of gravity and physics."[33]

The boys created their own neighborhood teams and played against teams from other neighborhoods on makeshift baseball fields, using rubber balls at first but then baseballs, which were more expensive than rubber balls so they had to improvise again. The boys played all day and into the evening and then woke up and did the same thing, slowly mastering their skills in half-rubber.[34] When the boys played with a harder ball, they also had to improvise because they did not have money for gloves. Brown used a paper bag or a modified cardboard box for a glove. He would put one side of his hand flat on a piece of cardboard and trace out his fingers with a pencil and use scissors to cut along the pencil marks. He would duplicate the process with the back of his hand on a separate piece of cardboard. He then put his hand between the pieces of cardboard and tied together the cardboard with a piece of twine.[35]

The boys could not afford to buy baseballs so they went to College Park, near Hampton Park, which was built in 1940 for the baseball teams of The Citadel and College of Charleston, and they would chase foul balls and home runs that left the park and take them back to their baseball fields.[36] The first game played at College Park was an exhibition game between the Boston Red Sox and the Cincinnati Reds. Ted Williams, in his second year in the big leagues, hit the first home run.[37] During the off-season, African American Major Leaguers would travel with Negro League teams throughout the South, and this included games at College Park. Jackie Robinson, Larry Doby, Roy Campanella, and Don Newcombe played in games in November 1949 and October 1950. An article in the *News and Courier* called the October 1950 game "the greatest negro baseball attraction ever offered here."[38]

African American boys often begged the Negro League teams for any balls or spare bats or gloves. One day Buck Godfrey and his friends saw what appeared to be the equipment manager for one of the teams putting bats, gloves, balls, and other items into a half dozen duffle bags. Godfrey and his friends told the man how much they loved baseball but were too poor to buy their own balls, gloves, or bats. They asked if the man could spare anything for them. The man handed them one of the duffle bags. The stunned boys thanked the man.

"Go have some fun," the man said with a wink.

When they opened the bag, they found two broken thirty-four-ounce Louisville Sluggers and two thirty-six-ounce Louisville Sluggers. There also was a chest protector, a pair of shin guards, a catcher's mask, and three unused baseballs. When they got home, they took some nails, sandpaper, and a roll of athletic tape and repaired the broken bats.[39]

11.

BROWN V. BOARD OF EDUCATION

O n May 17, 1954, the U.S. Supreme Court ruled in *Brown v. Board of Education* that state-sponsored segregation in public schools was unconstitutional. In its unanimous decision, Chief Justice Earl Warren, who wrote the court's opinion, raised the question: "Does segregation of children in public schools solely on the basis of race . . . deprive the children of the minority group of equal educational opportunities?" Warren then answered the question: "We believe that it does." The chief justice then provided the court's rationale for ending separate schools for African American students. "To separate them from others of similar age and qualifications solely because of their race generates a feeling of inferiority as to their status in the community that may affect their hearts and minds in a way unlikely ever to be undone."[1]

Warren wrote that it was impossible to go back in time to understand why the court decided as it did in *Plessy v. Ferguson*, which established "separate but equal." But, he said, it was possible to rectify the mistakes of the past. "We conclude that, in the field of public education, the doctrine of 'separate but equal' has no place," the court said. "Separate educational facilities are inherently unequal." The court concluded its relatively short opinion by declaring that segregated public education was inherently unequal because it violated the "equal protection clause" of the U.S. Constitution. "Separate educational facilities are inherently unequal. Therefore, we hold that the plaintiffs and others similarly situated for whom the actions have been brought are, by reason of the segregation complained of, deprived of the equal protection of the laws guaranteed by the Fourteenth Amendment."[2]

The Supreme Court did not reference Waties Waring's dissent in *Briggs v. Elliott*, but it used his argument, cited the same court decisions, and came to the same conclusion as Waring. The court said, "Separate educational facilities are unequal." Waring said, "Segregation is per se inequality." Waring later acknowledged that the court had wisely not attacked the South as he had. "He knew the South would never accept a ruling with his name attached, not after the ferocity of his attacks on Southerners," Brian Hicks wrote in his biography of Waring. "He'd been too strident, too harsh, and recognized the Supreme Court managed to accomplish the same goal without sparking riots." Waring understood the court had succeeded where he had failed and yet reached the same conclusion. "Without considerable gratification, I sometimes laughingly say that nine Supreme Court justices were just as big damn fools as I was, apparently, because they happened to decide my way," he said.[3]

In his 1975 book *Simple Justice*, Richard Kluger said that *Brown* occupies a "high place in the literature of liberty" because it "marked the turning point in America's willingness to face the consequences of centuries of racial discrimination."[4] Historians, judges, and others have responded with near unanimity to the *Brown* decision's significance. J. Harvie Wilkinson III called *Brown* "the story . . . of a thousand tales of human suffering and sacrifice subsumed in the winning of a principle."[5] But newspaper editors and journalists— unlike historians—do not have the luxury of time to contemplate the gravity of the court's decision. "The first rough draft of history," as journalism has been called, represented the country's gut reaction to the decision.[6]

To a lot of northern newspapers, the *Brown* decision meant America had finally addressed the hypocrisy it had long ignored. How could a country preach equality to the rest of the world without practicing it itself? "What the Justices have done," the *Cincinnati Enquirer* said, "is simply to act as the conscious of the American nation."[7] The *Washington Post* agreed. "It is not too much to speak of the Court's decision as a new birth of freedom. It comes at a juncture in the affairs of mankind when this reaffirmation of basic human values is likely to have a wonderfully tonic effect," the *Post* said in an editorial. "America is rid of an incubus which impeded and embarrassed it in all its relations with the world. Abroad as well as home, this decision will engender a renewal of faith in democratic institutions and ideals."[8]

Georgia governor Herman Talmadge, however, said the court had reduced the Constitution to a "mere scrap of paper." The justices, Talmadge said, "had blatantly ignored all law and precedent and usurped from the Congress and the people the power to amend the Constitution."[9] South Carolina governor James Byrnes expressed "shock at the decision."[10] Senator Burnet Maybank of Charleston called the ruling "shameful." Congressman L. Mendel Rivers called the decision a "tragic mistake that creates one of the gravest problems to confront the white people of the South since the days of Reconstruction."[11]

Charleston Post and Courier editor Tom Waring wrote in a front-page editorial that the court had "cut deep into the sinews of the Republic" and attacked the natural order of life in the South that had peacefully existed since the end of Reconstruction. "It was too early to secede and start another War Between the States," Waring said. He called for calm but added that he had no intention of accepting racial integration in the South. He said that whites and African Americans "live in harmony" in most of the South, but that the court's decision jeopardized that. He blamed assertive Blacks for upsetting that harmony by insisting on rights they did not have.[12]

The newspaper quoted Waties Waring, who had retired from the federal bench and moved with his wife, Elizabeth, to New York City, and who said the decision would "erase the shame" of *Plessy v. Ferguson*. "The Court has affirmed our belief in the Declaration of Independence and the Constitution and has finally killed the hypocrisy of those who practice a vicious form of racial bias under the sophistry of the so-called 'separate but equal' doctrine," Waring said.[13]

The Warings surrounded themselves with like-minded racial progressives in New York City. He became a popular lecturer and guest on television and radio programs. In 1957 he appeared on a PBS talk show, *The Open Mind*, where he discussed the challenges facing "the new negro" with a young and then relatively unknown Alabama minister named Martin Luther King Jr.[14]

Waring died on January 11, 1968, and was returned to Charleston to be buried. Few whites came to his funeral service. When the hearse carrying the judge passed through the gates of Magnolia Cemetery, hundreds of Black residents lined up behind it and walked with Waring's body to its grave. His final request was to return to Charleston and be buried in a shaded plot next to the water in the same cemetery but separate from where so many of his ancestors and family had been laid to rest. The dead did not complain about him living among them—as his relatives had complained about him living among them. His relatives had wanted nothing to do with him when he was alive and now they would have to share a cemetery with him in death. Waring had forced himself upon his family and his hometown "for all eternity," Brian Hicks said, and "again, he would have the last word."[15]

Tom Waring and others in the family and in Charleston high society would later claim that their enmity toward the judge had everything to do with him leaving his wife to marry someone else and little to do with his judicial opinions. "It was my feeling," Tom Waring said in an interview, "that the so-called ostracism of Judge Waring on account of his racial decision was a complete distortion of fact."[16] Judge Waring's affair with Elizabeth and his divorce from Annie and subsequent marriage to Elizabeth were scandalous and embarrassing to the Waring name. The judge's private life may have reflected poorly on the Waring name. But Waties's judicial opinions reflected directly on the white supremacist beliefs of southern aristocracy and everything his family and most of the people in their social class believed was wrapped up in that.

"People weren't burning crosses in Waties's yard because he divorced Annie," Hicks said.[17]

In 2015 the Hollings Judicial Center in Charleston was renamed the J. Waties Waring Judicial Center. Hollings asked Congress to remove his name from the building and add Waring's. "They put my name on the courthouse because I got funding for it," Hollings said. "I want to put it in the name of the guy who did justice here."[18]

THOMAS WARING JR.'S LIFE was a monument to white privilege, and his journalism was a paean to white supremacy. He was born May 30, 1907, and grew up in Charleston the son of a newspaper editor and attended the prestigious Porter Military Academy. At age sixteen, he entered the University of the South in Sewanee, Tennessee, where he served as editor of the campus newspaper and graduated Phi Beta Kappa. He then returned to Charleston and applied for a job with his father, Thomas Sr., editor of the *Evening Post*. His father turned him down, telling his son he needed more experience.

Upon leaving his father's office at 134 Meeting Street in downtown Charleston, Waring saw his uncle, William Watts Ball, who was editor of the *News and Courier*, the city's morning newspaper. Ball, who was on his way to see his brother-in-law, Waring's father, asked his nephew what he was doing at the newspaper. Waring told him he had gone to see his father about a job but his father had turned him down.

"You're hired," Ball told him.

The two of them left the *Evening Post*'s office and walked to the *News and Courier* building several blocks away at 19 Broad Street. Ball introduced Waring to the newspaper's city editor and told the editor to put him to work.[19]

Waring worked for the *News and Courier* for two years before he was told he had a job with the *New York World*. But when he got to New York, there was no job. He stayed in New York and was hired at the *Herald Tribune*, where he worked until returning to Charleston to become city editor of the *News and Courier* in 1931.[20] He became the newspaper's managing editor in 1942 and then succeeded Ball when he retired in 1951 and remained editor more than two decades.[21]

Tom Waring may have gotten his name from his father, but he

got his politics from his more conservative uncle, who took seriously the words on the newspaper's masthead, "the most outspoken newspaper in South Carolina." In his book about the history of the *News and Courier*, Herbert Ravenel Sass, who wrote for the newspaper when Ball was editor, compared the editor to John C. Calhoun. "One might almost say that Ball is Calhoun brought down to date."[22]

Ball defended the southern aristocracy from either poor, uneducated whites or African Americans. "The aristocracy didn't like the idea of lowlifes horning in on their deal," Gene Roberts and Hank Klibanoff wrote in *The Race Beat*, "and they especially didn't like it when they saw the next wave of people banging on the door was not even white."[23] Sid Bedingfield agreed in his book *Newspaper Wars*. "Ball was obsessed with the notion of hierarchy in society," Bedingfield said, and "he believed all classes had their 'place,' with aristocratic elites in charge and working-class near the bottom, just one step above the former slaves."[24] The editor of the *Anderson (SC) Independent* characterized the newspaper as follows: Ball and the "chronic dyspepsia run together to form the *News and Courier.*"[25]

Strom Thurmond and other segregationist politicians in the state and elsewhere had no better friend than the editors of the *News and Courier*, Ball and Thomas Waring, who agreed with Thurmond's condemnation of President Harry S. Truman's call for civil rights legislation in 1947 and defended Thurmond's presidential run in 1948.[26] Thurmond could not run for reelection as governor because South Carolina law forbade governors from seeking successive terms. Thurmond then ran as a write-in candidate for the U.S. Senate in 1954 and won in part on the *News and Courier*'s endorsement.[27] Thurmond wrote Waring a letter of appreciation.[28]

Waring agreed with Ball that class distinctions were necessary to maintain aristocratic rule. He defended segregation for upper-class whites to maintain the power they had long had.[29] Bedingfield wrote that when the Supreme Court announced its decision in *Brown v. Board of Education*, Waring did what other *News and Courier* editors, including W. W. Ball, had done before him: "He led his newspaper deep into political battle."[30] His editorials attacked federal meddling to end segregation and African Americans in Charleston who dared challenge what Waring referred to as the "natural order."[31] Waring urged southern politicians and other newspaper editors to organize and resist the *Brown* decision.[32]

To Waring white supremacy sustained the South, and without it the region would become like so many other forgotten civilizations. Waties Waring called the *News and Courier* the "bible of the supremacists."[33] Roberts and Klibanoff said Waring "was as forceful a spokesman for segregation as there was in the South."[34] Reed Sarratt, editor of the *Winston-Salem (NC) Journal*, said Waring was without rival for the "sheer volume and variety of his fusillades against the Supreme Court."[35]

The South had disregarded elections and court decisions that did not serve their self-interests before and would do so again following the *Brown* decision. They would simply bide their time until laws were changed, while uppity African Americans were lynched by mobs or beaten by white law enforcement officers, the rest of Blacks were intimidated into silence, and things returned to normal. Until then, the South would resist any pressure to obey the Supreme Court. Tom Waring wrote that few southern newspapers agreed with the *Brown* decision. "We cannot name one at the moment," Waring said in an editorial on April 29, 1955.[36]

Waring raged against the Supreme Court, the NAACP, northern progressives, racial activists, communists, and anyone else who called for racial equality. He wrote essays in national magazines and toured the South on his one-man white supremacy tour. The KKK and its public displays of racism made Waring uncomfortable, though not enough to keep him from running lengthy stories about the organization on the front page of his newspaper. Nevertheless, he warned southern politicians that they must respond to *Brown* or else Klan violence would do "immeasurable" harm to the South in the court of public opinion.[37]

Waring called for the creation of Citizens' Councils to replace the KKK, which had sullied the reputation of respectable racists like himself. The first White Citizens' Council was created in Mississippi in the weeks after *Brown* to defend segregation. Citizens' Council members served on city councils and school boards and owned businesses and small-town newspapers. The Mississippi Citizens' Council said they were organized in more than a hundred towns and had twenty-five thousand members, a claim that would grow to sixty thousand members a few months later.[38]

Waring, who described Citizens' Councils as a better class of white people than the KKK, promoted the councils in his newspaper and even contributed editorials to the organization's newspaper.[39] The Citizens' Councils were nothing more than Klansmen with cleaner sheets. They sought revenge against those who had challenged segregation. The Reverend Joseph DeLaine and his family had left Summerton and moved to Lake City. But the harassment continued. Police did nothing after DeLaine's house was vandalized again and again. In early October, DeLaine's church was burned to the ground when he was in Charleston for an AME conference. Police refused to call it arson. They told DeLaine that a member of his congregation may have set the fire accidentally.[40]

On October 10, 1955, members of the White Citizens' Council fired upon DeLaine's home and he returned gunfire.[41] Police filed charges against DeLaine. No charges were filed against the men who fired at his house. DeLaine had had enough. He and his family moved to Buffalo. The state of South Carolina issued extradition orders to bring DeLaine back to the state to face justice. The state of New York refused to comply with the order. Gov. George Bell Timmerman dropped the extradition matter. "South Carolina is well rid of this professional agitator," Timmerman said.[42] DeLaine, speaking from the safety of New York, said, "The cowards now operating in the name of white supremacy would lynch Christ if it would serve their ungodly purpose."[43]

BROWN V. BOARD OF EDUCATION is widely considered the most important civil rights decision in American history. It also was one of the most difficult to implement. On May 31 the Supreme Court returned to *Brown* in what became known as *Brown II*, which confirmed that segregation was unconstitutional. It told states they had to desegregate their schools "with all deliberate speed."[44] The vagueness of the court's language appeared to tell states they could desegregate at their own discretion. This was intended as a compromise.

But the South was in no mood to compromise.[45]

Neither was Tom Waring.

Waring directed a sustained attack on racial equality during the summer of 1955 as few metropolitan newspaper editors had done since the Civil War. His arguments were as full of sound and fury and unrestrained bigotry as they were empty of facts, reason, and decency. Just a mile or so away from Waring's newspaper office, the Cannon Street Little League played its second season. Neither coaches nor players had any idea that they, too, would find themselves in Waring's crosshairs.

On June 2, four days after the *Brown II* decision, Waring responded with an editorial, "Segregation for the Whites," that said that Clarendon County had closed their schools rather than be forced to integrate them. Waring told whites to segregate themselves. "White people may not be permitted by law to segregate Negroes," he said. "but they can segregate themselves."[46] Nine days later, the *News and Courier* ran a front-page story on a KKK rally in Sumter County in what it called the first open meeting of the Klan in two years. The article reported that a thirty-foot cross illuminated the sky at the meeting where five hundred men, women, and children listened to the organization's imperial wizard, E. L. Edwards of Atlanta, call for a rebirth of the organization to confront the Supreme Court's decision. "These nine buzzards up there all but destroyed our Supreme Court with that one ruling," Edwards said. "If we are made to mix races in schools, they'll think it right that the Negroes should grow up and marry whites and you won't be able to stop them."[47]

ON JULY 4 WARING responded to a story in Waco, Texas, where rumors of an African American uprising followed the sentencing of a Black man for killing a white soldier. He wrote that there was racial equality in the courts and blamed the NAACP for trying to upset race relations.[48] On July 5 Waring said that northern newspapers that criticized segregation were run by communists.[49] On July 6 Waring recommended the book *Weep No More My Lady*, by North Carolina radio commentator W. E. Debnam, which was a response to former First Lady Eleanor Roosevelt's criticism of the South.[50]

On July 15 the *News and Courier* published a front-page story reporting that the Charleston NAACP had petitioned school trustees to take "immediate steps" to end segregation in the public schools. The petition asked trustees to reorganize schools on a nondiscriminatory basis. The document was signed by forty-seven parents of children enrolled in the school district's twenty schools.[51] The newspapers published the names and addresses of all the petitioners in hopes of intimidating them to withdraw from the lawsuit.[52] Another Waring editorial said South Carolina needed to root out "communists" from the teaching profession by doing what Georgia had done and ban schoolteachers from joining the NAACP. Waring said the newspaper believed in "individual liberty," but this, he said, did not include militant teachers who belonged to the NAACP. Membership in the organization, he said, "destroys the freedom to teach the unbiased truth."[53]

On July 21, 1955, the newspaper reported in a front-page story that an organization had been created to fight integration. It quoted A. O. Weeks, the founder and organizer of the yet-to-be-named organization, who said he would not accept the *Brown v. Board of Education* decision.[54] The article did not mention that Waring and the newspaper's statehouse correspondent, William D. Workman Jr., were among the group's organizers.[55] Waring wrote an editorial the next day, which began, "One of the saddest aspects of the argument over mingling the races is the fanning of racial hate." The editorial then accused the NAACP of "destroying racial harmony." It was up to whites to convince African Americans that they must "protect themselves against the bad leadership from the NAACP," the editorial said.[56]

The *News and Courier* reported on July 24 that Charleston attorney John H. Wrighten and J. Arthur Brown, president of the

Charleston chapter of the NAACP, had filed suit to open state-owned parks to Blacks.[57] Two days later, William Workman wrote a page-one story that said the state might eliminate its state parks as a result of the lawsuit.[58] On July 27 Waring wrote an editorial with the headline "Phony Word," which said that "desegregation," a word used by the Supreme Court in *Brown* and *Brown II*, was not a word. "Like many of the arguments for 'desegregation,'" he said, "it is synthetic, made up of the dreams of sociologists. What 'desegregationists' are talking about, of course, is mixing the races, but somehow they don't like the sound of those words. Too much truth, we guess."[59]

On July 30 Waring wrote that "militant" Blacks were demanding "first-class citizenship." He said that many Blacks did not deserve first-class citizenship because they reported false information on their tax returns by claiming more dependents than they had. Blacks also did not observe marriage laws and customs because so many Black children were illegitimate. And finally, he said, Blacks violated the requirements of first-class citizenship because they did not observe the peace or obey laws because "most of the crimes of violence tried in southern courts were committed by Negroes." He did not include a source for any of those observations.[60]

The *News and Courier* continued its campaign of intimidation against Blacks on August 10 by publishing the names and addresses of 250 people who signed a petition submitted to the Cooper River School Board calling for the integration of the school district. The article said that J. Arthur Brown had distributed the petition.[61] Waring criticized the signers in an editorial, "Who Are the Signers?" He asked: How many of them had children in the school district? Who persuaded them to sign the petition? "Do they understand they may be hoping to break down the public school system and even friendly race relations?" he asked. Waring called on white people to pressure anyone who signed the petition.[62]

On August 19 Waring praised the document that had been released from the anti-integration organization, which called itself "the Committee of 52," presumably because it was composed of what Waring called "a panel of 52 outstanding South Carolinians."

Waring tried to assure his readers of the character of the document's signers. "The signers of the racial separation manifesto are not crackpots, extremists, Klansmen, rightests or leftists," he said. "In other words, they are a cross-section of the better-class, moderate white people of South Carolina."[63] The manifesto served as the basis for White Citizens' Councils as the primary organization to defend segregation.[64] The "Manifesto of Southern Rights" called for white South Carolinians to "stand firm" against the Supreme Court's decision ordering the integration of schools.[65] The manifesto would serve as the basis for what would become known as the South's campaign of "massive resistance" to civil rights.[66]

Waring and his newspaper made no attempt during the summer of 1955 to recognize that there was anything other than one side of the argument. The newspaper published scores of letters to the editor that summer repeating the same language found in Waring's editorials: the South needed to resist the *Brown* ruling; race relations had been good until the NAACP began interfering; most Blacks did not want integration; anyone who supported integration was either a member of the NAACP or a communist or a northerner or all three; and segregation was God's plan. The newspaper published the names of Blacks who signed petitions calling for integration but did not identify letter writers who said all African Americans should be removed from the South and sent to northern cities.[67] This opinion was repeated six weeks later in another letter, which said that African American laborers could be replaced by mechanical farm equipment. This, the letter said, "would relieve our burden of a race who have never been self-supporting, that is only a few of their race [*sic*]. They have contributed to keeping us poor."[68]

One letter writer, who identified herself as a Black woman but was not named, said Blacks did not want integration.[69] Another said that the South was a "good place to live" until the NAACP started interfering.[70] Another compared the NAACP to Hitler's Germany.[71] Another said the Supreme Court's decision to integrate schools was part of a "highly successful plot of godless Communism against the nation as a whole."[72] Another said that the

NAACP was trying to destroy the "fine schools" that whites had built for Blacks. "I have four children and they will never go to school with Negroes," he said.[73] Other writers agreed. "My child will not attend school with a Negro, today, tomorrow or ever."[74] Another letter said that *Plessy v. Ferguson* was still the law of the land. The writer called "unconstitutional" the Supreme Court's decision to desegregate schools in *Brown*. "If the Southern people bow to this decision or allow it to disrupt their public school system, then they deserve to lose their heritage in the grand march of communism," the letter said.[75]

On August 7 one letter, appearing under the headline "Mixed Baseball," included an observation of what the writer had seen a few days earlier as she rode on the Rutledge Avenue–Heriot Street bus line at about noon. "Who can explain why Negroes boys and white boys were playing baseball behind the museum on Ashley Avenue," she said. "I could not help but exclaim and I am sure all who were on the bus heard me when I said, 'Why look, those are white and Negro boys playing baseball out there.'"[76]

12.

"A DASTARDLY ACT"

Allen Tibbs, the Cannon Street Y's executive secretary, completed the application for a charter with Little League Baseball and it was sent to Williamsport. Little League Baseball notified the Cannon Street YMCA that it had approved its application for a league for boys aged ten to twelve for the spring of 1954. The Y needed sponsors for teams and the teams needed coaches and players. The YMCA sent out word it needed coaches, Rufus Dilligard said. Dilligard and Lee Bennett agreed, and so did other men, including Ben Singleton, Archie Graham, and Walter Burke, one of the city's few African American police officers. The Harleston Funeral Home, the Fielding Funeral Home, the Pan Hellenic Council, and Police Athletic League each agreed to sponsor teams. If you did not have a baseball glove, someone would find one for you. Vermort Brown did not have to use his cardboard glove.

Burke coached the Police Athletic League team; Bennett and Dilligard the Pan Hellenic Council; Graham the Harleston Home; and Singleton the Fielding Funeral Home. Dilligard took the responsibility of seeing to it that the Harmon Field infield was raked. Burke did a lot of the umpiring. Allen Tibbs, who did not have a car, sometimes carried a duffle bag full of bats and balls from the Y to Harmon Field, almost a mile away, where he would find coaches and parents and players mowing the lawn, raking the infield, or putting down the chalk for the base lines.[1] Little League rules required an outfield fence that stood four feet high and stood the requisite distance from home plate. "We had little or no money and we needed things. Especially a portable fence," Godfrey said. "We went to Sears and Roebuck and from our own pockets, we bought this folding, portable fence," which was put up before every game and then taken down afterward.[2]

Morrison did not have to make phone calls or knock on doors to let the boys know about the league. The boys who played baseball on the empty lot behind the Y were probably among the first to hear. They told their friends. Word spread throughout the peninsula. There had been talk about a league but now there was a league. "There would be coaches and uniforms and real Little League equipment. There would be real bases and a fence for home runs," Buck Godfrey remembered. "What started as a subdued whisper now became a loud roar. The news had bumpety bumped into an avalanche of frenzied activity."

Tryouts for the 1954 Cannon Street Little League were on March 15 at Harmon Field.[3] The season began six weeks later.[4] Competition was fierce for a spot on one of the four teams. A hundred boys tried out and there were only spots for sixty—fifteen per team. Many of the boys knew each other from school or from pickup games. They knew who was good and who was not. The coaches, each wanting to get a drop on the other, scoured the neighborhood ballfields, looking for hidden talent. Walter Burke found Allen Jackson, who grew up on American Street on the eastern end of the peninsula. He was hitting pitches thrown by his father. Burke looked closer and Jackson was a rare find indeed—a switch-hitter with a powerful throwing arm.[5]

Leroy Major drew scrutiny because he was so tall for his age—nearly six feet tall. The coaches said he could not be twelve years old. Major had already learned about discrimination against African Americans. But that day he learned he was discriminated against for another reason. "I was discriminated against by the coaches," he remembered with a laugh. "They said I couldn't be twelve. They made me get my birth certificate."[6]

The *News and Courier* published a story on April 12 about opening night for the Cooper River Parks and Playground Commission Little League and Pony League programs. Forty teams of uniformed boys and six girls' softball teams walked in parade onto the North Charleston Athletic Field. A color guard of the American Legion followed and a marching band played while the field filled up with players and coaches. And then, the article said, it was "Play Ball."[7]

There was a separate ceremony for the Cannon Street Y League at Harmon Field more than two weeks later.[8] Before the first game, the boys all walked in a parade. This continued informally throughout the season as the boys walked from their homes to Harmon Field. "You would arrive at the park and you'd smell the freshly cut grass," John Rivers said. "That's what sticks in my mind."[9]

To the boys, being part of Little League Baseball—putting on a uniform and playing on a field with regulation bases and umpires and coaches in front of their mothers and fathers and relatives and other spectators—resonated in a magical way that had been the case since Carl Stotz created the first league for his nephews and their friends. John Rivers said he sat the bench during his first year in 1954, but he felt like the team's best player when he put on his uniform and walked to Harmon Field where the league played its games. "Putting on the uniform was the most invigorating experience of my life. When I walked to the ballpark from my house it was like I was floating," Rivers said.[10]

To the parents, the Cannon Street Little League provided a chance to get together on a warm spring or summer night, sit on bleachers, and chat and cheer for their boys. There were no lights at Harmon Field so games started in the early evening. Some of the parents had to skip dinner and go straight from work to be at the field before the game started. Mel Middleton remembered the evenings at Harmon Field. "How I wish you could have experienced a night at Harmon Field," he said. "The bleachers were packed. All the parents were there. They passed a hat to help pay for equipment when we needed it. Oh, it was a wonderful time."[11]

Baseball was segregated through Charleston. It was only integrated in small print in the *News and Courier* and the *Evening Post*, which ran results and line scores of the youth baseball leagues. The boys in the Cannon Street League had their names in a newspaper that rarely published the names of African Americans unless they were arrested. If you looked close enough at a line score, in eight-point type, you would see the names of white boys and Black boys in the line scores. John Rivers kept the box score of the first game he pitched.

The newspapers also printed the standings of the different youth leagues. Rivers's team, Pan Hellenic, coached by Dilligard, won the championship, but then its best players aged out and the team fell to the bottom of the standings the next year. Rivers, who worked hard on his fielding between the two seasons, became the team's shortstop and star player. "Nothing got by me," he said.[12]

THE CANNON STREET YMCA team couldn't register a team in the 1954 district tournament because first-year leagues were ineligible. But as Robert Morrison, once a star athlete himself, watched the boys play during the first half of 1955 season, he liked what he saw. Things were progressing according to his plan. Morrison told the league's coaches to select an All-Star team to play in the district tournament.

The first-half win-loss standings were as follows:
Fielding, 7-2.
Police Athletic League, 6-3.
Harleston, 3-6.
Pan Hellenic, 2-7.[13]
This meant that Fielding had the most All-Stars and Pan Hellenic had the fewest.

Morrison knew that the Cannon Street Y All-Stars met the qualifications to play in the tournament. He also knew that African American teams played against white teams in Little League tournaments in other states. The Cannon Street team could not be kept out of the tournament without violating Little League Baseball rules that barred racial discrimination. The coaches told the All-Stars they would keep playing baseball as long as they kept winning—all the way to the Little League World Series.

When John Bailey learned the news, he ran the eleven blocks from the Cannon Street Y to his family's two-story home on Strawberry Lane where he found his mother in the kitchen.

"Mama! Mama!" Bailey shouted. "I made it! I made the team!"

Fifty years later, Bailey recalled in an interview with *Post and Courier* sportswriter Gene Sapakoff the day he found out he had made the Cannon Street YMCA All-Star team.

Flossie Bailey handed her son a peach, told him to calm down, and asked him to repeat what he had said so she could understand him.

"An All-Star team," John Bailey said. "We play in a state tournament and then if we win that, we go to Georgia. And if we win that, we go to Pennsylvania, to Williamsport, for the World Series!"

Mrs. Bailey still did not quite understand what her son was saying. But she was pretty sure her husband would. He had arranged to get off early from his job at the naval yard to drive his son to baseball practices and games.[14]

Danny Jones, the director of the East Cooper Parks and Playground Commission, learned at some point that Robert Morrison had signed up the Cannon Street All-Star team for the Little League district tournament in Charleston. Jones must have known his life was about to get a lot more complicated. He knew Little League Baseball prohibited racial discrimination and he knew that the state of South Carolina prohibited integration.

It was at this point, the Cannon Street players remembered decades later, that white men started coming to their practices and games. Allen Jackson was in the on-deck circle one day when his father motioned for him to look down the leftfield line. "Do you know who those people are?" his father asked. "They're scouting you guys."[15] Leroy Major said one of the men was Danny Jones. "Jones was the big reason we didn't get to play," Major said. "He came down and scouted us. He stood on the leftfield line and watched us play."[16] Major said Jones may not have objected to the Cannon Street team in the tournament until he saw them practice or until he heard from politicians who said he could not allow the integration of a tournament so soon after the *Brown* decision. "That's why they canceled the contest," Major said.[17]

Rufus Dilligard, one of the team's coaches, said he heard rumors that Jones came to Harmon Field, but he said he never saw him.

"Other whites came and they could have scouted us, but I didn't care." Dilligard said. He said he knew his All-Stars were good and that they were probably good enough to beat the white teams. "I know the worst thing that could have happened to them was to play us and get whipped. They probably did not want to risk that. White fellas used to be at practices and games and that All-Star team was a bunch no one could take lightly."[18]

Jones did not have to see the All-Stars practice to know he had a problem on his hands. If the team was allowed to play in the tournament, it would cause an outcry among the segregationists who opposed any mixing of the races. Maybe one of the white teams would beat the league's All-Stars. Maybe the Black team was not that good or maybe it would collapse under the pressure of playing in its first tournament. What if the Cannon Street team defeated one of the white teams? What if the Cannon Street Y team defeated all the white teams? Gus Holt, who revived the story four decades later, answered the question with his own question. "Who wants to be the first white team to lose to a Black team in the all-American sport of baseball?"[19]

South Carolina politicians and the parks and playgrounds commission could not take that chance. Jones was not a politician and his position was not a political one. Jones's children do not remember their father having much of an interest in politics.[20] *Brown v. Board of Education* had made a lot of things political that had never been political and Jones found himself in the middle of something far bigger than himself.

THE SUPREME COURT'S DECISION in *Brown* and in *Brown II* resulted in hundreds of segregation laws in the South over the next decade. This ran counter to increasingly flexible policies in the years immediately preceding *Brown*. "For embattled segregationists, maintaining racial purity in athletics now became a crucial battle in the larger war to defend the entire Jim Crow system," historian Charles H. Martin, wrote. Hugh Locke, an Alabama judge, barred interracial football and baseball games in one city, warning that "allowing a few Negroes to play baseball here will wind up with Negroes and whites marrying." In 1955 Georgia governor Marvin Griffin offered this warning: "The South stands at Armageddon. The battle is joined. We cannot make the slightest concession to the enemy in this dark and lamentable hour of struggle. There is no more difference in compromising the integrity of race on the playing field than in doing so in the classroom. One break in the dike and the relentless seas will rush in and destroy us."[21]

Robert Morrison, Danny Jones, and Peter McGovern, president of Little League Baseball, found themselves on different sides of a story that played out in sports pages and editorial pages of newspapers throughout the country, including the *News and Courier*. Tom Waring seethed at the travesty of African American boys being forced on white boys on a baseball field. The story would be reported by wire services and published in international newspapers. John Rivers's father, who was in the army, read about the story while being stationed in South Korea.[22] Journalists writing about the story included Sam Lacy, the well-known columnist of the *Baltimore Afro-American*, who had been confronting racism in his columns for twenty years, and Jimmy Breslin, who was at the beginning of a career that would make him one of the more famous writers in the country.

Jack Bass, who became a journalist, a biographer of Strom Thurmond, and a chronicler of southern history, was a college student during the summer of 1955, working as a sportswriter for the *News and Courier*. He said that the presence of the Cannon Street All-Star team in the Charleston tournament represented an immediate danger to segregation in the state.[23] Gus Holt said that the court's decision in *Brown* no doubt had a part in the response to the Cannon Street All-Stars. "We may not be able to control the schools but we can control this," Holt said.[24] Holt wonders if the Y All-Stars would have been allowed to play in the tournament if *Brown* had not punctured the sensibilities of the white men who ran the recreation department and the white politicians and newspaper editors who said whites must do anything they could to resist integration. "I think so," Holt said.[25]

Waring may very well have spoken to Thurmond or certainly

others in the higher levels of South Carolina politics. Thurmond let Jones know that any tournament could not include an African American team. "Jones made the announcement but he didn't make the decision," Bass said. "If he made the decision, he was under pressure from a higher authority. He may have been directed to make it. He was taking orders. He got it on higher authority." Jones probably did not hear directly from Thurmond but through an intermediary. "We can't do anything to break the color line," Jones was told.[26]

Jones's children remember a lot of evenings when adults came to their house and talked behind closed doors. The children were too young to remember what was said or who was there, but they knew something was wrong because of the presence of so many people they did not know and the hushed voices they did not understand.[27] Jones knew if he forbade the Cannon Street Y team from playing in the district tournament, he would violate Little League rules, and the organization's president Peter McGovern would be justified in firing him as the state's director. But if Jones let the Cannon Street Y team play, he would anger not only many white coaches, parents, friends, and relatives but also city and state politicians. He would risk losing his job.

Jones's children, Sallie Frenkel, Tesa Livingston, and Bubba Jones, insist their father would have allowed the Cannon Street team into the district tournament.[28] Gus Holt, who came to know more about this story than anyone else, called Jones a good man who found himself caught between diametrically different positions and he had to choose one. Holt agrees with Jones's children. Jones would have let the Cannon Street All-Stars play in the tournament if the decision had been left to him. "Danny Jones would have been fine on his own," Holt said. But "he was being paid" by the county "and he had a family to support."[29] John Rivers, the shortstop on the Cannon Street team, also said he thinks his team would have played if it had been up to Jones, who, as an athlete himself, understood competition.[30] Historian Jack Bass, author of a biography of Strom Thurmond, also says Jones has been a scapegoat. "Danny Jones was willing to play the Black team," Bass said.[31]

"A DASTARDLY ACT"

THE CANNON STREET Y team won the district tournament by forfeit when all the teams withdrew in protest and advanced to the state tournament in Columbia. The Cannon Street coaches told the boys that the canceled district tournament would give them more time to practice for the state tournament. Leroy Major learned from Walter Burke, one of the coaches, that he would pitch the first game. "'We'll be playing the white kids,' he told us. 'Major, you'll be pitching. You think you can handle it?' 'Yes, sir,' I said."[32]

Sixty-two teams qualified for the tournament, which was scheduled to run from August 8 to 11.

Jones had resolved one issue in Charleston only to face the same one at the state tournament.[33] On July 6 Jones, as head of the state's Little League and a board member of the South Carolina Recreational Society, which organized the tournament, had a meeting in Columbia with managers from most of the white teams in the tournament to discuss how they would respond to the inclusion of the Cannon Street team. The managers voted 40–15 to oppose the Cannon Street team playing in the tournament.[34] Jones notified Peter McGovern, president of Little League Baseball, in Williamsport. "It is impractical for Negro teams to compete at this time," he said. Jones asked McGovern for permission to have an all-white tournament with the winner representing the state in the regional tournament in Rome, Georgia.[35]

McGovern rejected the suggestion by saying that this would violate Little League Baseball's rules. "We have no alternative except to abide by the rules that exist," he said.[36] Little League Baseball moved the state tournament to Donaldson Air Force Base in Greenville, because it was a military base and under federal regulations. Jones said that fifteen teams had registered for the tournament. The Cannon Street team was scheduled to play the winner of the first-round game between Batesburg-Leesville and North Augusta.[37]

Wire services, including the Associated Press, the United Press, and the Newspaper Enterprise Association, distributed the story of the white teams' protest against having the Cannon Street Y team in the state tournament.[38] Jones said the South Carolina Recreational Society would have its own tournament for the white teams that did not want to play in the Little League tournament.[39] Many of the remaining teams left the Little League tournament. North Augusta and Batesburg-Leesville notified Jones they "do not choose to participate in the Greenville tournament or in Little League." They both entered the "Little Boys" tournament. Jones called the withdrawal of the teams "a blow to the Greenville tournament."[40]

On July 24 the *News and Courier* ran a banner headline: "NAACP Asks U.S. Court to Open Park to Negroes." The story said that John Wrighten and J. Arthur Brown of the NAACP had filed suit demanding that all state parks be open to Blacks. The headline that ran directly below the story was no less provocative: "Jones Resigns as S.C. Little League Head." In a letter to McGovern, a defiant Jones said he believed that the northern press was using the participation of a Black team in the state tournament "as an opening wedge to abolish segregation in recreational facilities in South Carolina." In addition, Jones called it a "dastardly act" to use young boys "to undermine the laws and customs of our people."[41]

This story quoted Morrison as saying he consulted Jones when the Y was applying for a Little League for African American boys on the peninsula and Jones had expressed no objection. Morrison said he told Jones he was interested in giving African American boys the same privileges given to white boys. Jones, Morrison said, did not object. Morrison criticized Jones for his hypocrisy for violating the rules he had agreed to obey as the state's director of Little League Baseball. "If anyone was guilty of undermining the laws and customs it was Mr. Danny Jones himself when he became connected with a national organization such as the Little League which demands that every boy between 9 and 12 should have an equal chance to play in their program," Morrison said.[42]

Tom Waring responded to the NAACP's lawsuit and to Jones's resignation in an editorial on July 26 by blaming both on the NAACP. The NAACP had no direct—or probably indirect—involvement with the entry of the Cannon Street team in ether the district or state tournament. He referred to the letter Jones wrote to Little League Baseball, which did not mention the NAACP. "He is urging South Carolinians to secede from a national organization to promote sport among boys because Negro zealots are pushing into it," Waring said.[43]

Jones's resignation was credited with other teams dropping out of the Greenville tournament.[44] The city of Greenville responded sharply to the withdrawal of most of the teams by saying that past winners of the state championship, including Clinton and North Charleston, had played against mixed competition when they played in the national tournament in Williamsport.[45] John Schofield, president of the Walhalla Little League, said he had spoken to McGovern, who had told him that the tournament would proceed as scheduled. Schofield disagreed with those who saw a connection between the integration of schools and the integration of a baseball tournament. "Baseball is not a close contact sport," he said. "I doubt that in any baseball game there would be any more contact than one would find on a shopping tour of downtown in the afternoon."[46] The *News and Courier* reported the next day that the remaining two white teams had withdrawn. The Greenville team dropped out after it took a poll of the players' parents. When Walhalla learned of this, it too withdrew, leaving Cannon Street as the only team in the tournament.[47]

By winning the tournament, this meant that the Cannon Street team should have advanced to the regional tournament in Rome, Georgia. Walter "Buck" Ransom, the director of the regional tournament, said that Cannon Street was ineligible because it had advanced by forfeit and not by winning on the field, as the organization rules stated. There would be no team from South Carolina in the tournament, Ransom said. Peter McGovern responded that no official decision had been made.[48] Morrison said he had no comment until he heard from Williamsport. He said that the teams in the Y league had played on its own baseball field and had made no attempt to play white teams. There was, he insisted, no connection between his league wanting to play in a tournament and the integration of schools. "We feel our children should have the same right as any other to at least attempt to go to Williamsport. If we lose, that's all right," he said. "I regret that the white citizens have taken this attitude."[49]

McGovern then announced that any team affiliated with Little League Baseball that played in a tournament run by another program would be in violation of Little League rules.[50] In addition, he affirmed Ransom's decision that the Cannon Street team was ineligible for the regional tournament. He said the decision was made "with extreme reluctance and heartfelt regard." By allowing a team to advance to the regional tournament without winning any games would create what McGovern called "unbalance and inequity."[51] In addition, McGovern indicated that he was concerned about the Cannon Street All-Stars' safety if they went to Rome, Georgia. "We felt they might be subjected to every hate and prejudice at Rome," he said in a wire-service story on July 29. "It could be courting disaster," he said, to send the boys "into a hotbed such as could be developed by the situation. We felt it would be betraying our program to do it."[52]

John Rivers said that Williamsport "caved" because of political pressure. "I think it was all politics," he said. "The heat was heavy on them."[53] Gus Holt insists this was the case. "There was a deal cut," he said. He's convinced that McGovern was threatened. Someone told McGovern, "If you send those n——s down there, there will be blood on your hands," Holt said. Holt says that it's a good thing that McGovern declared the Cannon Street team ineligible. "It was a damn blessing they didn't go down and force themselves on those people," Holt said. "Something would have happened to that bus if they went to Rome."[54] Holt admitted he could not prove that McGovern ended the Cannon Street team's season because of the threat of violence. "There's no doubt in my mind that this conversation took place," he said.[55]

McGovern, threat or no threat, had reason to worry about sending an African American team to play white teams in a rural town in north Georgia.

ON AUGUST 2 WARING again addressed the Cannon Street story in an editorial, "Agitation and Hate." "The case of the South Carolina Little League could well be cited by sociologists as a textbook example of why racial relations in the South are becoming increas-

"A DASTARDLY ACT"

ingly difficult," he wrote. He said that more than sixty white teams were playing harmoniously in their own league in a national organization. "Along comes a single team, composed of Negro children," Waring said. "Some Negro adults, knowing that the colored children weren't wanted in the all-white state league, nevertheless decided to force the colored team into the league."[56]

Danny Jones said he had received a lot of letters of support after resigning from Little League Baseball. He also received criticism. "You and South Carolina as a whole should realize by now that if you are to continue in Little League you must accept Negro teams," Bob Williams, sports editor of the *Rocky Mount (NC) Evening Telegram*, said. Jones responded sharply. "I believe you and your colleagues in North Carolina fail to see the real significance in the entrance of a Negro team in competition in the Little League program. It is a much bigger thing at stake than Little League Baseball," Jones said. "It is just another step to break down the customs of our people, and thank God, the people of our great state have presented to the Nation a united front."[57]

McGovern wrote a letter criticizing Jones and the other managers who quit the tournament by refusing to play against the Cannon Street team even though they had signed affidavits to play "any team regardless of race, color or creed."

"Many South Carolina leagues had signified their willingness to compete under terms of signed affidavits, pleading adherence to the rules which recognize no racial barriers," McGovern wrote Jones from Williamsport. "For the boys of these teams there are no barriers of race, creed, or color. Again, here is the adult frame of reference. For the boys, baseball is a game to be played with bat, ball and glove. They became innocent victims of alien influences that have deprived them of beneficial associations and opportunity to meet and know other boys in Little League Baseball."[58]

Jones announced the creation of a segregated youth baseball league, the Little Boys League, that would compete with Little League Baseball. If Jones had once been ambivalent about whether he would stand with the racists or not, this was no longer the case.

And the Cannon Street Y All-Stars had become, without their knowing it, cause célèbres.

JET MAGAZINE PUBLISHED A story about how the South Carolina teams had boycotted the Cannon Street team. The *Pittsburgh Courier*, one of the top African American weeklies in the country, published a photo of the Cannon Street team across the top of its front page with the headline, "These Little Leaguers were Slapped Down by Ugly Segregation Laws." An editorial took issue with Jones's quote calling it a "dastardly act" to challenge the segregation laws of the state. "We believe it is dastardly for adult Americans, such as Danny Jones, to instill into boys from eight to twelve years of age, the outmoded, unchristian ideas of racist superiority," it said. The editorial said that children were not taught prejudice. They learned it from their parents. "The dastardly act of Jones is against the white boys, the colored boys, negro boys and all the youth of America," it added.[59]

African American newspapers had long condemned racial discrimination. But this was not the case for white newspapers, which had long participated in a conspiracy of silence on the subject of racial discrimination.[60] But the story of the Cannon Street All-Stars broke that silence. Editors and other journalists and much of white America might not have wanted to talk about the vastness of racism in the country but they could get their hands around something as objectionable as a team of eleven- and twelve-year-old African American boys being deprived the opportunity of playing in a baseball tournament because of the color of their skin. The fact that this was a story about children and it involved something as good and decent as Little League provoked outrage from cautious editors and columnists who directed their indignation at Jones and South Carolina obstructionists but also at McGovern and Little League Baseball for not doing more on behalf of the Cannon Street team.

The *Trentonian* newspaper in Trenton, New Jersey, published an editorial on August 11 that praised Morrison for defending the rights of an African American team to play in the tournament.

"We regret that the South Carolina grown-ups thought there was anything dangerous about a Little League tournament open to all comers," the editorial said. "The boys, we imagine, would never have kicked up a fuss. Prejudices, especially of the racial variety, are come by with age and practice." Someone sent Tom Waring a clipping of the editorial with a note that said, "I do not agree with it."[61] When Waring received an editorial from the *Seattle Times* that had criticized South Carolina teams for refusing to play the Cannon Street team, Waring defended himself in a note to the editor. "While we Southern reactionaries may be wrong in our race politics," Waring said. "we deplore the refusal of the metropolitan press as a rule to admit our side of the story."[62]

Waring's archives include a letter written on *Baltimore Sun* stationery that ridiculed South Carolina's overreaction to a team of African American boys who just wanted to play baseball. "I'm sure that team wasn't trying to alter the path of Southern psychology toward the negro race," it said. "I'd imagine they just wanted to play baseball." The writer sarcastically asked if the refusal to play the Cannon Street team was because the young players had "particularly nasty" morals or character. "Please don't tell me they were left standing alone because their skins were black," it said. "If you won't let them play toward a goal, as white teams do, maybe those little boys will see the hopelessness of playing at all and revert to the streets, where they might find out how to really hurt white people."[63]

Dick Herbert, sports editor of the *Raleigh News and Observer*, criticized white adults in South Carolina for sacrificing the dreams of their sons for their own racial bigotry. "Wonder if the youngsters were consulted when about fifty Little League teams in South Carolina withdrew from playoff participation because one Negro team entered?" he asked. "Chances are the players were wondering about why they were deprived of a chance at the big time."[64] An editorial in the *Elmira (NY) Advertiser* criticized the creation of the Little Boys League for "injecting adult bigotry" into boys' baseball. Neither white nor Black boys would object to integration unless their parents did, it said.[65]

On August 2 an editorial ran in the *Delaware County Daily Times* in Chester, Indiana. "If ever the race bigots had reason to hang their heads in shame, this is it! What was done to the young, impressionable minds of these youngsters is far more tragic than the blow suffered by the Cannon Street team. True, it was a bitter disappointment to the Negro boys," it said. "At least, the Cannon Street boys don't have to apologize or hang their heads when someone talks of good sportsmanship." But what is the lesson that the white ballplayers learned from their fathers, the editorial asked. If one of the white players who was denied the chance to play against African American players ends up playing in professional baseball, will he reject a contract because he will have to play with or against an African American ballplayer?[66]

Bill Beck, sports editor of the *Tampa Bay (FL) Times*, wondered how the mother of a Cannon Street player would explain to her son that he could not play in a tournament because he was African American. "Inversely," he added, "A number of white mothers must be trying to explain to their sons why they withdrew from the tournament just because a Negro team had entered." Beck directed his strongest criticism at McGovern and Little League Baseball who initially supported the team before abandoning it. Adults, he said, had once again become involved in the lives of kids, "and as usual," he said, "they have messed it up."[67]

John Fox, the sports editor of the *Binghamton (NY) Press and Sun Bulletin*, questioned McGovern's reason for affirming the Rome tournament's decision to prohibit the Cannon Street team because it would result in the inequality of competition. Fox said the real reason why McGovern denied the Cannon Street team's entry into the tournament was because of pressure put on him by southern whites. "Every decent Little League official and player must be thoroughly ashamed," he said.[68] The *Oneonta (NY) Star* said Little League Baseball was no better than the southern teams that refused to play the Cannon Street All-Stars. "Little League, which has always preached Americanism on the highest plane, now appears guilty of bigotry on the lowest plane," he said.[69] A Vermont Little League said it was considering resigning from Little League Baseball because of the action taken by Peter McGovern.[70] The Chelsea (Massachusetts) Little League sent a letter to the Little League organization accusing it of violating its own rules by practicing racial discrimination by not allowing the Cannon Street team to play in the Little League World Series. It asked the organization to explain its action.[71]

Ruth P. Koshuk, a retired sociologist who had studied the impact of racial prejudice on children, wrote a letter to Peter McGovern criticizing him for saying he had affirmed the forfeit of the Cannon Street team because it "would create unbalance and inequity." That outcome, Koshuk said, had already been accomplished by the South Carolina teams who withdrew from the tournament rather than play the Cannon Street team. "You have an opportunity to stand for the democratic principles of fair play and 'no discrimination based on race, color, of creed,' before a watching world, more attentive to such issues now than ever before. American integrity and sincerity in the principles as advocated is judged by every such incident, as I am sure you must realize."

"The 'extreme reluctance,' which you admit feeling," Koshuk continued, "is evidence that you know the action you take is wrong. . . . How many thousand young boys will know of the incident, and how will it be interpreted to them, in this year following the Supreme Court's decision on desegregation? Your regret and 'heartfelt regards' should go to all the other teams in the national tournament—not to the Cannon Street boys. It is the white boys who are most injured by the unreasoning prejudice of their elders. I hope the decision may be reversed, for the good of all concerned."[72]

Koshuk wrote a separate letter to Robert Morrison, in which she said she was "deeply disturbed" by the action taken by Little League Baseball. "I hope your Cannon Street boys are in good spirits, and that they realize they just happen to be cast in a role which may result in substantial gains for true brotherhood and sportsmanship, in the long run."[73]

ON JULY 31 SPORTS columnist Dick Young of the *New York Daily News*, which had a daily circulation of two million, interviewed

Jackie Robinson of the Brooklyn Dodgers about how white teams in South Carolina had quit the state tournament rather than play the Cannon Street team. "How stupid can they be? I had to laugh when I read the story," Robinson said. Young said it was not the fault of the boys playing for the white teams. Prejudice is not something you are born with, he said; you learn it from your parents. Young's column quoted Danny Jones as saying that including an African American team in the state tournament was "an attempt to undermine the laws and customs of our people."

Young said he felt a bit sorry for Jones but not for Peter McGovern, who had a chance to be "a big man in the showdown" and to say he was not intimidated by South Carolina's customs. McGovern, Young argued, could have said: "Okay, the Cannon Street YMCA wins the state title by default. It now goes to the regionals at Rome, Georgia, and if that is defaulted, the Cannon Street boys will go to Williamsport, Pennsylvania, for the Little League World Series." Instead, McGovern ruled that the team was ineligible to compete at the regionals in Rome.

Young said McGovern "should resign."[74]

The season was over for the Cannon Street YMCA All-Stars.

They did not play a game.

1. Pensacola Jaycees team, 1955. Courtesy of Common Pictures.

2. Ben Tillman. Bain News Service, Library of Congress.

3. Cannon Street YMCA. Courtesy of Paul Stoney.

4. Cannon Street YMCA All-Stars assistant manager Walter Burke addresses his players the night they arrived in Williamsport, Pennsylvania, for the Little League World Series. Courtesy of Little League Baseball and Softball.

5. Cannon Street YMCA players and coaches watch the Little League World Series championship game. Courtesy of Little League Baseball and Softball.

6. An unidentified man hands a pair of baseball cleats to Norman Robinson as Robert Morrison, president of the Cannon Street YMCA, and other players look on. Courtesy of Little League Baseball and Softball.

7. John C. Calhoun. Photograph by Mathew Brady, 1849. Wikimedia Commons.

8. John Rivers in uniform, 1955. Courtesy of John Rivers.

9. John and Robenia Rivers in Cuenca, Ecuador. Courtesy of John Rivers.

10. Gus Holt (*right*) with his brother, Lamar, and sister-in-law, Brenda. Courtesy of Lamar Holt.

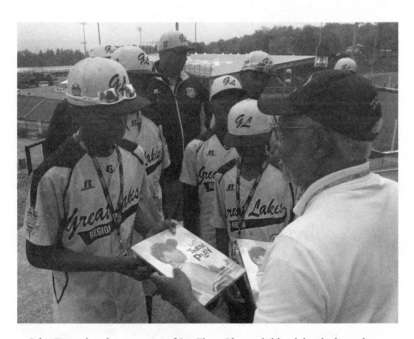

11. John Rivers hands out copies of *Let Them Play*, a children's book about the 1955 Cannon Street All-Stars, to members of the Jackie Robinson Little League West team at the Little League World Series in 2014. Courtesy of John Rivers.

12. (*opposite top*) Gus Holt, David Middleton, John Bailey, John Rivers, and Allen Jackson at the Little League World Series. Courtesy of John Rivers.

13. (*opposite bottom*) Peter McGovern talks to John Rivers and Vermort Brown during the 1955 Little League World Series. Courtesy of Little League Baseball and Softball.

14. (*above*) Isaac Woodard. Library of Congress.

(AX1)CHARLESTON,S.C.,JULY 13--UPHOLDS NEGRO
VOTE--U.S. DISTRICT JUDGE J.WAITES WARING
(ABOVE) RULED YESTERDAY THAT NEGROES ARE EN-
TITLED TO BE ENROLLED TO VOTE IN SOUTH CARO-
LINA DEMOCRATIC PRIMARIES. (AP WIREPHOTO)
(VB11400FLS) 1947.

15. J. Waties Waring. Courtesy of Harlan Greene.

16. Leroy Major. Courtesy of John Rivers.

17. Peter McGovern. Courtesy of Little League Baseball and Softball.

18. Robert Morrison. Courtesy of the Avery Research Center for African
American History and Culture, College of Charleston.

19. (*above*) Carl Stotz. Courtesy of Little League Baseball and Softball.

20. (*opposite*) Carl Stotz. Courtesy of Little League Baseball and Softball.

21. Vermort Brown.
Courtesy of John Rivers.

22. Carl Johnson. Courtesy
of John Rivers.

23. Gus Holt with his son, Lawrence, after Lawrence received a plaque for demonstrating courage for his fight against brain cancer. Courtesy of Lamar Holt.

24. A reunion of the players from the Pensacola Jaycees and Orlando Kiwanis teams that played in the Florida state Little League tournament in 1955. Courtesy of Common Pictures.

25. The statue of John Calhoun being removed from Marion Square in downtown Charleston. Photo by Rob Byko; used with permission.

13.

A LONG TIME COMING

In the 2018 documentary *Long Time Coming*, Willie Preyer, who was then in his seventies, remembered growing up in segregated Pensacola, Florida, in the 1940s and 1950s, where he often looked up at a thirty-foot granite Confederate memorial in the city's downtown. The statue, like the one of John Calhoun in Charleston, was constructed in the decades after the end of Reconstruction when whites reasserted their dominance. "Uncrowned heroes of the Southern Confederacy whose joy was to suffer and die for a cause they believed to be just," the inscription under the Confederate soldier says.[1] To Preyer, the statue depicted a Confederate soldier addressing African Americans who passed by. "In other words, this is me, this is mine," he said. "This is my domain. I rule here. I don't think whites can ever understand what we went through."[2]

Pensacola, like so many other American cities, was a different place depending on whether you were white or African American. Black kids were restricted to a designated part of town, and curfews meant they were not allowed on downtown streets after six o'clock. White kids could stay downtown until the store closed. "We had curfews," Willie Stromas, who also grew up in Pensacola, said. "I stayed where I was supposed to stay."[3]

African Americans learned either from their parents or perhaps by their own experience that nothing could protect them from the hatred that lingered in the humid air and exploded with no warning. Cleveland Dailey, who later played on the same Little League All-Star team with Preyer and Stromas, said he was walking on a street with his shoeshine box when white guys passed by in a convertible and whistled at some white girls. Suddenly, a white man came out of a store and pulled a knife on Dailey and asked, "Did you whistle at the girl?"[4] Willie Robinson said his family's paper boy taunted him with racial expletives on his daily rounds. "He came by our house and he said, 'Here's your paper n——!'" The paper boy then hurled the paper at the house. "He just hit the house so hard. It was like being bitten by a rattlesnake. It was stinging and it was poisonous."[5]

Stromas recalled a man with the last name Nash, whose wife was murdered. Her husband didn't commit the murder, Stromas said, but he was arrested by white police officers. "They arrested him and beat him up in front of his family. And locked him up," Stromas said. Nash stayed in jail for ten or fifteen years. "And then they decided to let him go," Stromas said. "And I don't think he lived too much longer after that. That really hurt him, you know." Admiral "Spider" Leroy said that bigotry left him scarred, literally and figuratively. He remembered taking part in a sit-in at a lunch counter in Pensacola—"People passing us and taking their cigarettes and putting their cigarettes out on our arms. As a result, I spent some years as a very, very militant angry young man."[6]

Preyer joined the air force and left Pensacola as soon as he was old enough. "I got on a bus and I began to see a difference," he said. "I found out what real freedom was, being a human being—I was treated like everyone else. It was the most wonderful feeling I ever had." Dailey, too, could not wait to leave Pensacola. "Segregation was so bad in my hometown," he said, "I had to leave town and I never moved back."[7]

The 2018 documentary *Long Time Coming*, which aired on Netflix, tells the story of an African American team from Pensacola, who played a white team in a Little League state tournament in Orlando on August 9, 1955. This story parallels that of the Cannon Street YMCA team. But the endings of the stories could not have been more different. More than sixty years after the game, several of the players on the Pensacola Jaycees and the Orlando Kiwanis teams met on a baseball field, shook hands and hugged, and reminisced about the game and the differences between growing up Black in the Florida panhandle and growing up white in Orlando in Orange County, in the central part of the state.

Stewart Hall, who played for the Orlando team, said he had thought a lot during those decades about playing in the game and what it meant to him and to history. He grew up in a white neighborhood and went to church and school only with whites and then attended the segregated Citadel, the Military College of South Carolina, in Charleston. After graduating from The Citadel, he went into the army and it was only then that he got to know African American men. As he got older he began thinking about racism. He thought about the kids on the Pensacola team when his mind flashed back to the state tournament. "What comes to my mind is with all the things that are going on around us today," Hall told Preyer during a scene in the film. "What was it like being a black child in the fifties? What was it that you wanted in life? What did you want out of life?"[8]

THERE WERE MORE LYNCHINGS in Florida per capita than any other state between 1880 and 1940, and there were more lynchings in Orange County than there were in any other county in Florida. It had the sixth-most lynchings of any county in America.[9] The history of Florida, like the history of so many southern states, is an infinite loop of cruelty against African Americans who learned—and still learn—that hatred hides in the humid air and explodes without warning.

In 1901 James Wheldon Johnson, who a year earlier wrote the lyrics for "Lift Ev'ry Voice and Sing," which would become the anthem of the NAACP, was a young teacher in Jacksonville, Florida. He remembered sitting on a park bench and talking to a white woman, who taught with him at a segregated school. He was unaware that he was being closely watched. As Johnson and the woman began walking toward a streetcar stop, they were confronted by a mob, which had been aroused by a rumor that someone had seen Johnson and the woman go into the park. Johnson found himself facing a lynch mob. "On the other side of the fence death was standing," Johnson later recalled. "Death turned and looked at me and I looked at death."[10]

Johnson's life was spared when the rumor of Johnson and the woman going into the park was discovered to be a misunderstanding. Philip Dray wrote in *At the Hands of Persons Unknown* that Johnson "remained deeply scarred by the impression of how the threat of total annihilation had risen so abruptly and from such seemingly ordinary events." Johnson became a prominent civil rights activist and the first Black to serve as executive secretary of the NAACP. But he said he was haunted by nightmares of that moment in Jacksonville for decades. Such nightmares were common. And so was the existential fear that one's life could end without any provocation. "There was good reason for the sense of constant vulnerability," Dray wrote. "A lynching could seem like some finely tuned spring-release trap, its jaws wired open, ready to clamp shut. It required only a victim to step into the mechanism."[11]

In early November 1918 a prosperous African American man, Mose Norman, went to vote in the town of Ocoee near Orlando but was denied doing so because he was told he had not paid the poll tax. He returned later in the day and when Klansmen, who were working at the polling station, saw a gun in Norman's car, they pistol-whipped him. The Klansmen went to find Norman that night but went instead to the house of another African American man, July Perry, who also was a voting rights activist. Two whites were shot to death—perhaps by friendly fire, according to one source. Perry was captured and lynched from a light post in Orlando. Whites began burning down houses in Ocoee. When people escaped from their burning homes, they were gunned down. Estimates of the dead ranged from six to sixty. All of Ocoee's five hundred Black residents left town. Ocoee became all white and remained that way for decades.[12] In January 2020 the judiciary committee of the Florida Senate approved reparations for descendants of Ocoee. It required the Ocoee massacre to be taught in schools.[13]

In 1934 Claude Neal, an African American farmhand, was accused of raping and killing a white woman in Marianna in the

Florida Panhandle. Neal was seized from his jail cell, beaten severely, castrated, and forced to eat his own genitals, and then shot to death with a 12-gauge shotgun. His corpse was then tied to a truck and dragged to the home of the dead girl's parents. The body was then dragged through the streets of Marianna and hanged from a tree not far from a Confederate memorial.[14] The city of Marianna also was the site of the Dozier School for Boys, or White House Boys, where generations of African American and white boys were used for slave labor, brutalized, sexually abused, murdered, and buried in unmarked graves.[15] Three times as many Blacks were murdered as whites.[16] Colson Whitehead's Pulitzer Prize–winning novel *The Nickel Boys* was based on the atrocities committed at the Dozier School.[17]

In October 1945 a white mob removed Jesse Payne—a thirty-year-old farmhand who had been accused of attacking the five-year-old niece of a Florida sheriff, Lonnie Davis—from an unguarded and unlocked jail cell in Madison. Payne was then taken to the outskirts of town and shot to death.[18] The coroner said that Payne was killed by "a person or persons unknown."[19]

Shortly after Payne's murder, a Suwannee County police officer took Sam McFadden, an African American prisoner, against his will from the jail to the Suwanee River, where, according to court documents, the police officer "did . . . whip, beat, abuse and otherwise cruelly maltreat" him by striking him with other weapons unknown. McFadden, who could not swim, tried to escape by jumping into the Suwannee River, where he drowned.[20] On October 30, 1945, police reportedly beat an African American Black man, George Floyd, to death with a blackjack in a county jail in St. Augustine, between Jacksonville and Daytona Beach on the Atlantic coast.[21]

A week earlier, on October 23, Branch Rickey, the president of the Brooklyn Dodgers, signed Jackie Robinson to a contract with the organization's top Minor League team, the Montreal Royals, making Robinson the first African American in white professional baseball since the 1880s. The Dodgers had a contract to have spring training in Daytona Beach, Florida, which had a reputation as a moderately progressive city. But Daytona Beach lacked enough accommodations for all the prospects and the different teams in the organization. Rickey dispatched the Montreal team to Sanford, a rural town between Daytona Beach and Orlando. After the second day of tryouts, a white man came to the house where Robinson was staying. Wendell Smith and Billy Rowe, African American sportswriters with the *Pittsburgh Courier* who had accompanied Robinson, were sitting on the front porch. The white man said he had a message from a meeting of a hundred townspeople. There would be trouble if Robinson was not "out of town by nightfall."[22] Robinson immediately returned to Daytona Beach, where he played his first game of the spring on March 17 before a capacity crowd at City Island Ballpark, which is now called Jackie Robinson Ballpark, making it the first time in the South that an African American played in a professional game with whites.

Five years after Robinson went to spring training in central Florida, Harry T. Moore, the executive director of the state's NAACP, and his wife, Harriette, were mortally injured when the KKK bombed their home in Mims in Seminole County in central Florida on Christmas Night in 1951. Harry died in a hospital on the way to an African American hospital in Sanford and Harriette died nine days later in the hospital. Moore was the first civil rights official killed in the civil rights movement. The state's governor did not condemn the murder of Moore and his wife. Instead, he condemned Walter White, the executive secretary of the NAACP, for coming to Moore's funeral "to stir up strife."[23]

The town of Sanford found itself the site of a racially motivated killing in 2012 when George Zimmerman, a neighborhood watch volunteer, thought Trayvon Martin, a seventeen-year-old African American with a bottle of iced tea and a bag of Skittles, represented a threat to the safety of the neighborhood. Zimmerman and Martin scuffled. Zimmerman shot and killed Martin. A jury found Zimmerman not guilty in the shooting.[24] Florida continues to practice racial discrimination at an alarming rate. The Brennan Center for Justice concluded in a 2016 report that no state disenfranchised more Blacks from voting.[25]

WILLIE PREYER DIDN'T FORGET the Confederate statue that taunted him. Cleveland Dailey never forgot the day he thought his throat would be slashed. Willie Stromas remembered what happened to Nash decades after the man died. Willie Robinson never forgot the sound of a newspaper hitting his house. And Spider Leroy never forgot the cigarette burns he received from protesting racial discrimination at a department-store lunch counter.

Therein lies the contrast between growing up Black and growing up white in the 1950s.

There were no such memories for the white boys who became the Orlando Kiwanis All-Star team. "I think it's a shame that every child can't grow up in a small town and have that small-town experience," Stewart Hall said. "I had a lot of great memories from my childhood, growing up in Orlando. Not many regrets. Maybe none." Bill Hudson said he was fortunate to grow up when he did because it was a "calmer, quieter, more peaceful world," he said. Jerry Cowart said he was free to do whatever he wanted and go wherever he wanted. "I was a twelve-year-old child in my own world," he said. "We went out on our bicycles at night and stayed out till ten o'clock and our parents never worried about us."[26]

Hall said baseball was still the national game, and it had a particular hold on boys who played after school and all day on Saturdays and after church on Sundays. The rules for baseball were the same for Blacks and white kids whether they played Little League Baseball or on one of countless sandlot fields. To Preyer, it didn't matter if the baseball was organized or not. They picked their teams and played the game. "It was just a makeup type thing, you know," he said.[27]

H. D. Goode, a dentist in Pensacola, Florida, who was president of the Negro Chamber of Commerce, suggested the organization of a Black baseball league. The Police Athletic League and the Negro Jaycees supported the idea and so did other civic leaders. Little League Baseball awarded the Pensacola Jaycees a charter. The boys wore uniforms and their parents and grandparents and uncles and siblings came to the ballfield and watched them play and cheered for them. The coaches became surrogate fathers to some of the boys and taught them to be better ballplayers and, when the time came, to be better men. "Things are the way they are," Dailey was told. "You have to deal with them accordingly. You have to stay out of trouble."[28]

THE PENSACOLA JAYCEES LEAGUE could not enter a team in the district tournament during its first year. The coaches selected an All-Star team the next summer and the team registered for the district tournament.[29] Peter McGovern, the president of Little League Baseball, authorized the Pensacola team to play in the tournament. Raymond Riddles, the director of the tournament, ignored the directive. He ruled the Pensacola team ineligible. The tournament began in Marianna. Arnold White, the director of Florida Little League Baseball, informed Riddles that the organization had invalidated the segregated tournament and it had declared the Jaycees the winner.[30] Doc Grant, president of the Marianna Little League, said there would be a tournament for white teams, as Danny Jones had organized in South Carolina. The winner of the Marianna tournament, Grant said, would play the winner of the South Carolina tournament.[31]

Peter McGovern's decision meant that the Jaycees All-Star team advanced to the state tournament in Orlando. The ruling almost came too late. Fred L. Hicks, the team's manager, received McGovern's decision on Saturday, August 6. Hicks learned he had to be at the San Juan Hotel in Orlando the next day by 3:00 p.m. for the coaches' meeting where the drawings would be done for the tournament bracket. If the Pensacola team was late it could be declared ineligible.[32]

The team left Pensacola early the next morning for the 450-mile trip to Orlando. By the time Hicks and the team's other coach, Nathaniel Black, entered the hotel room where the tournament officials and the other managers and coaches were waiting, it was several minutes after three. "It was shaved so close, we had our hearts in our mouths," Hicks told the *Baltimore Afro-American*. "They could have disqualified us, had they wished to do so, but they didn't." Instead, several of the men in the room introduced themselves to Hicks and Black. The tournament director checked the team's roster and the birth certificates of its players and found nothing improper. The Jaycees became the final team in the six-team tournament.[33]

The *Orlando Sentinel* reported that the question remained whether the city of Orlando would allow an integrated game to be played at the city-owned Optimist Park at Lake Lorna Doone. City recreation director Tommy Sterling said that Orlando had previously banned competition between African Americans and whites. Mayor J. Rolfe Davis said he would not say if the tournament would be allowed until an emergency meeting of the city council on Monday morning, August 8. Donald T. Senterfitt, the city attorney, told the council that custom rather than law prohibited the mixing of Blacks and whites on the field. "I don't see where we have any authority in the case," he said. "The park has been committed for this tournament and I don't see what we can do about it."[34]

This did not resolve the issue of whether the white teams in the tournament would play the Pensacola team. What if all the white teams refused to play the Pensacola Jaycees? If this happened, the Jaycees would win the state tournament on forfeit, as the Cannon Street Y did, but would not be allowed to advance to the regional tournament in Rome, Georgia. The Pensacola team stayed at the segregated Walker Hotel, where they waited to hear when—or if—they would play. Hicks said that the tournament director told him to disregard anything he might hear or read unless it came from him. "We were not in on any sessions where the racial question was an issue," Hicks said. "I am sure there were some heated discussions."[35]

The issue of whether any or all of the white teams would boycott their game against the Jaycees was delayed when the team drew a first-round bye. The Jaycees would play the winner of the game between Orlando and Tallahassee on Monday, August 8. Miami, who also received a first-round bye, would play the winner of the St. Petersburg–Fort Lauderdale game. Orlando and St. Petersburg each won their games. The Pensacola Jaycees learned they would play Orlando on Tuesday. If they won, they would play the winner of the St. Petersburg–Miami game in the semifinals on Wednesday. The winner of those games would play in the tournament's championship game. Miami's manager said his team would play Pensacola if both teams won their semifinal game. The St. Petersburg manager, Harry Repaid, however, said his team would not play Pensacola. "If Orlando doesn't win," Repaid said, "we will refuse to take the field."[36]

The Orlando boys voted on whether they would play Pensacola. The team voted to play. It was not unanimous. The team's co-manager, Dwight Devane, resigned in protest. Mel Rivenbark, the other manager, whose son had been the winning pitcher in the team's first-round game, said he opposed playing the game but deferred to his players. "I don't like the idea of playing the game, personally," he said. "But I feel I owe it to the boys."[37] Stewart Hall, the team's first baseman remembered Devane's response more than sixty years later. "Mr. Devane resigned because he would not coach a game against a Black team," Hall said, "and he made a big stink about it and he had a lot of ugly things to say."[38]

Joe K. Rukenbrod, a sports columnist of the *Orlando Sentinel,* said the game between Orlando and Pensacola was the first time in organized sports that a Black team took the field at Optimist Park.[39] The crowd began showing up early at the Lake Lorna Doone ballpark, and it became apparent that the bleachers would be insufficient to seat the 750 or so spectators.[40] The Orlando players remembered watching the Pensacola team exit their bus and walk to the baseball field. The team came off the bus in single file and walked to the dugout, and then they got in a circle and said the Lord's Prayer. "That was kind of impressive to us," Danny Rivenbark said. Cleveland Dailey remembered his impression of the Orlando team. "I looked at the white team and thought, 'They're big.'" He then paused and chuckled, "They're really big."[41]

Neither Hicks nor Black nor the Pensacola players knew what would happen when they entered the stadium. To their surprise, and perhaps relief, the team received a standing ovation. "This was all the evidence I needed to assure me we had been accepted and these people were interested in making history," Hicks said.[42]

Pensacola's pitcher Robert East, his arm hurting from wrestling with his teammates the night before, struggled with his control in the first inning, walking four batters and giving up four runs. Orlando's Danny Rivenbark hit a home run in the second inning to extend the lead. The *Orlando Sentinel*'s game story mentioned that the crowd responded with cheers when Willie Preyer made a diving catch in the second inning. By then, the Orlando team had what would become an insurmountable lead. Orlando won the game, 5–0.[43] Pensacola had just one hit.[44]

Before the game, the players and coaches were advised to leave the field as soon as the game was over to avoid any danger that might come from unruly fans angry about the mixing of African Americans and whites on the field.[45] When the game ended, the two teams could not do as they were told because spectators came onto the field to congratulate ballplayers, the *Pittsburgh Courier* and *Baltimore Afro-American* reported. Hicks told the *Baltimore Afro-American* that the Orlando manager warmly shook his hand and that neither he nor his team could have been treated any better in Orlando.[46]

In his column, *Baltimore Afro-American* sports editor Sam Lacy wrote that the result of the game was far more meaningful than the game itself. He said that Pensacola may have lost on the field but they won "on the scoreboard of human relations." If things were left to children, Lacy added, there would be no color lines in the South. Lacy wrote that when the Orlando Little Leaguers were asked whether they should play the Pensacola Jaycees, they voted unanimously to play the game. "One of their managers resigned in protest against their decision, and the youngsters said, 'Sorry about that but . . . well, it was nice knowing you,'" Lacy said.[47] Lacy compared what happened in Florida to what happened in South Carolina where the adults pulled out of a tournament when an African American team registered. "After it was pointed out that the admittance of the colored boys was entirely legal, the South Carolinians decided they'd have none of that, so they broke up the league," Lacy said.[48]

The Orlando team lost their next game in the tournament.

IN EARLY AUGUST, AN all-Black Little League team from Marshall, Texas, in Harrison County in the eastern part of the state, registered for a district tournament in Denison, Texas. The team advanced to the tournament finals by winning five games by forfeit when opponents refused to play them. Sulphur Springs, a white team, agreed to play Harrison County after a vote of players and their parents. Harrison County won, 6–5.[49] The Denison newspaper reported that the Harrison County team came from behind to "win the game with ability and spirit most admirable."[50] Harrison County won their first game in the sectional tournament in Greenville, Texas, on forfeit when a team from Helena, Arkansas, refused to take the field. It then lost 8–1 in the tournament finals to Alexandria, Louisiana, which advanced to the regional tournament in San Antonio, Texas. Alexandria won the tournament and became one of the eight teams in the Little League World Series.[51]

The integrated team from Delaware Township, New Jersey, qualified for the Little League World Series by winning their regional tournament in the segregated city of Front Royal, Virginia. The boys on the Delaware Township team grew up in the same neighborhoods, went to the same schools, and played in the same Little League Baseball league. Its All-Star team included three Blacks—Billy Hunter, Wilbur Robinson, and Bob Cook. "We went to school with black kids, ate dinner with them, played ball with them," Herb Harrison, a white right-handed pitcher remembered decades later. Harrison said he thought this was how it was everywhere until his team won the state Little League tournament and traveled to Front Royal, seventy miles west of Washington DC, in the Shenandoah Valley, and the players found themselves in a different world.[52]

The Delaware Township team was supposed to stay with local families. But that plan went awry as soon as one of the white men, who had agreed to host the players, saw that the team had African American players. Hunter, Robinson, and Cook stayed with an African American man and his family in the segregated part of town. The man owned a restaurant. "That's where we ate all our meals," Hunter said. While the team was in Front Royal, the boys went to a theater to see the movie *Chief Crazy Horse*. An employee stopped them before they got to their seats and said that Hunter, Robinson, and Cook had to sit in the segregated section in the balcony. The boys were escorted to an outside entrance into the balcony, where they watched the movie through chicken wire. "They took us up to a rear staircase to a place they called 'the bird's nest,'" Hunter said. "I think they used chicken wire so blacks wouldn't throw trash down on the white people."[53]

The bigotry in Front Royal left an impression on the impressionable boys. Tommy Trotman, a white player, was reprimanded by one of his host parents for putting his arm around Hunter before a game. "The man I was staying with told me I couldn't touch a Negro," Trotman said, adding, "I didn't know why." The stunned Trotman asked his father what he had done wrong. "I asked my dad about it and he said it was okay and that we'd talk about it later," Trotman said. Herb Harrison said he was hit by a pitch in one game in retaliation for having African American teammates. Bill Slimm, the team's white third baseman, remembered how the umpires were against the New Jersey team. "I have a picture of one of us sliding into third base and the umpire is calling him out before the third baseman even has the ball," Slimm said. "It shows you how much hatred they had for us." Billy Hunter remembered hearing an angry voice in the crowd when his team was batting that said, "Get those n——s out!"[54]

The Delaware Township team—playing before a hostile crowd and perhaps partisan umpires—left little to chance. Trotman threw a perfect game in Delaware Township's 9–0 victory in the tournament's semifinal.[55] The Delaware Township coaches and players sat in the bleachers and watched the Carlstadt, New Jersey, team win its semifinal game to advance to the championship game against Delaware Township. The team's manager, Elmer Bauer, asked Hunter what he thought of the team. Hunter, who had not allowed a single run in each of his four games since the team played its first game in the district tournament, told his coach he thought he would shut them out.[56] Hunter threw a no-hitter—the second straight game that the team's pitchers gave up no hits—and drove in the team's only run with a double that scored Wilbur Robinson as the team won the championship game, 1–0.[57]

In Williamsport there were no racial epithets, no racial incidents. White and African American boys talked to one another. There were no adults telling the boys who they could talk to or with. There was no chicken wire in the movie theaters. Hunter said he had a chance to talk to white boys on other teams, which may have meant more to the white boys who played on southern teams than it did to Hunter. Hunter said he once received a letter from a player on the Auburn team, who had become a doctor. He told Hunter that the 1955 World Series was the first encounter he had with a Black person. "He said it was a positive experience for him," Hunter said, "and that he appreciated what he learned. Even though we beat them, it had a positive impact on his life."[58]

14

THE TRIP TO WILLIAMSPORT

Peter McGovern's decision to uphold the ineligibility of the Cannon Street All-Stars from the Rome tournament left him with an uneasy feeling. He wanted to do something to express that regret. He invited the team to be guests of Little League Baseball at the World Series in Williamsport from August 23 to 26. He said the players would be treated the same as the other boys in the tournament. They would stay in the same Lycoming College dormitory and eat in the same cafeteria. They would have reserved seats in the bleachers and would be invited to the closing ceremonies. They would be treated like all the other players on the other teams in the tournament.[1]

Except the Cannon Street All-Star team would not play.[2]

McGovern had tried to negotiate a compromise to appease the southern resisters while remaining true to the organization's principles that forbid racial discrimination. Having failed on both accounts, he invited the Cannon Street All-Stars to Williamsport to watch the Little League World Series. They could watch the game but they could not play. It was yet another compromise, and, like the other compromises, it failed. "The compromise was, let them come but don't let them play," John Rivers said. "You know, try to walk the fence. All right, that would satisfy everybody. Well, it didn't."[3]

A United Press story reported that Little League Baseball offered to pay the team's expenses. But Robert Morrison said that the team would pay its own way. He said the team had raised money to go to the state and the regional tournaments, which it had not needed. Morrison said he would ask parents and businesses for additional contributions to pay the expenses for the team, coaches, and a delegation from the YMCA. Morrison contributed his own money.[4] Jimmy Breslin, who was then a twenty-six-year-old columnist for the Newspaper Enterprise Association wire service, quoted Morrison as saying the YMCA thought the players deserved to go to Williamsport even though they were not going to play. "We just want them to see the series and we feel they deserve the chance to go to Williamsport," Morrison said.[5]

Ben Singleton and the other coaches told the players they could go to Williamsport but only as spectators. They would not play. The words did not make sense to the eleven- and twelve-year-olds. In interviews decades later, the former Cannon Street players said they thought they were going to play until they got to Williamsport and learned otherwise—even though they were told by their coaches they were not going to play, even though they did not bring their uniforms or bats or cleats, even though the tournament had not only already started, it was nearly finished.

"In our mind we were going to play. They were going to let us play," Vernon Gray said—though it was not clear how this would happen.[6] "We were so young. We were twelve," Maurice Singleton, Ben's son, said. "We didn't know what was going on."[7] John Bailey also said he thought they were going to play when they got to Williamsport. "We thought we were going to play."[8]

Ben Singleton and the other coaches knew that Little League Baseball had invited the team to Williamsport to ease the pain of being denied their chance to play in the regional tournament and perhaps to relieve their own guilt by being a part of it. "We knew the kids weren't going to play," Lee Bennett, one of the coaches, said. "The league was trying to say they were sorry. But the kids were disappointed. They held on to a glimmer of hope."[9]

Why would Morrison bring his team so far to sit on bleachers and watch white boys play in the championship in the Little League World Series? Why travel so far to be snubbed in Pennsylvania when they could have stayed in Charleston and been snubbed there? Because Morrison saw beyond the baseball field. He had hoped the team would advance to the Little League World Series by winning their way there. But his real objective was to advance the cause of racial equality. He knew he could achieve more by going to Williamsport—even if it meant not playing—than if his All-Stars had played and lost at the district, state, or regional tournaments. If they had lost, the story would have ended, as it did for the Pensacola Jaycees and the Harrison County teams, and they would have dropped from the sports pages and that would have been the end of the story.

By going to Williamsport, Morrison was playing the long game. The Cannon Street Y team would remain players in a bigger story about the unfairness of racial bigotry. As things turned out, the most publicized team in the tournament was the one that did not play. Morrison had his reasons for going. But the boys' parents had their reasons for keeping their sons in Charleston. They knew—or at least probably knew—about the worsening state of race relations since *Brown v. Board of Education*. The Charleston newspapers, the *News and Courier* and the *Evening Post*, told their readers about the rising popularity of the Ku Klux Klan and the Citizens' Councils. The *News and Courier* put stories about two Klan rallies on the front page and excluded stories of African Americans from the newspaper.[10]

THE PARENTS OF THE All-Stars knew about the dangers involved in sending their sons hundreds of miles—most of them on country roads that ran through rural towns, where the boys and their coaches would not be allowed to eat in restaurants or use public bathrooms. And yet the parents let their boys go—perhaps because their boys begged them or perhaps because they thought their boys had earned the trip. Buck Godfrey's father, however, told his son, who was one of the best players on the team, that he could not go if he was not going to play. Mr. Godfrey did not understand the point of exposing his son to the dangers of going where he was not wanted for nothing more than being recognized at a baseball game he was not allowed to play.[11]

To travel to Williamsport, Morrison needed a bus. Fortunately, Morrison knew Esau Jenkins, who was familiar with going where he was not wanted. Jenkins had a bus and he, too, was a race man— and he, too, understood the long game. Jenkins taught African Americans the Constitution so they could pass the literacy test required for them to vote. He then drove them to Charleston to register to vote.

A person could get killed for doing that.

The Reverend George Lee was one of the first Blacks registered to vote in Humphreys County, Mississippi. Lee, the head of the Belzoni, Mississippi, branch of the NAACP, used his pulpit to urge others to register to vote. This put him in conflict with the white Citizens' Council, which ordered him to stop registering Blacks to vote. Lee refused.[12] On May 7, 1955, Lee was driving late at night on a rural road when another car pulled up next to his and a man in the passenger seat fired three times from a shotgun striking Lee in his face. Lee lost control of his car and crash. He died at the scene.[13] The sheriff, Ike Shelton, wanted to call the incident a traffic accident and close the case. He said the buckshot pellets were dental fillings torn loose by the impact of the crash.[14] Lee's widow, Rosebud, insisted that her husband have an open casket. The *Chicago Defender* published a photo of Lee's mutilated corpse. No one was arrested for the murder.[15]

On August 13, three months after Lee's murder, Lamar Smith, who organized Blacks to vote in Brookhaven, Mississippi, was shot to death on the courthouse lawn as he went to register to vote. Dozens of whites witnessed a white man shoot Smith and then walk away with Smith's blood on his hands and his clothes. But all the witnesses stayed quiet. "Nobody knows nothing," the sheriff, Robert Case, said.[16] Three men were charged in the murder but a grand jury of white men made no indictments.[17]

ON THE NIGHT OF Wednesday, August 24, Esau Jenkins's well-traveled bus pulled into the parking lot at the Cannon Street YMCA, where the boys and their parents were anxiously waiting. Morrison and the other adults on the bus knew that a bus full of Black men and boys might draw suspicion as they drove through a southern town or on one of the rural highways so he decided to leave at twilight and drive through the night. The bus included fourteen players: Charles Bradley, Norman Robinson, Leroy Carter, Carl Johnson, Allen Jackson, Arthur Peoples, Leroy Major, John Mack, John Bailey, John Rivers, David Middleton, Vermort Brown, Maurice Singleton, and Vernon Gray. The delegation also included Benjamin Singleton, the manager; Walter Burke, the assistant manager; Robert Morrison and other adults with either the Little League or the YMCA, including Lee Bennett and Archie Graham.[18]

Mothers and fathers shed tears when they saw their boys off on the bus. John Rivers knew his mother was uneasy about him going away. He did not have any such fears. To him, this was the trip of a lifetime. Many of the boys had never been out of Charleston or had been away from their parents for a night. Some of the boys had never worn pajamas before. "It was the first time I ever had a new pair of pajamas," Vernon Gray said.[19] Once on the road, the boys played cards and bingo and listened to a transistor radio, and cracked jokes.[20] "This was the greatest adventure of our lives," John Rivers said. "Just the idea of getting on a bus with your friends for a long trip was more exciting than Christmas."[21]

The boys were told to pack enough food for the trip because there was no guarantee that restaurants would serve them. The boys' mothers provided sandwiches, chicken, and snacks. John Bailey's mom, Flossie, was known for her sandwiches. "She made the best sandwiches in town and everyone knew it," John Bailey said. "I had to guard my rations; I could hardly sleep." Most of the boys had trouble sleeping because they were so excited. Norman Robinson could not get comfortable on the hard seat so he slept on the floor of the bus.[22] Robert Morrison told the team when they left that when they got to Williamsport they would be met "with fire trucks and bands and everything."[23]

THE OPENING CEREMONIES FOR the eighth Little League World Series began on Tuesday, August 23, with eight teams from San Diego, California; Winchester, Massachusetts; Hamtramck, Michigan; Delaware Township, New Jersey; Glens Falls, New York; Morrisville, Pennsylvania; Auburn, Alabama; and Alexandria, Louisiana. Eighty-eight-year-old Cy Young, the winningest pitcher in Major League history, threw out the first ball. This was the last appearance for Young, who had attended each of the Little League World Series. He died three weeks later. Stotz was one of the pallbearers. Other guests of Little League Baseball included Pennsylvania's governor, George M. Leader, and General George C. Marshall, then secretary of defense.

The press in Williamsport included Ted Husing, who broadcast the game on CBS radio; local sportswriters; wire service reporters; Bob Considine, one of the most famous journalists in the country; and Sam Lacy, of the *Baltimore Afro-American*, the country's best-known sportswriter working for a Black newspaper. Lacy and Considine had known each other since they were teenagers in Washington DC. Both were talented athletes who wanted to be journalists. Lacy remembered when they were playing tennis one day. "Sam, you know it's a shame," Considine told him. "When we grow up, I'm going to be able to go a lot farther than you."[24] Considine was right. He became one of America's best-paid journalists—a syndicated newspaper columnist, prolific author, war correspondent, screenwriter, and commentator. Lacy spent his life working for modest wages for African American newspapers. But he became as well known to his readers as Considine was to his.

Lacy, who was born in 1903, grew up in Washington DC near the home of Griffith Stadium, home of the Major League team, the Nationals, who would later change their name to the Senators. Lacy's father, Sam Sr., a researcher at a law firm, introduced his love of baseball to his son. The two regularly attended games at Griffith Stadium, where they sat in the segregated section in right field.[25] When Lacy was a teenager, he began working at Griffith Stadium during Nationals' games—shagging flies during batting practice before the games and then either selling concessions or operating the scoreboard during the games. When the Nationals were on the road, the team's owner, Clark Griffith, leased the stadium to Negro League teams. Lacy, therefore, saw both African American and white teams. He said he saw many African American players who were equal or better than whites in the Major Leagues. This experience shaped his lifelong interest in racial equality. Segregation deprived the best African American players of playing in the big leagues, Lacy said, but it also deprived white players of playing against them and white spectators of watching those players.[26]

After Lacy attended Howard University, the *Washington Tribune* hired him to be a staff reporter and promoted him to sports editor. In 1935 Lacy went to see Griffith, who he knew from working at the ballpark, and asked the Senators' owner why African Americans were not in the big leagues. He told Griffith that the perpetually low-achieving Senators could became the best team in the American League if it signed players like Satchel Paige, Josh Gibson, Buck Leonard, and Cool Papa Bell. Griffith ignored him. He said this would destroy the Negro Leagues, which would deprive him of the gate receipts from renting his ballpark to African American teams.[27]

Over the next several years, Lacy was joined by other African American sportswriters who repeatedly challenged the white baseball establishment's claim that only "ability" and "character" prevented a ballplayer from playing in the Major Leagues. Lacy wrote that baseball's history clearly demonstrated that character had never been a requirement for wearing a Major League uniform.[28] Major League Baseball commissioner Kenesaw Mountain Landis, who—with *Sporting News* editor J. G. Taylor Spink and the rest of the baseball establishment—had kept baseball segregated since taking office in 1921, died in 1944.

The Baseball Writers' Association had its own color line, which meant African American sportswriters were denied membership in the organization and therefore were denied press cards, which prohibited them from press boxes, dugouts, and dressing rooms. In 1948 Lacy became the first African American sportswriter to become a member of the Baseball Writers' Association. A half century later, Lacy, who had reported on many, if not most, of the important stories on race and sports in the twentieth century, was awarded the J. G. Taylor Spink Award for his "meritorious contributions" to baseball writing and recognized in the writers' wing of the Baseball Hall of Fame in Cooperstown in 1997.[29]

A year later Lacy wrote in his autobiography, *Fighting for Fairness*, about how the Cannon Street YMCA and the Pensacola Jaycees tried to integrate Little League tournaments. The Jaycees got to play but the Cannon Street Y did not. The book quoted a column he wrote on August 30, 1955.[30] To Lacy, the story of the Cannon Street All-Stars was important enough for him to drive two hundred miles or so from his home in Washington DC to see the tournament in Williamsport, Pennsylvania.

THE LITTLE LEAGUE WORLD SERIES began after the opening ceremonies with Winchester, Massachusetts, defeating Hamtramck, Michigan, 8–5, and then Morrisville, Pennsylvania, won 4–3 over Glens Falls, New York. A day later, Delaware Township, New Jersey, beat Alexandria, Louisiana, 4–2, and Auburn, Alabama, beat San Diego, California, 4–1. The field of eight was cut to four. In Thursday's semifinal games, Morrisville won 3–0 against Winchester, and Delaware Township defeated Auburn, 6–4. It was the integrated Delaware Township's second win against an all-white team from the Deep South in as many days.

Lacy interviewed a father with two sons who played for the Auburn team before the game with Delaware Township. Robert Salter, a radio station manager, said he was opposed to his sons sharing a field with African American kids. "I'm just not ready to accept them," Salter said, adding that integration will happen when the country is ready for it. "We don't like the idea of being told we've got to do something, that's all."

Lacy asked Salter if African Americans had not been waiting for whites to extend equal rights to them for more than a century. Salter ignored the question and continued:

"You know, there are people in your race," Salter said, "that you don't want anything to do with yourself. Well, we feel that way in the South."

Lacy said that every group had its share of undesirables. The colored group did not have a monopoly on undesirables, he said.

"You're right about that," Salter said. "But in the South we don't have many of that kind in our race and they predominate among the colored people."

Lacy then asked if he thought African American boys should be allowed to play with white boys in Little League Baseball.

"Let 'em play among themselves. That's the way it should be. Sure, there's a lot of agitation about this thing, but that doesn't help matters any," Salter said. "It just serves to make things worse."

Lacy then asked Salter's sons, identical twins George and Frank, what they thought about playing against Africa Americans.

"It didn't make any difference to me," one of them told Lacy, who admitted he could not tell the brothers apart.

"To me, either," the other said.[31]

Lacy also interviewed a white father and son, Sam Despine and Sam Jr., from the Alexandria, Louisiana, team, whose team had lost to Delaware Township.

Sam Despine Sr., the team's manager, said his team qualified for the regional tournament by defeating a Black team, Harrison County, Texas, in the state tournament. His son pitched the game.

"The colored kids played in our regional," Despine said. "It was no choice of ours but the Little League rules said we had to play them to qualify for the World Series. So we played against them. I can't say that we wanted to play with them or didn't want to play with them. It was the rules, that's all."

Sam Jr. said it made no difference to him whether he pitched against white boys or African American boys.

"It wasn't any different," he said. "I struck them out, too."[32]

Delaware Township would play Morrisville in the championship on Friday, August 26.

THE CANNON STREET TEAM arrived in Williamsport after 9:00 p.m. on Thursday night, twenty-four hours after it left Charleston. The bus was delayed because of bad weather and then got lost in the mountains. The bus broke down a few times. One of the coaches then tinkered around under the hood and the bus started again. Just inside the Pennsylvania state line, the bus came to a stop. Ben

Singleton and Lee Bennett helped get the engine started again. And then a few miles south of Williamsport, smoke began coming from under the hood. In the haste to get back on the road, the emergency brake was left on. The brakes caught fire. South Williamsport firefighters came and put out the fire.

Robert Morrison had told the boys on the team when they had left that they would be met "with fire trucks and bands and everything."[33] There was no band.

The bus was towed into town and, shortly thereafter, the Cannon Street All-Stars arrived at Lycoming College in Williamsport. The team checked into a residence hall at Lycoming College, where the other Little League teams were quartered. When they got to their rooms, they found Little League World Series shirts and baseball caps waiting for them—the same gifts that had awaited the players who were playing in the Little League World Series.[34]

There is a photo of Walter Burke, one of the team's coaches, addressing the boys, who are in their pajamas, crowded into one of the rooms in the residence hall.

15.

"LET THEM PLAY!"

T he Cannon Street players woke up the next morning and went
to the cafeteria for breakfast, where players and coaches from
the other teams were seated. They found an empty table. But before
they sat down, someone with the Little League organization led
them to a table where the San Diego, California, team was sitting.

"Sit here," the Cannon Street team was told.

Little League Baseball wanted the boys in the tournament to
socialize with other boys from throughout the country—and they
could not do that if each team sat at their own table. This made
Leroy Major feel like he was indeed part of the tournament. "'No,
no, no, sit with all the teams," he said they were told. "They treated
us like real All-Stars."[1]

The boys from Charleston and San Diego probably did not
know what to say to one another at first. But then the conversation turned to the lingua franca of boys—baseball.

"Who's your home-run hitter?" one of the California boys asked.

A grin came to the face of Allen Jackson, the Cannon Street's
center fielder and pitcher. He raised his hand and said, "Here he
is, fellow, here he is."[2]

Jackson's quote appeared in a wire-service story that reported that
the team had been invited to Williamsport for the championship
game and had arrived the night before after a long and difficult bus
trip. One newspaper article said the team would go on a sightseeing
trip of Williamsport and then go to Bowman Field after the Little
League championship game for an Eastern League game between

Williamsport and Binghamton. "We're going to see as much as we can and do as much as we can before we go home," Jackson said.[3]

When the Cannon Street boys finished breakfast, they mingled with the boys from the other teams, as they had done the night before at dinner. Vermort Brown later said this was one of the things he remembered about the trip. "We got to mix with the white kids, the other players," Brown said.[4]

When they met with the New Jersey team, the talk turned to grits. One of the Cannon Street boys remembered that when they asked the New Jersey kids if they liked grits, one of them asked what grits were. The Cannon Street boys looked at each other with disbelief, momentarily considering the possibility of a world without grits. "We had a nice conversation about grits and oatmeal," Major said.[5]

The Williamsport newspapers published a number of stories and photographs about the team, including one of the boys and adults with the team standing on the Lycoming College campus; one of Peter McGovern talking with Vermort Brown and John Rivers; and another of the boys smiling and waving from their seats at the Original Little League Field.

THE CANNON STREET TEAM took a bus to the Original Little League Field for the consolation game and then the championship game. The World Series was moved to Howard J. Lamade Stadium in South Williamsport in 1959.[6]

Sam Lacy reported that the standing-room-only crowd applauded the Cannon Street team as it entered the ballpark and walked to its reserved seats. He noted that the Salter brothers from the Auburn team, whom he had interviewed, were among those applauding. There was another standing ovation when Ted Husing, the public address announcer who broadcast the game on radio, introduced the team. Lacy wrote that the introduction was simple and sincere. "There was no come-on-now-give-em-a-big-hand business," he said.[7]

When the Cannon Street team got to their seats, they looked out at the field in awe. "We were mesmerized," Leroy Major said. "They had a real stadium. A real stadium!"[8] John Rivers said the field was nothing like the one at Harmon Field. "God, I've never been on a field like that," he said. "You walk out and look at this well-manicured baseball diamond again and the grass was like a carpet. Where we played in Charleston, it was crabgrass and clay and rocks."[9]

Rivers said the big hitters on the team looked at the outfield fences and saw home runs. "Our home-run hitters were looking at those short fences and thinking they could hit them over those fences every time up," he said. Rivers added with a chuckle that the fences were no closer than they were at Harmon Field because Little League Baseball required that all fences be the same distance from home plate.[10] The permanent fence was different from the portable one at Harmon Field, which had to be put up and taken down after every game.[11]

Alabama defeated Massachusetts, 1–0, in extra innings in the consolation game.

The Cannon Street Y players said they were told to go onto the field and practice between games while the players on the Pennsylvania and New Jersey teams warmed up outside the foul lines. Rivers said the short practice consisted of one of the coaches hitting grounders to the infielders and fly balls to the outfield.[12]

"They were willing to allow us to warm up on the diamond. And we got out there and we warmed up," Rivers said. "And we were just awesome. The crowd started to get excited. And they started to chant. And it was just something overwhelming."[13]

Allen Jackson, the boys remembered, picked up a misplayed throw by one of the teams warming up. He then threw a one-hop strike to the catcher.[14]

The players remembered the crowd's applause. The players say that what happened next left an impression as intense as anything that's ever happened to them.

"Let them play!" one of the spectators yelled.

And then others joined in, the players said.

"Let them play!"

"Let them play!"

"Let them play!"[15]

The boys were told they had to leave the field because it was time for the championship game. They said the applause followed them as they walked off the field. By the time the boys got to the bleachers, they said they could hear the vibrations from the spectators stomping on the bleachers as they chanted, "Let them play!" Maurice Singleton said the spectators "jumped up and started saying, 'Let them play!'" He said he could feel the stadium "shaking."[16]

Rivers said he, too, could feel the vibrations of the bleachers. He, too, remembers the cheers.

"The chanting," he said. "You know, the 'Let them play.' 'Let them play.'"

He said he hears the cheering to this day.

"I can hear it now," he said.[17]

Gene Sapakoff, sports columnist for the *Charleston Post and Courier*, said the cheers the players heard from the crowd convinced them that the spectators thought they were good enough to be on that field. "A chant became one last gasp of hope for the team no one would play," Sapakoff wrote.[18]

Neither Sam Lacy nor any of the other journalists at the game mentioned the brief practice or the crowd yelling, "Let them play!"

The former All-Stars still talk about the disappointment of leaving the field and watching two other teams play in the championship game when they thought they deserved to be in one of the dugouts. The Cannon Street team was so close to their dreams of playing, but then when they reached out to touch those dreams, there was nothing there but air and dust. That disappointment is unmistakable in a photograph of the team that was taken right after they took their seats. The players, coaches, and Y executives are all staring into the camera. Hardly anyone is smiling. Vermort Brown said the photo was taken right after they had left the field. "It was heartbreaking," Brown said. "It was really sad. We had real support from the audience."[19]

The Cannon Street players who had been denied the chance to play in the Little League tournament because of racial discrimination looked out from their seats onto the field and saw the African American boys on the New Jersey team and had to wonder, if those boys were allowed to play, why weren't they? "This ain't right," Rivers said to himself.[20]

Once the game started, members of the St. John's Masonic Lodge brought them food and drinks, and spectators asked for their autographs. Vernon Gray remembered signing autographs. "I figured I was live at the Apollo," he said. Rivers said that they were well treated. "We gave out our autographs and we had fun," he said. "But we never got a chance to see how good we actually were."[21] Major remembered witnessing an act that would have met with severe consequences if it had happened in the South—when girls asked two of the players, Maurice Jackson and David Middleton, to sign their names on the bottoms of their pants. Other players then signed the pants. "I was shocked!" he said. "I don't know what happened to those pants to this day, but I know we signed them."[22]

Some of the boys remained immersed in their celebrity while others watched the game between Morrisville, Pennsylvania, and Delaware Township, New Jersey. It turned out to be one of the greatest championship games in the history of the Little League World Series.

THE PLAYERS AND COACHES on the Morrisville, Pennsylvania, and the Delaware Township, New Jersey, teams lived a half hour apart but played in different regional tournaments. The teams rode on the same bus to the stadium. Some of the boys remembered walking from the parking lot to the field as thousands of spectators cheered them.[23]

The starting pitchers, Tom Kaczor for Morrisville and Herbie Harrison for Delaware Township, each pitched the limit of six innings. Delaware Township scored in the first inning when Billy Hunter drove in Tommy Trotman. Morrisville scored twice in the bottom of the first. Jim Wiedenhafer walked and scored on a double by Dick Hart. Maurice Foulke then drove home Hart with a single. Delaware Township scored again in the second inning to tie the game and went ahead in the fourth inning. Morrisville tied the game, 3–3, in the bottom of the inning on a home run by Foulke. The score remained 3–3 at the end of six innings. The game went into extra innings.[24]

Vince Straszynski pitched a scoreless seventh for Morrisville. Delaware Township manager Elmer Bauer sent out Tommy Trotman, who was described as the team's "freckled-faced catcher," to pitch the bottom of the seventh. Bauer and his players later questioned the decision to bring in a catcher—who had a tired arm from trying to throw out baserunners on the hot August day—to pitch under such stressful circumstances.[25]

The first batter was Rich Cominski, who was normally the team's catcher but had injured his hand while horsing around with his teammates and was playing right field instead. Cominski swung hard and connected on Trotman's third pitch, and the ball sailed over the left-field fence, ending the game.[26]

Cominski's mother reportedly fainted as he ran around the bases. Trotman's mother dropped to the ground and wept.[27]

"When Cominski's drive soared into the left-field standards," wrote Carl Lundquist of the United Press, "Little Tom dropped to the ground, wailing, 'It's my fault. I lost it.'"[28]

AFTER THE GAME, SAM LACY interviewed the Cannon Street boys, who told him they could have beaten either of the teams. "Oh sure," said catcher Norman Robinson, "we could've licked both of those teams—I know that." "We wouldn't be scared of none of them, that's for sure," David Middleton, the team's second baseman, said. "And I think we could have beat them, too." Maurice Singleton said, "We'd beat any of the teams they have here if they'd let us play 'em."

His father, Ben, the team's manager, was more circumspect.

"I don't know whether those boys could beat those kids or not," he said. "They're some pretty good youngsters here. I do know, though, that they'd most certainly give a good account of themselves. I wouldn't have to leave here the least bit shamed. If they didn't win, they'd make it close."[29]

But there is still no answer to the question: How would they have done if they had played?

"We will never know," Rivers said. "But what if?"[30]

If they had been able to play, they would have had an answer to that question. If they had been able to play in Williamsport, win or lose, they would have achieved something they did not get a chance to do. "If we had played, if we had won or if we had lost, we would have moved to another level of acceptance of who can play on a broader scale," Rivers said. "It would have been a gut punch to segregation."[31]

When you are deprived of something, as the Cannon Street Y team was, you are left wondering what would have happened if you had had the chance, and you are left with nothing but what if's. If they had won the championship, Allen Jackson said, it would have made a difference in their lives—not just for them but for other African American kids. "This is what bothers me, and I think all of us," Jackson said. "What if, all right, we were World Series champions, an all-black team from Charleston, South Carolina? Do you know what that does to motivate a kid and what it does for racism? You know what I mean, what if?"[32]

This question remained with some of the Cannon Street players until they died and will remain with the surviving members until they die. There are of course no guarantees that the Cannon Street team would have won their first game in the district tournament in Charleston, let alone all the other games they would have had to have won to play in the Little League championship game. There is no guarantee that winning the championship would have meant they would have better lives. But the fact that they were denied that possibility is etched in their minds. In that sense, the Cannon Street All-Stars are no different from millions and millions of African Americans who were—and still are—denied by racial discrimination the possibility of chasing after their dreams.

TWO YEARS LATER, IN 1957, a Little League team from the industrial city of Monterrey, Mexico, won an invitation to play in a tournament in Texas. They raised money by working odd jobs and even donated their blood. They carried little beyond their bats, gloves, and uniforms. They took a bus to the border town of Reynosa, where they crossed the border by foot and walked several more miles to McAllen, Texas, for their first game. The team did not anticipate going far in the tournament. They only sought a three-day visa. "We didn't know Williamsport existed," pitcher José "Pepe" Maiz said.[33]

The Monterrey Industrials won their first game in McAllen and they kept winning. Their visas expired. The Mexican ambassador to the United States got their visas extended. They ran out of money and food and had to rely on strangers for both. They slept in churches and kept winning, even though they weighed thirty to forty pounds less than the players on the opposing teams. They won the Texas state tournament and then the regional tournament in Louisville, Kentucky. This qualified the Industrials to go to Williamsport, Pennsylvania, where they would play on the Original Field in the Little League World Series. The Industrials won their way to the championship game when Angel Macias, an ambidextrous player who was five feet tall and weighed eighty-eight pounds, threw a perfect game in a World Series championship game. Monterrey won, 4–0. It was the only time a pitcher threw a perfect game in the World Series and the first time a team from outside the United States won the championship.

It took a month once the Industrials left Monterrey until they got to Williamsport. It took another month for them to return to Monterrey. They went to New York to see a Brooklyn Dodgers game, and they went shopping at Macy's department store. Macy's gave each of them $40. They went to Washington DC, where they met President Dwight D. Eisenhower and his vice president, Richard M. Nixon. When they returned to Monterrey, they were the guests at a parade in their honor before a crowd of hundreds of thousands of people.[34]

The Los Angeles Angels of the American League signed Macias to a professional contract. He played in the Minor Leagues before returning to Mexico to play in the Mexican League. He said that playing in the World Series changed the trajectory of his life. "All the doors opened and everywhere we went somebody would point us out or want an autograph," he said.[35]

The Monterrey Industrials won the Little League World Series again the next year.

16.

EMMETT TILL

The Cannon Street team got on Esau Jenkins's repaired bus on Saturday, August 27, and began their trip back to Charleston.[1] Gone was the boys' giddiness of a few days earlier—the laughing and the wisecracking. Gone was the excitement of going on a long trip with your friends to somewhere you had never been. Gone was the hope that they would play when they got to Williamsport—and they would win and return to Charleston as champions of Little League Baseball; and that they would prove to those who had refused to play them that they were not just the equal of any team of white boys, they were better than any of the white teams who played them and any of the white teams who would not play them.

"We had come all the way up here for nothing," Allen Jackson said.[2]

Vermort Brown remembered the sense of disappointment that filled the bus on the return trip. "It took a lot out of us," he said. "We weren't able to get what we wanted." Brown said he and his teammates were changed by what happened. "Even as we got older and we'd get together and we looked back over our lives, and sometimes we would talk about it," he said, "and tears would come to our eyes."[3]

John Rivers said the bus was quiet on the way back to Charleston. Nobody wanted to talk about what had happened to them. "We were embarrassed," he said. "We were hurt." He said that he and the other players suppressed the memories of the trip because it hurt too much to think about them. "It was like it never happened. We got rid of the pain by pushing it to the back of our minds."

John Rivers asked his future wife, Robenia, whom he met in the eighth grade, if she remembered if he told her about what happened in Williamsport. "Not a word," she told him.

Rivers asked his teammates if they talked about it to their friends or family. "No," they said. "We didn't talk about it."[4]

"Nobody ever talked about it again," Maurice Singleton said.[5]

Buck Godfrey, who did not go to Williamsport, said his friends were different when he saw them again.

"Something happened to them in Williamsport," he said, "Something happened up there that was devastating."[6]

Godfrey, writing in the first person, even though he did not go on the trip, once described the mood of the bus as it returned to Charleston as that "of a wake with the accompanying emptiness one feels in the pit of the stomach after viewing the remains of someone close." He said it took decades for the players to comprehend what had happened in Williamsport, where "reality—steel hard and ice cold—had smacked us in the face."[7]

"Broken forever was the innocence that had steadied us all our lives. Its loss opened the floodgates of cold knowledge, cynical and brutal," he said. "Because of this, a little boy became a man-child and never again would he surrender his complete trust to any adult. Skepticism bordering on cynicism now stood at the fore. The blister of not playing became a sore. The sore became a hardened callous. The callous became a man-child."[8]

After graduating from Burke High School, Godfrey attended Delaware College, which became Delaware State University, where he became captain on the baseball and football teams. He batted a conference best .511 during his junior year and was inducted into the university's sports hall of fame.[9] He then returned to the South where he began teaching English at a high school in rural Georgia. He eventually received a master's degree in the subject at Georgia State.[10]

Godfrey transferred to Southwest DeKalb High School in Decatur, near Atlanta, where he coached baseball, swimming, and foot-

EMMETT TILL

ball for thirty years. He became one of the most successful high school football coaches in Georgia, winning a state title, finishing runner-up, and winning thirteen regional championships. He retired in 2012 after winning 273 games.[11] Southwest DeKalb now plays its football games at William "Buck" Godfrey stadium.[12] Shortly after retiring in 2012, Godfrey was inducted into the Georgia Athletic Coaches Association Hall of Fame. Two hundred and seventy of his players received college scholarships.[13] "He probably sent more kids to college than anyone I know of," said Richard Adams Jr., who played football for Godfrey, and said the coach became a father figure to him. "I didn't have a lot of direction," Adams said. "He taught so many of us to be responsible. To do whatever we wanted to do, but to be the best at it. He taught me how to be a man."[14]

To do so, Godfrey taught his students the same kind of things that Robert Morrison had been taught at Avery Institute nearly a century earlier. "We taught kids how to tie a tie," Godfrey said. "We taught them eye contact, strong body language, how to present themselves."[15] Godfrey's mentors taught him how to maneuver through a racist society when he was a boy, and then as a man he did the same for other young men. Godfrey taught his students, including his athletes, that racism would shadow them so they needed to work harder. "I'm never surprised at anything the other race did to keep us back or hold us down," he said.[16]

Godfrey, the All-Star who did not go to Williamsport, was the only one of the team who played college baseball. Some of the boys played Pony League Baseball when they turned thirteen. But others never played organized baseball again. The boys who were eleven may have returned to play another year in the Cannon Street Y League. But there was no district or state tournament the next year because there were no leagues. The white teams joined the Little Boys League. After the 1956 season, the Cannon Street Y League faded away as the segregated Little Boys League flourished.

Only a few of the All-Stars—the ones who were eleven during the 1955 season—were able to play baseball in high school. This had less to do with their ability than with the racism in schools.

White high schools had baseball teams. The all-Black Burke High School did not have a baseball team until the year after most of the Cannon Street All-Stars had graduated.

Buck Godfrey's father was not the only African American parent who feared for his or her children—especially their sons—because of what might happen at the hands of white racists.

"We came back on the bus the day they lynched Till," Rivers said.[17]

EMMETT TILL'S MOTHER, MAMIE, had the same concerns about her son, who had turned fourteen on July 25. The mother and son were close. He was her only child during a brief marriage to her abusive husband, Louis Till. The Tills separated a year after the birth of Emmett, or "Bobo," as he was called. Louis was executed while serving in the U.S. Army for "willful misconduct" after he was convicted of raping a women while stationed in Italy. The army sent Till's belongings home. They included a silver ring with the initials "L.T.," which Mamie gave to Emmett when he got older.[18]

Like many boys his age, Emmett loved baseball. He grew up in Chicago, where the Cubs and White Sox played, but, like many African American boys his age, he rooted for the Brooklyn Dodgers. His favorite player was the team's star pitcher, Don Newcombe. His mother remembered when she sent him to the store to buy a load of bread. Emmett got involved in a baseball game on his way home. When Mamie found Emmett, he was playing ball and the bread looked like it had been used for second base.[19]

Till left Chicago to visit his great uncle Moses Wright in Money, Mississippi, a small town in the Delta. His mother, Mamie, warned her son to watch his behavior. She told Emmett, who was big for his age, that he could get into a lot of trouble if he talked back to whites and told him he should not speak to whites unless spoken to and should always say, "Yes, sir," and, "Yes, ma'am." When Emmett left Chicago on the train, he was wearing his father's ring.[20]

On August 24, a few days after arriving in Money, and the day the Cannon Street boys left Charleston, Till went with his cousins to Bryant's Grocery and Meat Market, which was run by a married couple, Carolyn and Roy Bryant. Roy was out of town. Carolyn was working at the store by herself. Till violated a southern custom by touching her hands when he gave her the money for some bubblegum and then by saying "goodbye" to her as he was leaving, Carolyn Bryant said. He then whistled at Carolyn Bryant, who then went to the car to retrieve a pistol. Emmett's cousins, realizing the danger they were in, sped away from the scene.[21]

When Roy returned, his wife told him what had happened. In the early morning of August 28, Bryant and his half-brother, J. W. Milam, went to Wright's house and dragged Emmett away. Bryant and Milam and several others tortured the boy before murdering him. They started by beating him with a .45 semiautomatic pistol, as Emmett pled for his life. His skull was crushed. His left eye was gouged out. Part of one ear was missing. And finally, he was shot through the head. In his book *The Blood of Emmett Till*, Timothy Tyson wrote that the torture of Till left injuries beyond comprehension. "They reveal a breathtaking level of savagery, a brutality that cannot be explained without considering rabid homicidal intent or a rage utterly beyond control," Tyson said. "Affronted white supremacy drove every blow."[22]

Bryant and Milam then threw Till's corpse into the Tallahatchie River, but not before using barbed wire to tie the body to a seventy-pound cotton-gin fan so it would sink to the bottom of the river and never be found. The body got hung up on some branches and did not sink. It was discovered on Wednesday, August 31. Emmett was identified by his father's ring on his finger. The murder would have ended up forgotten like so many murders of African Americans in Mississippi and elsewhere in the South. But Mamie, like Rosebud Lee, insisted on an open casket because she wanted the rest of America to see what had happened to her son. The *Chicago Defender* reported that two hundred and fifty thousand people viewed Emmett's body. *Jet* magazine published photos of Emmett's corpse.[23]

The story of Till's murder, which was supposed to lay buried in a river, provoked outrage from civil rights activists and from Black newspapers. Roy Wilkins, executive secretary of the NAACP, condemned Till's murder in a statement. "It would appear by this lynching that the state of Mississippi has decided to maintain white supremacy by murdering children," he said. "The killers of the boy felt free to lynch him because there is in the entire state no restraining influence of decency, not even in the state capital, among the daily newspapers, the clergy nor any segment of the so-called better citizens."[24] On September 18, 1955, Tom Waring published an opinion piece masquerading as a news story by Nicholas Stanford, who was identified as a special writer, that criticized Wilkins's statement that "Mississippi was trying to maintain white supremacy by murdering children." Wilkins, Stanford wrote, was using propaganda to gin up northern public opinion against the South.[25]

Nicholas Stanford was a pseudonym, a privilege Waring afforded contributors who shared his white supremacist values so they could be free to express their vile opinions without fear of retribution. The murder and kidnapping trial of Bryant and Milam began on Monday, September 19.[26] The fate of Bryant and Milam rested in the hands of twelve of their fellow white Mississippians. The *News and Courier*'s coverage of the trial was no more objective than the trial itself. The newspaper reported a story from Mississippi that said the sheriff investigating Till's disappearance said he did not believe the boy found in the river was Till. The sheriff, H. C. Strider, said he thought the body found in the river was put there by the NAACP. The wire service story in the newspaper did not mention that a finger on the dead body was wearing Emmett Till's ring.[27]

The *News and Courier* published the most salacious details about the trial at the top of its front page. On September 23 the newspaper reported court testimony under the headline, "Mrs. Bryant Said Negro Sought Date." The story reported that Bryant had testified that Till had bought candy and then grabbed her hand and said, "How about a date, baby?" She said he then put both hands around her waist, "What's the matter, baby, can't you take it? You need not be afraid of me." After she got free of his grip, he told her he had been with white women before.[28]

In an editorial, Thomas Waring called for Till's murderers to be punished. But he also wrote that the NAACP was in part responsible for the murder. "Had it not been for the constant dinning in the ears of colored people about denial of their 'rights,' the boy might never have made a remark that caused animosity in the rural community where he was visiting," Waring wrote. "The death of this boy should remind all who tamper lightly with deep mass emotions that voluntary, friendly approaches are the only way the races can live together in peace."[29]

The NAACP had nothing to do with the murder of Emmett Till. He was tortured and murdered by racist sociopaths who went on trial for the boy's kidnapping and death; and an all-white jury exonerated them. *Look* magazine paid Bryant and Milam $4,000 for an interview that appeared in January 1956. Bryant and Milam admitted they had murdered Till. "Chicago boy, I'm tired of 'em sending your kind down here to stir up trouble," Milam said. "God-damn you, I'm going to make an example of you—just so everybody can know how me and my folks stand."[30]

Bryant and Milam would go unpunished because of double jeopardy, the procedural defense that prohibits someone being charged twice for the same crime if they had been formally acquitted. In 2017 Carolyn Bryant told author Timothy Tyson that Till had not said the things she said he did. "Nothing that boy did could ever justify what happened to him," she said.[31] This admission came as no comfort to Emmett Till, who had been dead for sixty-two years, or to his mother Mamie, who died in 2003.

Gene Roberts and Hank Klibanoff wrote that Till's murder was unrelated to the NAACP's legal challenges, school segregation, voting rights, or the campaign for civil rights. It was, they said, just another grisly murder in an unceasing line of grisly murders of African Americans in the South. "But no single event intensified the interest of the Negro press," Roberts and Klibanoff said, "more than the story of the Chicago kid visiting his mother's uncle in the late summer of 1955 and the trial of the two white men accused of beating him, shooting him in the head, and ditching him in a river with a seventy-pound cotton gin tethered to his neck with barbed wire."[32]

The brutal murder of a fourteen-year-old horrified the African

American press and galvanized the northern white press in a way that had perhaps never happened before, whether it was the photo of Till's mutilated corpse, the viciousness of the crime, or the obscenity of the jury's verdict. "Emmett Till not only brought Negro reporters into the heart of the white man's kingdom—the courtroom—but he brought white reporters into the Deep South in unprecedented numbers to cover a racial story," Roberts and Klibanoff said. "Northerners were shocked and shaken by what they read."[33]

So was Rosa Parks, who wrote to a friend shortly after the acquittal of Bryant and Milam that what had happened to Till happens regularly in Mississippi, Alabama, Georgia, and Florida. She attended a speech by the Reverend Martin Luther King Jr. at the Dexter Avenue Baptist Church in Montgomery. King introduced a Mississippi doctor who talked about the assassinations of George Lee and Lamar Smith and the murder of Till.[34]

On December 5, four days after listening to the Mississippi doctor and a little more than three months after Till's murder, Rosa Parks refused to give up her seat to a white man on a bus in Montgomery, Alabama. This inspired the Montgomery bus boycott, where Blacks refused to ride on buses for the next year. On November 13, 1956, the U.S. Supreme Court affirmed a lower-court ruling outlawing segregation on public buses.[35]

The Cannon Street team perhaps heard about Emmett Till but they were probably not quite old enough to fully comprehend the sheer magnitude of racism in America. The boys were too young and the news was too horrific and their parents did what they could to protect them from something that evil. Till's murder had an impact on John Rivers. "I'd see a white woman coming down the street," he said, "and I'd cross the street."[36]

BY THE TIME THE Cannon Street boys returned, summer was nearly over and school was about to begin. Many of the boys and their fathers were following the Brooklyn Dodgers, who had won the National League pennant by almost twenty games. It was their fifth pennant since Robinson joined the team in 1947. The Dodgers had played the New York Yankees in each of their previous

World Series. The Yankees won each time. To come so close to becoming World Series champions and to lose each time to the Yankees must have been particularly vexing to the competitive Robinson, who hated losing, and he particularly hated losing to the Yankees. When Robinson played the Yankees, he looked into their dugout and saw all white men and heard the racial epithets they screamed at him.[37]

By October 1955 Robinson must have wondered how many more chances he would have to win a World Series. He was thirty-six years old and his body was breaking down. He played in the fewest games and hit the lowest average of his career. But Robinson could look in his own dugout and see progress in racial equality. The Dodgers had five African Americans on their roster—more than any other Major League team: pitcher Don Newcombe, who won twenty games, Joe Black, Jim Gilliam, Sandy Amoros, and Robinson.

On October 4 the Dodgers and Yankees, tied three games apiece, played in the decisive seventh game. Brooklyn led 2–0 in the bottom of the sixth inning but the Yankees had runners at first and second when the team's catcher, Yogi Berra, sliced a ball toward the left-field line. Amoros, one of the fastest men in the league, raced toward the ball, and running hard, with his right arm fully extended, caught the ball. He then threw the ball into the infield to double baserunner Gil McDougald off first for a double play, ending the inning.

Brooklyn won the game and the series. It was perhaps the greatest single day in the history of the franchise.

Robinson played one more year for the Dodgers, who lost again to the Yankees in the 1956 World Series. Brooklyn general manager Walter O'Malley, who had succeeded Branch Rickey, traded Robinson to the team's hated intercity rival, the New York Giants. Robinson retired. Robinson had long been active as a mentor at the Harlem YMCA and would continue to do so the rest of his life. His retirement from baseball allowed him to spend more time at the Y, whether it was playing basketball with the boys, talking with them, or serving as a father figure.[38]

Robinson became active in the civil rights movement and would express himself on bigotry in America in a way he had not been able to do as a ballplayer, in a way that expressed his frustration with racism, in a way that was brutally honest for its time. He remembered in his 1972 book, *I Never Had It Made*, standing for the national anthem during Game One of the 1947 World Series, the first African American to play in a World Series. "There I was, the Black grandson of a slave, the son of a Black sharecropper, part of an historic occasion, a symbolic hero to my people," he said. "The band struck up the national anthem. It should have been a glorious moment for me as the stirring words . . . poured from the stands." Yet it was not, as Robinson described twenty-years years later in his autobiography. "I cannot stand and sing the anthem. I cannot salute the flag," Robinson said. "I know that I am a Black man in a white world. In 1972, in 1947, at my birth in 1919, I know that I never had it made."[39]

TO SOUTHERN CITIES AND states, the only response to demands for racial equality was not integration but more segregation. In August Danny Jones and three other men formerly involved with Little League Baseball in South Carolina announced the incorporation of Little Boys League, Inc., which was the name given to the segregated tournament for teams who withdrew from the Little League Baseball tournament after the national organization ordered them to allow the Cannon Street All-Stars.[40] The Little Boys League released a statement that said it was doing so because Little League Baseball had made a "political football" out of youth baseball. The statement did not mention that Jones and the managers of white Little League teams in South Carolina had withdrawn from the district and state tournaments because an African American team had registered for the tournaments. Peter McGovern said that any "political footballing," as he put it, was done on the part of those who refused to play in a tournament because "of race." He repeated that the South Carolina teams had signed affidavits promising that anyone could play in Little League Baseball, "regardless of race, color, or creed."[41]

News and Courier sports editor Ed Campbell quoted Jones as saying the rules for the organization would not differ much from those of Little League Baseball except that it would exclude African American boys.[42] The Little Boys League's charter mandated that the organization be segregated. "The Organizers hereof are of the opinion it is for the best interest of all concerned that this program be on a racially segregated basis; they believe that mixed teams and competition between the races would create regrettable conditions and destroy the harmony and tranquility that now exists."[43]

The Little Boys League became part of the southern resistance to desegregation. The Little Boys League waved the Confederate flag, and more than five hundred teams in 122 leagues joined the organization when it began its first season in the spring of 1956. The league increased to 390 leagues in eight southern states by 1962.[44] In 1958 Little League Baseball sued the Little Boys League for copyright infringement over their name.[45] A judge ruled on the side of Little League Baseball. The Little Boys League changed its name to Dixie Youth Baseball.[46]

Jones remained the organization's commissioner until his death in 1966.[47] He can be credited for much of the organization's success. He was a popular and respected figure in youth baseball and then became a hero in the South for defying Little League Baseball and creating his own segregated league. When Jones died suddenly in 1965, tributes came from throughout the South. The *Charleston Evening Post* recognized Jones's legacy by noting how he had defended southern custom in its obituary. "Mr. Jones sprang into national prominence when he resigned and urged all of South Carolina's communities to follow," the obituary said.[48] Jones is remembered in his hometown. Dixie League Baseball also remembers him. The Danny Jones Sportsmanship Award is given annually to the team in the Dixie League World Series that "fully embodies the principles and ideals of its namesake."[49]

But those principals and ideals included segregation.

Dixie League Baseball didn't become integrated until after Jones's death.

Fifty years after its creation, Dixie Youth Baseball continued to play down its racist past. In fact, it was founded by segregationists for the purpose of segregating youth baseball. Its rule books had a Confederate flag. So did its uniforms, until Gus Holt took his fight to city hall in Charleston. When Holt was asked about Dixie Baseball, he said, "I don't think much of it. No one is saying it is a bad organization, but there is a legacy and a stigma behind it."[50]

BY NOVEMBER 1955 LITTLE League Baseball's civil war had spread to a second front as the tensions between the organization's executive director, Peter McGovern, and its commissioner, Carl Stotz, deteriorated into a power struggle between the two men and their contrasting visions of the organization. Stotz believed that the terms of the 1950 charter gave him the autonomy to make decisions about rules and regulations, to select regional directors, and to rule on the eligibility of leagues and teams. McGovern said the board of directors, which included Stotz, later amended the charter, giving McGovern the authority that Stotz believed was rightfully his.[51]

Stotz challenged McGovern for control of the organization during a board meeting on November 21, 1955, at the Lycoming Hotel in downtown Williamsport. Stotz demanded McGovern's immediate resignation. He demanded that the organization return to the bylaws that gave him most of the power. The board rejected both resolutions. Stotz's attorney immediately filed suit against Little League Baseball. A judge ordered the closing of Little League's building at 120 West Street in Williamsport. A sheriff's deputy ordered everyone out of the building and padlocked its doors. Little League officials had the padlock removed the next morning.[52]

The *Williamsport Sun-Gazette* published Stotz's statement, which said that McGovern had breached the 1950 contract giving him control over the organization. Stotz sued the organization for $300,000. McGovern described Stotz's actions as "unnecessarily dramatic." He said Stotz had refused to accept board decisions that were made in the best interests of the boys who played Little League Baseball. McGovern replaced Stotz as commissioner and replaced him with his assistant, John Lindemuth.[53] Other Little League officials stood by Stotz and resigned from the organization. Stotz created a separate youth baseball organization called the "Original Little League," which is what Stotz had first called Little League Baseball. Stotz wrote all Little League presidents inviting them to a meeting in Pittsburgh to join his organization. McGovern and Little League Baseball sued to stop Stotz from taking action "to cripple Little League Baseball by setting up a rival organization in violation of his contract with Little League Baseball, Inc."[54] U.S. district court judge Frederick Follmer issued an injunction to prevent Stotz from appearing at the Pittsburgh meeting. Stotz dropped the lawsuit.[55]

Stotz lived in Williamsport for the next thirty-six years, separated from Little League Baseball but also inextricably connected to it. He became a tax collector for Lycoming Township. The *Los Angeles Times* reported in a 1985 story that Stotz got little recognition for creating the organization. The World Series brochures did not mention his name and there was little mention of him in the Little League Museum, which was named for Peter McGovern.[56] Stotz, who was often invited to the annual World Series and to the Little League Museum, always declined. He formed a baseball league for Williamsport and created his own museum in a converted toolshed that includes a glass case with the lilac bush that inspired him to create Little League Baseball. By the time of his death in 1992, Little League Baseball was played by more than 2.5 million boys and girls in more than thirty countries.[57]

17

"PAPER CURTAIN"

In November 1955 Tom Waring wrote an editorial for the *Mast-head*, a newsletter of the National Conference of Editorial Writers, where he criticized northern newspapers and magazines for abandoning objectivity by slanting stories to advance racial equality and integration. "A paper curtain shuts out the Southern side of the race relations story from the rest of the country," Waring said. He called on northern editors to publish more balanced news articles—that is, articles like his newspaper did, that defended segregation, questioned the patriotism of those advocating racial equality, and published the names and addresses of those African Americans who advocated for civil rights. "Waring turned his 'paper curtain' accusation into a battle cry as he launched a campaign to present the segregationist view in the national media," Sid Bedingfield wrote.[1]

John Fischer, the editor of *Harper's* magazine, was looking for a pro-segregation essay that could become "a starting point for rational discussion" on the issue of racial equality. He asked Waring to write it.[2] In January 1956 *Harper's* published Waring's essay, "The Southern Case Against Desegregation," which said the mingling of the races would subject white southerners to the inferior race of African Americans and their higher rates of "venereal disease," "illegitimate" births, "divorce," and "crime" and their lower rates of what he called "intellectual development." He wrote that northern readers would be infuriated by his essay, adding, "What I am saying is documented by facts and statistics. If these should seem to the reader to add up merely to bias, bigotry, and even untruth, I shall regret it."[3]

There is no evidence Waring regretted a word of what he wrote. He repeated these words over and over in other essays, in speeches, and in interviews until his death.[4] Waring promised he would include documentation to support his facts. But he then admitted he could not verify any of his statements. "The incidence of venereal disease for instance is much greater among Negroes than among whites," Waring wrote. "Statistics to document this statement are difficult to come by, though the statement itself would be generally accepted in the South."[5] Such statements were generally accepted in the South because Waring and other editors and politicians repeated them over and over until they were so well known they *became* generally accepted.

Waring said that the reason for the high crime in the South was because of the high amount of violence among Black people. "Interracial homicide is relatively rare," he said. This, he added, was why the murder of Emmett Till had been so widely reported.[6] Waring ignored the fact that the publicity about Till's murder had to do with his mother Mamie's insistence that her son have an open casket to demonstrate the viciousness of the murder. He did not mention that the *Chicago Defender* and *Ebony* published photos of the boy's mutilated corpse. He did not mention that northern newspapers, which had previously dismissed lynching and violence against African Americans as a regional issue, saw the murder as so brutal, so cruel, so inhuman, they could no longer ignore it. Waring did not mention that his own paper had questioned whether the murdered boy was really Till. The *News and Courier* instead perpetuated the myth of the lecherous African American male preying on the defenseless white female in its reporting on Bryant's testimony.

In his *Harper's* essay, Waring blamed the racial unrest in the country on the NAACP and other racial agitators. He repeated the southern myth that race relations were good until the Supreme Court ended school segregation in *Brown v. Board of Education*. If the mingling between the races was encouraged, he said, it would lead to interracial marriages and the downfall of southern society. African American southerners, he added without evidence, preferred being segregated and objected to the interference of the NAACP, who, he insisted, served the interests of white liberals and communists.[7]

Waring said he felt compelled to write the essay to correct misunderstandings and false perceptions that appeared in the northern metropolitan and African American press. "While less violent than the Negro press—which understandably presents only the militant anti-segregation case—the metropolitan press almost without exception has abandoned fair and objective reporting of the race story," Waring said. "For facts, it frequently substitutes propaganda."[8] He did not cite any examples of such propaganda but instead included paragraph after paragraph of his own propaganda. Waring, for his part, could not be accused of ever abandoning "fair and objective reporting on the race story" because he had never practiced it himself.

He said African Americans lagged behind whites in seemingly all quality-of-life issues because they were inferior to whites. "For whatever reason," Waring wrote, "Southern Negroes usually are below the intellectual level of their white counterparts." He said African Americans were inferior because they were shiftless, ignorant, and immoral. He did not mention that they were deprived of decent schools and decent jobs and decent living conditions.[9] He did not mention the institutional racism that had enchained Blacks—either literally or metaphorically—since the editor's ancestors had run a plantation in the seventeenth century.

Waring's editorial made him a celebrity in the South, and he was invited to speak at colleges and universities. He defended segregation on radio and television programs.[10] His "paper curtain" argument, however flawed and dishonest, gained currency in the South and among conservatives in the rest of the country because, as Wade Hampton did after the Civil War, it deflected the focus of the South from a region clinging to poverty, ignorance, bigotry, and white supremacy to one that was victimized by northern oppression. Southern politicians and journalists were revising history again—as they did during and after Reconstruction. War-ing's ideology would prove useful to future political conservatives who would later project the failure of their ideas to win approval by blaming the liberal media.

Senator Strom Thurmond and Congressman L. Mendel Rivers of Charleston praised Waring for tearing down the "newspaper curtain" and giving northerners the southern argument for segre-gation.[11] Rivers praised Waring's essay on the floor of the House of Representatives. "Too little has been said," Rivers argued, "entirely too little written about the fine things the Southern states have been doing to help the Negroes, to improve their educational facilities, to raise their economic and cultural status, all within the frame-work of segregation that contributes to a peaceful society in the South." Rivers said he agreed with Waring's reason for opposing the integration of schools because of the low health standards, illegit-imacy, crime, and lesser intellectual development among Blacks.[12] Thurmond read Waring's essay into the *Congressional Record*.[13] Rivers lacked either the pure malevolence or sexual defiance of some of the state's other politicians but he gave no ground when it came to demagoguery. In a speech in late November 1955, Rivers defended the supremacy of white men and denounced "the unholy alliance" between the Supreme Court and the NAACP, which he called "the National Association for the Advancement of Com-munist Propaganda."[14]

Waring worked with other like-minded southern newspaper editors, like James J. Kilpatrick of the *Richmond (VA) News Leader*, to plot their strategy on resisting the implementation of *Brown v. Board of Education*, which they believed was a consequence of northern newspapers' opposition to segregation. Waring wrote Kilpatrick on July 27, 1955, asking for advice on how to "fight the enemy on his own ground." Waring suggested that they enlist a syndicate of southern newspapers to send reporters into the North to "expose" segregation there. If enough southern newspapers pub-lished these stories, then maybe the Associated Press would cir-culate the story to sympathetic newspapers.[15]

A study of press coverage during the 1950s soundly contradicts Waring's argument of a "paper curtain." Newspapers and magazines were inundated with manuscripts espousing conservative propaganda that tried to delegitimize racial progressives. In a November 1956 *Atlantic Monthly* article, identified by an editorial note as "the fundamental case for the white South," Charlestonian Herbert Ravenel Sass, who had spent much of his career working for the *News and Courier* and wrote a fawning history of the newspaper, maintained that the United States was "overwhelmingly a pure white nation" and ought to stay that way. Desegregation of the schools would inevitably lead to "widespread racial amalgamation."[16]

Waring was determined to prove his conspiracy of a "paper curtain," regardless of whether it existed or not. So you can imagine his joy when he found someone working for a northern newspaper who agreed with him. It did not matter—at least initially—that John W. Briggs hid behind a pseudonym and that he was a raging racial bigot and anti-Semite. Waring was looking for a journalist who shared his views on race. He could not afford to be selective. If Waring would not have found Briggs he would have had to invent him. Which, one could argue, is what he did.

Waring obviously liked what Briggs sent him during the Till trial and published it under the byline Nicholas Stanford. In 1956 Waring began publishing the byline of Stanford, who claimed to understand the workings of the northern media because he worked among them. As it turned out, Nicholas Stanford was a pseudonym for John W. Briggs, a classical music critic of the *New York Times*. Briggs, who was born in North Carolina, was, like Waring, an avowed anticommunist who believed that left-wing newspapers of the North, including his own, were slanting newspaper coverage on the side of integration. Sid Bedingfield wrote that Waring, Briggs, and other southern segregationists helped sow the "liberal media" argument to discredit northern journalists covering the civil rights movement in the South.[17]

Waring and Briggs shared letters during the next few years where Briggs acted as a spy in the *Times*' newsroom. Waring, at some point, began to distance himself from Briggs as his language became more and more bigoted. Briggs hated Blacks and he hated Jews—and he sometimes juggled both in the same sentence. He called the *Times'* liberal columnist Murray Kempton "the great n— lover" and described people living in West Harlem as "vermin." He frequently criticized the Jewish influence in the New York news media. Briggs's anti-Semitism made Waring uncomfortable. The Charleston editor may not have had any African American friends but he had Jewish friends. Waring urged Briggs to stick to racial issues. Briggs disregarded the order. The *News and Courier* finally quit publishing Briggs's work.[18]

Briggs's opinions were racist but were no longer mainstream. Waring's opinions were racist but still mainstream.

On March 12, 1956, Strom Thurmond presented what would be called the Southern Manifesto. Signed by more than a hundred southern members of Congress, it criticized "outside agitators" for destroying race relations in the South. Thurmond said that "the white people of the South are the greatest minority in the Nation. They deserve consideration and understanding instead of the persecution of twisted propaganda." Waring praised the document in the *News and Courier*.[19] When the U.S. Senate considered a civil rights bill in 1957, Thurmond would have no part of it. He conducted the longest speaking filibuster ever by a single senator at twenty-four hours and eighteen minutes. Waring again praised Thurmond in a front-page editorial.[20]

The NAACP registered nine Black students to attend segregated Little Rock Central High School in the Arkansas capital in response to the Supreme Court's decision in *Brown v. Board of Education*. When the state's governor, Orval Faubus, resisted, President Dwight Eisenhower ordered federal troops to escort the "Little Rock Nine" past an angry mob of more than a thousand white protestors into Central High School.[21] Harry Ashmore, editor of the *Arkansas Gazette*, which was published in Little Rock, argued that Faubus and Arkansas were obligated to obey a judge's order to implement the decision in *Brown*. Ashmore received the Pulitzer Prize in 1958. But Tom Waring and other newspaper editors condemned the integration of Little Rock Central High School or of any other school. To Ashmore, Waring was an extremist who was a danger to the country. "The *News and Courier* feels like what's wrong with this country is democracy," Ashmore said.[22]

On August 24, 1957, William F. Buckley, editor and founder of the *National Review*, wrote a column, "Why the South Must Prevail," praising the South for restricting voting rights for African Americans. Buckley's editorial called whites "the advanced race" in the South and said therefore that they should be allowed to "take such measures as necessary to prevail, politically and culturally, in areas in which it does not predominate numerically." In Buckley's view, "the claims of civilization supersede those of universal suffrage." Waring agreed: "The right to vote is not more basic than civilization," he said.[23]

Waring and William Workman joined Buckley and conservative politicians, including U.S. senator Barry Goldwater of Arizona, in challenging the GOP's more liberal politicians, like Nelson B. Rockefeller in 1964, and sought to redefine the Republican Party as what William Loeb, the editor of the *Manchester Union-Leader*, called "the white man's party."[24] Workman resigned from the *News and Courier* to run for the U.S. Senate as a pro-segregationist Republican in 1962. His campaign rested on the argument that African Americans were inferior to whites and that the mixing of races would be disastrous for whites and African Americans. He lectured southern Blacks to quit being so sensitive to the term "n——," which, rather than an epithet, Workman said, was meant as a term of endearment.[25] Sid Bedingfield said Workman became the progenitor for right-wing politicians on talk radio, television news networks, and websites that used racial demagoguery to unite political conservatives.[26] He also forged a path for pro-segregation politicians like Thurmond to abandon the Democratic Party for the GOP. Thurmond's announcement signaled the start of what was called the "great white switch" or Southern Strategy.[27]

By the late 1970s, former California governor Ronald Reagan had united former segregationists with economic and social conservatives to create a political movement that would dominate American politics. Reagan built this coalition in part through the use of coded rhetoric connecting race to such issues as crime, welfare, and government spending.[28] In 1980 he launched his fall presidential campaign at the Neshoba County Fair near Philadelphia, Mississippi, where three civil rights workers, Michael Schwerner, Andrew Goodman, and James Cheney, had been murdered and buried in an earthen dam. Reagan declared his support for states' rights—a phrase indelibly linked to Thurmond's Dixiecrat campaign of 1948—and said he would use whatever power he had "to restore to states and local governments the powers that properly belonged to them."[29]

In 1981, the year Reagan became president, Lee Atwater, who grew up in Aiken and had spent the last decade working as a political operative for the Republican Party in South Carolina, told an interviewer how the GOP could win votes of racists without appearing to be racist. "You start out in 1954 by saying, 'N——, n——, n——.' By 1968, you can't say 'n——'—that hurts, backfires. So you say stuff like, uh, forced busing, states' rights, and all that stuff, and you're getting so abstract," Atwater said. "Now, you're talking about cutting taxes, and all these things you're taking about are totally economic things, and the byproduct of them is, blacks get hurt worse than whites. . . . 'We want to cut this' is much more abstract than even the busing thing, uh, and a hell of a lot more abstract than 'N——, N——, N——.'"[30]

The Republican Party used coded—and sometimes uncoded—messages to stoke fears of the predatory African American man, as the Democrats had done decades earlier. Atwater, then working as campaign manager for Vice President George W. H. Bush's presidential campaign in 1988, approved a television ad blaming Democratic presidential candidate Michael Dukakis, the former governor of Massachusetts, for a furlough program in the state that released a first-degree murderer, Willie Horton, who then "repeatedly raped" a "white woman." George H. W. Bush won the election. Atwater later said he regretted saying that he would make Horton into Dukakis's running mate "because it makes me sound racist, which I am not."[31]

When George W. Bush, the son of George H. W. Bush, ran for

president in 2000, he found himself trailing U.S. senator John McCain going into the South Carolina primary. The Bush campaign engaged in a smear campaign during the primary that spread lies that McCain's wife, Cindy, was a drug addict and that the couple's adopted daughter from Bangladesh was the product of an extramarital affair by the senator.[32] George W. Bush won the GOP nomination and was elected president in October 2000. In 2016 Donald Trump won the GOP's presidential nomination and then the presidency by using racially divisive rhetoric that lacked abstraction.

WARING CONTINUED TO WRITE editorials perpetuating myths, fabrications, distortions, and lies, and his friends in Congress saw that his words were published in the *Congressional Record*. In April 1959 it published a Waring editorial that repeated much of what the editor had been saying for several years or more. African Americans wanted separate schools and they were happy with segregation, he said. Integration, he added, would ruin education and the country. "While I do not pose as a spokesman for the colored people, and do not pretend to read their minds," he said, "I believe that most of them are happy and satisfied. I do not believe the NAACP by any means represents a unanimous feeling among the southern Negroes." He charged that the NAACP was responsible for the poor race relations and for censoring news about the horrible conditions in Black America. "With its political allies, it has set up a virtual censorship on race. Negro crime in cities is appalling, but the facts are being deliberately disguised in the 'paper curtain' press," Waring said.[33]

Waring was not just an unrepentant racist and a dangerous demagogue; he was a bully. He made a personal crusade out of trying to close the Highlander School and to ruin Septima Clark, who had worked closely with the school to train civil rights workers to register African Americans to vote.[34] Clark fought for civil rights and racial equality with the same passion that Waring had opposed it. But Waring had a metropolitan newspaper to publish his opinions and punish his enemies. Arthur Clement Jr., president of the Charleston branch of the NAACP, wrote Waring on August 20 to complain about the newspaper's condemnation of Clark because "her ideas may be at variance with yours." Clement pointed to how the newspaper published a story that said she had been charged with possessing "illegal whiskey" even though she did not drink alcohol. "Bear in mind that Mrs. Clark has no way to fight back at this veritable character assassination technique," Clement said.[35]

Waring's personal papers include letters from those who condemned him for his tactics. On July 15, 1957, Albert Varner of Johns Island wrote Waring after hearing an interview with U.S. senator John Sherman Cooper of Kentucky, who said that he may not agree with the U.S. Supreme Court's decision in *Brown* but that in the South it "must be regarded as the law of the land." Waring, Varner said, would no doubt begin a "character assassination" against Cooper. "You know the routine well: call him a 'communist,'" Varner said, and then ridicule him "for being out of touch with the real facts, say that he's misguided. You know the whole rotten series of moves you have to go through (having done it so many times)."[36] William F. Buckley eventually abandoned his segregationist views. Waring took his white supremacist view to the grave. When Waring died in 1993, James J. Kilpatrick praised him for his gentility in his fight against integration. "Even during the peak of the desegregation fight," Kilpatrick said, "he was never mean about it. He would never cast black people down."[37]

Waring, for all his bluster about his expertise on race relations, spent little time around African Americans, less time talking to them, and even less listening. By his own account, he did not eat with a Black person until well into the 1960s, and even then, it was not by choice. President Henry Hill of Peabody College deliberately assigned Waring to sit next to the president of an African American college at a dinner event in Nashville. Waring told Hill he was initially uncomfortable because he had never sat next to an African American person at a meal. As the evening went on, Waring said, he found his dinner companion charming and ended up enjoying the experience.[38]

It is not known whether Waring ever dined with another African American.

18.

THE CIVIL RIGHTS MOVEMENT
IN CHARLESTON

F our first-year students at North Carolina Agricultural and Technical College in Greensboro, North Carolina, Joseph McNeil, Franklin McCain, Ezell Blair Jr., and David Richmond, dressed in coats and ties, walked into the Woolworth department store on South Elm Street in Greensboro at 4:30 p.m. on February 1, 1960. They bought several items and then sat down at the lunch counter. They were ignored. If they could buy toothpaste at one counter, why couldn't they buy a cup of coffee at another? The store's manager, Clarence Harris, ordered them to leave. When that did not happen, Harris called the Greensboro police. The young men did not leave until the store closed at 5:30. They said they would return the next day.[1]

The men returned the next morning with two dozen of their classmates and, before entering the store, stood in a circle and recited the Lord's Prayer. They then sat at the lunch counter, ordered coffee, and were refused service. One of the students told an Associated Press reporter they were "prepared to keep coming for two years" until they were treated the same as white customers in stores and restaurants in Greensboro.[2] The men came back the next day and the day after and the day after that, and each day, more people joined them and the number of journalists at the Woolworth store increased. The story went from a brief account on an inside page to page one. Word of the protest spread throughout the South, and African American students began their own sit-down strikes, first in other cities in North Carolina, including Durham, Winston-

Salem, Charlotte, and Raleigh, and then to other cities through-out the South, including Charleston.[3]

Gene Roberts and Hank Klibanoff wrote that the reporting was initially sparse and tentative but that it changed as whites began to harass African Americans who sat quietly at the lunch counter. Whites who had previously ignored racial bigotry as a regional issue began to read articles and see photographs in newspapers and see images on television that shook them out of their complacency. "The picture they began to paint for a national audience was of nicely attired, soft-spoken, well-behaved young men and women, most clutching Bibles or textbooks, sitting passively at counters, surrounded by unruly white people," Roberts and Klibanoff said. "The stories were clear in pointing out that every act of aggression came from the whites; they threw eggs and ammonia and knocked the Negroes off lunch counter stools."[4]

Northern newspapers included such snapshots of racial discrimination. But because their staffs were largely restricted to white editors, reporters, and photographers who lacked the understanding of institutionalized bigotry, the stories and articles deprived readers of the context to understand why African Americans were demanding equal rights. Claude Sitton of the *New York Times* reported from Greensboro and then from other sit-down strikes in other cities, describing for readers that African Americans were responding to America's long legacy of racial discrimination and, in particular, the sluggishness of the desegregation of schools, which had been mandated by *Brown v. Board of Education* and again in *Brown II*.[5]

By February 1960, nearly six years had passed since *Brown v. Board of Education*. African Americans still went to segregated schools and could not attend white colleges and universities in the South. They were restricted from voting. They were still denied jobs and decent housing. They still drank from Blacks-only water fountains and were still prohibited from sitting down at a department store lunch counter and, like any white person, having something to eat or drink.

Young African Americans had heard enough.

They ignored the threats of white politicians, cops, and newspaper editors. They ignored the warnings of their elders that things would get worse and not better if they confronted Jim Crowism. They listened instead to the words of a young minister, Martin Luther King Jr., who preached nonviolent resistance. King also directed his words at the white supremacists who had maintained control for generations in the South. "We will wear you down by our capacity to suffer," King told whites. "One day *we shall win freedom*, but not only for ourselves. *We shall* so *appeal* to *your heart* and *conscience* that *we shall win you* in the *process*." Roberts and Klibanoff wrote that young African Americans became the "frontline embodiment of the philosophy" King preached.[6] C. Vann Woodward, writing in *The Strange Career of Jim Crow*, wrote that "all but the most incorrigible white resistance was vulnerable to such a weapon."[7]

Charleston was part of the struggle for civil rights in the South during the decade of the 1960s, beginning with a sit-down strike at a department store two months after the one in Greensboro, when Burke High School students, including one of the former Cannon Street players, would protest that they could buy items in one part of the store but could not be served food or coffee at another. The decade included lawsuits so that African American children could go to white schools in Charleston and high school graduates could go to a white university in the state. King came to Charleston to preach at Emanuel AME Church, and a couple years later, so did his wife, Coretta, to march with hundreds of others for a living wage for striking hospital workers.

The 1960s and 1970s lay bare the breadth and depth of bigotry in Charleston.

JOHN RIVERS AND ABOUT two dozen other Burke High School students began meeting secretly in the basement of the Reed Community Center and at the home of J. Arthur Brown, president of the Charleston branch of the NAACP, in early March, a month or so before they would sit down at the lunch counter at the S. H. Kress Department Store on King Street to protest racial discrimination.[8]

Rivers said he became more and more anxious in the days preceding the protest. He was afraid of what might happen when he sat down at the lunch counter and refused to move when ordered to do so. He was afraid of being arrested or having a police officer strike him with a billy club. But he also did not want to let down his classmates. "I didn't want my fear to take over. I didn't want other kids to say, 'John is chickening out.' The night before, I couldn't sleep," he said. When his mother asked him what was wrong, he told her what he was going to do. "'No, you're not,' she said. 'You'll end up going to jail. There'll be violence. You're not going.' I was relieved. I was so frightened." He did not join the protest.[9]

Rivers's classmate, Harvey Gantt, who had played baseball in the Cannon Street Y League in 1955, was one of the organizers of the protest. Gantt belonged to the NAACP's youth council, which met at the Cannon Street Y. He said he had been following what was happening in civil rights, including the lunch counter sit-in in Greensboro, and was looking for a way to protest segregation. "When the Greensboro college students sat in on February 1, we found a way we could get involved directly," Gantt said.[10] The protesters included John Bailey, one of the Cannon Street All-Stars, and Minerva Brown, the daughter of J. Arthur Brown.[11]

On April 1, 1960, sixteen boys, in suits and ties, and eight girls, in dresses, entered the Kress Department Store at 10:45 a.m., sat down at the lunch counter, each put a quarter on the counter in front of them, and they waited to be served. They were ignored. They sat for the next seven or so hours. Each student carried a copy of the Gospel of St. Mark and small cards titled "The Poet's Code of Ethics." They periodically recited the Lord's Prayer and the Twenty-Third Psalm. When the store owner demanded that the students leave the building, they refused. They were then arrested by Charleston police.[12]

This became the city's first civil rights "sit-in" and the beginning of the broader civil rights movement in Charleston.

King had implored a crowd at Emanuel AME Church in 1962 to register to vote.[13] When King returned in 1967 he was one of the most admired people in the world, having won the Nobel Peace Prize for his practice of nonviolent resistance to demand racial justice. The Associated Press reported that the Ku Klux Klan said that eight thousand protesters would protest King's speech outside Charleston County Hall on King Street. The story quoted a Klansman who called on King to be shot. There was no protest. There was no violence.[14]

On February 8, 1968, two months before King's assassination, law enforcement officers in Orangeburg, South Carolina, between Columbia and Charleston, open fired on unarmed African American college students who were protesting racial discrimination at a bowling alley. Harry Floyd, the owner of the bowling alley, refused to serve African Americans in the establishment's diner even though the 1964 Civil Rights Act had outlawed discrimination based on race, color, religion, or national origin. When African Americans again tried to sit down at the counter, they were arrested. In response, hundreds protested outside the bowling alley that evening. Governor Robert McNair called in the National Guard. When an Orangeburg police officer was struck in the face by a thrown object, state highway patrolmen and police began firing, killing three and injuring twenty-eight protesters. No law enforcement officers were charged. The so-called Orangeburg Massacre received little attention in the mainstream newspapers.[15] The *Orangeburg Times and Democrat* described the action as a "fire fight" between police and protesters.[16] The Associated Press, Governor McNair, and other politicians and law enforcement officers also reported this version of events. They provided no evidence.[17]

In mid-May, a few months after the "Orangeburg Massacre," a few thousand demonstrators, including Esau Jenkins and Septima Clark, began marching at Saint Andrews shopping center in West Ashley, a section of town that sits west of the Ashley River from downtown. They marched through the downtown streets to County Hall as part of the Southern Christian Leadership Council's "Poor People's Campaign," which addressed poverty and other economic issues faced by African Americans and other minorities.[18] "If the Charleston Poor People's March represented the potential to redress many of the shortcomings of local civil rights activities," historian Stephen O'Neill wrote, "a protracted hospital strike that began less than one year later fulfilled much of that potential."[19]

African American employees at the Medical College Hospital on Calhoun Street had become increasingly frustrated because they were paid thirty cents an hour less than the federal minimum wage. The frustrations boiled over after twelve demonstrators were fired and the president refused to meet with the disgruntled employees. Dozens of workers, many of them single mothers who barely had enough to feed their families, given their paltry wages, went on strike, one worker said, for "the right to be treated like human beings." A *News and Courier* columnist called for the "use of force" against the hospital workers. Whites in Charleston supported the hospital administration.[20]

Coretta Scott King addressed the crowd of three thousand at the Emanuel AME Church on April 29, a little more than a year after her husband was assassinated while supporting striking sanitation workers in Memphis. Coretta then joined a march of fifteen hundred protesters the next day who walked down Calhoun Street and then to the hospital on Ashley Avenue. Governor Robert McNair said the state would not negotiate with the striking workers and ordered hundreds of National Guardsmen to patrol the streets of Charleston, wearing fatigues, combat helmets, and carrying rifles with bayonets.[21] The guardsmen were there, as they had been in Orangeburg, to respond by force if need be. The demonstrators gave them no reason to do so. The strike ended on June 27, a hundred days after it began, after the Medical College Hospital agreed to hire back the employees they had fired and pay workers the federal minimum wage.[22]

J. ARTHUR BROWN AND THE NAACP filed a lawsuit against Charleston schools to allow his daughter, Minerva, and other African American children to attend the all-white Rivers High School.[23] Justice moved slowly. Minerva graduated and went to college. On August 23, 1963, federal judge J. Robert Martin Jr. ordered Charleston schools to desegregate. Martin's decision was restricted only to the students named in the lawsuit. Millicent Brown, Minerva's sister, and ten other plaintiffs began attending the previously white Rivers High School.[24] Nine years after *Brown v. Board of Education*, South Carolina desegregated its public schools. Millicent Brown said she did not encounter the problems other African American schoolchildren did.[25] By 1963 South Carolina school officials had dragged their feet so long on integration that history had practically passed them by. South Carolina lagged behind other southern states in desegregating its public colleges and universities. The University of North Carolina was integrated in 1955. The University of Georgia was integrated in 1961. The University of Mississippi was integrated in 1962.

Harvey Gantt applied to Clemson University after graduating as valedictorian from Burke. Clemson rejected his application. Gantt sued the university claiming that he was denied admission because of racial discrimination. He attended Iowa State University as his lawsuit played out in the courts. A federal appeals court ordered Clemson to admit Gantt.[26] After graduating with honors with a degree in architecture, Gantt earned a master's degree at MIT before he started a successful architecture company in Charlotte, North Carolina. He became involved in local politics, serving on the city council before being elected the city's mayor.

David Folkenflik, who now works as a reporter for National Public Radio, was a summer intern at the *News and Courier* when Gantt ran for the U.S. Senate in North Carolina in 1990 against the incumbent, Jesse Helms, an avowed segregationist. Folkenflik was assigned to write a profile about Gantt. He remembered looking through the newspaper's library for material about Gantt but could not find anything. There was no file for "Gantt." There was nothing about him in the files marked "Clemson" or "civil rights" or "integration." Folkenflik finally found what he was looking for—in a file called "Negro agitation."[27]

Tom Waring was still influencing the judgment of his newspaper from his grave.

WHITE SUPREMACISTS STILL CONTROLLED The Citadel and the College of Charleston—the two four-year universities on the peninsula, which resisted until they could no longer do so. The Citadel, or the Military College of South Carolina, as it is also called, began as a garrison that was constructed after the Denmark Vesey slave rebellion to protect white Charleston against another rebellion but also to intimidate African Americans living nearby. It was converted to a military academy, the South Carolina Military Academy, in 1842.[28]

The Citadel moved to Hampton Park in the early 1920s and continued to uphold the same Confederate values it did when the college's cadets fired on Fort Sumter. In April 1951, six months after a brick was thrown through a window at the Warings' Meeting Street home, Elizabeth Waring was giving a speech to an African American sorority near The Citadel when a baseball came crashing through the window. The Citadel told the press that it was investigating whether the incident was deliberate or whether it was an accident. The commander of the cadet corps said that he believed that the ball came from a baseball game between The Citadel and Clemson. This would have been the longest foul ball in baseball history. Septima Clark, who was attending the speech, had a more plausible explanation. She said she looked out the window and saw a Citadel cadet fleeing the scene.[29]

In 1952 General Charles P. Summerall, the eighty-five-year-old president of The Citadel and former U.S. Army chief of staff, castigated the college's cadets after a case of beer was found in one of the barracks. "N——s were made to lie and steal and cheat and the cadets of The Citadel have proved themselves to be no better than n——s," he said.[30] Mark Clark, a retired four-star U.S. Army general, became president of the college three years later in 1955, a year after *Brown v. Board of Education*. Clark denounced *Brown* and vowed to keep the college segregated. The Citadel remained segregated until 1966.

Citadel cadets made life as miserable as possible for the school's first African American cadet, Charles Foster, who grew up in Charleston and had attended Charles A. Brown High School. The Citadel's president, Hugh Harris, did not want him at the school but knew if Foster was run out of The Citadel it would hurt the institution's reputation. Foster's first roommate, who was from New Jersey, remembered he would hear the same question whenever he went into another cadet's room: "The question was always, 'Did you kill him yet?'"[31]

Foster survived his years at The Citadel but not without sustaining emotional damage. He had been an honors student in high school but struggled at The Citadel. There was no support network for him. His brother Bill said Charles received threatening letters, got the silent treatment, was harassed—physically and emotionally. If Foster dared sit down at the same dining table as other cadets, they would stand up and move to another table. Novelist Pat Conroy, who was a senior when Foster was a freshman, observed what happened to Foster. "Charles was brutalized. I've never heard one kid called 'n——' more in my entire life," he said.[32]

Foster's brother Bill saw what became of Charles after enduring four years at The Citadel. "Those four years made him a completely different person—no doubt about it," Foster's brother Bill said. "Charles was intense after he graduated. You could really tell when he talked, especially when he was making a point. His demeanor had changed. I'm sure something happened and it was so traumatic," Bill Foster said. "He refused to talk about it." Charles Foster graduated, was commissioned a lieutenant in the army, spent three years in the army, and was then discharged. He never returned to The Citadel but never escaped from what happened there. He died in a fire near Dallas, Texas, in 1986.[33]

Conroy's 1980 book *Lords of Discipline* depicts racism, brutality, and dishonor inside a fictionalized military college, Carolina Military Institute in Charleston, during the year the university admitted its first Black student. The central character and narrator is an aspiring writer who learns about a secret society that conspires to drive the African American cadet from the school.[34] Conroy denied that the brutal conditions at Carolina Military Institute were based on his own experiences at The Citadel. But such protests were hardly convincing. Conroy attended The Citadel and the school had once been called the South Carolina Military Academy. Conditions at Carolina Military Institute were indeed eerily similar to those at The Citadel. Administrators banned the book from campus for several years.[35]

It has been more than fifty years since Charles Foster graduated from The Citadel. But harassing African American cadets remains as much a part of the college as the song "Dixie" and flying the Confederate flag. A 1977 photo shows most of the cadets in one of the companies dressed in full Ku Klux Klan regalia while they stood around an African American cadet who was wearing a noose.[36] In 1986 cadets, dressed as Klansmen and carrying lit paper crosses, broke into the room of an African American cadet, Kevin Naismith, and began yelling racist epithets at him until they were chased off by Naismith's roommate. Naismith left the college when the school did not expel the students. Naismith's brother Alonzo, a Citadel graduate, quit his position on the school's Board of Visitors, calling the incident "an act of terrorism."[37] Citadel president James A. Grimsley, a retired army major general, responded: "I would like to write it off as a college prank that got out of hand."[38]

The Citadel continued to do little or nothing to break from its racist—and sexist—past. It did not admit its first woman until 1995.[39] Jordyn Jackson, an African American, said she was a victim of racial harassment at the military college almost from the moment she walked through its doors during the fall of 2012. She was the target of racial epithets like "jungle monkey" and racist notes like "KKK" were hung on her door. She quit the school rather than endure more insults.[40]

Austin Gray, an African American who received his bachelor's and master's degrees from The Citadel, remembered a white upperclassman who forced an African American freshman—or knob as they are called—to dress as a Klansman. Gray said he had to explain to his classmate why the joke was not funny. "It makes you as an alumni feel ashamed, feel embarrassed, and question, 'Do I really matter in the grand scheme of things of what The Citadel stands for?'" Gray said.[41]

In early 2016 fourteen Citadel cadets were suspended for wearing Klan hoods for a skit called "The Ghosts of Christmas Past." Lieutenant General John Rosa, the president of the college, responding by saying that the cadets "did not intend to be offensive."[42] Two years later, a cadet wrote on a Facebook post, "A n—— just stole my friend's bike who lent it to me to go rock climbing." Rosa responded by saying, "These statements represent the exact opposite of The Citadel's core values of Honor, Duty, and Respect that we teach and expect from the entire Citadel family."[43] In 2018 *News and Courier* sports columnist Gene Sapakoff called for the university to remove the Confederate flag—the Naval Jack—from inside Summerall Chapel. The university told him it could not take down the flag or it would violate the state's Heritage Act, which required that no war memorial or monument in the state could be removed without a two-thirds vote by each chamber of the state legislature. "So what if the school would be in technical violation of something called the Heritage Act?" Sapakoff asked. "If Citadel officials remove the flag, would the state's Heritage Act police scale the gate of The Military College of South Carolina?"[44]

THE CONFEDERATE BATTLE FLAG has been a symbol of white supremacy in the South since it was flown by General Robert E. Lee's Army of Northern Virginia. The flag began flying on top of the state's capitol in the early 1960s. Supporters argued that the flag was put on top of the capitol to commemorate the centennial anniversary of the Civil War. Critics disagreed. They said the flag was hoisted onto the capitol in response to the civil rights movement and court decisions to desegregate schools. If indeed the flag was posted to commemorate the Confederacy, it would have come down after the centennial of the war. But the flag remained. "The Confederate flag symbolizes more than the civil war and the slavery era," wrote James Forman Jr., a professor at Yale Law School. "The flag has been adopted knowingly and consciously by government officials seeking to assert their commitment to black subordination."[45]

In late 1986 James Clyburn, the state's Human Affairs commissioner, wrote an op-ed column in the *News and Courier* criticizing The Citadel for flying the Confederate flag and playing "Dixie" during its football games. Clyburn received death threats. The newspaper was filled with letters to the editor supporting the flag and "Dixie." "It was an ugly reminder that civil rights were still a struggle in South Carolina," Brian Hicks wrote.[46]

Mayor Joseph Riley, a moderate on race relations, tried to mitigate the controversy by writing a conciliatory op-ed.[47] The Far Right would have nothing of it. The Ku Klux Klan requested a permit to march in Charleston. Riley agreed, but under his conditions. He set the date for August 2 because he knew it would be one of the hottest days of the summer and he knew the marchers would sweat underneath their white sheets. The Klansmen then learned that Charleston police chief Reuben Greenberg, a Black Jew, would lead the parade. "As the sweating, white-robed members of the Ku Klux Klan walked along Charleston streets, getting spit on and yelled at by black and white protesters," Hicks wrote, "they were forced to look straight ahead at a Jewish black man— and a horse's ass."[48]

DURING THE EARLY 1990S, African Americans in South Carolina and sympathetic whites elsewhere in the South began demanding that the Confederate flag be removed from the state capitol and other state buildings. South Carolina remained the only state that flew the flag over its capitol.[49] The NAACP and African American ministers began an economic boycott to pressure for the removal of the flag.[50] Business leaders, many of them white, supported the NAACP because the perception of racism hurt the tourism industry and discouraged businesses from moving to the state. The NCAA was among the national organizations supporting the boycott; athletic tournaments were moved to other states.[51] Riley led a march against the flag by walking from Charleston a hundred miles to Columbia.[52]

White Charleston state legislators, including state senators Glenn McConnell, who owned a store that sold Confederate memorabilia, and Arthur Ravenel Jr., were among those criticizing the NAACP for its economic boycott. Ravenel called the NAACP "the National Association for Retarded People."[53] When an apology was demanded, Ravenel, who had a special needs son, apologized to "retarded people."[54] McConnell said the economic boycott "has strengthened the resolve for a presence of the flag."[55] McConnell worked toward a compromise that removed the flag from the capitol and moved it to the nearby Confederate Soldiers Monument. The legislature also made Martin Luther King Jr's birthday an official state holiday, making it the last state to do so.[56] The legislation created a separate Confederate Memorial Day holiday for state workers on May 10.[57] It also created the Heritage Act, which forbid the removal from public property of any flags or memorials without a two-thirds vote of the legislature.[58]

19

GUS HOLT'S CRUSADE

During the summer of 1993, Lawrence Holt made his first Dixie Youth League All-Star team. His father, Gus, who had coached Lawrence's team, was proud of what his son had accomplished. Gus and Lawrence had spent hours practicing on a baseball field in the Lenevar subdivision in Charleston where the Holts lived. But when Gus saw Lawrence in his All-Star uniform, he nearly gasped and his pride turned to indignation.

The uniform included a patch of the Confederate flag.

This, Holt said, was yet another reminder of what Holt was up against, trying to raise Lawrence to be proud of his Black skin in a city where African Americans were constantly exposed to symbols of white supremacy.

"What in the hell is this?" Holt said to himself when he saw the flag.[1]

Holt, who spent much of his childhood in segregated Charleston, became conscious of the toxicity of institutional racism while serving in the army. He tried to raise Lawrence to believe that he was inferior to no one and to confront racial discrimination. "If I see a disparity, I call it out," Holt said.[2]

Holt brought a petition to city hall demanding that the Confederate insignia be removed from all Dixie Youth Baseball uniforms. He began investigating why there was no Little League Baseball in Charleston and learned about the 1955 Cannon Street YMCA Little League.[3] In doing so, Holt made the connection between Dixie Youth Baseball and the Cannon Street All-Stars. Holt brought Little League Baseball back to Charleston and sought to revive the story of the Cannon Street YMCA All-Stars. "I began to research the Dixie Leagues and discovered it had been founded on the tears of the Cannon Street players," Holt said.[4]

Until Holt did his research, he did not know that Dixie Youth Baseball had prohibited integration in its charter and included the Confederate flag on the cover of its rulebooks and on the uniforms of its players.[5] By the time Holt became involved in Dixie Baseball, the organization had ended segregation and dropped the Confederate flag from uniforms—except for those of the players who made the All-Star team.[6] By the time Holt saw the Confederate flag on his son's uniform, he had coached in the Dixie Leagues for several years and had grown increasingly impatient with what he called "the institutional racism" in the Charleston Recreation Department.[7]

Howard Silverstein, president of the department, denied Holt's team a second-place trophy because it had played one less game than the team awarded second place.[8] Holt refused to play a makeup game unless it was moved from Martin Park, where parents of an opposing team had been abusive after a game that Holt's team won on forfeit because the other team had not had enough players at the start of the game. When Holt's team packed up its equipment and went to the parking lot to leave, the absent players showed up and the other team wanted to play the game. When Holt said it was too late, some of the parents began using abusive language and then tried to intimidate Holt and other parents of children on his team.[9]

The other team asked Silverstein if they could play Holt's team in a makeup game at Martin Park. Silverstein approved the game. Holt objected. "I was not going to put my players and their parents in harm's way," he said. He asked Silverstein to move the game to another field. Silverstein denied the request. The makeup game was never played, the forfeited win was dropped, and the team finished a half game out of second place. Holt wrote a letter of protest to Silverstein, who responded with a patronizing letter that criticized Holt's attitude. "How dare you treat me like this," Holt thought.[10]

Holt took the letter to a meeting of the Recreation Commission Board. The *Charleston News and Courier* reported that Silverstein was deeply apologetic and awarded Holt and his team the second-place trophy. The trophy and the apology satisfied Holt. But the sting over the Confederate flag remained.[11]

This put Holt in the middle of a statewide debate over the flag's divisiveness.

Holt took his grievance to the *Charleston Chronicle*, the African American newspaper in Charleston, which published a story. He then went to the daily newspaper, which had become the *Post and Courier* after the merger of the *News and Courier* and *Evening Post*. The city hall reporter told Holt his complaint about the flag wasn't newsworthy.

"I made it news," he said.[12]

In February 1994 Holt met with his city council representative, Maurice Washington, who introduced him to Mayor Joe Riley. When Holt told Riley about the Confederate flag on the uniforms, Riley initially did not believe him. Holt then showed Riley a photo of Lawrence, the flag plainly visible on his uniform. Riley's face turned red. Holt left Riley's office not knowing whether he had the powerful mayor's support.[13]

HOLT PROBABLY DID NOT know it at the time but he and Riley shared a love of baseball and an affection for Jackie Robinson.

Riley, who grew up in relative affluence in downtown Charleston, spent his summers at the family's home on Sullivan's Island. As a young boy, his grandfather took him to his first professional baseball game at College Park.[14] Riley sat on his grandfather's knee and listened to Major League Baseball games on the radio. Riley became a Dodgers' fan and Robinson was his favorite player. "I listened to the games on the radio," Riley said. "Every day during baseball season, I thought about Jackie Robinson and all that he could do."

Riley, who was the same age as the Cannon Street YMCA All-Stars, admitted he was not a very good ballplayer but this did not detract from his love of the game. "Baseball was my life," he said.[15]

As Riley grew up into his teens, he became aware of the racism in Charleston and became "troubled by the fact" that if Robinson came to Charleston, he would not be allowed to eat in the same restaurants as Riley and his family.[16] After graduating from college, Riley went to law school, became a lawyer, and entered politics. In 1974, he was elected mayor of Charleston after being the first mayoral candidate in the city's history to actively campaign for African American votes. Whites in Charleston derisively called him "Little Black Joe."[17] Riley served as mayor for the next forty years. Riley hung a photo of Martin Luther King Jr. at city hall. He was responsible for a bust of J. Waties Waring that was installed in city hall chambers and a portrait of Denmark Vesey that hangs at the Gaillard Auditorium, which sits across Calhoun Street from Mother Emanuel Church.[18] Riley had a photo of Jackie Robinson in his office.[19]

GUS HOLT WAS BORN on Friday, September 13, 1946, in the African American wing at Roper Hospital in Charleston. He was the fifth of ten children born to Isabelle and Robert Holt, who lived on the city's east side. Gus described his father, a sergeant in the air force, as being like Sergeant Bilko, the wisecracking, card-playing Phil Silvers television character who was always trying to put one over on everyone else. Gus said his superstitious, poker-playing father was pleased that his son was born on a Friday the thirteenth. "You couldn't have done any better than this," Robert Holt told his wife and then repeated the quote to his son when he got older.[20]

Holt remembers riding with his grandfather, who had a hauling and moving business. Gus, who was then six or seven, saw white boys in their white uniforms playing Little League Baseball in Hampton Park on the west side of the peninsula. Holt wondered why there were no Black kids playing. This experience became one of his first lessons about racial inequality. When he asked why he could not play baseball with the white kids, he was told, "That's just the way things are."[21]

Holt said he didn't know about the Cannon YMCA League because Holt and his family lived on the east side of the peninsula. Before the end of Holt's third-grade year in 1955, his father was transferred to Hickam Air Force Base in Honolulu, Hawaii. The Holts lived on an integrated military base and the children attended integrated schools. Gus and his older brother, Jerome, played on the same Little League team, the Dodgers. Jerome was good enough to make the All-Star team. Gus, who was two years younger, played second base for the Dodgers, like his hero Jackie Robinson had done.[22]

The Holt brothers were the only African Americans on the team, but Gus does not remember feeling excluded, whether on or off the baseball field. The players and their parents would have post-game cookouts, where hot dogs were grilled and marshmallows were roasted. "There were no racial problems with other kids," Holt said. "We were kids. If there was a problem, we would deal with it."[23] During that summer in Charleston, white adults prevented a team of African American boys from playing in a post-season Little League Baseball tournament. Holt did not know any of this at the time. "Little did I know that there was all this hell-raising going on in Charleston," he said.[24]

The Holts returned to Charleston in 1957—the same year, Holt said, that the NAACP registered nine Black students to attend segregated Little Rock Central High School.[25] The Holts moved into Jenkins Terrace, an African American subdivision in North Charleston.[26] Gus began school in segregated Charleston and then had moved to Hawaii, where schools where integrated. Now he was back in the segregated South. "I left Jim Crowism and moved into an integrated society," he said. "And then I moved back into Jim Crowism."[27]

By this time Little League Baseball had disappeared from Charleston, replaced by the Little Boys League, which became Dixie Youth Baseball. African Americans kids played on whatever fields they could find. "We played baseball on vacant lots all over the city," Holt said.[28] Sometimes, he and his friends played with white boys, if there were not adults around to tell them otherwise. Baseball became an important part of Holt's teenage years because, he said, it forced him to socialize with kids from different neighborhoods, most of them were African American but some were white.[29]

Holt graduated from Bonds Wilson High School in 1964. He was aware of the limited opportunities for African Americans in a country that was still largely segregated. The United States was expanding its presence in the Vietnam War, and African Americans—because they were less likely to qualify for draft deferments—were drafted at a disproportionate rate into the army. Holt knew a lot of young Black men who went to Vietnam and came back different men. Some used drugs or alcohol to deal with the trauma of injuries—physical, mental, and emotional. "Some of them were messed up," when they got back to Charleston, Holt said. Others did not return. When Holt was drafted, he said, he broke up with his girlfriend because, he said, "I feared I would not return home the same person."[30]

While in the army, Holt became more conscious of racial bigotry and, in particular, of the double standard for white and Black soldiers. There was not an "equal application of the law," he said. White soldiers were far more likely to be promoted. Black soldiers were far more likely to be wounded or killed in action.[31] In 1967, while Holt was at Fort Hood, heavyweight champion Muhammad Ali, citing religious reasons, refused induction into the army. "I ain't got no quarrel with them Viet Cong," Ali told America's white establishment. "I was impressed with Muhammad Ali and his defiance. He was telling whites, 'That yellow man didn't call me a n——,'" Holt said. "How could he be so goddamn bold!"[32]

Holt was transferred to Heidelberg, Germany, a long way from the fighting in Vietnam but not far enough from the racism in America or in the military. He spent much of his free time in the base library, reading about how African Americans had been brutalized and marginalized since the slave ships came to America. He read how white supremacy was perpetuated—often subconsciously—in American life. He heard a speech by Kathleen Cleaver, wife of Black Panther leader Eldridge Cleaver, at the University of Heidelberg. He learned about the white power structure from political education classes taught by Black Panthers. He read the Little

Red Book by Chairman Mao. "I came into an understanding of the ramifications of institutionalized racism," he said.[33]

After seven years in the U.S. Army, Holt returned to Charleston a different person because of the racism he experienced in the military, his younger brother, Lamar, said. "The military opened his mind up and made him stronger," Lamar Holt said. "He was almost a militant" when he returned home.[34] He began working at the Charleston shipyards, married his wife, Debra, had a son, Lawrence, and bought a house in the Lenevar subdivision in West Ashley, west of the Ashley River in Charleston, on land once owned by Arthur Ravenel's family.[35]

Holt remembered his own upbringing in segregated Charleston, where baseball had provided a sanctuary from the bigotry of the outside world. Holt passed onto his son his love of baseball. "I wanted to share the game that had been good to me with my son," he said.[36] The father and son bonded through the game and they talked about life while they played catch at one of the baseball fields in the subdivision. Holt looked for ways to influence Lawrence outside the home. Holt wondered how he could raise Lawrence to be a confident Black man in a racist country, where white men were in positions of authority in all parts of society. He signed up to coach Lawrence's Dixie Youth teams. "My son is being exposed to the white power structure," Holt said. "I can at least be his coach."[37]

Lawrence became good enough to become an All-Star, good enough to wear a uniform with the Confederate flag on it.

AS HOLT BEGAN DOING his research on the Cannon Street team, tears came to his eyes as he learned what whites had done to them. "I said, 'How can they do that?'"[38] Holt went to the Cannon Street YMCA and asked if there was anyone who could tell him more about the 1955 All-Star team. Robert Morrison, who had been the Y's president, had died in 1972. Someone told Holt about Allen Tibbs, who had assisted Morrison in writing Little League Baseball to start a league. Tibbs told Holt to go to the Avery Research Center, an archive for Black history and culture in Charleston, to look at his personal papers that he had donated. Holt learned that

Dixie League Baseball had begun in North Charleston. "When I found out that the Dixie Leagues started in North Charleston under Danny Jones," Holt said, "that's when the rubber hit the road."[39]

Holt began inquiring to see if anyone knew how he could contact the coaches. He was told that Lee Bennett and Dilligard were active in the Boys' Club. He talked to them and tracked down some of the players. The former All-Stars told Holt about their admiration for their coaches. The players remained devoted to Ben Singleton, who managed the team that won the league championship in 1955 and then managed the All-Star team. Vermort Brown praised Singleton. "He could run around the bases faster than we could," Brown said. "He taught us how to control the ball for bad hops. He challenged us to get in front of the ball. He took time with us."[40] John Bailey added this: "Ben Singleton is a god to me. He was smart enough to be rich had he gone into business, but he spent his time on kids."[41]

Nobody could tell Holt what had happened to Singleton—if he had moved away or whether he was even still alive. Holt finally learned that Singleton was working as a custodian at the College of Charleston and living in the Gadsden Green housing projects. When Holt finally saw Singleton, he said, he became emotional.

"Tears came to my eyes," Holt said.[42]

Nearly forty years had passed since white teams had refused to play the Cannon Street YMCA All-Stars. Hardly anyone remembered the team. Several of the former All-Stars had moved far away. A few of the players—Leroy Major, Vermort Brown, Arthur Peoples—still lived in Charleston. Holt tracked down one player after another. During a joint class reunion for Charleston inner-city high schools of the 1960s, Holt talked to Arthur Peoples, one of the Cannon Street players, who talked about his trip to Williamsport in 1955. "We went all the way up there and didn't get to play," Peoples told Holt. Peoples's voice still stung with hurt and disappointment, Holt said.[43]

ON MARCH 8, 1994, Holt and several other Black Charlestonians went to the city council to protest the Confederate flag on Dixie

League uniforms. Holt asked why the city used tax dollars to support an organization where players wore the Confederate flag. He asked the city council to replace its affiliation with Dixie Youth Baseball with Little League Baseball.[44] Holt circulated his petition. "We the undersigned believe that the Confederate flag is a divisive element in our community and should not be supported by tax dollars," the petition said. "Further, that to continue to place the burden of this issue on our youth is unacceptable. It's time to move on to Little League Baseball where all young citizens of our community can fulfill the purpose of organized sports without intimidation."[45] Onica Fields, one of the signers of the petition, asked the council: "Will my son be subjected to wearing this logo?"[46]

Holt said that Charleston youth should be playing in Little League Baseball, where they would be a part of an international organization, with the hope of playing in the Little League World Series in Williamsport, Pennsylvania, and not be a part of Dixie Youth Baseball, a regional organization that had once been segregated. "Dixie Youth came out of the resistance of white leaders not wanting their children playing with blacks," Holt said.[47] Riley said he understood the racial sensitivity about the Confederate flag and was unaware of the flag on the Dixie Youth Baseball players' uniforms until Holt told him. Riley also said he did not know about the organization's history.[48]

Riley said it was unacceptable to have the Confederate flag on baseball uniforms. Howard Silverstein said the city had a long and mutually beneficial affiliation with the Dixie Leagues. He said that the city had already sent in its dues for the season. If it withdrew from Dixie Baseball, it would lose that money and, more importantly, obstruct hundreds of children from playing baseball that spring and summer. Riley said he was committed to having as many children as possible play baseball. But he would not perpetuate racial inequality to do that. He told Silverstein that if the insignia was not removed the city should change its affiliation from the Dixie Leagues to the Little Leagues.[49] Riley said that the city of Charleston would support Little League Baseball regardless of what happed with Dixie Baseball and make available any field it made available to the Dixie Leagues. The Confederate flag was removed from uniforms before the start of the next season. "As a result, we were able to make a southern institution give up a divisive symbol of a bygone era," Holt said.[50]

Shortly after Holt went to city council, he met with two businesses—First Citizens Bank and Harleston-Boags Funeral Home—who agreed to be corporate sponsors in the American Little League.[51] Little League Baseball approved Holt's charter for the league and he became its president. It included leagues for ages nine through ten; ages eleven through twelve; a girls' softball league; and a senior league, ages thirteen through fifteen. Holt, like Carl Stotz in Williamsport, Pennsylvania, in 1939, willed the organization into existence, calling anyone he could think of—friends, colleagues, or strangers, to coach or to contribute either their time or their money—or both. He passed out fliers and put signs in store windows to get the word out about the league. Mayor Riley proclaimed December 14, 1994, Little League Baseball Day.[52]

As Holt worked on reviving Little League Baseball, he worked on reviving the story of the Cannon Street All-Stars. On February 24, 1995, Holt wrote a column for the *Post and Courier* that repeated the story that Arthur Peoples had told him about going to Williamsport but not playing. "After all those years I sensed a disappointment and a hurt in his replay."[53] Holt organized a reunion for the fortieth anniversary of the Cannon Street YMCA All-Stars at the International Longshoreman's Association Headquarters on Morrison Drive. Ben Singleton said he appreciated being acknowledged after so many years. "Nobody ever talked about it after it happened," he said. Singleton's son, Maurice, remembered the disappointment as he and the others sat in the bleachers watching the championship game. "Our feelings on that day were inexpressible. Tears came to our eyes," Maurice said. "We were a hurting bunch of young men, yet we held our heads up because we were proud of what we had achieved. We were so good we could have beat the New York Yankees."[54]

In Holt's speech, he told the crowd about the stars of the Negro Leagues—men like Satchel Paige, Josh Gibson, and Buck Leonard who became heroes in Black America. Jim Crowism relegated these men to playing in the shadows of white baseball for far less pay and recognition. They played because baseball was more than a game to them. "It was their life," Holt said.

This was true for the Cannon Street All-Stars, Holt added. He summarized the story of the Cannon Street All-Stars and then asked: "Whatever happened to those brave men and boys that challenged the Jim Crow policies of the South?" He said that history could not ignore the "courageous actions" of the Cannon Street YMCA All-Star team. He ended his speech by quoting from Langston Hughes's poem "What Happens to a Dream Deferred?"[55]

Holt had an organizational meeting at Arthur Christopher City Gym on February 9, shortly after the reunion for Cannon Street players and before the newspaper column he wrote about the team, for parents and other volunteers who were interested in becoming involved in the Charleston American Little League.[56] He announced tryouts for interested boys and girls. Lawrence, Gus's son, was one of the one hundred or so boys and girls—most of them were African American but some of them were white.[57] Lawrence played that season for the Harleston-Boags Funeral Home team. He wore number 42, Jackie Robinson's number.[58] Holt did whatever he could for the Little League. He made phone calls. He hired umpires and coaches. He drove kids to games and practices. He encouraged the players and thanked the coaches and parents. He picked up trash after games. He resolved disputes. All this took time. "Management at the shipyard was a little worried about the amount of time I was spending" on the organization, Holt said. "I even used my annual leave."[59]

The Charleston newspapers, the *News and Courier* and the *Evening Post*, had opposed the Cannon Street YMCA Little League. But the *Post and Courier* supported the Charleston American Little League. In a column, Elsa McDowell praised Holt for using baseball to unite parents and their children in the Black community. "He worries that black parents aren't involved," McDowell wrote. But, because of Little League Baseball, parents became more involved in their children's lives, she added: "The boys learned the adults in their lives were willing to go to bat for them. They gave up their afternoons and vacation time to make sure [their boys] learned about sportsmanship and citizenship; about respect for others and for themselves."

Holt told McDowell he became involved because someone had to do something and if it wasn't him, then who?[60]

AS GUS HOLT ACHIEVED the improbable, he was confronted with the unthinkable. Lawrence had a seizure at school one day during his freshman year of high school in 1995. An MRI revealed a tumor in his brain. Doctors removed the tumor but it came back. A stroke in 1998 left Lawrence partially paralyzed and unable to go to school. A tutor came to his house and so did a physical therapist.[61]

"I'm worried, 'Can this cancer take me out at any time?'" Lawrence Holt told a reporter. "I was thinking about having the complete balance of a family—wife, son, daughter, white picket fence on the back. Allowing myself to dream is about as much as I can do right now. It gives me a little hope.

"There's still the possibility that I won't gain full strength back," he said. "I'm hoping that I will because I want a future playing professional baseball."[62]

When Lawrence became ill, Gus quit his job at the shipyards and stayed home with his son. Debra worked days as a bank teller. While Gus cared for Lawrence he continued to publicize the story of the Cannon Street All-Stars and run the Charleston Little League. He equated things in his life to a baseball game. "Nine innings is a long day," he told the *Charleston Post and Courier* in 1998. "What I enjoy about baseball is the deliberate slowness of the game, which says 'sit down, relax, and enjoy what God has given you.'" He talked about his love for baseball and how it played out in his love for his son. "When you think of Little League, the first thing that comes to your mind is a father playing catch with his son," he said.[63]

When the Holts heard a television story about an experimental drug for brain cancer, they flew to New York and met with the doctor. The Medical University of South Carolina Hospital treated Lawrence.[64] While Lawrence underwent radiation treatments, Gus was interviewed for a story in the *Post and Courier*, where he was asked about the sacrifices he and Debra had made for their son. "There is no sacrifice," he said. "Spending time with your child is a blessing."[65]

IN JUNE 1999 LAWRENCE, in a wheelchair, graduated with his high school class from Garrett Academy of Technology. Soon after, the city of Charleston renamed Lenevar Field for Lawrence Holt. Mayor Riley spoke at the dedication.[66]

Lawrence died December 26, 1999. He was eighteen.

Gus and his wife, Debra, created the Lawrence A. Holt Memorial Scholarship, an annual scholarship for an African American senior at Garrett Academy of Technology who planned to study architecture or engineering at a two- or four-year college. "I would always emphasize to Lawrence that we should be of service. If you want a good community, then you have to go out and serve and give back," Holt said. "The scholarship endowment underlines that principle of giving that I tried to instill in Lawrence."[67]

Twenty years passed and Gus Holt continued doing what he could to keep alive Lawrence's memory. He hoped he had been a good example for his son. "My son died tragically of cancer," Holt said. "But he got to see his father stand for something."[68]

Holt kept a memorial for Lawrence in the den of his house. It includes photographs of Lawrence. He decorated a Christmas tree with ornaments with Lawrence's image. The walls had his son's framed baseball jerseys—most of them had Jackie Robinson's number 42.[69]

"That hurt him, watching his son get sicker and sicker and eventually die. It was so traumatic. He never got over it," Lamar said.

Lamar tried to tell his brother to take down the tree and put away the photos, jerseys, and ornaments and move on as much as is possible. "I can recall sitting in the den and saying, 'Man, why don't you take that stuff down and move on with your life?'" Gus did not say anything and he left the memories of Lawrence where they were. "I concluded," Lamar added, "that this is how you deal with loss. I made up my mind not to address it anymore."

20.

RETURN TO WILLIAMSPORT

The Cannon Street YMCA All-Stars returned to Williamsport, Pennsylvania, on August 16, 2002, for the opening ceremonies of the Little League World Series at Howard J. Lamade Stadium. Forty-seven years had passed since they had gone to Williamsport in one of Esau Jenkins's well-traveled buses. The men, now in their late fifties, returned in an air-conditioned bus, accompanied by their wives and children and grandchildren and decades of pent-up bitterness and regret.

"You know what? All the way on that bus, they're reliving the past, they're talking about the trip they made forty-seven years ago," Barbara Brown, the wife of Vermort Brown, said.[1]

When the former teammates walked onto the Original Little League Field, which was now a sandlot field but was the site of the Little League World Series in 1955, they become overwhelmed by the memories of that summer so long ago.

John Bailey, a developer who lived in Washington DC, remembered the pain in his gut as he sat in the bleachers and watched the championship game between Morrisville, Pennsylvania, and Delaware Township, New Jersey—not quite understanding why his teammates and he were not sitting in one of the dugouts. "It was very, very painful for some of us," said Bailey, choking up at the memory. "Most of us gave up on our hopes and dreams right here on this field."[2]

Leroy Major, the talented pitcher who was so big for his age during the summer of 1955 that he must have appeared to be ten feet tall as he looked down on batters from the pitcher's mound, had grown into manhood and then into middle age trying to repress what had happened. Not long before he left for Williamsport, the schoolteacher received a letter from a boy in Pennsylvania who thanked him for his contributions to the civil rights movement. "Tears came to my eyes," Major said.[3]

A group of boys, who had come to play baseball, watched the African American men and women as they stood on the field talking back and forth.

Norman Robinson, who had been the team's catcher and was now an architect, asked one of the spectators, an eight-year-old boy, if he could borrow his bat. With the bat in his hand, Robinson became a boy again. Vermort Brown borrowed a baseball and went to the pitcher's mound. Robinson stepped up to the plate and Brown threw him a pitch. Robinson lifted a home run over the fence. He hugged and high-fived his teammates on his way around the bases.

Grown men cried and children looked in awe.[4]

Leroy Major laughed at the memory of Norman Robinson's home run.

"It was something," he said. "He's still got it."[5]

The Cannon Street All-Stars then went to Howard J. Lamade Stadium for the opening ceremonies of the World Series. Steven Keener, president of Little League Baseball, told the crowd that the Cannon Street Y All-Stars had been denied the opportunity of playing in the South Carolina tournament because all the other teams withdrew. Keener said the Cannon Street All-Stars had won the tournament, but their championship was nullified because they had won it by forfeit. Keener then awarded the team the 1955 South Carolina state championship banner—decades after they had rightfully won it. "There is no way to undo the wrongs perpetrated on people throughout history because of the color of their skin," Keener said.[6]

When Keener handed the players the state banner, the crowd applauded and gave them a standing ovation. The banner and the applause provided the aging men a measure of satisfaction. The players recognized the crowd with appreciative waves. Buck Godfrey, who did not go to Williamsport in 1955, accompanied the team when it returned. Godfrey said his teammates would never part with the bitterness they went through as boys, but, he added, the return trip to Williamsport had put salve on those wounds. "This was the end of a long journey for a lot of boys," Godfrey said. "It seems like America is always trying to make up for things it did in the past."[7]

The former All-Stars then toured the Peter J. McGovern Little League Museum, which includes an exhibit about the Cannon Street teams. John Rivers donated the bat he had used during the season. You can listen to an interview with John Bailey.

Vermort Brown stayed in Charleston long after most of his teammates moved away. He worked at Lockheed Aircraft Company for thirty years and served as a military instructor in the Army Reserves for twenty-six years. He served in the deacon's ministry at Mount Moriah Missionary Baptist Church. When he was asked to describe the difference between going to Williamsport as a boy and then returning as a middle-aged man, he drew on his religious background. God, he said, had taken the team to Williamsport for one reason and then brought them back for another.

"It may not have been our time. He took us there so we could see and be there. Then He turned around and gave us another way. He took us back to get our reward. They gave us the banner," Brown said. "There were spectators there like there was the first time and they cheered us again. It was a blessing for us. It was more joyful coming back the second time."[8]

THE STORY OF THE Cannon Street All-Stars got a lot of attention for a few weeks in 1955. But then "it went dark," as John Rivers said.[9] It disappeared until Gus Holt got hold of it, and it spread with every telling, with every newspaper article or column and every radio and television interview. Gene Sapakoff, the newspaper's sports columnist, gave the story national exposure with an article on the team's fortieth anniversary for *Sports Illustrated*. "The bittersweet story of a most remarkable season is scarcely known outside of a downtown Charleston neighborhood," Sapakoff said. "Surely you have never heard of the players—John Bailey, Leroy Major, Buck Godfrey, Maurice Singleton, Allen Jackson, John Rivers, Vermort Brown and Norman Robinson, among others—a bunch of twelve-year-olds drafted into a baseball civil war. But in the space of three months, the Cannon Street All-Stars changed youth baseball in the South."[10]

"Little League's Civil War," the headline said, was the greatest crisis in the organization's history.[11] Creighton Hale, who preceded Keener as the organization's president, said the only crisis comparable to Danny Jones and the secession of the South came when King Hussein of Jordan refused let his team play Israel in baseball if the two were slated to play one another in a 1994 international tournament. Hale said this reminded him of what had happened in 1955, but the Jordan-Israel incident was resolved with more equanimity than the one in 1955.[12] King Hussein was easier to negotiate with than Danny Jones, the *Sports Illustrated* article said.[13] As it turned out, the two countries did not play in the tournament in 1994. But they played one another the next year and exchanged baseball caps after the game.

Hale called Little League Baseball's response to Jones's demands that the South Carolina state tournament be segregated "our darkest yet finest hour." The organization rejected Jones's demands to have a segregated tournament in South Carolina. "It was the first time we had been confronted with such overt racism," Hale said. "We wanted to make a statement."[14] Hale defended the organization's decision to declare the Cannon Street team ineligible. "The rules provide that a team must play to advance in tournaments," he said. The organization, he added, was required to follow its own rules.[15]

The issue of whether Little League Baseball did all it could remains an open question. The Cannon Street players wonder why some consideration was not given to the fact that they advanced by forfeit because white teams refused to play them because of racial discrimination and not because of anything the team had done. Peter McGovern feared the organization would lose the South if

RETURN TO WILLIAMSPORT

the Cannon Street team was allowed to play. McGovern upheld the ban against the team and ended up losing hundreds of teams in the South anyway.

The All-Star team found themselves victims of a conflict between a national organization and a southern way of life. "I think it was cruel because adults used Little Leaguers, twelve-year-olds, to promote segregation," Norman Robinson said.[16] The players say Little League Baseball should have demanded that their team be included in the regional tournament in Rome, Georgia. "It was in the Little League charter not to discriminate based on race, creed or color. But they did it," Bailey said. "It broke our little hearts."[17]

The Cannon Street team did not forget what happened when they went to Williamsport in 1955. And neither did Little League Baseball. "This was something we kind of resolved to not let die," Van Auken said.[18] In 2000 Van Auken, Creighton Hale, and other Little League officials traveled to Charleston to meet with the team at a Charleston RiverDogs Minor League game at Joseph P. Riley Jr. Ball Park. The Cannon Street Y hosted a reception for the team.[19] "It's an honor to be recognized after so many years," Vermort Brown said. "It's never too late."[20] A plaque about the team now hangs just inside the ball park, which sits not far from Harmon Field and the neighborhood where many of the players grew up.

The RiverDogs acknowledge the Cannon Street team before a game every year. One year, the former Cannon Street players had a chance to talk to some of the players on the white teams that did not get to play because the recreation department canceled the tournament. "We had an opportunity to meet some of the players that we didn't play. And lo and behold, we discovered that they had different feelings from their parents," John Bailey said. "We shared our common stories and backgrounds and they said, 'Well, look, you know, it was our parents' fault.' I mean, we shook hands and it made things better," Bailey said.[21]

When Leroy Major was twelve years old, he did not understand what was happening. He said the crowd had cheered, "Let them play! Let them play!" for his teammates and him on that field in Williamsport. It took a lifetime for him to realize how right the fans were and how wrong the world was. "It was the adults that took the world away," Major said. But it was one particular adult, he said, "Danny Jones."[22]

To others, Jones had no choice but to prohibit the Cannon Street team. If it had been up to Jones, Holt, Rivers, and others say, the team would have played in the Charleston and state tournaments. But Major and Godfrey disagree. "I don't know him, but I knew he was what the South meant and what it symbolized," Godfrey said. "He became who he was because he was raised that way. People like him who get to where they are, they get there with the ability to inflict pain without impunity. They're a little ignorant and antagonistic."[23]

THE CANNON STREET ALL-STARS returned to the Original Field in 2005 on the team's fiftieth anniversary. The team was honored at the opening game of the Little League World Series at Howard J. Lamade Stadium. Gus Holt threw out the first ball and the former players received a standing ovation and then signed autographs. Holt said his dream was to have his son Lawrence with him. "When I was sitting in the stands, I was thinking of Lawrence," he said. "That was part of my dream, making it here with him."[24]

John Bailey sat on the first base line with his two grandsons—Louis, thirteen, and Tyler, twelve—and explained to them, as best as he could, what had happened. "They understand some of it, but not the whole impact of what happened to us." Bailey said. "This was a baseball story, but it was also a civil rights story. In due time, I'm going to get them to understand that."[25] Bailey said one of his grandsons was the same age he was in 1955. "That's the same age I was when this terrible thing happened to me. This despicable thing. This unconscionable thing," Bailey said. "But we survived. I mean, we're here in celebration of many, many years of agonizing and trying to put together what happened to us."[26]

Leroy Major explained how his perspective on what happened had changed over a half century. "We just wanted to play ball," Major said. "We never expected to be on *Nightline* fifty years down the line just because of that."[27]

But that is what happened.

Ted Koppel, who hosted the long-running, late-night news program, had his own moral to the story on *Nightline* in 2005. "It was just a little story, really. Nobody got hurt. Nobody got arrested," Koppel said in the segment's introduction. "Nobody got killed. In fact, you can even argue that in the overall context of racism in America, what happened back in 1955 was progress."[28]

Koppel said Little League Baseball took the position that if South Carolina's white teams would not play against the all-Black Cannon Street team, the Cannon Street team would win those games by forfeit. This meant that the Cannon Street team won the state championship and then should have advanced to the regional tournament and a chance to play in the Little League World Series. "But that's where the national Little League organization lost its nerve," Koppel said.[29]

Two days later, ABC *World News Tonight* did a story on the Cannon Street team. What if the team had won the Little League World Series? Allen Jackson was asked. "Do you know what that does to motivate a kid and what it does for racism?" Jackson said. "You know what I mean, what if?"[30] The *Boston Globe*, *Baltimore Sun*, ESPN, and National Public Radio did stories on the team. The All-Stars were acknowledged before a Major League game in Washington DC between the Philadelphia Phillies and the Washington Nationals.[31] Margot Theis Raven wrote a children's book, called *Let Them Play*.[32] At some point, Gus Holt suggested the players wear blue blazers and striped ties to public events—something newspaper columnist George Will referred to in his 2012 column "The Little League All Stars Who Were Never Beaten." Will praised the men, who were nearly seventy, "who," he said, "were determined to keep telling their story for the benefit of old people who only dimly remember it, and for the edification of young people who cannot imagine it."[33]

In 2012 U.S. senator Tim Scott (R-SC), one of the few Black senators in the country and the only one in the South, read a tribute to the Cannon Street YMCA All-Stars into the *Congressional Record*. Scott mentioned how racial bigotry had denied the team the opportunity to play in any of the postseason tournaments:

"The team would advance to the Charleston City Little League playoff games but would never be given the opportunity to earn a spot in the Little League World Series. It was not because they were unworthy players or because they could not afford to go. The color of their skin stifled the dreams of these twelve-year-old boys," Scott said. "As children, they embodied the very characteristics that organized sports aim to impart—teamwork, courage, and respect. As adults they have worked in productive and valuable careers such as architecture, law enforcement, and education. As they have grown older, they are now volunteers in their communities—giving back, yet again. While they never had the opportunity to compete, their story has demonstrated where we have come from as a nation."

Scott's resolution ended as follows: "The boys of the Cannon Street Little League team are men who through their careers and service to the community have become assets to their neighborhoods. In spite of the adversity they encountered and the challenges they confronted, these young people illustrated to the world the absurdity of segregation and the hatred inherent in racism. In the fifty-five years since they were excluded from competing to earn a spot at the Little League World Series in their own right, America has matured. I would like to believe that a handful of twelve-year-olds contributed to our maturity."[34]

21.

NO CITY OWES ITS SUCCESS MORE
TO THE WHIPPING OF SLAVES

Writer Toni Morrison, winner of the Nobel Prize for Literature, went to Sullivan's Island near Charleston in July 2008 to honor the millions of men, women, and children who were forcibly removed from Africa and brought to work as enslaved people in other parts of the world. To the sounds of "Swing Low, Sweet Chariot," Morrison tossed a wreath made of yellow daisies into the Atlantic Ocean in memory of the slaves. "It's never too late to honor the dead," Morrison said, as she sat on a six-foot-long, twenty-six-inch-deep black steel bench facing the water. Morrison dedicated the first memorial in her Bench by the Road project, a nonprofit organization that puts benches at sites from African American history and fiction.[1]

In Morrison's much-praised novel *Beloved*, the protagonist, Sethe, and her children escape from a Kentucky plantation by crossing the Ohio River into the free state of Ohio in the 1850s. Sethe and her children are pursued and captured by slave hunters. Sethe tries to murder her children rather than have them returned to the plantation. Her youngest child dies. The slave owner, believing Sethe insane, leaves her in Ohio. Years later, when Sethe and her children are living as free Blacks after the Civil War, they are haunted by a woman named Beloved, who is the ghost of the murdered daughter.[2] Morrison's *Beloved* was inspired by the story of the slave Margaret Garner, who killed her daughter to prevent her from returning to her brutal master's Kentucky plantation.[3]

Morrison's *Beloved* won the Pulitzer Prize for Fiction and was adapted into an opera and a movie. This gained Garner a measure of fame and perhaps redemption a century and a half after her death. Such recognition eluded most African American slaves, many of whom are buried in unmarked graves in neglected cemeteries.[4] Morrison acknowledged the need to remember enslaved people and the history of slavery in the United States. "There is no place you or I can go, to think about or not think about, to summon the presences of, or recollect the absences of slaves," she said. "There is no suitable memorial, or plaque, or wreath, or wall, or park, or skyscraper lobby. There's no 300-foot tower, there's no small bench by the road."[5]

But there was a 115-foot monument of John Calhoun, who defended slavery with his last breath. There is a park named for Wade Hampton III, who restored rule to whites after the Civil War. There is a Confederate Defenders of Charleston memorial near the Battery. There is a bridge named for one modern-day Confederate, Arthur Ravenel Jr., and a highway and a college residence hall named for another, Glenn McConnell, who longed for special occasions when he could walk the streets of Charleston in a Confederate general's uniform. A highway is named for Mark Clark, the general who resisted calls to integrate The Citadel as long as he served as its president. The former rice plantations and the mansions of the elite class of antebellum Charleston remain today as monuments to the brutality of slave traders, flesh peddlers, and plantation masters. Charleston owes enslaved people for its plantations, mansions, churches, graveyards, cobblestones streets, and its billion-dollar annual tourism economy.

No American city owes its history more to the whipping of slaves than Charleston.

No city engages more profitably in a pathology to deny its part in America's greatest sin—slavery. In doing so, it denies its responsibility to make amends for its crimes against African Americans for four hundred years. Racism metastasized into the Charleston consciousness and it passed like inherited money from generation to generation, poisoning the minds and the souls of the

NO CITY OWES ITS SUCCESS MORE

generations of whites who lived here, who fooled themselves into believing that their wealth came from their own toil, their own shrewdness, and their own industriousness. The *New Republic* once referred to the "whitewashing" of the slavery issue in Charleston.[6] Little is said on tours of plantations and historic homes that enslaved people created much of what makes the city so charming and seductive. Charleston, like much of the South, clings to a sanitized—and counterfeited—version of the past so they do not have to acknowledge the reality that they owe their wealth and their beloved history to slavery and to enslaved peoples. "They created the wealth that made all this possible," said a descendent of a slave who worked on Middleton Plantation.[7]

If there is ever an argument for reparations for the families of former slaves, it is in Charleston. The city is not merely ground zero in the story of slavery in the United States but its primary industry, tourism, relies on preserving that history. In Charleston, the past is so much a part of the present they are indistinguishable. As novelist William Faulkner, himself a son of the South, once said: "The past isn't dead. It isn't even past." Newspaper columnist Walter Williams, an African American economics professor at George Mason University, opposes reparations. "What people are suggesting is that we help a black person of today by punishing a white person of today for what a white person of yesterday did to a black of yesterday," said Williams. "That's a perverse sense of justice in my opinion."[8]

Williams's critique of reparations is not merely grotesquely over-simplified; it is grotesquely inaccurate and obfuscates rather than illuminates what should be a serious question. The argument for reparations is not just about slavery and it is not just about the past. It is about centuries of racial discrimination that kept African Americans from voting, going to decent schools, and having decent jobs where they could afford good living conditions and their children could look forward to better lives. It is about equal justice and racial equality, where dreams are not deferred and where African Americans can live free without having to worry about the centuries-old fear of white supremacy and police brutality.

The argument for reparations cannot be restricted to the nineteenth and eighteen centuries.[9] It may be a "perverse sense of justice" to punish people in the present for what their ancestors did in the past. But this not the case here. Whites continue to profit from the land and labor of African Americans. White families in the old-money city of Charleston live in the mansions and on the plantations owned by their slave-owning ancestors who made their money on the blood and sweat of enslaved people.

The story of racial discrimination in America includes how African Americans were denied—and are still denied—the same education, housing, and jobs as whites and this, in part, explains why the net worth of a white family is ten times higher than a Black family.[10] It helps explain why the gap between white and African American home ownership is more than thirty percentage points.[11] White students receive a college education at a rate of twenty percentage points more than African Americans.[12] Racism explains the disparities between whites and African Americans in crime, health, infant mortality, and longevity of life. It explains why there are comparatively few African Americans at the highest rung of politics, business, education, technology, sports, and the media.

Sixty-five years ago, the Cannon Street All-Stars looked out at a baseball field in Williamsport, Pennsylvania, and wondered why they were not on the field. How many other African American boys and girls have asked themselves the same question as they looked at America? How many continue to do so today? What was the collective damage over generations of newspapers like the *Charleston News and Courier*?

What is the going rate on centuries of deferred dreams?

Much of the wealth in Charleston is old money, inherited from ancestors who made that money from the hard work of enslaved people and from the Jim Crow era where African Americans were prohibited from pursuing the same education and jobs as whites. There continues to be two Americas, one for whites and one for African Americans.

Perhaps you shouldn't be punished for the sins of your ancestors.

But you shouldn't be rewarded for them either.

CONDÉ NAST TRAVELER REGULARLY names Charleston the best city to visit in the United States and one of the best cities in the world. Tourism translates into an estimated $8 billion annually as millions come to stroll on the beaches where millions of slaves were dragged ashore.[13] Visitors tour downtown Charleston on horse-drawn carriages or by foot, and then pay $20 or so to walk through the antebellum mansions of slave merchants and plantation owners, including Nathaniel Russell, William Aiken, Robert Rhett, John C. Calhoun, William Blacklock, William Gibbes, Robert William Roper, Daniel Ravenel, and Joseph Manigault, whose family has owned newspapers in Charleston for more than a century.[14]

Not far from the historic homes, boutique shops, and pricey restaurants is the Charleston Battery, which was constructed as a defensive seawall in the Charleston Harbor, where you can see Fort Sumter. The Battery is famous for its imposing antebellum homes, including the Charles Drayton House, the Edmondston-Alston House, William Ravenel House, and the Colonel John Ashe House, which sold for $7.72 million in 2015.[15] Nearby is Rainbow Row and its multicolored mansions. According to one story, the homes were painted in bright colors so their occupants could find their own home after a night of heavy drinking.[16]

When tourists finish their fanciful history tour of downtown Charleston, many drive to one or more of the former rice plantations—Middleton, Drayton Hall, Magnolia, or Boone Hall. Tourists sit or stand in the shade of the Spanish moss hanging from centuries-old oak trees, and smiling women in bonnets and hoop skirts long regale their visitors with stories of benevolent slave owners and happy slaves who sang Negro spirituals while working in the fields. A few of the visitors smile in recognition because they, too, may have been told something like it on their tour of the former homes of slave merchants and slave owners in downtown Charleston.

You get a different spiel at the McLeod Plantation, which lies on Wappoo Creek, across the Ashley River from downtown Charleston, where visitors hear the slave perspective. One of the guides, an African American woman, says visitors are often surprised by what they hear on her tour because they have been given a counter narrative during their other tours. "Slavery was not that bad," she says visitors tell her. The tour guide shakes her head when recalling how some visitors seem to think that working on a plantation was like going with your family to a dude ranch. "To my face, people have said, 'Well, they had a place to sleep. They had meals. They had vegetables.'"[17]

A TOUR OF CHARLESTON'S history should not begin with a tour of a plantation or a historic home or a horse-drawn carriage near the downtown market but perhaps on Sullivan's Island, where many enslaved people were quarantined before being taken to Gadsden's Wharf in downtown Charleston.

As you stand on the beach at Sullivan's Island, stare out into the harbor and imagine what it would have been like to be forcibly removed from your home in Africa and chained and packed into the bowels of a ship, where there is little or no room separating one shackled body from another. The shackles prevent captives from sitting up or changing positions for hour after hour, day after day, week after week. There is little to drink and to eat. The heat is stifling below deck and there is no ventilation, leaving you to inhale the stench from urine and defecation and decaying corpses for the next several weeks.

Africans on the Middle Passage suffered from dysentery, seasickness, and starvation, and when one died, he or she remained shackled to one of the living until one of the crew noticed and tossed the corpse off the ship. Some of the enslaved tried to commit suicide by refusing to eat what little they were offered. The crew often tortured those who refused to eat. "I think in terms of hell on earth," Barry Unsworth, author of *The Sacred Hunger*, said. "That must have been as near as anyone ever comes."[18]

For those who survived the weeks-long journey—and many did not—life did not get any better upon arrival on the Charleston coast, where they were stripped of their names, separated from their families, and escorted in shackles to a slave market, where they were poked and prodded and sold before they were branded with hot irons and dragged away, where they lived the rest of their lives in captivity, sentenced to a life of hard labor for the unpardonable sin of being born with a dark skin in a land far away.

Once you try to imagine the unimaginable, you leave Sullivan's Island by driving over the Ben Sawyer Bridge to Mt. Pleasant, where you take Coleman Boulevard to Highway 17 and then across the Cooper River and the impressive, two-and-a-half-mile-long Arthur Ravenel Jr. Bridge, which, at a cost of nearly $750 million, is the longest and most expensive Confederate memorial ever constructed. The bridge is named for a snarling, Confederate flag–waving politician who spent most of his life running for political office and was sometimes elected, most notably to the U.S. House of Representatives.

While serving in the state Senate, Ravenel, or "Cousin Arthur" as the folksy politician is affectionately known, vilified the National Association for the Advancement of Colored People, who wanted to remove the Confederate flag from the grounds of the state capitol in Columbia, by calling the NAACP "the National Association for Retarded People." When a reporter asked Ravenel if he was a racist, he responded that he could not be a racist because he shared a Senate office with a "very fine black senator."[19] When Ravenel left the state legislature, he was elected to the Charleston County School Board, the culmination of an impressive political career that took him from the U.S. Congress all the way to the Charleston County School Board. While on the school board, Ravenel gloated that he had intimidated the board's Black president into leaving her job and then told her successor, a white woman, that he gotten rid of one "bitch" and would get rid of her too.[20]

Ravenel used his political influence to get his son Thomas elected state treasurer in South Carolina in 2006. Soon after taking office, however, Thomas was charged with cocaine distribution and subsequently pled guilty, serving ten months in prison.[21] The Cooper River bridge may be named for Arthur but its white lines, the joke goes, are named for Thomas. Will Moredock, the longtime columnist of the alternative weekly the *Charleston City Paper*, wrote that the Ravenels represented the city's aristocratic past. "They are living proof of the plantation mentality that has held this state back for centuries. They are the dead weight of an unreconstructed past, which all of us haul around like a ball and chain in the 21st century," Moredock wrote. "They are the haughty remnant of an arrogant class which has misruled this state from the beginning. The good news is that the Ravenels seem to be finished in politics, hoisted on their own julep-scented petards, undone by their own presumption and their own intellectual inertia."[22]

But Thomas Ravenel had a second act. After being released from prison, he became a star on the television reality show *Southern Charm*, until he was fired after his children's nanny accused him of rape. Ravenel pled guilty to third-degree assault and battery in September 2019.[23] Several months earlier, Ravenel had sold his $4 million former plantation on Edisto Island to pay legal bills resulting from his custody suit after his girlfriend and *Southern Charm* castmate, Kathryn Dennis, moved out of the house she shared with Ravenel and their two children.[24] In May 2020 Dennis apologized for sending an emoji of a monkey to Charleston radio host Tamika Gadsden, an African American activist, who criticized a local white salon owner for holding a rally in support of President Donald Trump. "This is what happens when a black woman in Charleston speaks up against white supremacy," Gadsden said.[25]

Once you cross the Ravenel Bridge, you are in Charleston, and you drive a mile or two on East Bay Street before turning onto Calhoun Street, where you pass the site of Emanuel AME Church, and then, across the street, you see Marion Square, where the statue of John C. Calhoun, the spiritual father of Confederate secession, once stood. Perhaps a hundred feet away is a memorial to Wade Hampton III, who orchestrated the Lost Cause movement and, according to legend, ran his gubernatorial campaign from the basement of a whorehouse, the Grace Peixotto House, at 11 Fulton Street.[26] The story is not true. But it makes for a good metaphor. One can hardly think of a more appropriate place to revive the Confederacy than the basement of a whorehouse in the presence of disease-carrying rodents.

The College of Charleston is so close to Marion Square that its students sunbathe on the grass during the spring and summer. It is one of the oldest campuses in America and was built using the work of enslaved people, although it would be almost two centuries before African Americans could attend the college.[27] The college was founded in 1770, chartered in 1785, and became the country's first municipal college in 1837. Its founders included signers of the Declaration of Independence and the U.S. Constitution. The campus includes a number of buildings that are registered as historic landmarks, including Randolph Hall, as well as brick walkways and live oak trees covered with Spanish moss.[28] *Travel and Leisure* named it the country's most beautiful college campus in 2017.[29]

Calhoun Street appropriately divides the College of Charleston because a color line restricted African Americans from attending the school until 1967. Beginning in the 1940s, civil rights activists pushed for the school's integration. In 1949 James Hinton, president of the South Carolina NAACP, said the organization was considering suing the college to force it to open to all qualified students, "regardless of color." College president George Grice responded by ending its affiliation with the city of Charleston and becoming a private institution, which brought about a steady decrease in the quality, reputation, and funding of the school.[30]

The college finally accepted Black students after the federal government told them it was in violation of the 1964 Civil Rights Act and would lose federal funds if it did not integrate. The college admitted its first African American student in 1967 and became a state institution in 1970. In the decades afterward, the percentage of Blacks attending the college remained low because of its reputation for being hostile toward them. One African American student who began attending the college in the early 2000s remembered the summer immediately before his freshman year when he came for orientation. While he was in the lobby of the residence hall, a Black security guard casually told him, "You're going to get arrested while you're here." The comment shook the student. He said he wanted to jump over the counter separating the guard and himself and grab the man's throat. It was not until he began attending the college that he realized the words had been a warning and not a threat.[31]

In 2012 the college introduced an initiative to increase its racial diversity. Such good intentions were undermined two years later when the school's board of trustees, under pressure from the state legislature, hired Glenn McConnell, the state's lieutenant governor and a graduate of the college, to be the school's president, against the recommendations of its search committee, faculty, staff, and alumni. It did not seem to matter to the board of trustees that McConnell was a divisive figure who would alienate not just faculty, students, and staff but prospective donors, faculty, and students—particularly northern out-of-state students who pay far more in tuition than in-state students. In addition, it did not seem to matter that McConnell had no experience in higher education and no presence at the college—except for the Glenn McConnell residence hall. McConnell, who was then sixty-five, was a graduate of the college and a popular figure in the legislature, which had long bristled at the progressive doings of the college and its faculty. Trustees wanted someone like them as president of the college and hired McConnell, a member of the Sons of the Confederacy, owner of a Confederate memorabilia store, and an enthusiastic defender of the Confederate flag. McConnell once characterized the effort to remove the flag from the state-house capitol as "cultural genocide."[32]

On December 20, 2010, McConnell strode through the streets of Charleston wearing the uniform of a Confederate general on his way to a formal ball at Gaillard Municipal Auditorium to mark the 150th anniversary of South Carolina seceding from the Union. Inside the auditorium, hundreds of men in Confederate uniforms or frock coats and women in hoop skirts waltzed and sang "Dixie" inside the auditorium and the NAACP protested outside. Joseph Darby, pastor of the Morris Brown AME Church, called the gala "disgusting." McConnell responded to the criticism as follows: "There was some criticism. But I don't let that bother me."[33] Inside the Gaillard, McConnell played the part of D. F. Jamison, president of the 1860 secession convention. "It was a fiery speech,"

McConnell said, "and I gave it verbatim because I was not gonna be part of sanitizing it or making it appear to be something other than it was."[34]

McConnell's appointment as president of the College of Charleston four years later brought condemnation from faculty and students. Students demonstrated against his selection in what was called "the largest campus protest in recent memory." Joe Kelly, an English professor who was co-director of the college diversity commission, wondered what signal McConnell's hiring sent to prospective students. "I'm worried about what is going on in the mind of that student when [they] see [that someone supportive] of the Confederate battle flag is now president," Kelly said. "There are a lot of subtleties to how you commemorate the Old South and a lot of those subtleties can be lost when you're deciding what college you're going to."[35]

Racism had not been as overt on the campus of the College of Charleston as it has been at The Citadel. But that, too, changed in the context of several high-profile deaths of African Americans at the hands of police officers. On April 12, 2015, Freddie Gray of Baltimore was arrested for possessing an illegal knife. Witnesses said that police used unnecessary force during the arrest. Gray suffered a spinal-cord injury while in police custody and later died as a result of the injury. The U.S. Justice Department ruled two years later that there would be no charges filed against the six police officers involved in Gray's death.[36]

Shortly after the Justice Department's announcement, a College of Charleston student posted a photo of himself on Facebook wearing an orange jumpsuit with the name "Freddie Gray." The words "ur going to jail tonight" were included on the jumpsuit. McConnell responded strongly to the incident. "Racism and intolerance of any kind have no place on our campus—and in our world," he said.[37] A year later, the college again found itself the subject of national criticism after a video appeared of three male students in the back of a pickup truck in the Francis Marion National Forest. One of the students on the video can be heard saying, "Yes, sir, we are here in the country about to visit my slave farm." One of the students on the video responded, "Leroy, I told you to get back to that plantation. Leroy!"[38]

McConnell resigned as president of the college in 2018. He was succeeded a year later by Andrew T. Hsu, a Chinese American with no connections to the state's good-old-boy political hierarchy. A profile of Hsu in the college's magazine mentioned that Hsu worked as a teenager harvesting cotton in a remote village in China while reading *Gone with the Wind* at night—a novel about a spoiled southern belle living in the last days of the plantation aristocracy that includes dozens of references to Charleston. "The universe has an ironic sense of humor," the writer of the article said. "It is not lost on Hsu."[39]

In late January 2020, the 250th anniversary of the university, a marker was erected on campus that referred to the fact that it did not admit women until 1918, that it resisted integration by going private, and that it did not admit its first African American student until 1967.[40] On June 11, Hsu sent a message to the college community that the college had long failed to address systemic issues of race. "As I learn more about Charleston and its history," he said, "I am seeing more clearly how deep the wounds of slavery, Jim Crow, and racial injustice truly are." He then announced a series of initiatives the college would take to address its past, including requiring mandatory diversity education and inclusion training for faculty and staff; developing a more robust mentorship program for underrepresented minorities; investing more in diversity programs; engaging more directly and deliberately with African American alumni; establishing a diversity advisory board made up of alumni, faculty, staff, students, and community members; and raising private funds to support initiatives for underrepresented minorities.[41]

The college's acknowledgment of its racist past followed the city of Charleston's apology for its part in the slave trade in June 2018. Mayor John Tecklenburg, who supported the apology, addressed how "enamored and intertwined" the city has been with slavery. "Do we have a reason to be sorry, to apologize?" he said. "We do." The resolution acknowledged that "fundamental to the economy of colonial and antebellum Charleston was slave labor, Charleston prospering as it did due to the expertise, ingenuity, and hard labor of enslaved Africans who were forced to endure inhumane working conditions that produced wealth for many, but which was denied to them." Many of those who spoke during the meeting, including council members, said if all the city did was apologize and erect a marker, this would be insufficient. They wanted to know how the city would address issues such as affordable housing, economic development, and criminal justice.[42]

WALKING DOWNTOWN YOU WILL see few reminders of the history of African Americans in Charleston. There is, though, the Old Slave Mart Museum, at 6 Chalmers Street, the only remaining structure in the city where slaves were sold. Ten thousand or so slaves were sold at what was then called Ryan's Mart—or "Ryan's n—— jail," which was named for a city councilman who opened a private slave market in 1858 after the city issued a ban against the public sale of slaves. At least ten thousand slaves were sold here. "You can hear heartbeats," Nicole Green, the director of the museum, said.[43]

Dozens of national historic landmarks exist in Charleston County but only a few—the site of the Stono Rebellion and the home of Denmark Vesey—recognize African Americans.[44] The Denmark Vesey House, at 56 Bull Street, is registered as an historic landmark—even though Vesey never lived at the house.[45] Few people go to Charleston for the irony, but it is easy to find if you're interested. There is a statue honoring Vesey, who was executed for organizing a slave revolt, in Hampton Park, which is named for a slave owner who came to political power after a campaign of intimidation and murder against African Americans. A marker was erected outside what was once the Kress Department Store to acknowledge the lunch counter sit-in by students at the all-Black Burke High School in April 1960. A delivery truck inadvertently destroyed the marker. It took more than a year to erect a replacement.[46]

The International African American Museum will open in 2021

on the site of Gadsden's Wharf where 40 percent of American slaves disembarked.[47] There is little to remember the African Americans who confronted white supremacy in Charleston. There is nothing to remember Robert Morrison who died in 1970. In his obituary, the *News and Courier*, which was no longer edited by Tom Waring, said that Morrison was one of the first African Americans in Charleston to receive a college degree, was the oldest member of the local chapter of the NAACP, and long served as a bridge between whites and African Americans. Morrison frequently came to the newspaper with articles for publication that expressed ideas to improve race relations. "We regarded Mr. Morrison as a counselor and a friend," it said. "We share deeply in his death at age 86. He deserves to be long remembered with honor and gratitude by Charlestonians of both races."[48]

The Cannon Street Y no longer exists on Cannon Street.

Emanuel AME Church remains where it has been for more than century, a monument to steadfastness in a violent maelstrom of history, where African Americans sought refuge from white supremacy for generations until the church itself became the site of a white supremacist's rage.

CANNON STREET PLAYERS MET at the Emanuel Church in December 2012 for the funeral of their last surviving coach, Lee Bennett, a member of the church.

In his eulogy, Clementa Pinckney, the minister of the church, talked about Bennett's love of baseball.

"Lee Bennett loved baseball," Pinckney said.

"He marched onto the field out of that heavenly dugout one day and as he did so, he remembered the rules of the game," Pinckney said. "And how the heavenly coach told him to live his life and round the important bases to be a good man."

Pinckney told the audience that Bennett belonged to the church for seventy years and that he and his wife raised six children. He said that Bennett had shouldered the unexpected burden of a civil rights standard-bearer as a coach of the Cannon Street All-Stars. Pinckney said that one of the lyrics in the song of Bennett's life was "Let them play," a line he repeated when told the story about when the team went to the 1955 Little League World Series.

"We heard of the legendary Brother Bennett, who said if a group of young men plays baseball and played hard, they deserved to play well and deserved to go as far as the game would let them go," Pinckney said. "Brother Bennett said, 'Let the boys play.'"

Pinckney reminded his listeners that the church was founded in 1818 and that one of the founding families was named Bennett and two of the Bennetts were among those executed with Denmark Vesey. He told the congregation that Hurricane Hugo had in 1989 torn away the church's steeple and left the support beams for the three-story, stained-glass window warping and cracking, in danger of collapsing. Bennett, who was then sixty-six, grabbed plywood, climbed a ladder, and saved the window.

In his eulogy, Pinckney returned to baseball.

"We are wanting to live our life on the field so that somebody in the stands can say, 'That was a good man.' We're going to want somebody to say, 'Look how he ran those bases, look how he rounded second, look how he moved past third on the way home. Look how he walks off the field, look how he makes it to the dugout.'

"But you know, when you get to the dugout, you're not concerned about the peanut gallery. You want to see the coach and what you want to hear is 'Servant of God, well done.'

"Brother Bennett has made it back to the dugout. His time is over. He knew the rules of the game. He understood this day would come. May we who are yet to finish our game know that he's cheering us on, waiting for us to reach him in the dugout."[49]

22.

THE "EMANUEL NINE"

Dylann Roof, a skinny, unemployed twenty-one-year-old white man with a bowl haircut and a ninth-grade education, pulled his black Hyundai into the parking lot of the Emanuel African Methodist Episcopal Church at about 8:15 p.m., June 17, 2015. He parked the car by a side door of the church. He entered the church and asked to see the pastor, the Reverend Clementa C. Pinckney. Roof was directed to a Bible study class, where he found Pinckney sitting with a group of people, including a few other ministers, in a large room on the church's lower level. Roof asked to sit next to Pinckney. Pinckney obliged.[1]

Pinckney, forty-one, a prominent minister who served in the South Carolina Senate, had recently called for laws requiring police and other law enforcement officials to wear body cameras in response to the death of Walter Scott, an unarmed Black man, who was shot eight times in the back by a police officer in North Charleston two months earlier.[2] Police officer Michael Slager pulled over Scott's car during the daylight of April 4 because it had a non-functioning brake light. An observer's phone captured Scott as he was shot in the back as he fled the scene.[3] "We were able to see the gunshots and we saw him fall to the ground," Pinckney said in a speech in the Senate, "to see him die face down on the ground as if he were gunned down like game. I believe as a legislator, as a state, we have the opportunity to allow sunshine into this process to allow us new eyes into seeing."[4]

Cell phone video of the killings of Scott and other men and

women of color at the hands of police provided white America a glimpse into the long and bloody history of white violence against unarmed minorities, whether it was committed by plantation owners, lynch mobs, or law enforcement officers.[5] Whenever an unarmed person of color was killed by a police officer in recent years, white Americans took a glimpse at their television, their computer, or their cell phone, grimaced, and then looked away as if each death was an aberration—a separate, isolated incident unrelated to the killing of another African American a day or week earlier or the lynchings a century earlier. Each time another African American died, whether by the hands of police or someone else for reasons motivated by race and hatred, and politicians did nothing, the chances increased that there would be another murder and one after that and one after that until one night this brutality exploded in one of the country's most historic African American churches.

Roof listened as one of the parishioners, the Reverend Myra Thompson, fifty-nine, led the discussion of the Parable of the Sower in the Gospel of Mark, where Jesus tells his disciples about the farmer who plants his seed. Some seeds grow, others do not. Some are eaten by birds.[6] "The sower sows the word," Jesus says in Mark 4:1–20. "And these are the ones along the path, where the word is sown: when they hear, Satan immediately comes and takes away the word that is sown in them. And these are the ones sown on rocky ground: the ones who, when they hear the word, immediately receive it with joy. And they have no root in themselves, but endure for a while; then, when tribulation or persecution arises on account of the word, immediately they fall away. And others are the ones sown among thorns. They are those who hear the word, but the cares of the world and the deceitfulness of riches and the desires for other things enter in and choke the word, and it proves unfruitful. But those that were sown on the good soil are the ones who hear the word and accept it and bear fruit, thirtyfold and sixtyfold and a hundredfold."[7]

Roof listened for about an hour. When the discussion ended, Thompson began the benediction, and most of the group bowed their heads and closed their eyes. "As eyes were closed and heads were bowed, the young man with the child's haircut"—as Herb Frazier, Bernard Powers, and Marjory Wentworth described him in their book *We Are Charleston: Tragedy and Triumph at Mother Emanuel*—pulled out a .45-caliber Glock semiautomatic pistol loaded with hollow-point bullets. "I have to do this. You rape our women, and you're taking over our country," he said. "And you have to go. It don't matter, I'm going to shoot you all."[8]

Roof shot Pinckney three times at point-blank range. His bleeding body lay face down on the ground. The Reverend Daniel L. Simmons Sr., a Vietnam War veteran who was born in Clarendon County a few years before George Stinney was executed and Harry Briggs filed a lawsuit challenging the constitutionality of school segregation, jumped toward Roof as he cried out for Pinckney. Roof shot Simmons four times. Simmons died at the Medical University Hospital.[9]

Roof, stopping only to reload several times, fired seventy-seven bullets, killing nine people. More than fifty bullets were removed from the dead bodies. The white tile floor of the fellowship hall was covered with bodies, blood, and spent shell casings.[10]

Susie Jackson, an eighty-seven-year-old, was shot eleven times. Doctors recovered four rounds from Tywanza Sanders; three from Clementa Pinckney; six from Cynthia Graham Hurd; seven from Ethel Lance; eight from the Reverend DePayne Middleton Doctor; four from the Reverend Daniel L. Simmons Sr.; five from Sharonda Coleman-Singleton; and eight from the Reverend Myra Thompson.[11]

Roof, who was now out of bullets, walked by Polly Shepherd, a seventy-year-old retired nurse who was hiding behind a table praying. Pinckney's wife and one of his daughters were in the church's office. They heard the shots that killed their husband and their father, respectively.[12] A security camera captured Roof leaving the church gripping a pistol at 9:07 p.m. He was arrested the next day in Shelby, North Carolina.[13] In January 2017 Roof was convicted of nine counts of first-degree murder and sentenced to death in Judge Richard Gergel's courtroom in the federal courthouse on Broad Street. Two days later, a jury deadlocked in the trial of police officer Michael Slager.[14]

The murder of the "Emanuel Nine," as they became known, came on June 17, one day and 193 years after the date of Denmark Vesey's purported slave rebellion. Roof told investigators and friends that he had hoped to start a race war. He addressed what he said was an epidemic of Black-on-white crime and that Blacks were taking over the United States.[15] Authorities released a manifesto written by Roof that said, among other things, "Integration has done nothing but bring Whites down to [the] level of brute animals."[16] Roof explained why he selected Charleston for his massacre. "I chose Charleston because it is [sic] most historic city in my state and at one time had the highest ratio of blacks to Whites in the country. We have no skinheads, no real KKK, no one doing anything but talking on the internet. Well, someone has to have the bravery to take it to the real world, and I guess that has to be me."[17]

Roof said he believed that he alone could right the wrong.[18]

Photos emerged from Roof's website of him at Confederate monuments and slave museums. One photo, which shows Roof holding the murder weapon in one hand and a Confederate flag in the other, left little doubt about his intentions.[19] The Emanuel Church tragedy prompted demands to remove the Confederate flag from the statehouse grounds in Columbia.[20]

Republican Party leaders in South Carolina, including Senator Lindsey Graham and Governor Nikki Haley, initially rebuffed calls to remove the flag because they said it was part of the state's heritage.[21] They changed their position under tremendous pressure from business leaders and from those within their own party, including a few candidates seeking the party's nomination in the 2016 presidential race. Haley, while saying she lacked the authority to remove the flag because of the Heritage Act, nevertheless called for its removal because "the events of this week call upon us to look at this in a different way."[22] Graham agreed. "I hope that, by removing the flag," he said, "we can take another step towards healing and recognition—and a sign that South Carolina is moving forward."[23]

South Carolina had indeed taken steps to recognize racism, and, as had happened in the past, the terms would be dictated by white politicians. The legislature voted to remove the flag.[24] But no other steps were taken to acknowledge the state's racist history or to heal the racial rift. To Lindsey Graham, Nikki Haley, and other conservative politicians in South Carolina, the removal of the Confederate flag was an equal trade for the gruesome murders of nine churchgoing African Americans.

Four years after the Emanuel tragedy, Haley, who became the U.S. ambassador to the United Nations halfway through her second term as governor, blamed Dylann Roof for hijacking the meaning of the Confederate flag from a symbol of "service, sacrifice, and heritage" to one of hatred and divisiveness. She accused the national media of "wanting to define what happened. They want to make this about racism." Haley received a sharp rebuke from Michael Steele, the African American former chair of the Republican Party. "Really, Nikki?!" Steele said. "The Confederate Flag represented 'service, sacrifice and heritage'? To whom? The Black people who were terrorized and lynched in its name? . . . Roof didn't hijack the meaning of that flag, he inherited it."[25]

To Gus Holt, seeing the insignia of the Confederate flag on his son's baseball uniform was enough to take his disgust to city hall and to compel him to examine how the flag had ended up on his son's uniform. To Lamar Holt, Gus Holt's brother, the flag stands not for "heritage" or "honor" but for "white supremacy" and "control."[26] The Reverend Joseph Darby, a friend of Clementa Pinckney's who has longed served as an AME minister and a member of the NAACP, began demanding the removal of the flag twenty years ago. When the flag was finally removed from the Confederate memorial on the statehouse grounds, Darby was not satisfied. He did not believe that this was the end of the conversation about racial inequalities, as some whites did or at least had hoped for. Darby said the state needed to do more to address other issues of inequality. If the flag was removed but nothing else was done to address racial issues, he said, nothing would have been accomplished. "If nothing else changes," he said, "it'll ultimately be cosmetic."[27]

In 2017 the Avery Research Center for African American Culture and History at the College of Charleston released a report that said institutionalized racism continued to be ubiquitous in the city of Charleston. Among the findings included were that African Americans were arrested 2.33 times as often as whites and they were arrested nearly seven times as often for marijuana possession. In 2016 African Americans represented 75 percent of all gunshot victims and 67 percent of suspects for violent crimes. The report recommended that Charleston County finally treat racism as a matter of priority. "Charleston County must commit itself to an inclusive and aggressive effort to end racism and poverty," it said.[28] In addition, *ProPublica*, an independent, nonprofit, online newspaper, examined U.S. Department of Education data and found staggering racial disparities between white and African American students on educational opportunities and discipline. African American students in Charleston, for instance, were enrolled in a lower percentage of gifted classes than their white counterparts, and they were disciplined six times more often than white students. Schools remained highly segregated.[29] In addition, about 45 percent of African American children in Charleston lived in segregated areas with a high concentration of poverty compared with just 5 percent of white children. Schoolchildren were taught about white men who fought for the Confederacy and not about African Americans who confronted white supremacy.[30]

A 2019 study by the Pew Research Center said that most Americans say the legacy of slavery continues to negatively affect African Americans in the United States. Most Americans in the survey also said that race relations were bad. A majority of Americans also said that President Donald Trump had made race relations worse, and two-thirds said they're more likely to make a racist statement since Trump became president. Four out of ten said making racist statements is more acceptable than it was before Trump became president. Those surveyed—particularly African Americans—are pessimistic about whether race relations will improve.[31]

Trump, a real estate billionaire from New York and former reality television star, does not necessarily follow the tradition of southern demagogues. But do not be fooled by his Queens accent. In an effort to undermine the legitimacy of the country's first Black president, Trump established himself as an early frontrunner for the Republican presidential nomination in 2012 by questioning whether President Barack Obama was born in the United States. The claim was patently false, and Trump dropped out of the race.[32]

On June 16, 2015, Trump announced his candidacy for the presidency with old-style demagoguery by stoking the fears of conservatives by attacking the influx of immigrants from Mexico that he said was ruining the United States. "The United States is becoming a dumping ground for everyone else's problems," he said. Trump blamed Mexico, in particular. "They're sending people that have lots of problems and they're bringing their problems," he said. "They're bringing drugs, they're bringing crime, they're rapists, and some I assume are good people."[33]

Trump's speech came the day before Dylan Roof's massacre at Emanuel Church. There is no evidence that Trump inspired Roof. But as Jamelle Bouie wrote in *Slate*, there are similarities between the two men, both of whom received their information from right-wing media and websites that said that minorities were taking over the country, whites were being persecuted, and the liberal media was suppressing the white perspective—just as Tom Waring and other white demagogues had done. Trump's campaign chair was Steve Bannon, who had been CEO of Breitbart, a news website that spouts racist propaganda and runs the work of "neo-Nazis and white supremacists," as Bouie wrote. "In the world of Bannon and Breitbart, white America is under siege by dark-skinned people and their white liberal editors."[34]

During his inauguration address, Trump, like Roof, said that only he could right the wrongs. "I alone can fix it," he said.[35]

TOM WARING WOULD HAVE liked Donald Trump.

Waring would not have liked what has happened to his former newspaper. He would be outraged at how the newspaper has committed itself to covering the issues of racism instead of serving as a voice for racists. He would have been outraged after seeing a 2018 story in his old newspaper that raised doubts about whether fourteen-year-old George Stinney had indeed committed the crime that he was executed for.[36]

Twenty years ago, the Manigault family, which owns the newspaper, hired a publisher and gave him the directive to improve the newspaper. The publisher then hired a like-minded editor who hired a projects editor who compiled a team of reporters who were given time to investigate and write stories and series that examined the issues and problems of the community.[37] The first of these high-profile series, "Tarnished Badges in 2005," exposed how local and state governments were compliant in allowing law enforcement officers who committed crimes to keep their jobs or to find jobs with other police departments. The series, which brought reforms and led to the dismissals of corrupt cops, won several state and national journalism awards, including a National Headliner Award for Investigative Reporting. Ron Menchaca, who worked on the series, praised the newspaper for giving editors, reporters, and editors the time and resources to investigate the story. "It is one of the only newspapers in the country that invested in investigative journalism," Menchaca said.[38] The family-owned newspaper, which is not susceptible to the demands of corporate or chain ownership, added to its staff and expanded its coverage when other newspapers gutted their staffs. "The family wants to do good journalism," said Brian Hicks, who has worked at the newspaper for more than thirty years.[39]

The newspaper continues to publish investigative stories and series that are nationally recognized for their quality. The *Post and Courier* won a Pulitzer Prize for "Public Service" in 2015 for a series that examined why South Carolina was the most dangerous state for women in the United States because of the high number of incidents of domestic abuse. The series criticized legislators and law enforcement departments for not doing enough to address domestic abuse.[40] In 2016 the newspaper was recognized in the category of "Breaking News" for its stories about the fatal shooting of Walter Scott.[41] The *Post and Courier* also became a Pulitzer finalist that year in "Feature Photography" for its coverage of the murders at Emanuel Church.[42]

23.

JOHN RIVERS'S DREAM

Gus Holt died on April 18, 2020, after a long illness. He was seventy-three.[1]

For Holt, who spent much of his life confronting racial inequalities, the cause of his death—sarcoidosis—was an ironic indicator of such racial inequalities. Sarcoidosis, a disease that usually affects multiple organs but mostly the lungs and lymph nodes, afflicts African Americans two and a half times more often than whites.[2]

Holt's obituary said that he spent the last quarter century of his life telling the story of the Cannon Street YMCA All-Stars. Charleston mayor Joe Riley said Holt made it a national story. "He was the keeper of the flame for the story and he spent his life making sure everyone knew about them," he said. John Rivers, one of the players on the team, said, "He was a unique and passionate human being who didn't do things for personal gain."[3]

Holt said he came to the story accidentally—by "divine intervention," he said. He did not want his son, Lawrence, wearing a uniform with a Confederate flag insignia. In confronting that issue, Holt's brother, Lamar, said, Gus learned about the Cannon Street story. "The Cannon Street story was not as important to him as his son being able to play baseball in a league that wasn't Dixie Youth Baseball," Lamar Holt said.[4]

Gus Holt convinced Riley and the city to pressure Dixie Youth Baseball to remove the Confederate flag from all Dixie Youth Baseball uniforms. Holt then brought Little League Baseball back to Charleston decades after segregationists had replaced it with an all-white youth organization. Holt revived the story of how racial bigotry had denied the Cannon Street team the opportunity of playing in the Little League World Series and, in doing so, brought redemption to a dozen or so middle-aged men.

"His intent was to right some of the wrongs," Lamar said.

Lamar did not understand why Gus kept a shrine to his son's memory in the den of his house. That is, until Lamar watched Gus die. "Watching him die," Lamar said, "I can appreciate what he did to keep his son's memory alive."

Lamar, who was a chemical technician with DuPont before becoming a realtor, remembers how his older brother dragged him out of the house on scorching summer days and hit him baseballs until he "couldn't get out of the heat fast enough." Lamar resented Gus for making him work so hard until he recognized the value of hard work. When Gus was in high school, he gave his brother money for clothing and kept an eye out on him. Gus went into the military, and when he returned he apologized to Lamar for "leaving" him. Their relationship changed as the men got older. "He started out as my big brother, became like a father figure, and then at the end he was my best friend," Lamar said.[5]

Gus was motivated by three things, Lamar said. He wanted to bring Little League Baseball back to Charleston. He wanted to bring recognition to the Cannon Street All-Stars. And he wanted to keep his son Lawrence's memory alive with a scholarship in his name. He accomplished all these things and continued to publicize the significance of the Cannon Street story even while he was dying.[6] Holt's good friend Steve Hoffius said that the former Cannon Street players did not always appreciate that "he was working overtime to tell their story."[7]

Gus Holt thought the Cannon Street story was a significant civil rights story during the 1950s. Hoffius, a South Carolina historian, disagrees. "I think the case in 1955 was just another horrible incident of racial discrimination, not worse and probably more innocent than refusing to let Black kids attend white schools," Hoffius said. "It became a civil rights case when Gus, a veteran and baseball fan, but most importantly a father, took up the team's story, though in the beginning he didn't know any of the players personally. He was just horrified that children could be targeted—'How could they do this to *kids*?'—and I think he always thought to himself, 'What would I do if something like this happened to my son, Lawrence?' He was determined to tell the story of the team whenever and wherever he could. His defense of the players—of all children who faced discrimination—made the story a civil rights case, and one of the most important in South Carolina."[8]

John Rivers said that he and some of the other Cannon Street players had once talked about having a reunion, but they never did, and eventually the story slipped from their conversations but remained etched in their consciousness until Holt began researching what had happened to Little League Baseball in Charleston by going to archives of the Avery Research Center. Rivers was asked what Holt meant to the Cannon Street team. He answered, "Everything. Were it not for him, our story would still be in the archives."[9]

Rivers—who was working as an architect in Jacksonville, Florida, in 1994—remembers when he got a phone call from Holt, who told him he had done a lot of research on the Cannon Street team. Holt told Rivers he wanted to honor the team.

"Okay," Rivers thought to himself. "Who is this guy?"

Holt contacted Little League Baseball. He talked with the Charleston RiverDogs, the city's Minor League team, about honoring the Cannon Street All-Stars. He talked to *Charleston Post and Courier* columnist Gene Sapakoff, who wrote a piece about the team for *Sports Illustrated.* Holt kept contacting people until they could not ignore him. "He didn't give up on anything," Rivers said.[10]

The story of the Cannon Street All-Stars is part of the history of racial bigotry in Charleston and in South Carolina and in the South. Leroy Major, the team's strapping pitcher, says the story of the Cannon Street team is still relevant sixty-five years after it happened. "Discrimination was going on then. Discrimination is still going on," he said. "I don't suspect it's ever going to go away."[11]

ON MAY 25, 2020, four Minneapolis police officers investigated a call from a convenience store employee who said an African

American man had paid for cigarettes with a counterfeit twenty-dollar bill. The man, George Floyd, was then arrested and hand-cuffed and constrained by police officers. Someone took a cell phone video of officer Derek Chauvin sitting on the street with his knee on Floyd's throat.

"I can't breathe," Floyd said.

Chauvin did not move his knee and appeared to stare nonchalantly as if he were daydreaming. Floyd pleaded again and again, "Please, please, please." Chauvin kept his knee on Floyd's throat for close to ten minutes—at least a minute after Floyd lost consciousness. Floyd could not be revived. Floyd's death incited protests in Minneapolis, which spread to other cities and eventually throughout the world. Within a week, the National Guard had been dispatched to about thirty states and dozens of cities had issued curfews to stop arson, looting, and other violence.[12]

More than one African American is killed by police in the United States every day, and African Americans are killed by police three times more often than whites. Floyd's death coincided with the deadly coronavirus pandemic—or Covid-19—that disproportionately killed far more people of color, and the pandemic's economic toll disproportionately cost more African Americans their jobs than it did whites. "It's either Covid is killing us, cops are killing us or the economy is killing us," says Priscilla Borkor, a thirty-one-year-old social worker who joined demonstrations in Brooklyn.[13]

Dylan Roof's murder of nine parishioners at Emanuel AME Church pressured South Carolina legislators to remove the Confederate flag and raised the issue of removing Confederate monuments.

On June 24, 2020, the statue of John C. Calhoun was removed from its pedestal in Marion Square. Brian Hicks, who has long been a columnist for the *Charleston Post and Courier* and has written a number of books on Charleston's history, wanted to see history as it was made. "When they took down the Calhoun monument, a couple of my buddies and I carried a case of beer on ice into the Francis Marion parking garage to watch," Hicks said. "Best beer I'd had in forever, just because we were sitting around bullshitting. Plus, it was humid and the beer was exceptionally cold."[14]

I LEARNED ABOUT GUS Holt's death from John Rivers, who had been living with his wife, Robenia, in Cuenca, Ecuador, since February 2017, a month after Donald Trump was inaugurated president. Rivers said the couple had planned to live abroad but that the Trump presidency "accelerated our move." Rivers said they had to go to a foreign country to find racial equality. "There's no racial baggage," he said. "You feel liberated."[15]

Rivers grew up in Charleston at a time when a monument of John C. Calhoun stood over the city, everything was segregated, and African Americans knew their place or risked being beaten or jailed or worse. "There is a lot of fear, a lot of fear, that at any moment you can become destroyed. What it does to you psychologically," Rivers said. "For some, it does permanent damage."

Rivers learned to fight against discrimination "by accomplishing things," he said. He became a successful architect. He said he wanted to be an architect by the time he was nine years old. He learned he had an ability to draw when he was eight. His mother, a domestic worker who did not have a lot of money, paid for her only child to take a correspondence course in drawing. When he got to Burke High School, he took mechanical drawing, carpentry, and geometry.

Rivers had to learn how to maneuver through the white world as an African American boy. He listened to adults who told him how he had to behave around whites "if you want to survive and not get killed, not get hurt, and not go to jail." Nobody had to tell him that whites thought Blacks were inferior. "You're pounded by racism. It does irrevocable damage to you," he said. "You're damaged goods."[16]

Adults, including his mother, his teachers, and his coaches, encouraged him.

"Adults see potential in you when you don't see it yourself," he said.

When Rivers was eleven years old, he played in the Cannon Street Little League, sitting on the bench during his first year but becoming an All-Star in his second year. But none of the white teams would play his team. The Cannon Street All-Stars traveled to Williamsport for the Little League World Series and sat in the bleachers and watched the championship game. Rivers and his teammates had the same dreams as the white boys on the other teams. Rivers and his teammates watched the other boys live out their dreams.

"Our dreams were taken away," Rivers said.

What does a twelve-year-old boy do without dreams?

Rivers knew he had to get out of Charleston, away from what he called the apartheid of the city. When he was fifteen, he spent a summer with his uncle and aunt in New York City. He worked at the YMCA in Queens, where he rode on buses and sat where he wanted. He could look white people in the eyes. He didn't have to say "Yes, ma'am" and "No, ma'am" to white adults. He knew he had to leave Charleston when he was old enough. "I couldn't wait to leave Charleston," he said. "I had to leave Charleston."[17]

Rivers, who graduated from Hampton Institute in Hampton, Virginia, worked as an architect on Park Avenue in New York City before starting his own architecture company. During his career, he worked on projects such as the Schomburg Museum and Sculpture Garden in Washington DC, the Schomburg Library for Research in Black Culture in New York City, and the Martin Luther King Jr. Center for Non-Violent Social Change in Atlanta.[18]

Norman Robinson also became an architect; John Bailey became a contractor; Leroy Major a teacher; Vermort Brown worked for Lockheed Aircraft and served in the Army Reserves; Vernon Gray became a chef; Allen Jackson became a corrections officer; and others worked in other jobs. One went to prison. Several players on the team have died.

Rivers left Charleston so many years ago—only to have his dreams take him back to Charleston. He has the blueprint for a meditation garden to be constructed near Harmon Field with plaques that honor Gus Holt, the Cannon Street YMCA Little League, and the Cannon Street Y All-Stars. Benches will be provided for visitors to sit and meditate.[19]

Rivers wants to make sure that Charleston doesn't forget the Cannon Street players as it has the likes of so many other African

Americans. He wants to make sure that the dreams of other African American children are not stripped away.

"It was a long time ago," Langston Hughes wrote in his poem "As I Grew Older."

"I have almost forgotten my dream."

Rivers was asked for the moral of the story of the Cannon Street YMCA All-Stars.

"It's a tragedy to take dreams away from youngsters," Rivers says. "I knew it then, I know it now, and I've seen to it that no one takes dreams away from me again."[20]

NOTES

1. "The Team Nobody Would Play"

1. Interview with John Rivers, April 30, 2015.

2. Abrams, "The Little League Champions Benched by Jim Crow in 1995," 53.

3. Jackson, "Sacrifices and Errors," 34.

4. Interview with Lee Drago, July 21, 2014.

5. Interview with John Rivers, April 30, 2015.

6. Godfrey, *The Team Nobody Would Play*.

7. Gene Sapakoff, "Little League's Civil War in '55: A Black All-Star Team Was Sidelined by a Racial Boycott in South Carolina," *Sports Illustrated*, October 30, 1995, https://vault.si.com/vault/1995/10/30/little-leagues-civil-war-in-55-a-black-allstar-team-was-sidelined-by-a-racial-boycott-in-south-carolina.

8. Interview with Gus Holt, July 28, 2014.

9. Rod Stodghill, "In Charleston, Coming to Terms With the Past," *New York Times*, November 15, 2016, https://www.nytimes.com/2016/11/20/travel/charleston-south-carolina-past-slave-trade-history.html.

10. Gergel, *Unexampled Courage*, 253.

11. "Brings Segregation Muddle to a Climax," *Charleston News and Courier*, July 24, 1955.

12. Sapakoff, "Little League's Civil War in '55," *Sports Illustrated*, October 30, 1995.

13. Dixie Youth Baseball, accessed July 8, 2020, http://youth.dixie.org/?nomobile=true&org=dixie.org.

14. "Agitation and Hate," *Charleston News and Courier*, August 2, 1955.

15. Brown v. Board of Education of Topeka, 347 U.S. 483 (1954).

16. Brown v. Board of Education, 349 U.S. 294 (1955).

17. Bass and Thompson, *Ol' Strom*, 158.

18. Abrams, "The Little League Champions Benched by Jim Crow in 1995," 53.

19. Sapakoff, "Little League's Civil War in '55," *Sports Illustrated*, October 30, 1995.

20. "Klan Wizard Lashes Out at NAACP, Daily Papers," *Charleston News and Courier*, August 21, 1955.

21. Interview with John Rivers, April 30, 2015; *Charleston News and Courier*, August 21, 1955.

22. Interviews with John Rivers, April 30, 2015, and April 20, 2020; Vermort Brown, June 2, 2018; Leroy Major, June 2, 2020.

23. Interview with John Rivers, April 30, 2015.

24. Stan Grossfeld, "Justice Delayed: Black Team Barred in 1955 a Big Hit in Little League '02," *Boston Globe*, August 20, 2002.

25. "Youth Baseball League Founded on Racism Flourishing as Integrated Program," ESPN, August 6, 2005, http://www.espn.com/espn/wire/_/section/mlb/id/2126814.

26. Patricia Jones, "It's 'Batter Up' for Little League," *Charleston News and Courier*, April 14, 1994.

27. Sapakoff, "Little League's Civil War in '55," *Sports Illustrated*, October 30, 1995.

2. America's Original Sin

1. Quoted in Kidada E. Williams, "Slavery, Survival, and Community Building," 9.

2. Berlin, "American Slavery in History and Memory," 1258; Wallis, *America's Original Sin*.

3. Nic Butler, "Nearly 1,000 Cargos: The Legacy of Importing Africans into Charleston," Charleston County Public Library, accessed July 24, 2020, https://www.ccpl.org/charleston-time-machine/nearly-1000-cargos-legacy-importing-africans-charleston.

4. Bob Janiskee, "Sullivan's Island Was the African American Ellis Island," *National Parks Traveler*, accessed July 24, 2020, https://www.nationalparkstraveler.org/2009/03/sullivan-s-island-african-american-ellis-island.

5. Brian Hicks, "Slavery in Charleston: A Chronicle of Human Bondage in the Holy City," *Charleston Post and Courier*, April 9, 2001, https://www.postandcourier.com/news/special_reports/slavery-in-charleston-a-chronicle-of-human-bondage-in-the-holy-city/article_54334e04-4834-50b7-990b-f81fa3c2804a.html.

6. See Peter Wood, *Black Majority*; Janiskee, "Sullivan's Island Was the African American Ellis Island," *National Parks Traveler*, accessed July 24, 2020; "Charleston's African-American Heritage: A Port of Entry for Enslaved Africans," *Charleston Chronicle*, March 4, 2016, https://www.charlestonchronicle.net/2016/03/04/charlestons-african-american-heritage-a-port-of-entry-for-enslaved-africans/.

7. Dray, *At the Hands of Person Unknown*, 29–30; "Master/Slave Relationship," National Humanities Center, accessed July 23, 2020, http://nationalhumanitiescenter.org/pds/maai/enslavement/text6/text6read.htm; "The Brutality of Slavery," Mises Institute, accessed July 23, 2020, https://mises.org/library/brutality-slavery; George Morris, "Unspeakable Cruelty: Former Slaves Tell Their Stories in Southern University Online Listings," *The Advocate*, accessed July 24, 2020, https://www.theadvocate.com/baton_rouge/entertainment_life/article_996926ae-579c-11e7-9d36-13d23afca32d.html.

8. "Incidents in the Life of a Slave Girl," PBS, accessed July 19, 2019, http://www.pbs.org/wgbh/aia/part4/4h2924t.html.

9. Williams, Williams, and Blain, *Charleston Syllabus*, 18–19.

10. Morris, "Unspeakable Cruelty," *The Advocate*, accessed July 24, 2020.

11. Dray, *At the Hands of Persons Unknown*, 31.

12. Kytle and Roberts, *Denmark Vesey's Garden*, foreword.

13. Stodghill, "In Charleston, Coming to Terms with the Past," *New York Times*, November 15, 2016.

14. Edgar, *South Carolina*, 80.

15. Hicks, "Slavery in Charleston," *Charleston Post and Courier*, April 9, 2001.

16. Edgar, *South Carolina*, 74–77; Ball, *Slaves in the Family*, 140–41.

17. Edgar, *South Carolina*, 76–77.

18. Frazier, Powers, and Wentworth, *We Are Charleston*, 54–55, 57, 61.

19. Kytle and Roberts, *Denmark Vesey's Garden*, 61.

20. Kelly, *America's Longest Siege*, 142–43; Edgar, *South Carolina*, 328–29.

21. Kytle and Roberts, *Denmark Vesey's Garden*, 61.

22. Kelly, *America's Longest Siege*, 143; Frazier, Powers, and Wentworth, *We Are Charleston*, 66–67; Kytle and Roberts, *Denmark Vesey's Garden*, 20.

23. Kelly, *America's Longest Siege*, 143.

24. Edgar, *South Carolina*, 328.

25. Kytle and Roberts, *Denmark Vesey's Garden*, 20; Edgar, *South Carolina*, 328; Kelly, *America's Longest Siege*, 154–55.

26. Kytle and Roberts, *Denmark Vesey's Garden*, 20, Edgar, *South Carolina*, 328; D. Egerton, *Wars of Reconstruction*, 164.

27. Ron Menchaca, "Bernard Powers on the Life and Legacy of Denmark Vesey," *The College Today*, accessed July 22, 2020, https://today.cofc.edu/2019/10/22/cofc-podcast-bernard-powers-on-the-life-and-legacy-of-denmark-vesey/.

28. Kelly, *America's Longest Siege*, 202–3, 227–28.

29. Carol Berkin, "Angelina and Sarah Grimke: Abolitionist Sisters," The Gilder Jehrman Institute of American History, accessed July 26, 2020, http://ap.gilderlehrman.org/history-by-era/slavery-and-anti-slavery/essays/angelina-and-sarah-grimke-abolitionist-sisters.

30. "A Brief History of The Citadel," The Citadel, accessed March 13, 2019, http://www.citadel.edu/citadel-history/brief-history.html.

31. "A Brief History of The Citadel."

32. Capers, *John C. Calhoun*, 1–2.

33. Paul Starobin, "The Cult of Calhoun," *Politico*, June 28, 2015, https://www.politico.com/magazine/story/2015/06/south-carolina-states-rights-119514_Page2.html.

34. Davis, *A Fire-Eater Remembers*, x–xi.

35. Frazier, Powers, and Wentworth, *We Are Charleston*, 96.

36. Blain Roberts and Ethan J. Kytle, "The South Carolina Monument That Symbolizes the Clashing Memories of Slavery," *What It Means to Be American*, accessed July 2, 2020, https://www.whatitmeanstobeamerican.org/places/the-south-carolina-monument-that-symbolizes-clashing-memories-of-slavery/.

37. Davis, *A Fire-Eater Remembers*, ix; "Rhett, Robert Barnwell," *South Carolina Encyclopedia*, accessed May 1, 2020, http://www.scencyclopedia.org/sce/entries/rhett-robert-barnwell/.

38. Davis, *A Fire-Eater Remembers*, xii–xiii.

39. *Charleston Mercury*, February 2, 1864.

40. Smith, *American Civil War*, 31.

41. Kelly, *America's Longest Siege*, 233.

42. Edgar, *South Carolina*, 307; Kelly, *America's Longest Siege*, 243.

43. Kelly, *America's Longest Siege*, 240.

44. "King Cotton," Mr Gray's History Emporium, accessed July 23, 2020, https://www.mrgrayhistory.com/united-states-history/the-south-slavery/king-cotton/.

45. Hicks, "Slavery in Charleston," *Charleston Post and Courier*, April 9, 2001.

46. Edgar, *South Carolina*, 352.

47. "Declaration of the Immediate Causes Which Induce and Justify the Secession of South Carolina from the Federal Union," Atlanta History Center, February 17, 2020, https://www.atlantahistorycenter.com/assets/documents/SCarolina-Secession-p1-13.pdf.

48. *Charleston Mercury*, December 21, 1860.

49. Cate Lineberry, "The Thrilling Tale of How Robert Smalls Seized a Confederate Ship and Sailed it to Freedom," *Smithsonian*, June 13, 2017, https://photocontest.smithsonianmag.com/photocontest/detail/dream-on/.

50. The story of the Fifty-Fourth Massachusetts Regiment is told in the 1989 movie *Glory*.

51. D. Egerton, *Wars of Reconstruction*, 2–3.

52. D. Egerton, *Wars of Reconstruction*, 1–5.

53. D. Egerton, *Wars of Reconstruction*, 8.

54. Frazier, Powers, and Wentworth, *We Are Charleston*, 84. See Mother Emanuel Church website, accessed July 29, 2020, https://motheremanuel.com/history-2/.

3. The Charleston Baseball Riot

1. The Citadel Green is now Marion Square.

2. *Charleston Daily News*, July 27, 1869, 3; Nic Butler, "The Charleston Baseball Riots of 1869," Charleston County Public Library, accessed June 17, 2020, https://www.ccpl.org/charleston-time-machine/charleston-baseball-riots-1869.

3. *Charleston Daily News*, July 27, 1869, 3.

4. Swanson, *When Baseball Went White*, 130.

5. *Charleston Daily News*, July 27, 1869, 3.

6. Butler, "The Charleston Baseball Riots of 1869."

7. "The Late Riot," *Daily Phoenix* (Columbia SC), July 28, 1869.

8. *Charleston Daily News*, July 27, 1869, 3.

9. *Charleston Daily News*, July 27, 1869, 3.

10. "Charleston Was Defeated and Why—Full Particulars; A Disgraceful Riot," *Charleston Courier*, July 29, 1869; "The Late Riot," *Daily Phoenix* (Columbia SC), July 29, 1869; Swanson, *When Baseball Went White*, 130–31.

11. Butler, "The Charleston Baseball Riots of 1869."

12. "Negro Riot in Charleston—Military Called Out," *New York Times*, July 28, 1869; Swanson, *When Baseball Went White*, 132; *Baltimore Sun*, July 29, 1869, 1.

13. *Nashville Republican Banner*, July 30, 1869, 1.

14. Ryan Swanson, "Charleston's Baseball Riot of 1869," National Pastime Museum, accessed November 3, 2019, https://sabr.org/latest/swanson-charleston-baseball-riot-1869.

15. Swanson, *When Baseball Went White*, 132.

16. Swanson, "Charleston's Baseball Riot of 1869."

17. Nic Butler, "The Charleston Baseball Riots of 1869, Part 2," Charleston County Public Library, https://www.ccpl.org/charleston-time-machine/charleston-baseball-riots-1869-part-2.

18. Swanson, *When Baseball Went White*, 132–33.

19. Swanson, *When Baseball Went White*, 132–33.

20. Woodward, *The Strange Career of Jim Crow*, 70.

21. The *Charleston News* and *Charleston Courier* were merged to create the *Charleston News and Courier*.

22. *Charleston News and Courier*, May 11, 1887, 8.

23. *Charleston News and Courier*, May 11, 1887, 8.

24. Kirsch, *Baseball in Blue and Gray*, xiv, 9, 11, 17, 26, 31, 34, 37, 39.

25. "The Man About Town," *Charleston Sunday News*, May 1, 1887.

26. Kirsch, *Baseball in Blue and Gray*, 35.

27. Swanson, *When Baseball Went White*, 22, 24.

28. "Sporting Tastes," *New York Times*, October 1, 1867.

29. Kirsch, *Baseball in Blue and Gray*, 122; Butler, "The Charleston Baseball Riots of 1869."

30. George Kirsch, "Blacks, Baseball, and the Civil War," *New York Times*, September 23, 2014, https://opinionator.blogs.nytimes.com/author/george-kirsch/.

31. Swanson, *When Baseball Went White*, 13; Charles R. Douglass, *Washington Times*, November 25, 1920, 6; "Student's Family in History Books," *Daily News-Journal* (Murfreesboro TN), March 5, 2014.

32. Swanson, *When Baseball Went White*, 24, 108–11.

33. "The Martyred Catto," *New National Era* (Washington DC), October 19, 1871; Swanson, *When Baseball Went White*, 50; Kirsch, *Baseball in Blue and Gray*, 124–25.

34. "The Martyred Catto," *New National Era*, October 19, 1871; Swanson, *When Baseball Went White*, 51, 142–43.

35. Swanson, *When Baseball Went White*, 144–45.

36. "The Martyred Catto," *New National Era*, October 19, 1871.

37. Swanson, *When Baseball Went White*, 144–45.

38. Helen Armstrong, "Philly Just Unveiled Its First Memorial to an African-American Figure," *Philadelphia*, September 26, 2017.

39. Lamb, *Conspiracy of Silence*, 32.

40. Lamb, *Conspiracy of Silence*, 32, 33, 34, 35.

41. Lamb, *Conspiracy of Silence*, 37.

42. Ribowsky, *Complete History of the Negro Leagues*, 20–21; "Fulton Base Ball Club," Wikipedia, accessed June 18, 2020, https://en.wikipedia.org/wiki/Fulton_Base_Ball_Club.

43. "Bullets Instead of Base Balls," *Charleston News and Courier*, August 2, 1883.

44. "A New Way to Run Bases," *Charleston News and Courier*, May 29, 1886.

45. "An Awful Example," *Charleston News and Courier*, June 3, 1886.

46. *Charleston News and Courier*, June 4, 1887, 8.

47. "The 'Secret History' of Baseball's Earliest Days," NPR, March 16, 2011, https://www.npr.org/2011/03/16/134570236/the-secret-history-of-baseballs-earliest-days.

48. Victor Salvatore, "The Man Who Didn't Invent Baseball," *American Heritage*, June/July 1983, https://www.americanheritage.com/man-who-didnt-invent-baseball#3.

49. "Reaper's Harvest," *Times-Tribune* (Scranton PA), January 28, 1893.

50. Joe Wilson, "Charleston May Have Fostered Baseball," *Charleston News and Courier*, July 6, 1969.

51. Lamb, *Conspiracy of Silence*, 60.

52. Lamb, *Conspiracy of Silence*, 67–67; Washburn and Lamb, *Sports Journalism*, 31–32.

53. Lamb, *Conspiracy of Silence*, 66, 67.

54. Tygiel, *Baseball's Great Experiment*, 16, 18.

55. Lamb, *Conspiracy of Silence*, 68.

56. "Inning Five: Shadow Ball," *Baseball: A Film by Ken Burns*, accessed October 1, 2018, https://www.pbs.org/kenburns/baseball/shadowball/oneil.html.

4. The Lost Cause

1. Edgar, *South Carolina*, 386, 388.

2. Edgar, *South Carolina*, 386–87.

3. D. Egerton, *Wars of Reconstruction*, 9.

4. Edgar, *South Carolina*, 386.

5. Edgar, *South Carolina*, 398–400.

6. Paul Duggan, "The Confederacy Was Built on Slavery: How Can So Many Southern Whites Think Otherwise?" *Washington Post*, November 28, 2018.

7. Edgar, *South Carolina*, 400–403.

8. Tillman got his nickname by attacking President Grover Cleveland as "bag of beef" and by threatening to stick a pitchfork in him.

9. Kantrowitz, *Ben Tillman*, 68–69, 74.

10. Kantrowitz, *Ben Tillman*, 76.

11. Budiansky, *The Bloody Shirt*, 1.

12. Quoted in Lamb, *Conspiracy of Silence*, 38

13. Simkins, *Pitchfork Ben Tillman*, 396.

14. Edgar, *South Carolina*, 416.

15. Woodward, *Strange Career of Jim Crow*, 88.

16. Woodward, *Strange Career of Jim Crow*, 87.

17. Edgar, *South Carolina*, 444, 445, 448.

18. Kantrowitz, *Ben Tillman*, 308.

19. Edgar, *South Carolina*, 468; Dray, *At the Hands of Persons Unknown*, 330.

20. Kantrowitz, *Ben Tillman*, 296.

21. Dray, *At the Hands of Persons Unknown*, 117; *Sumter (SC) Watchman and Southron*, April 5, 1899, 6.

22. Dray, *At the Hands of Persons Unknown*, 117.

23. Dray, *At the Hand of Persons Unknown*, 117–19.

24. *Sumter (SC) Watchman and Southron*, April 5, 1899, 6; Dray, *At the Hands of Persons Unknown*, 117.

25. Dray, *At the Hands of Persons Unknown*, 119.

26. Quoted in Dray, *At the Hands of Persons Unknown*, 117.

27. Briggs v. Elliott, 342 U.S. 350 (1952).

28. Plessy v. Ferguson, 163 U.S. 537 (1896).

29. Woodward, *Strange Career of Jim Crow*, 67–68, 98; Edgar, *South Carolina*, 448.

30. Edgar, *South Carolina*, 449.

31. Will Moredock, "Remembering Daniel Duncan," *Charleston City Paper*, July 6, 2011, https://www.charlestoncitypaper.com/charleston/remembering-daniel-duncan /Content?oid=3525778.

32. Yvonne Wenger, "100 Years Later, Pardon Is Being Sought," *Charleston News and Courier*, January 25, 2011, https://www.postandcourier.com/news/100-years -later-pardon-being-sought/article_be7360e7-35d2-53e2-bdc5-e98b4cc90506.html.

33. "Lynchings: By State and Race, 1882–1968," University of Missouri–Kansas City School of Law, accessed February 1, 2020, http://law2.umkc.edu/faculty/projects /ftrials/shipp/lynchingsstate.html; "History of Lynchings," NAACP, accessed February 1, 2020, https://www.naacp.org/history-of-lynchings/.

34. "A Brute Lynched," *Orangeburg Times and Democrat*, December 2, 1903, https:// www.newspapers.com/image/343746867/?terms=lynching%2BDorchester%2BCounty.

35. "Hung by a Mob," *Marlboro (SC) Democrat*, January 22, 1904.

36. "Nation's Premier Civil Rights Organization," NAACP, accessed July 2, 2020, https://www.naacp.org/nations-premier-civil-rights-organization/.

37. Kytle and Roberts, *Denmark Vesey's Garden*, 34, 178.

38. See Wilkerson, *The Warmth of Other Suns*.

39. W. E. B. Du Bois, "Closed Ranks," *The Crisis* 16, no. 3 (July 1918): 111, accessed at https://www.blackpast.org/african-american-history/w-e-b-du-bois-close-ranks -editorial-from-the-crisis-july-1918/.

40. Franklin, *From Slavery to Freedom*, 478–79.

41. Woodward, *Strange Career of Jim Crow*, 114–15.

42. Woodward, *Strange Career of Jim Crow*, 14.

43. Drago, *Charleston's Avery Center*, 164.

44. Drago, *Charleston's Avery Center*, 165.

45. Nic Butler, "The Charleston Riot of 1919," Charleston County Public Library, accessed July 19, 2020, https://www.ccpl.org/charleston-time-machine/charleston-riot -1919; Damon L. Fordham, "Forgotten History—The Charleston Race Riot of 1919," *Charleston Chronicle*, February 14, 2018, https://www.charlestonchronicle.net/2018 /02/14/forgotten-history-the-charleston-race-riot-of-1919/; see "2 Dead 27 Wounded in Street Rioting," *Charleston News and Courier*, May 12, 1919; "Unruly Sailors Pursue Negroes in Charleston," *Orangeburg (SC) Times and Democrat*, May 13, 1919.

46. Fordham, "Forgotten History," *Charleston Chronicle*, February 14, 2018.

47. "2 Dead, 27 Wounded," *Charleston News and Courier*, May 12, 1919.

48. Drago, *Charleston's Avery Center*, 165.

49. Fordham, "Forgotten History," *Charleston Chronicle*, February 14, 2018.

50. Drago, *Charleston's Avery Center*, 165–67.

51. O'Neill, "From the Shadows of Slavery," 73.

5. The Accommodationist

1. Interview with Lee Drago, June 16, 2020.

2. Drago, *Charleston's Avery Center*, 16, 17, 18, 49, 57, 156; "R. F. Morrison, Civic Leader, Dies at 87," *Charleston News and Courier*, April 22, 1970.

3. Drago, *Charleston's Avery Center*, 49.

4. Drago, *Charleston's Avery Center*, 17–18.

5. Drago, *Charleston's Avery Center*, 17.

6. Drago, *Charleston's Avery Center*, 17–18.

7. Interview with Lee Drago, July 6, 2014.

8. "Booker T. Washington Delivers the 1895 Atlanta Compromise," History Matters (George Mason University), accessed June 29, 2020, http://historymatters.gmu.edu/d/39/.

9. Dray, *At the Hands of Persons Unknown*, 197–98.

10. Quoted in Wallenfeldt, *Africa to America*, 143.

11. Drago, *Charleston's Avery Center*, 106.

12. Drago, *Charleston's Avery Center*, 106.

13. Kytle and Roberts, *Denmark Vesey's Garden*, 107–8.

14. Drago, *Charleston's Avery Center*, 106; Williams and Hoffius, *Upheaval in Charleston*, 252.

15. Erin Blakemore, "The Woman Who Schooled the Civil Rights Movement," *Time*, February 16, 2016.

16. Drago, *Charleston's Avery Center*, 156.

17. Jackson, "Sacrifices and Errors," 69.

18. Brown, "Civil Rights Activism in Charleston," 137.

19. Robert Morrison obituary, Robert Morrison File, Avery Research Center, Charleston.

20. Drago, *Charleston's Avery Center*, 142.

21. Drago, *Charleston's Avery Center*, 155–56.

22. Drago, *Charleston's Avery Center*, 155; Brown, "Civil Rights Activism in Charleston," 137.

23. Brown, "Civil Rights Activism in Charleston," 137.

24. "John Henry McCray," *South Carolina Encyclopedia*, accessed June 19, 2020, http://www.scencyclopedia.org/sce/entries/mccray-john-henry/.

25. Bedingfield, *Newspaper Wars*, 20; "John Henry McCray," *South Carolina Encyclopedia*.

26. John Henry McCray, "States the Position for Southern Negroes," *Charleston News and Courier*, April 13, 1937.

27. Drago, *Charleston's Avery Center*, 221.

28. Bedingfield, *Newspaper Wars*, 21.

29. Jackson, "Sacrifices and Errors," 47.

30. Bedingfield, *Newspaper Wars*, 22.

31. O'Neill, "From the Shadow of Slavery," 107; "John Henry McCray," *South Carolina Encyclopedia*.

32. Bedingfield, *Newspaper Wars*, 21–22; "John Henry McCray," *South Carolina Encyclopedia*.

33. O'Neill, "From the Shadow of Slavery," 74.

34. O'Neill, "From the Shadow of Slavery," 74.

35. Hicks, *In Darkest South Carolina*, 158–59.

36. Gergel, *Unexampled Courage*, 178.

37. Jackson, "Sacrifices and Errors," 48–49.

38. Brown, "Civil Rights Activism in Charleston," 138–42, 145–46.

39. Brown, "Civil Rights Activism in Charleston," 140–42, 144.

40. Brown, "Civil Rights Activism in Charleston," 142; Jackson, "Sacrifices and Errors," 80.

41. Abrams, "Little League Champions Benched by Jim Crow in 1955," 56.

42. Brown, "Civil Rights Activism in Charleston," 148.

43. Brian Hicks, "An Honor for Septima Clark 120 Years in the Making," *Charleston Post and Courier*, May 2, 2018; Itabari Njeri, "Black Educator, 89, Wrote the Book on Civil Rights," *Los Angeles Times*, May 4, 1987; "Septima Clark's Memories Preserved: College Buys Scrapbook of Rights Activist," *Charleston Post and Courier*, December 20, 2006; Drago, *Charleston's Avery Center*, 166.

44. Billy E. Bowles, "Esau Jenkins Engineers Changes for Negroes," *Charleston News and Courier*, July 28, 1968; "Esau Jenkins: A Retrospective View of the Man and His Times," Esau Jenkins File, Avery Research Center.

45. "Esau Jenkins: A Retrospective View."

46. "Esau Jenkins: A Retrospective View."

47. Jack Leland, "Retired Railway Mail Service Employee Runs Filling Station," *Charleston News and Courier*, October 10, 1948.

6. The Blinding of Isaac Woodard

1. Isaac Woodard deposition, April 23, 1946, University of South Carolina Upstate, http://faculty.uscupstate.edu/amyers/deposition.html; Chris Lamb, "The Police Beating That Opened America's Eyes to Jim Crow Brutality," *The Conversation*, February 11, 2016, https://theconversation.com/the-police-beating-that-opened-americas-eyes-to-jim-crows-brutality-53932.

2. Susan Bragg, "Isaac Woodard (1919–1992)," Black Past, September 7, 2013, https://www.blackpast.org/african-american-history/woodard-isaac-1919-1992/.

3. Isaac Woodard deposition, April 23, 1946.

4. "Federal Jury Clears Shull Police Chief," *Times and Democrat* (Orangeburg SC), November 6, 1946; Bragg, "Isaac Woodard (1919–1992)."

5. Isaac Woodard deposition, April 23, 1946.

6. Lamb, "The Police Beating That Opened America's Eyes," *The Conversation*, February 11, 2016.

7. Isaac Woodard deposition, April 23, 1946.

8. "Orson Welles Commentary: Affidavit of Isaac Woodard," July 28, 1946, https://www.youtube.com/watch?v=P1IsW1sXNbs.

9. "NAACP Discovers Eyewitness in Woodard Case; Servicemen Feared for Safety," *New York Age*, August 1946; *Alabama Citizen* (Tuscaloosa), August 24, 1946.

10. Isaac Woodard deposition, April 23, 1946; Bragg, "Isaac Woodard (1919–1992)."

11. Isaac Woodard deposition, April 23, 1946.

12. "U.S. Jury Frees Cop in Jury Blinding," *New York Daily News*, November 6, 1946.

13. Isaac Woodard deposition, April 23, 1946.

14. Isaac Woodard deposition, April 23, 1946.

15. Isaac Woodard deposition, April 23, 1946.

16. Isaac Woodard deposition, April 23, 1946.

17. Bragg, "Isaac Woodard (1919–1992)."

18. Lamb, *Blackout*, 62–63.

19. J. Williams, *Thurgood Marshall*, 132–33; Lamb, *Blackout*, 9–11.

20. "The Columbia Race Riot (1946)," Black Past, August 29, 2019, https://www.blackpast.org/african-american-history/the-columbia-race-riot-1946/.

21. Lamb, *Blackout*, 11.

22. J. Williams, *Thurgood Marshall*, 135–42.

23. Lamb, *Conspiracy of Silence*, 243–44.

24. The *York (PA) Daily Record* was among white newspapers that printed Woodard's deposition. "Funds Raised Here Will Aid Arrest, Conviction of Blind Vet's Attacker," *York Daily Record*, August 7, 1946; Bragg, "Isaac Woodard (1919–1992)."

25. Ludlow Werner, "Across the Desk," *New York Age*, July 27, 1946.

26. Bedingfield, *Newspaper Wars*, 97.

27. Bragg, "Isaac Woodard (1919–1992)"; "Isaac Woodward, Officer X, and Orson Welles," *ITALKYOUBORED*, September 2, 2014, https://italkyoubored.wordpress.com/2014/09/02/isaac-woodard-officer-x-and-orson-welles/.

28. Lamb, "The Police Beating That Opened America's Eyes," *The Conversation*, February 11, 2016.

29. "Orson Welles Commentary: Affidavit of Isaac Woodard."

30. "Orson Welles' Film Barred in Aiken," *Pittsburgh Courier*, August 24, 1946; "The Aiken Case Should Be Proved or Apologies Made," *Aiken (SC) Standard*, August 14, 1946.

31. "Isaac Woodard, Officer X, and Orson Welles," *ITALKYOUBORED*, September 2, 2014.

32. "Negro Vet Blinded by Vet at Batesburg, Not Aiken, Drunk, Obscene on Bus, Charge," *Greenville (SC) News*, August 18, 1946. The Associated Press account wrongly identifies Shull as "Shaw."

33. "N.Y. Rally Provides $22,000 for Negro Blinded in S.C," *Greenwood (SC) Index-Journal*, August 19, 1946.

34. "NAACP Discovers Eyewitness in Woodard Case; Servicemen Feared for Safety," *New York Age*, August 24, 1946; *Alabama Citizen* (Tuscaloosa), August 24, 1946, 1.

35. Dray, *At the Hands of Persons Unknown*, 376–83; "Two Negro Couples Shot to Death by Mob," *New York Daily News*, July 27, 1946.

36. "Truman Is Urged to Take Action," *Pittsburgh Courier*, August 3, 1946.

37. Dray, *At the Hands of Persons Unknown*, 374–76.

38. "Gruesome Lynching," *Pittsburgh Courier*, August 24, 1946.

39. J. Egerton, *Speak Now Against the Day*, 414.

40. "Isaac Woodard Benefit Show," *New York Daily News*, August 15, 1946; "Concert for Isaac Woodard at Lewisohn Stadium," *The Hi de Ho Blog*, accessed July 9, 2020, http://www.thehidehoblog.com/blog/2015/08/august-16-1946-concert-for-isaac-woodward-at-the-lewisohn-stadium.

41. "Isaac Woodard, Officer X, and Orson Welles," *ITALKYOUBORED*, September 2, 2014.

42. Lamb, "The Police Beating That Opened America's Eyes," *The Conversation*, February 11, 2016.

43. Gergel, *Unexampled Courage*, 72–75.

44. Bragg, "Isaac Woodard (1919–1992)."

45. Bragg, "Isaac Woodard (1919–1992)."

46. Bragg, "Isaac Woodard (1919–1992)."

47. Bragg, "Isaac Woodard (1919–1992)."

48. Gergel, *Unexampled Courage*, 128–29.

49. Lamb, "The Police Beating That Opened America's Eyes," *The Conversation*, February 11, 2016.

50. Alfred Duckett, "Column Right," *New York Age*, November 16, 1946.

51. McCullough, *Truman*, 589.

52. "Truman Exhorts World to Join in Bill of Rights," *Salt Lake (UT) Tribune*, June 29, 1947.

53. Bass and Thompson, *Ol' Strom*, 84–85.

54. J. Egerton, *Speak Now Against the Day*, 415–16; "Special Message to the Congress on Civil Rights," Truman Library, accessed June 17, 2020, https://www.trumanlibrary.gov/library/public-papers/20/special-message-congress-civil-rights.

55. Bass and Thompson, *Ol' Strom*, 112.

56. Gergel, *Unexampled Courage*, 260.

57. Gergel, *Unexampled Courage*, 261.

58. Audra D. S. Burch, "Why a Town Is Finally Honoring a Black Veteran Attacked by Its White Police Chief," *New York Times*, February 8, 2019, https://www.nytimes.com/2019/02/08/us/sergeant-woodard-batesburg-south-carolina.html.

59. Gergel, *Unexampled Courage*, 261.

7. "It's Time for South Carolina to Rejoin"

1. Yarborough, *Passion for Justice*, 52; Hicks, *In Darkest South Carolina*, 139.

2. Yarborough, *Passion for Justice*, 52–53.

3. Yarborough, *Passion for Justice*, 52; Hicks, *In Darkest South Carolina*, 139–40; Gergel, *Unexampled Courage*, 131.

4. Hicks, *In Darkest South Carolina*, 139.

5. Yarborough, *Passion for Justice*, 53.

6. Hicks, *In Darkest South Carolina*, 139–41; Gergel, *Unexampled Courage*, 131–32.

7. Yarborough, *Passion for Justice*, 53; Hicks, *In Darkest South Carolina*, 142–43.

8. Hicks, *In Darkest South Carolina*, 143–44.

9. Yarborough, *Passion for Justice*, 3.

10. Hicks, *In Darkest South Carolina*, 28–30; Gergel, *Unexampled Courage*, 94–95; interview with Brian Hicks, May 30, 2018.

11. Hicks, *In Darkest South Carolina*, 33–35; Gergel, *Unexampled Courage*, 95–96.

12. Hicks, *In Darkest South Carolina*, 54, 55; Gergel, *Unexampled Courage*, 96–97.

13. Hicks, *In Darkest South Carolina*, 81; interview with Brian Hicks, May 30, 2018.

14. Hicks, *In Darkest South Carolina*, 84, 90.

15. Duvall v. Seignous, U.S. Court of Appeals for the Fourth Circuit-112 F.2d 992 (4th Cir. June 18, 1940); Hicks, *In Darkest South Carolina*, 103, 105, 107; Gergel, *Unexampled Courage*, 102.

16. Hicks, *In Darkest South Carolina*, 103–9; Gergel, *Unexampled Courage*, 102–5.

17. Yarborough, *Passion for Justice*, 33–36.

18. Smith v. Allwright, 321 U.S. 649 (1944) 64 S. Ct. 757; 88 L. Ed. 987.

19. J. Williams, *Thurgood Marshall*, 114.

20. Hicks, *In Darkest South Carolina*, 114.

21. Elmore v. Rice, 72 F. Supp. 516 (E.D.S.C. 1947).

22. "Negroes May Vote in S.C. Primaries, Judge Here Holds," *Charleston News and Courier*, July 13, 1947.

23. "Rejoining the Union," *Charleston Evening Post*, July 15, 1947; Hicks, *In Darkest South Carolina*, 163–64.

24. "Federal Court Decisions," *Charleston News and Courier*, July 14, 1947.

25. "Could Teach 'White Folks,'" *Charleston News and Courier*, July 14, 1947.

26. "Youths Fire Shotguns into Southern Boy Scout Camp," *Honolulu (HI) Advertiser*, July 15, 1947.

27. "3 White Youths Wound Negroes," *Greenville (SC) News*, July 15, 1947.

28. "Stormy Protests Voiced Against Judge J. W. Waring," *Times and Democrat* (Orangeburg SC), August 5, 1948.

29. Gergel, *Unexampled Courage*, 209–10.

30. Gergel, *Unexampled Courage*, 184.

31. See Samuel Grafton, "Lonesomest Man in Town," *Collier's*, April 29, 1950, 20–21, 49, J. Waties Waring File, Charleston County Public Library.

32. Yarborough, *Passion for Justice*, 130–31.

33. Yarborough, *Passion for Justice*, 127, 135.

34. Yarborough, *Passion for Justice*, 135.

35. Yarborough, *Passion for Justice*, 154–55.

36. Gergel, *Unexampled Courage*, 210–11.

37. Hicks, *In Darkest South Carolina*, 248.

38. Hicks, *In Darkest South Carolina*, 265.

39. Kluger, *Simple Justice*, 4.

40. See "An Undying Mystery," a series about George Stinney that appeared in the *Charleston Post and Courier*, accessed July 17, 2020, https://www.postandcourier.com/news/special_reports/stinney/.

41. Kluger, *Simple Justice*, 4; Gergel, *Unexampled Courage*, 217.

42. Gergel, *Unexampled Courage*, 221.

43. Yarborough, *Passion for Justice*, 174.

44. Gergel, *Unexampled Courage*, 218.

45. Gergel, *Unexampled Courage*, 218.

46. Interview with Brian Hicks, May 30, 2018.

47. Gergel, *Unexampled Courage*, 218.

48. Gergel, *Unexampled Courage*, 220; Yarborough, *Passion for Justice*, 175.

49. Gergel, *Unexampled Courage*, 220.

50. Yarborough, *Passion for Justice*, 177, 118.

51. Hicks, *In Darkest South Carolina*, 282.

52. Bedingfield, *Newspaper Wars*, 118.

53. McCullough, *Truman*, 297.

54. Bedingfield, *Newspaper Wars*, 119–21.

55. Bedingfield, *Newspaper Wars*, 119–21.

56. Gergel, *Unexampled Courage*, 227.

57. Bedingfield, *Newspaper Wars*, 123.

58. Gergel, *Unexampled Courage*, 228.

59. Yarborough, *Passion for Justice*, 179.

60. Yarborough, *Passion for Justice*, 180–84.

61. Gergel, *Unexampled Courage*, 238–39.

62. Gergel, *Unexampled Courage*, 241.

63. Hicks, *In Darkest South Carolina*, 304.

8. The Story of Little League Baseball

1. Van Auken and Van Auken, *Play Ball!*, 18.

2. Stotz and Loss, *Promise Kept*, 2, 4; Van Auken and Van Auken, *Play Ball!*, 18.

3. Stotz and Loss, *Promise Kept*, 3.

4. Stotz, and Loss, *Promise Kept*, 3, 5, 6, 14; Van Auken and Van Auken, *Play Ball!*, 22.

5. Stotz and Loss, *Promise Kept*, 11, 18; Van Auken and Van Auken, *Play Ball!*, 22, 24, 25.

6. Stotz and Loss, *Promise Kept*, 26; Bill Hewitt, "Little League Game Changers: Three Trailblazers on What It Meant to Play Ball," *Parade*, May 30, 2014, https://parade.com/298887/billhewitt/little-league-game-changers-three-trailblazers-on-what-it-meant-to-play-ball/.

7. Van Auken and Van Auken, *Play Ball!*, 28; Stotz, *Promise Kept*, 22–29.

8. Van Auken and Van Auken, *Play Ball!*, 34.

9. Van Auken and Van Auken, *Play Ball!*, 38–39; Frommer, *Growing Up at Bat*, 20–21. Little League Baseball prohibited girls until 1974.

10. Interview with Lance Van Auken, June 30, 2018.

11. Stotz and Loss, *Promise Kept*, 43; Van Auken and Van Auken, *Play Ball!*, 35–36, 41; Frommer, *Growing Up at Bat*, 21.

12. Van Auken and Van Auken, *Play Ball!*, 23, 29.

13. Frommer, *Growing Up at Bat*, 24.

14. *Long Time Coming: A 1955 Baseball Story*, directed by Jon Strong, Common Pictures and Strong Films, 2018.

15. Van Auken and Van Auken, *Play Ball!*, 70–71.

16. Interview with Lance Van Auken, October 10, 2019.

17. Van Auken, and Van Auken, *Play Ball!*, 52–53.

18. Interview with Lance Van Auken, October 10, 2019.

19. *Williamsport (PA) Sun-Gazette*, August 28, 1950, 3.

20. Stotz and Loss, *Promise Kept*, 172.

21. Van Auken and Van Auken, *Play Ball!*, 52–53.

22. Van Auken and Van Auken, *Play Ball!*, 58.

23. Van Auken and Van Auken, *Play Ball!* 58, 59.

24. "National Tourney Stays Here; Carl Stotz Named Director," *Williamsport (PA) Sun-Gazette*, December 3, 1948.

25. "Little League Baseball," *Canton (PA) Independent-Sentinel*, May 26, 1955.

26. Interview with Lance Van Auken, October 10, 2019.

27. Van Auken and Van Auken, *Play Ball!*, 55, 56.

28. Van Auken, and Van Auken, *Play Ball!*, 69; Frommer, *Growing Up at Bat*, 26.

29. Van Auken and Van Auken, *Play Ball!*, 68, 70; Stotz and Loss, *Promise Kept*, 178.

30. Interview with Lance Van Auken, June 30, 2018; Van Auken and Van Auken, *Play Ball!*, 70–71.

31. Van Auken and Van Auken, *Play Ball!*, 70–71; Stotz and Loss, *Promise Kept*, 178–81.

32. Interview with Lance Van Auken, June 30, 2018.

33. Stotz and Loss, *Promise Kept*, 173.

34. Van Auken and Van Auken, *Play Ball!*, 71; Fine, *With the Boys*, 7.

35. Interview with Lance Van Auken, June 30, 2018.

36. Frommer, *Growing Up at Bat*, 29–30.

37. Van Auken and Van Auken, *Play Ball!*, 64.

38. Van Auken and Van Auken, *Play Ball!*, 64.

39. Carriere, "'A Diamond Is a Boy's Best Friend,'" 352.

40. Frommer, *Growing Up at Bat*, 24.

41. Carriere, "'A Diamond Is a Boy's Best Friend,'" 354.

42. Frommer, *Growing Up at Bat*, 26, 28.

43. Carriere, "'A Diamond Is a Boy's Best Friend,'" 352.

44. Carriere, "'A Diamond Is a Boy's Best Friend,'" 356.

45. Carriere, "'A Diamond Is a Boy's Best Friend,'" 356; Fine, *With the Boys*, 196.

46. Fine, *With the Boys*, 197.

47. Fine, *With the Boys*, 197.

48. "Danny Jones, Recreation and Sports Official, Dies," *Charleston Evening Post*, September 28, 1966; "Daniel H. Jones Dies at Age 56," undated newspaper clipping, Danny Jones File, Charleston County Public Library.

49. "Danny Jones, Recreation and Sports Official, Dies," *Charleston Evening Post*, September 28, 1966.

50. "Danny Jones, Recreation and Sports Official, Dies," *Charleston Evening Post*, September 28, 1966.

51. Interview with Sallie Frenkel, March 9, 2018.

52. Ed Harrill, "Sports Background Aided Park, Playground Director," *Charleston Evening Post*, January 25, 1958. USO refers to United Service Organizations, an organization that supports active-duty servicemen and servicewomen and their families.

53. Ed Harrill, "Sports Background Aided Park, Playground Director," *Charleston Evening Post*, January 25, 1958; Bob Heeke, "Jones' Kids Cost $71,000 Per Year," *Charleston News and Courier*, April 4, 1957, Danny Jones File, Charleston County Public Library.

54. J. Douglas Donehue, "Pool Is Named for Jones," *Charleston News and Courier*, May 17, 1959.

55. Donehue, "Pool Is Named for Jones," *Charleston News and Courier*, May 17, 1959; "Daniel H. Jones Dies at Age 56," Danny Jones File, Charleston County Public Library.

56. Interview with Sallie Frenkel, Tesa Livingston, and Charles "Bubba" Jones, March 9, 2018.

57. Interview with Bubba Jones, March 9, 2018.

58. Warren Koon, "He Got the Job Done," *Charleston Evening Post*, October 1, 1966; interview with Jones's children, March 9, 2018.

59. Interview with Tesa Livingston, July 6, 2020.

60. Interview with Sallie Frenkel and Bubba Jones, March 9, 2018.

61. Interview with Bubba Jones and Tesa Livingston, March 9, 2018.

62. Interview with Tesa Livingston and Bubba Jones, March 9, 2018.

63. Koon, "He Got the Job Done," *Charleston Evening Post*, October 1, 1966; interview with Tesa Livingston, July 7, 2020.

64. "Daniel H. Jones Dies at Age 56," Danny Jones File, Charleston County Public Library.

65. "Time In," *Charleston News and Courier*, August 25, 1949.

66. Interview with Sallie Frenkel and Bubba Jones, March 9, 2018.

67. "Negro Little League Team Will Compete," *Charleston News and Courier*, June 22, 1955.

68. Interview with Sallie Frenkel and Bubba Jones, March 9, 2018.

69. Interview with Bubba Jones and Sallie Frenkel, March 9, 2018.

70. Interview with Tesa Livingston, July 6, 2020.

9. The YMCA

1. Certificate of Incorporation, August 2, 1941, Charleston YMCA Collection, South Carolina Historical Society, Addlestone Library, College of Charleston; Jackson, "Sacrifices and Errors," 67–68.

2. Interview with Paul Stoney, July 19, 2018.

3. Interview with Paul Stoney, July 19, 2018.

4. There is confusion over whether the first African American Y was created in 1852 or 1853.

5. Nina Mjagkij, *Light in the Darkness*, 1.

6. Nina Mjagkij, *Light in the Darkness*, 7.

7. Charleston YMCA website, https://www.ymcagc.org/about-us/.

8. Mjagkij, *Light in the Darkness*, 18.

9. Charleston YMCA website, https://www.ymcagc.org/about-us/.

10. "$5,000 Will Assure Building on Lots Acquired in 1916," *Charleston News and Courier*, November 1, 1948; Jackson, "Sacrifices and Errors," 66–67. Herb Frazier, "Cannon Street Y Is No Stranger to Conflict, Change," *Charleston News and Courier*, December 21, 2003.

11. Drago, *Charleston's Avery Center*, 128.

12. Drago, *Charleston's Avery Center*, 132.

13. Frazier, "Cannon Street Y," *Charleston Post and Courier*, December 21, 2003.

14. Jackson, "Sacrifices and Errors," 67.

15. Interview with Paul Stoney, July 19, 2018.

16. "$5,000 Will Assure Building on Lots Acquired in 1916," *Charleston News and Courier*, November 1, 1948.

17. "Negroes to Build YMCA; Opening Planned in February," *Charleston News and Courier*, November 23, 1947.

18. "Ground Breaking for Negro YMCA Announced for Monday," *Charleston News and Courier*, December 17, 1949.

19. Frazier, "Cannon Street Y," *Charleston Post and Courier*, December 21, 2003.

20. "Negroes to Build New YMCA; Opening Planned in February," *Charleston News and Courier*, November 27, 1948, Charleston YMCA Collection, South Carolina Historical Society, Addlestone Library, College of Charleston.

21. "Negroes to Build New YMCA; Opening Planned in February," *Charleston News and Courier*, November 27, 1948.

22. Elsa McDowell, "YMCA Alumni Work to See Facility Return to Glory," *Charleston Post and Courier*, April 16, 1987, Charleston YMCA Collection, South Carolina Historical Society, Addlestone Library, College of Charleston.

23. Jackson, "Sacrifices and Errors," 73.

24. Robert L. Morrison, letter to the editor, "Cutting Into Negro Playground," *Charleston Post and Courier*, June 5, 1953.

25. "Burke High School Accrediting Move Makes Progress," *Charleston News and Courier*, August 22, 1945.

26. Dan T. Henderson to Thomas R. Waring, Thomas R. Waring Jr. Papers, South Carolina Historical Society, Addlestone Library, College of Charleston.

27. "Negro Businessman Offers Ideas on County's Schools," *Charleston News and Courier*, October 9, 1955, Lee Drago Papers, Avery Research Center.

28. Jackson, "Sacrifices and Errors," 74–75.

29. Gene Sapakoff, "Cannon Street All-Stars Get to Smile," *Charleston Post and Courier*, August 6, 2000.

30. Interview with Paul Stoney, July 19, 2018.

31. "Seven More Teams Withdraw from Little League Tourney," *Charleston News and Courier*, July 26, 1955.

10. Even the Ocean Was Segregated

1. Godfrey, *The Team Nobody Would Play*, x.

2. Stephen L. Nelson, ed., *Charleston Looks at Its Services for Negroes*, quoted in Jackson, "Sacrifices and Errors," 70. Robert Morrison was a member of the Charleston Welfare Council.

3. Godfrey, *The Team Nobody Would Play*, 4.

4. Interview with John Rivers, April 30, 2015.

5. Interview with John Rivers, April 20, 2020.

6. Interview with Gus Holt, July 28, 2014.

7. Myrdal, *American Dilemma*, 41.

8. Taeuber and Taeuber, *Negroes in Cities*, 45–48.

9. Interview with Leroy Major, June 2, 2020.

10. Interview with John Rivers, April 30, 2015.

11. Godfrey, *The Team Nobody Would Play*, x.

12. Godfrey, *The Team Nobody Would Play*, 4.

13. Dray, *At the Hands of Persons Unknown*, 83.

14. Moredock, *Banana Republic*, 63–64; Will Moredock, "Atlantic Beach Once Thrived as S.C.'s Only Black-Friendly Beach, Now Home to Dreaded Black Bike Week," *Charleston City Paper*, September 10, 2014.

15. Moredock, *Banana Republic*, 63–64.

16. Interview with John Rivers, April 20, 2020.

17. Leroy Major, information presentation, "The 1955 Cannon Street YMCA in Uniform," Patriots Point Naval and Maritime Museum, February 11, 2016.

18. Godfrey, *The Team Nobody Would Play*, xii, xiii, 2.

19. Godfrey, *The Team Nobody Would Play*, xiii; Hanna Raskin, "Downtown Charleston House Used to be Popular Restaurant for African-American Politicians," *Charleston News and Courier*, May 23, 2018.

20. Ellison, *Invisible Man*, 3.

21. Godfrey, *The Team Nobody Would Play*, xi.

22. Thomas Waring to William Browder, Thomas R. Waring Jr. Papers, South Carolina Historical Society, Addlestone Library, College of Charleston.

23. *New York Herald Tribune*, October 25, 1945, quoted in Lamb, *Conspiracy of Silence*, 290.

24. *Sporting News*, November 1, 1945, quoted in Lamb, *Conspiracy of Silence*, 291.

25. Rampersad, *Jackie Robinson*, 179.

26. Eig, *Opening Day*, 217.

27. Eig, *Opening Day*, 4–5.

28. Godfrey, *The Team Nobody Would Play*, xiii.

29. Godfrey, *The Team Nobody Would Play*, 4.

30. Sapakoff, "Little League's Civil War in '55," *Sports Illustrated*, October 30, 1995.

31. Interview with John Rivers, April 20, 2020.

32. Godfrey, *The Team Nobody Would Play*, 6, 9; interview with Vermort Brown, June 2, 2018.

33. Godfrey, *The Team Nobody Would Play*, 9–10; interview with Vermort Brown, June 2, 2018.

34. Godfrey, *The Team Nobody Would Play*, 5.

35. Interview with Vermort Brown, June 2, 2018.

36. Godfrey, *The Team Nobody Would Play*, 11.

37. "Ted Williams Slams Homer, Bagby is Best Moundsman," *Charleston News and Courier*, April 2, 1940.

38. "Major Leagues Negro Stars to Play Here Monday," *Charleston News and Courier*, November 4, 1949; "Stars to Play Here Tonight," *Charleston News and Courier*, October 14, 1950.

39. Godfrey, *The Team Nobody Would Play*, 11.

11. *Brown v. Board of Education*

1. Brown v. Board of Education, 397 U.S. 483 (1954).

2. Brown v. Board of Education, 397 U.S. 483 (1954).

3. Hicks, *In Darkest South Carolina*, 327, 328; Gergel, *Unexampled Courage*, 247.

4. Kluger, *Simple Justice*, x.

5. Abrams, "The Little League Champions Benched by Jim Crow in 1955," 52.

6. The quote has been attributed to *Washington Post* publisher Philip Graham.

7. Kluger, *Simple Justice*, 710.

8. Abby Phillip, "How the Washington Post Covered Brown v. Board of Education in 1954," *Washington Post*, May 16, 2014.

9. Kluger, *Simple Justice*, 710.

10. W. D. Workman, "Gov. Byrnes 'Shocked' by Court Ruling," *Charleston News and Courier*, May 18, 1954.

11. "Decision Is Denounced by S.C. Congressmen," *Charleston News and Courier*, May 18, 1954.

12. "The Court's Decision," *Charleston News and Courier*, May 18, 1954.

13. "Democracy Prevails," *Charleston News and Courier*, May 18, 1954.

14. *The Open Mind*, PBS, aired February 10, 1957, https://www.pbs.org/video/the-open-mind-the-new-negro/.

15. Hicks, *In Darkest South Carolina*, 354–55.

16. Jack Bass interview with Thomas Waring, February 19, 1974, Thomas R. Waring Jr. Papers, South Carolina Historical Society, Addlestone Library, College of Charleston.

17. Hicks, *In Darkest South Carolina*, 353.

18. "Courthouse Renamed for Civil Rights Hero," United States Courts, October 14, 2015, https://www.uscourts.gov/news/2015/10/14/courthouse-renamed-civil-rights -hero#:~:text=The%20Hollings%20Judicial%20Center%20in,Waties%20Waring.

19. "50-Year News Career in Family Tradition," *Charleston Evening Post*, June 17, 1977.

20. "50-Year News Career in Family Tradition," *Charleston Evening Post*, June 17, 1977.

21. "50-Year News Career in Family Tradition," *Charleston Evening Post*, June 17, 1977.

22. Sass, *Outspoken*, 59.

23. Roberts and Klibanoff, *The Race Beat*, 37.

24. Bedingfield, *Newspaper Wars*, 13–14.

25. Sass, *Outspoken*, 107.

26. Roberts and Klibanoff, *The Race Beat*, 40–41.

27. Bass and Thompson, *Ol' Strom*, 144.

28. Strom Thurmond to Tom Waring, November 7, 1954, Thomas R. Waring Jr. Papers, South Carolina Historical Society, Addlestone Library, College of Charleston.

29. Bedingfield, *Newspaper Wars*, 37.

30. Bedingfield, *Newspaper Wars*, 151.

31. O'Neill, "From the Shadows of Slavery," 127–28.

32. Bedingfield, *Newspaper Wars*, 158.

33. Bedingfield, *Newspaper Wars*, 127–28.

34. Roberts and Klibanoff, *The Race Beat*, 37.

35. O'Neill, "From the Shadows of Slavery," 127–28.

36. "Speaking for the South," *Charleston News and Courier*, April 29, 1955.

37. Bedingfield, *Newspaper Wars*, 158.

38. Roberts and Klibanoff, *The Race Beat*, 71.

39. Thomas Waring, "Mississippi's Citizens Councils," Thomas R. Waring Jr. Papers, South Carolina Historical Society, Addlestone Library, College of Charleston.

40. Hicks, *In Darkest South Carolina*, 308, 338–40.

41. Hicks, *In Darkest South Carolina*, 308, 338–40.

42. Hicks, *In Darkest South Carolina*, 347. In 1963 playwright Loften Mitchell wrote a play based on DeLaine's story called *Land Beyond the River*. In 2008 actor Ossie Davis wrote a short play about DeLaine called *The People of Clarendon County*, which starred Davis as DeLaine and costarred Ruby Dee and Sidney Poitier.

43. "Fugitive Pastors Relates 'Land of Terror' in S.C.," *Florence (sc) News*, October 21, 1955.

44. Brown v. Board of Education of Topeka, 349 U.S. 294 (1955).

45. Bedingfield, *Newspaper Wars*, 154.

46. "Segregation for Whites," *Charleston News and Courier*, June 2, 1955.

47. "Sumter Klu [*sic*] Klux Klan Rally First in S.C. in Two Years," *Charleston News and Courier*, June 12, 1955.

48. "Color Blind Justice," *Charleston News and Courier*, July 4, 1955.

49. "The National Brain Washing," *Charleston News and Courier*, July 5, 1955.

50. "A Handbook for Southerners," *Charleston News and Courier*, July 6, 1955.

51. "Charleston Schools Asked to End Racial Segregation," *Charleston News and Courier*, July 15, 1955.

52. "Negro Petitioners' Names Are Released by Gaines," *Charleston News and Courier*, August 5, 1955.

53. "Combating the Negro Bias," *Charleston News and Courier*, July 15, 1955.

54. "Anti-Integration Group to Organize," *Charleston News and Courier*, July 21, 1955.

55. Bedingfield, *Newspaper Wars*, 154.

56. "Destroying Racial Harmony," *Charleston News and Courier*, July 22, 1955.

57. "NAACP Asks U.S. Court Here to Open Parks to Negroes," *Charleston News and Courier*, July 24, 1955.

58. W. D. Workman, "S.C. May Eliminate State Parks as Result of Negro Court Action," *Charleston News and Courier*, July 26, 1955.

59. "A Phony Word," *Charleston News and Courier*, July 27, 1955.

60. "First Class Citizenship," *Charleston News and Courier*, July 30, 1955.

61. "Petition Signers' Names Are Listed," *Charleston News and Courier*, August 10, 1955.

62. "Who Are the Signers?" *Charleston News and Courier*, August 11, 1955.

63. "Manifesto of Southern Rights," *Charleston News and Courier*, August 19, 1955.

64. Bedingfield, *Newspaper Wars*, 154–55.

65. "Manifesto of Southern Rights," *Charleston News and Courier*, August 19, 1955.

66. Bedingfield, *Newspaper Wars*, 154–55.

67. "Invite Them North," *Charleston News and Courier*, June 27, 1955.

68. "Send Negroes North," *Charleston News and Courier*, July 31, 1955.

69. "What Negroes Want," *Charleston News and Courier*, July 10, 1955.

70. "Never Will Integrate," *Charleston News and Courier*, July 28, 1955.

71. "NAACP's Goal," *Charleston News and Courier*, July 31, 1955.

72. "North Must Be Told," *Charleston News and Courier*, July 10, 1955.

73. "Negro Schools," *Charleston News and Courier*, August 5, 1955.

74. "Hold Color Line," *Charleston News and Courier*, August 9, 1955.

75. "Resist the Court," *Charleston News and Courier*, July 16, 1955.

76. "Mixed Baseball," *Charleston News and Courier*, August 7, 19552.

12. "A Dastardly Act"

1. Godfrey, *The Team Nobody Would Play*, 14–15, 21; Jackson, "Sacrifice and Errors," 80.

2. Godfrey, *The Team Nobody Would Play*, 21, 80.

3. "Colored Boys Prepare for Little League," *Charleston Evening Post*, March 8, 1954.

4. "Negro Little League Opens Wednesday at Harmon Field," *Charleston Evening Post*, April 17, 1954.

5. Godfrey, *The Team Nobody Would Play*, 17–18.

6. Interview with Leroy Major, June 2, 2020.

7. "1,500 Attend Opening Ceremonies of Cooper River Youth Baseball," *Charleston News and Courier*, April 13, 1954.

8. "Cannon Street Y Little Loop Sets Opening Monday," *Charleston News and Courier*, April 28, 1954.

9. Interview with John Rivers, April 20, 2020.

10. Interview with John Rivers, April 20, 2020.

11. Sapakoff, "Cannon Street All-Stars Get to Smile," *Charleston Post and Courier*, August 6, 2000.

12. Interview with John Rivers, April 20, 2020.

13. "Youth Leagues," *Charleston News and Courier*, July 4, 1955.

14. Gene Sapakoff, "The Most Significant Team You've Never Heard From," *Charleston Post and Courier*, October 25, 1995.

15. Sapakoff, "Little League's Civil War in '55," *Sports Illustrated*, October 30, 1995.

16. Quoted in Jackson, "Sacrifices and Errors," 84.

17. Godfrey, *The Team Nobody Would Play*, 34.

18. Godfrey, *The Team Nobody Would Play*, 33.

19. Interview with Gus Holt, March 3, 2018.

20. Interview with Bubba Jones and Sallie Frenkel, March 9, 2018.

21. "Regent Blasts Griffin on Tech-Pitt Games," *Atlanta Constitution*, December 1, 1955; Charles H. Martin, "Integrating New Year's Day: The Racial Politics of College Bowl Games in the American South," published in Lamb, *From Jack Johnson to LeBron James*, 283–84.

22. Interview with John Rivers, April 20, 2020.

23. Interview with Jack Bass, August 18, 2014.

24. Interview with Gus Holt, June 12, 2013.

25. Interview with Gus Holt, September 23, 2019.

26. Interview with Jack Bass, August 18, 2014.

27. Interview with Sallie Frenkel, Tesa Livingston, and Bubba Jones, March 9, 2018.

28. Interview with Sallie Frenkel, Bubba Jones, and Tesa Livingston, March 9, 2018.

29. Interview with Gus Holt, June 21, 2018.

30. Interview with John Rivers, July 30, 2015.

31. Interview with Jack Bass, August 18, 2014.

32. Interview with Leroy Major, June 2, 2020; Patrick Obley, "Segregation Holds Back Cannon Street All-Stars," *The State* (Columbia SC), July 15, 2007.

33. "White Little League Teams Bolt Tourney," *Charleston News and Courier*, July 8, 1955.

34. "White Little League Teams Bolt Tourney," *Charleston News and Courier*, July 8, 1955.

35. "Little Loop Tourney May Have 5 Teams," *Charleston News and Courier*, July 10, 1955.

36. "Little Loop Tourney May Have 5 Teams," *Charleston News and Courier*, July 10, 1955.

37. "15 S.C. Teams to Compete for Little League Crown," *Charleston News and Courier*, July 21, 1955.

38. "Negro Dispute Halts Play in Little League," *Times Standard* (Eureka CA), July 8, 1955.

39. "Donaldson Air Base to be Host," *Charleston News and Courier*, July 14, 1955.

40. "Two More Teams Quit LL Tourney," *Charleston News and Courier*, July 22, 1955.

41. "Jones Resigns as S.C. Little League Head," *Charleston News and Courier*, July 24, 1955.

42. "Seven More Teams Withdraw from Little League Tournament," *Charleston News and Courier*, July 26, 1955.

43. "Race Issue in Recreation," *Charleston News and Courier*, July 26, 1955.

44. *Charleston News and Courier*, July 26, 1955, 1.

45. "Seven More Teams Bolt LL Tourney," *Charleston News and Courier*, July 26, 1955.

46. "Seven More Teams Bolt LL Tourney," *Charleston News and Courier*, July 26, 1955

47. "S.C. Little Loop Tourney Disintegrates," *Charleston News and Courier*, July 27, 1955.

48. "S.C. Little Loop Tourney Disintegrates," *Charleston News and Courier*, July 27, 1955.

49. "S.C. Little Loop Meet Abandoned," *Charleston News and Courier*, July 27, 1955.

50. Peter McGovern, letter to South Carolina Little Leagues, July 27, 1955, courtesy of Lance Van Auken, Little League Baseball and Softball, Williamsport, Pennsylvania.

51. "Cannon Street Team Left in Cold," *Charleston News and Courier*, July 27, 1955.

52. "South Carolina White Little League Teams May Lose Franchises Next Year," *Hartford Courant*, July 30, 1955.

53. Grossfeld, "Justice Delayed," *Boston Globe*, August 20, 2002.

54. Interview with Gus Holt, June 12, 2013.

55. Interview with Gus Holt, November 10, 2012.

56. "Agitation and Hate," *Charleston News and Courier*, August 2, 1955.

57. Ed Campbell, "Soup's On," *Charleston News and Courier*, August 2, 1955.

58. Peter McGovern, letter to South Carolina Little Leagues, July 27, 1955.

59. "A Dastardly Act," *Pittsburgh Courier*, August 6, 1955.

60. Lamb, *Conspiracy of Silence*, 14.

61. "Now Batting, Jim Crow!" *The Trentonian* (Trenton NJ), August 11, 1955, Thomas R. Waring Jr. Papers, South Carolina Historical Society, Addlestone Library, College of Charleston.

62. Thomas Waring to Russell McGrath, editor, *Seattle Times*, Thomas R. Waring Jr. Papers, South Carolina Historical Society, Addlestone Library, College of Charleston.

63. Ed Brandt to Thomas R. Waring, July 28, 1955, Thomas R. Waring Jr. Papers, South Carolina Historical Society, Addlestone Library, College of Charleston.

64. Dick Herbert, "The Sports Observer," *Raleigh News and Observer*, July 15, 1955.

65. "Adult Bigotry," *Elmira (NY) Advertiser*, September 1, 1955.

66. "Bigotry in the Little League," *Delaware County Daily Times* (Chester IN), August 2, 1955.

67. Bill Beck, "It Won't Be Easy to Explain to an 8-Year-Old," *Tampa Bay Times* (St. Petersburg FL), July 29, 1955.

68. John W. Fox, "Little League Ban on Carolina Entry Victory for Bigots," *Binghamton (NY) Press and Sun-Bulletin*, July 31, 1955.

69. "We Were Shocked," *Oneonta (NY) Star*, August 1, 1955.

70. "Vermont Loop May Quit Little League in Protest Over Stand on Negroes," *Lowell (MA) Sun*, July 29, 1955.

71. "Chelsea L.L. Asks Decision on Racial Bias," *Boston Globe*, August 25, 1955.

72. Ruth Koshuk to Peter McGovern, August 13, 1955, courtesy of Lance Van Auken, Little League Baseball and Softball, Williamsport, Pennsylvania.

73. Ruth Koshuk to Robert Morrison, August 13, 1955.

74. Dick Young, "Sports of Kings and Queens," *New York Daily News*, July 31, 1955.

13. A Long Time Coming

1. "Real History of How Pensacola's Confederate Statue Came to Be," *Pensacola News Journal*, August 23, 2017, https://www.pnj.com/story/news/2017/08/23/real -history-how-pensacola-confederate-statue-came/592196001.

2. *Long Time Coming*, directed by Jon Strong.

3. *Long Time Coming*, directed by Jon Strong.

4. *Long Time Coming*, directed by Jon Strong.

5. *Long Time Coming*, directed by Jon Strong.

6. *Long Time Coming*, directed by Jon Strong.

7. *Long Time Coming*, directed by Jon Strong.

8. *Long Time Coming*, directed by Jon Strong.

9. Amy R. Connolly, "Report: Florida Led Southern States in Per Capita Lynchings," United Press International, Florida, February 11, 2015, https://www.upi.com/Top _News/US/2015/02/11/Report-Florida-led-Southern-states-in-per-capita-lynchings /4551423676057/; Jeff Kunerth, "Report: Orange County Ranks Sixth in Lynching from 1877–1950," *Orlando Sentinel*, February 11, 2015, https://www.orlandosentinel .com/news/breaking-news/os-lynchings-report-orange-county-20150211-story.html.

10. Dray, *At the Hands of Persons Unknown*, 83–84.

11. Dray, *At the Hands of Persons Unknown*, 83–84.

12. Stephen Hudak, "Ocoee, Where Massacre Occurred in 1920, Aims to Shed Past Reputation as 'Sundown' Town," *Orlando Sentinel*, November 19, 2018; Paul Ortiz, "Ocoee, Florida: Remembering 'the Single Bloodiest Day' in Modern U.S. Political History," *Facing South*, May 14, 2010; Andrew Maraniss, "Legacy of Bloody Election

Day Lingers in Florida Town," *The Undefeated*, November 4, 2016; "Several Killed in Election Riot at Ocoee, Florida," *Jacksonville (IL) Daily Journal*, November 4, 1920.

13. "Florida Senate Panel Backs Reparations for Descendants of Ocoee Massacre Victims at White Mob's Hands," *FlaglerLive*, January 22, 2020, https://flaglerlive.com/149292/ocoee-massacre/.

14. Dray, *At the Hands of Persons Unknown*, 344–50.

15. Greg Allen, "Florida's Dozier School for Boys: A True Horror Story," NPR, October 15, 2012.

16. Amari Jackson, "Murder, Forced Labor, and the Forgotten Black Boys of Florida's Dozier School for Boys," *Atlanta Black Star*, May 9, 2017.

17. Whitehead, *The Nickel Boys*, 2019.

18. "Senator Kicks on New Probe," *Tallahassee (FL) Democrat*, October 25, 1945.

19. "Florida Governor Orders Probe of Lynching of Farm Hand Removed from Jail," *New York Age*, October 20, 1945.

20. "Constable Accused of Driving Negro Prisoner to Death," *Miami Herald*, June 20, 1946.

21. "Three Lynchings Are Reported in 1945," *Pittsburgh Courier*, December 29, 1945.

22. Lamb, *Blackout*, 88.

23. "Warren Declares NAACP Head Came to State to Stir up Strife," *Orlando Sentinel*, December 30, 1951.

24. Lizette Alvarez and Cara Buckley, "Zimmerman Is Acquitted of Trayvon Martin Killing," *New York Times*, July 13, 2013.

25. Erika L. Wood, "Florida: An Outlier in Denying Voting Rights," Brennan Center for Social Justice, December 16, 2016, https://www.brennancenter.org /our-work/research-reports/florida-outlier-denying-voting-rights.

26. *Long Time Coming*, directed by Jon Strong.

27. *Long Time Coming*, directed by Jon Strong.

28. *Long Time Coming*, directed by Jon Strong.

29. Albert J. Dunmore, "Little League Champs Overcome Opposition to Reach Title," *Pittsburgh Courier*, August 27, 1955.

30. "District 1 LL Tilt Canceled—Riddles," *Pensacola (FL) News Journal*, August 3, 1955.

31. "Negroes to Play at Least 1 Game," *Pensacola (FL) News Journal*, August 9, 1955.

32. "Fla. Little League Has Mixed Playoff," *Baltimore Afro-American*, August 16, 1955.

33. "Fla. Little League Has Mixed Playoff," *Baltimore Afro-American*, August 16, 1955.

34. Kent Chetlain, "Race Issue Decision Delayed in Little League Tournament," *Orlando Sentinel*, August 8, 1955; Harold Albert, "City Little Leaguers Okay Negro Game," *Orlando Sentinel*, August 9, 1955.

35. "Fla. Little League Has Mixed Playoff," *Baltimore Afro-American*, August 16, 1955.

36. "City Little Leaguers Okay Negro Game," *Orlando Sentinel*, August 9, 1955.

37. "Council Bows Out of Row," *Orlando Evening Star*, August 9, 1955.

38. *Long Time Coming*, directed by Jon Strong.

39. Joe K. Rukenbrod, "Orlando Little Leaguers Win in 1st Interracial Game Here," *Orlando Sentinel*, August 10, 1955; "Fla. Little League Has Mixed Playoff," *Baltimore Afro-American*, August 16, 1955.

40. "Pensacola Negro Team Bows at Orlando, 5–0," *Pensacola Journal*, August 10, 1955.

41. *Long Time Coming*, directed by Jon Strong.

42. "Fla. Little League Has Mixed Playoff," *Baltimore Afro-American*, August 16, 1955.

43. Rukenbrod, "Orlando Little Leaguers Win," *Orlando Sentinel*, August 10, 1955.

44. Sam Lacy, "A to Z," *Baltimore Afro-American*, August 16, 1955.

45. Dunmore, "Little League Champs Overcome Opposition," *Pittsburgh Courier*, August 27, 1955.

46. "Fla. Little League Has Mixed Playoff," *Baltimore Afro-American*, August 16, 1955; Dunmore, "Little League Champs Overcome Opposition," *Pittsburgh Courier*, August 27, 1955.

47. Lacy, "A to Z," *Baltimore Afro-American*, August 16, 1955.

48. Lacy, "A to Z," *Baltimore Afro-American*, August 16, 1955.

49. "Negro Team Wins in Little League," *Paris (TX) News*, August 3, 1955.

50. "County All-Star Nine Gains Fans' Praise," *Marshall (TX) News Messenger*, August 4, 1955.

51. "County Team Topped in Meet Final," *Marshall (TX) News*, August 7, 1955.

52. Chuck Gormley, "Little Leaguers Faced Racial Injustices," *Camden (NJ) Courier-Post*, July 24, 2005.

53. Gormley, "Little Leaguers Faced Racial Injustices," *Camden (NJ) Courier-Post*, July 24, 2005.

54. "Little," *Philadelphia Inquirer*, August 20, 1995.

55. "Delaware Twp. LL Wins 1–0 for Reg. 4 Title," *Camden (NJ) Courier-Post*, August 15, 1955.

56. "Delaware Twp. LL Wins 1–0 for Reg. 4 Title," *Camden (NJ) Courier-Post*, August 15, 1955.

57. "Delaware Twp. LL Wins 1–0 for Reg. 4 Title," *Camden (NJ) Courier-Post*, August 15, 1955.

58. "Delaware Twp. LL Wins 1–0 for Reg. 4 Title," *Camden (NJ) Courier-Post*, August 15, 1955.

14. The Trip to Williamsport

1. "S.C. Negro Team to See LL Series," *New York Daily News*, August 9, 1955.

2. "Cannon Street All-Stars May Visit Williamsport," *Charleston News and Courier*, July 31, 1955.

3. "America in Black and White," *Nightline*, ABC, transcript, August 11, 2005.

4. "Reject Free Little Leagues Series Trip," *Logansport (IN) Pharos-Tribune*, August 9, 1955.

5. "Little Leaguers," *The Rhinelander* (Rhinelander WI), August 10, 1955.

6. Obley, "Segregation Holds Back Cannon Street All-Stars," *The State*, July 15, 2007.

7. Gene Sapakoff, "Never Too Late: 55 Cannon Street All-Stars to be Honored," *Charleston Post and Courier*, August 5, 2000.

8. Robert E. Pierre, "Left Out in 1955, Little League World Series is Bittersweet for South Carolina Team," *Washington Post*, August 11, 2011.

9. Grossfeld, "Justice Delayed," *Boston Globe*, August 20, 2002.

10. "Ku Klux Klan Rally First in S.C. in Two Years," *Charleston News and Courier*, June 12, 1955; "Klan Wizard Lashed Out at NAACP, Daily Papers," *Charleston News and Courier*, August 21, 1955.

11. Interview with John Rivers, April 20, 2020; quoted in Jackson, "Sacrifices and Errors," 105.

12. "Order FBI Probe of Lee Lynching," *New York Age*, June 4, 1955; "Exclusive!" *Pittsburgh Courier*, December 10, 1955.

13. Sam Johnson, "Atmosphere of Racial Hate Blamed for Belzoni Killing," *Jackson (MS) Clarion-Ledger*, May 23, 1955.

14. David T. Beito, "The Grim and Overlooked Anniversary of the Murder of the Rev. George Lee, Civil Rights Activist," History News Network, accessed July 11, 2020, http://hnn.us/articles/11744.html.

15. Beito, "The Grim and Overlooked Anniversary."

16. "White Farmer of Lincoln County Surrenders Self," *McComb (MS) Enterprise Journal*, August 15, 1955.

17. "But White to Take Closer Look at Brookhaven Race," *Delta Democrat-Times* (Brookhaven MS), August 22, 1955; "Aug. 13, 1955: Lamar Smith Murdered," Zinn Education Project, accessed July 11, 2020, https://www.zinnedproject.org/news/tdih/lamar-smith-murdered.

18. "South Carolina Team Accepts LLB Series Invitation," *Williamsport Sun*, August 20, 1955.

19. "America in Black and White," *Nightline*, ABC, transcript, August 11, 2005.

20. Godfrey, *The Team Nobody Would Play*, 18; interview with John Rivers, July 30, 2015.

21. Sapakoff, "Little League's Civil War in '55," *Sports Illustrated*, October 30, 1995.

22. Sapakoff, "Never Too Late," *Charleston Post and Courier*, August 5, 2000.

23. Sapakoff, "Never Too Late," *Charleston Post and Courier*, August 5, 2000.

24. Lacy and Newton, *Fighting for Fairness*, 99.

25. Lacy and Newton, *Fighting for Fairness*, 24.

26. Interviews with Sam Lacy, May 20, 1999, and May 27, 1995. See Lamb, *Conspiracy of Silence*, 57–59.

27. Reisler, *Black Writers/Black Baseball*, 12.

28. Lamb, *Conspiracy of Silence*, 59.

29. "1997 J. G. Taylor Spink Award: Sam Lacy," National Baseball Hall of Fame, accessed July 11, 2020, https://baseballhall.org/discover-more/awards/spink/sam-lacy.

30. Sam Lacy, "A to Z," *Baltimore Afro-American*, August 30, 1955.

31. Lacy, "A to Z," *Baltimore Afro-American*, August 30, 1955.

32. Lacy, "A to Z, " *Baltimore Afro-American*, August 30, 1955.

33. "Southern Little Leaguers Arrive for Series Finale," *Williamsport (PA) Sun-Gazette*, August 26, 1955.

34. Godfrey, *The Team Nobody Would Play*, 37.

15. "Let Them Play!"

1. "Black Little Leaguers Recognized at Last," *Indiana (PA) Gazette*, August 10, 2002.

2. Sapakoff, "Little League's Civil War in '55," *Sports Illustrated*, October 30, 1995.

3. "Cannon St. Team Attends Finale of LL World Series," *Charleston News and Courier*, August 27, 1955.

4. Interview with Vermort Brown, June 2, 2018.

5. Obley, "Segregation Holds Back Cannon Street All-Stars," *The State*, July 15, 2007.

6. David Maher, "A Place in Time: The Original Little League Field," Pennsylvania Historic Preservation, March 18, 2015, https://pahistoricpreservation.com/a-place-in-time-the-original-little-league-field/.

7. Lacy, "A to Z," *Baltimore Afro-American*, August 30, 1955.

8. Interview with Leroy Major, June 2, 2020.

9. Grossfeld, "Justice Delayed," *Boston Globe*, August 20, 2002; interview with John Rivers, April 30, 2015.

10. Interview with John Rivers, April 30, 2015.

11. Interview with Leroy Major, June 2, 2020.

12. "America in Black and White," *Nightline*, ABC, transcript, August 11, 2005.

13. "America in Black and White," *Nightline*, ABC, transcript, August 11, 2005.

14. Godfrey, *The Team Nobody Wanted to Play*, 37.

15. Interview with Vermort Brown, June 2, 2020; interview with Leroy Major, June 2, 2020; "America in Black and White," *Nightline*, ABC, transcript, August 11, 2005; Sapakoff, "Little League's Civil War in '55," *Sports Illustrated*, October 30, 1995.

16. "America in Black and White," *Nightline*, ABC, transcript, August 11, 2005.

17. Interview with John Rivers, April 20, 2020.

18. Sapakoff, "Never Too Late," *Charleston Post and Courier*, August 5, 2000.

19. Interview with Vermort Brown, June 2, 2018.

20. Interview with John Rivers, April 20, 2020.

21. Grossfeld, "Justice Delayed," *Boston Globe*, August 20, 2002.

22. Quoted in Ramon Jackson, "Sacrifices and Errors," 109.

23. Paul Franklin, "Little League World Series," *Lansing (MI) State Journal*, August 20, 1975.

24. "Jersey Nine Bows in Title Final, 4–3," *New York Times*, August 27, 1955.

25. "Delaware Twp. Team was First Integrated Team in Series," *Courier-Post* (Camden NJ), July 24, 2005.

26. Carl Lundquist, "Injured Player Hits Game-Winning Home in LL Series Climax," *Franklin (PA) News-Herald*, August 27, 1955.

27. Lundquist, "Injured Player," *Franklin (PA) News-Herald*, August 27, 1955.

28. Lundquist, "Injured Player," *Franklin (PA) News-Herald*, August 27, 1955.

29. Lacy, "A to Z," *Baltimore Afro-American*, August 30, 1955.

30. Godfrey, *The Team Nobody Would Play*, 42.

31. Interview with John Rivers, April 30, 2015.

32. Godfrey, *The Team Nobody Would Play*, 41.

33. Jim Morrison, "The Little League World Series' Only Perfect Game," *Smithsonian*, April 5, 2010, https://www.smithsonianmag.com/history/the-little-league-world-series-only-perfect-game-12835685/; Steve Wulf, "As Williamsport Opened Its Arms to Mexico's Team, Its Players Embraced the Legacy of Their Predecessors from Monterrey," ESPN, August 24, 2016, https://www.espn.com/moresports/story/_/id/17337253/little-league-world-series-mexico-little-league-world-series-team-embraces-legacy-legendary-little-giants; Olloa, "The Perfect Game."

34. Morrison, "The Little League World Series' Only Perfect Game," *Smithsonian*, April 5, 2010; Wulf, "As Williamsport Opened Its Arms to Mexico's Team," ESPN, August 24, 2016; Olloa, "The Perfect Game."

35. Morrison, "The Little League World Series' Only Perfect Game," *Smithsonian*, April 5, 2010.

16. Emmett Till

1. "Little Leaguers Give $52,587 to Polio Fund," *Williamsport Sun-Gazette*, August 27, 1955.

2. Godfrey, *The Team Nobody Would Play*, 38.

3. Interview with Vermort Brown, June 2, 2018.

4. Interview with John Rivers, April 30, 2020.

5. Gus Holt, "Team Demonstrated Its Courage," *Charleston Post and Courier*, February 23, 1995.

6. Obley, "Segregation Holds Back Cannon Street All-Stars," *The State*, July 15, 2007.

7. Godfrey, *The Team Nobody Would Play*, 40–41.

8. Godfrey, *The Team Nobody Would Play*, 41.

9. The Official Site of Delaware State Athletics, accessed July 11, 2020, https://dsuhornets.com/sports/HOF/roster/william-godfrey/800.

10. Godfrey, *The Team Nobody Would Play*, back cover.

11. Elizabeth Florio, "Longtime Southwest DeKalb Football Coach Buck Godfrey Honored with GACA Hall of Fame Nod," *Atlanta Magazine*, May 30, 2014, https://www.atlantamagazine.com/news-culture-articles/longtime-southwest-dekalb-football-coach-buck-godfrey-honored-with-gaca-hall-of-fame-nod/.

12. Craig Sager, "Mays Tops SW DeKalb in Newly Named 'Buck' Godfrey Stadium," *Atlanta Journal-Constitution*, September 19, 2015, https://www.ajc.com/blog/high-school-sports/mays-tops-dekalb-newly-named-william-buck-godfrey-stadium/QalL5HIroDeV8Q3r49rIEO/.

13. Florio, "Longtime Southwest DeKalb Coach," *Atlanta Magazine*, May 30, 2014.

14. John Kessler, "Holiday Hero: William 'Buck' Godfrey," *Atlanta Journal-Constitution*, September 21, 2015, https://www.ajc.com/lifestyles/holiday/holiday-hero-william-buck-godfrey/21U60JeSEioUnGbQHHdcTL/.

15. Florio, "Longtime Southwest DeKalb Coach," *Atlanta Magazine*, May 30, 2014.

16. Obley, "Segregation Holds Back Cannon Street All-Stars," *The State*, July 15, 2007.

17. Interview with John Rivers, April 20, 2020.

18. Tyson, *The Blood of Emmett Till*, 28–29.

19. Tyson, *The Blood of Emmett Till*, 15–16.

20. Tyson, *The Blood of Emmett Till*, 34.

21. Tyson, *The Blood of Emmett Till*, 52–54.

22. Tyson, *The Blood of Emmett Till*, 205–6.

23. Tyson, *The Blood of Emmett Till*, 260–61.

24. Tyson, *The Blood of Emmett Till*, 125–26.

25. Nicholas Stanford, "Another Scottsboro Case?" *Charleston News and Courier*, September 18, 1955.

26. Tyson, *The Blood of Emmett Till*, 123.

27. "Mississippi Sheriff Doubts Identity of Negro Boy," *Charleston News and Courier*, September 4, 1955.

28. "Mrs. Bryant Said Negro Sought Date," *Charleston News and Courier*, September 23, 1955.

29. "Mississippi Murder," *Charleston News and Courier*, September 2, 1955.

30. Tyson, *The Blood of Emmett Till*, 77. See also "Killers' Confession," *American Experience*, PBS, accessed May 10, 2020, https://www.pbs.org/wgbh/americanexperience/features/till-killers-confession/.

31. Tyson, *The Blood of Emmett Till*, 7; Richard Perez-Pena, "Woman Linked to 1955 Emmett Till Murder Tells Historians Her Claims Were False," *New York Times*, January 27, 2017.

32. Roberts and Klibanoff, *The Race Beat*, 86.

33. Roberts and Klibanoff, *The Race Beat*, 86.

34. Tyson, *The Blood of Emmett Till*, 210–12.

35. J. Williams, *Eyes on the Prize*, 88.

36. Interview with John Rivers, June 20, 2020.

37. Eig, *Opening Day*, 254.

38. Rampersad, *Jackie Robinson*, 204.

39. Jon Meacham, "'I Am a Black Man in a White World," *New York Times Book Review*, August 2, 2020; Robinson, *I Never Had It Made*, xxii.

40. "Little Boys Baseball Loop Formed by Columbia Group," *Orangeburg (SC) Times and Democrat*, August 10, 1955.

41. "South's Hassle with Little League Growing," *Charleston News and Courier*, August 18, 1955.

42. Ed Campbell, "Too Much of a Good Thing," *Charleston News and Courier*, August 26, 1955.

43. Sapakoff, "Little League's Civil War in '55," *Sports Illustrated*, October 30, 1995.

44. "Civil Rights Era Racism Still Haunts Youth Leagues," *Bluffton Today*, July 10, 2013, https://www.blufftontoday.com/article/20130710/NEWS/307109825.

45. J. Douglas Donehue, "Little League to File Cancellation Petition; Jones Prepared to Fight," *Charleston News and Courier*, October 23, 1958.

46. "Baseball," *South Carolina Encyclopedia*, accessed August 3, 2020, https://www.scencyclopedia.org/sce/entries/baseball/.

47. "Daniel H. Jones Dies at Age 56," undated newspaper clipping, Danny Jones File, Charleston County Public Library.

48. "Danny Jones, Recreation and Sports Official, Dies," *Charleston Evening Post*, September 28, 1966.

49. Danny Jones Sportsmanship Award, accessed 4 July 2020, https://s3.amazonaws.com/files.leagueathletics.com/Images/Club/22268/2019%20DANNY%20JONES%20SPORTSMANSHIP%20AWARDS-Revised.pdf.

50. "Dixie Youth League Wraps Up 50th Year," Ocala.com, April 7, 2005, https://www.ocala.com/news/20050807/dixie-youth-league-wraps-up-50th-year.

51. Van Auken and Van Auken, *Play Ball!*, 74–76.

52. Van Auken and Van Auken, *Play Ball!*, 73–75.

53. Van Auken and Van Auken, *Play Ball!*, 75–76.

54. "Little League Baseball in Court," *New York Times*, November 30, 1955.

55. Van Auken and Van Auken, *Play Ball!*, 76, 77, 80, 85.

56. "Founder of Little League Still Shunned; Organization Refuses to Recognize Carl Stotz's Contribution," *Los Angeles Times*, August 26, 1985, https://www.latimes.com/archives/la-xpm-1985-08-26-sp-26503-story.html/.

57. "Carl Stotz, 82, Founder of Little League Baseball," *New York Times*, June 5, 1992, https://www.nytimes.com/1992/06/05/sports/carl-stotz-82-founder-of-little-league-baseball.html.

17. "Paper Curtain"

1. Bedingfield, *Newspaper Wars*, 175.

2. Bedingfield, *Newspaper Wars*, 175.

3. Thomas R. Waring, "The Southern Case Against Desegregation," *Harper's Weekly*, January 1956, Thomas R. Waring Jr. Papers, South Carolina Historical Society, Addlestone Library, College of Charleston.

4. Interview with Thomas Waring, "Eyes on the Prize Interviews," October 25, 1985, http://digital.wustl.edu/e/eop/eopweb/war0015.0978.107thomasrwaring.html.

5. Waring, "The Southern Case Against Desegregation," *Harper's Weekly*, January 1956.

6. Waring, "The Southern Case Against Desegregation," *Harper's Weekly*, January 1956.

7. Waring, "The Southern Case Against Desegregation," *Harper's Weekly*, January 1956.

8. Waring, "The Southern Case Against Desegregation," *Harper's Weekly*, January 1956.

9. Waring, "The Southern Case Against Desegregation," *Harper's Weekly*, January 1956.

10. "50-Year News Career in Family Tradition," *Charleston (sc) Evening Post*, June 17, 1977.

11. No headline, article published in the *News and Courier*, not dated, Charleston County Public Library; Thomas R. Waring Jr. Papers, South Carolina Historical Society, Addlestone Library, College of Charleston.

12. "Segregation Article by Editor Praised by Rivers in House," *Charleston News and Courier*, January 6, 1956, Charleston County Public Library; Thomas R. Waring Jr. Papers, South Carolina Historical Society, Addlestone Library, College of Charleston.

13. Thomas R. Waring Jr. Papers, South Carolina Historical Society, Addlestone Library, College of Charleston.

14. "Rep. Rivers Labels Supreme Court and naacp as 'Unholy,'" *Charleston News and Courier*, November 29, 1955.

15. Thomas R. Waring to Wayne Freeman and James J. Kilpatrick, July 27, 1955, Thomas R. Waring Jr. Papers, South Carolina Historical Society, Addlestone Library, College of Charleston.

16. Carol Polsgrove, "Silencing Voices for Radical Change During the 1950s," *Nieman Reports*, September 15, 2001, https://niemanreports.org/articles/silencing -voices-for-racial-change-during-the-1950s/; see Sass, *Outspoken*.

17. Bedingfield, *Newspaper Wars*, 177–78.

18. Bedingfield, *Newspaper Wars*, 181.

19. Bedingfield, *Newspaper Wars*, 165–66; Bass and Thompson, *Ol' Strom*, 157–60.

20. Bedingfield, *Newspaper Wars*, 172–73.

21. J. Williams, *Eyes on the Prize*, 100–143, 118–19.

22. Jonathan Yardley, "Two Journalists Recall the Reporters Who Covered Some of the Nation's Most Hard-Fought Battles," *Washington Post*, November 26, 2006.

23. Kevin B. Schulz, "William F. Buckley and The National Review's Vile Race Stance: Everything You Need to Know About Conservatives and Civil Rights," *Salon*, June 7, 2015; Bedingfield, *Newspaper Wars*, 184–85, 187.

24. Bedingfield, *Newspaper Wars*, 187–90.

25. Bedingfield, *Newspaper Wars*, 187–90.

26. Sid Bedingfield, "Before Breitbart, there was the Charleston News and Courier," *The Conversation*, November 27, 2017.

27. Lee Edwards, "The Last Dixiecrat," *Heritage Foundation*, August 31, 2012; "Thurmond Joins the gop," *New York Times*, September 17, 1964; Jack Bass, *Ol' Strom*, 202–5.

28. Bedingfield, *Newspaper Wars*, 211–12.

29. Andrew Young, "The Cruel Record of States Rights," *Miami News*, August 11, 1980.

30. Rick Pearlstein, "Exclusive: Lee Atwater's Infamous 1981 Interview on the Southern Strategy," *The Nation*, November 13, 2012 .

31. Peter Baker, "Bush Made Willie Horton an Issue in 1988, and the Racial Scars Are Still Fresh," *New York Times*, December 3, 2018.

32. Jennifer Steinhauer, "Confronting Ghosts of South Carolina in 2000," *New York Times*, October 19, 2007.

33. Thomas R. Waring Jr., from a statement submitted to the Subcommittee on Constitutional Rights of the Senate Judiciary Committee on April 14, 1959, Congressional Record, p. 31, Thomas R. Waring Jr. Papers, South Carolina Historical Society, Addlestone Library, College of Charleston.

34. Mellinger, "Saving the Republic," 212.

35. Arthur Clement Jr. to Thomas R. Waring, August 20, 1959, Thomas R. Waring Jr. Papers, South Carolina Historical Society, Addlestone Library, College of Charleston.

36. Albert Varner to Tom Waring, July 15, 1957, Thomas R. Waring Jr. Papers, South Carolina Historical Society, Addlestone Library, College of Charleston.

37. "Thomas R. Waring Jr.," *Charleston Post and Courier*, March 10, 1993.

38. Bass and Thompson, *Ol' Strom*, 194.

18. The Civil Rights Movement in Charleston

1. Roberts and Klibanoff, *The Race Beat*, 223–24.

2. "Negroes Seek Diner Service," *Charlotte Observer*, February 3, 1960.

3. Roberts and Klibanoff, *The Race Beat*, 223–24.

4. Roberts and Klibanoff, *The Race Beat*, 224.

5. Roberts and Klibanoff, *The Race Beat*, 224–26.

6. Roberts and Klibanoff, *The Race Beat*, 225.

7. Woodward, *The Strange Career of Jim Crow*, 170.

8. Interviews with John Rivers, April 30, 2015, and April 20, 2020; Adam Parker, "The Sit-in That Changed Charleston," *Charleston Post and Courier*, August 2, 2013, https://www.postandcourier.com/archives/the-sit-in-that-changed-charleston/article _6a817d6e-e67b-53d8-8ec0-7fb0345b51cf.html. Other sources said meetings also took place at Emanuel AME Church.

9. Interviews with John Rivers, April 30, 2015, and April 20, 2020.

10. Parker, "The Sit-in That Changed Charleston," *Charleston Post and Courier*, August 2, 2013.

11. "24 Negroes Arrested in Sitdown," *Charleston Evening Post*, April 2, 1960.

12. "24 Negroes Arrested in Sitdown," *Charleston Evening Post*, April 2, 1960.

13. "FLASHBACK: Dr King Visited Charleston in 1962 and 1967," Live 5 WCSC, January 15, 2018, https://www.live5news.com/story/37266288/flashback-dr-king-visited -charleston-in-1962-july-1967/.

14. "'Build Baby Build,' King Tells Negroes," *Greenwood (SC) Index-Journal*, July 31, 1967.

15. Lorraine Boissoneault, "In 1968, Three Students Were Killed by Police, Few Remember the Orangeburg Massacre," *Smithsonian*, February 7, 2018.

16. Frank Myers, *Orangeburg (SC) Times and Democrat*, February 9, 1968.

17. Boissoneault, "In 1968, Three Students Were Killed by Police," *Smithsonian*, February 7, 2018.

18. O'Neill, "From the Shadows of Slavery," 248–49.

19. O'Neill, "From the Shadows of Slavery," 252.

20. O'Neill, "From the Shadows of Slavery," 263–68, 275, 277; "Marker Notes 1969 Charleston Hospital Strike," *The State*, October 1, 2013.

21. Stewart King, "Coretta King Pledges Support for Striking Hospital Workers," *Charleston News and Courier*, April 30, 1969; Jack Leland and Fred Rigsbee, "Issues Are Drawn, Stakes Are Big," *Charleston News and Courier*, May 13, 1969; Jack Bass, "1st Joint Statement in a Year," *Charlotte Observer*, April 21, 1969; Brian Hicks, "Coretta Scott King at Charleston at Hospital Strike March: Like Selma, Memphis, 'a National Test,'" *Charleston Post and Courier*, June 9, 2019; Hicks, *The Mayor*, 27–33.

22. Hicks, *The Mayor*, 40.

23. Adam Harris, "The Persistence of Segregation in Charleston," *The Atlantic*, September 29, 2020.

24. "City Schools Ordered to Integrate This Fall," *Charleston News and Courier*, August 23, 1955.

25. Doug Pardue, "A Walk That Changed History," *Charleston Post and Courier*, September 1, 2013; see Brown, "Civil Rights Activism in Charleston."

26. "Court Orders Gantt's Entry Into Clemson," *Charlotte Observer*, January 17, 1963.

27. David Folkenflik, "For Southern Papers, a Divisive Beat and History," NPR, November 29, 2006.

28. "A Brief History of the Citadel," The Citadel, July 1, 2012, https://www.citadel.edu/root/brief-history.

29. "Ball Crashes Negro Talk at S.C. College," *New York Daily News*, April 18, 1951.

30. "News from the South," undated letter to the editor, Thomas R. Waring Jr. Papers, South Carolina Historical Society, Addlestone Library, College of Charleston.

31. Linda L. Meggett, "Citadel of Trauma, the Untold Story of the Citadel's First Black Graduate," *Diverse Issues in Higher Education*, July 5, 2007, https://diverseeducation.com/article/8050/.

32. Meggett, "Citadel of Trauma," *Diverse Issues in Higher Education*, July 5, 2007.

33. Meggett, "Citadel of Trauma," *Diverse Issues in Higher Education*, July 5, 2007.

34. See Conroy, *The Lords of Discipline*.

35. Charles McGrath, "Reconciliation at the Citadel, Through Basketball," *New York Times*, March 2, 2009, https://www.nytimes.com/2009/03/03/sports/ncaabasketball/03citadel.html.

36. Robert Behre, "A 1977 Citadel Yearbook Photo Still Haunts Cadets," *Charleston Post and Courier*, March 10, 1919.

37. David Treadwell, "Outrage Refuses to Die Down in Scandal Over Hazing of Black Cadet at Citadel," *Los Angeles Times*, December 26, 1986; Behre, "A 1977 Citadel Yearbook Photo Still Haunts Cadets," *Charleston Post and Courier*, March 10, 2019.

38. Treadwell, "Outrage Refuses to Die Down in Scandal Over Hazing of Black Cadet at Citadel," *Los Angeles Times*, December 26, 1986.

39. Richard Fausset, "The Citadel Fought the Admission of Women; Now a Female Will Lead the Corps," *New York Times*, May 4, 2018.

40. Glenn Smith, "Ex-Cadet Alleges Racial Incidents," *Charleston Post and Courier*, March 13, 2013, https://www.postandcourier.com/archives/ex-cadet-alleges-racial-incidents-citadel-officials-mum-on-claims/article_ae358453-94e0-5b3e-9d80-4e00434e51e3.html.

41. Deanna Pan, "One Year After Cadets Don White Hood, The Citadel Recommits to Diversity and Racial Inclusion," *Charleston Post and Courier*, December 27, 2016, https://www.postandcourier.com/news/one-year-after-cadets-don-white-hoods-the-citadel-recommits-to-diversity-and-inclusion/article_fbadef82-c16c-11e6-88b0-d3c3f7e4aafd.html.

42. Christine Hauser, "Citadel Punishes Students for Costumes Evoking the KKK," *New York Times*, January 25, 2016; "KKK or Ghosts of Christmas Past: Citadel Cadets Suspended for White Hoods," AL.com, March 7, 2019, https://www.al.com/news/2015/12/kkk_or_the_ghosts_of_christmas.html.

43. Noah Feit, "Citadel Investigating 'Abhorrent Racist Statements' Made by Cadet on Social Media," *The State*, January 31, 2018.

44. Gene Sapakoff, "Sapakoff: The Citadel Should Stop Kneeling and Remove the Confederate Flag from its Chapel," *Charleston News and Courier*, November 2, 2017.

45. Justin Worland, "This is Why South Carolina Raised the Confederate Flag in the First Place," *Time*, June 22, 2015, https://time.com/3930464/south-carolina-confederate-flag-1962/.

46. Hicks, *The Mayor*, 195–96.

47. Joseph P. Riley, "Our Heritage and Our Future," *Charleston News and Courier*, April 4, 1987.

48. Hicks, *The Mayor*, 198–99.

49. "National NAACP Blasts Plan to Fly Black, Battle Flags Together," *Greenville (SC) News*, March 11, 1994.

50. Dan Hoover, "Economic Boycott of State Still Possible," *Baltimore Sun*, June 15, 1994.

51. Paul Shepard, "NAACP May Expand Sanctions Against States with Flag Symbols," *Orangeburg (SC) Times and Democrat*, July 13, 2000.

52. Hicks, *The Mayor*, 283.

53. "Criticism for Ravenel's Comments Continues," *Orangeburg (SC) Times and Democrat*, January 14, 2000.

54. "Flag Issues Dominates Legislature's Week," *Greenville (SC) News*, January 16, 2000.

55. Chris Burritt, "Flag Boycott in S.C. Takes Toll on Some Blacks," *Atlanta Constitution*, March 29, 2000.

56. Steven Reynolds, "Banner Faces House Scrutiny in Face of NAACP Opposition," *Greenwood (SC) Index-Journal*, April 13, 2001.

57. "Hodges Signs Bill Into Law," *Times and Democrat* (Orangeburg SC), May 2, 2000; "MLK Holiday Passes First House Hurdle," *Greenwood (SC) Index-Journal*, February 3, 2000.

58. Fleming Smith, "SC Heritage Act Stands in the Way of Removing Confederate Memorials," *Charleston Post and Courier*, June 11, 2020.

19. Gus Holt's Crusade

1. Interview with Gus Holt, March 3, 2018.

2. Interview with Gus Holt, March 3, 2018.

3. Interview with Gus Holt, March 3, 2018.

4. Interview with Gus Holt, March 3, 2018.

5. Interview with Gus Holt, March 3, 2018.

6. Jones, "It's 'Batter Up!' for Little League," *Charleston Post and Courier*, April 14, 1994.

7. Interview with Gus Holt, March 3, 2018.

8. Jones, "It's 'Batter Up!' for Little League," *Charleston Post and Courier*, April 14, 1994.

9. Interview with Gus Holt, March 3, 2018.

10. Interview with Gus Holt, March 3, 2018.

11. Interview with Gus Holt, March 3, 2018; Patricia B. Jones, "Holt Starts Second Baseball League," *Charleston Post and Courier*, April 14, 1994.

12. Interview with Gus Holt, March 3, 2018.

13. Interview with Gus Holt, March 3, 2018.

14. Hicks, *The Mayor*, 48–49.

15. "Remembering the 1955 Cannon Street All-Star Team," presentation, Patriots Point, Mt. Pleasant, South Carolina, February 11, 2016, https://livestream.com/patriotspointlive/cannonstreet/videos/112068548.

16. "Remembering the 1955 Cannon Street All-Star Team," February 11, 2016.

17. Debbie Elliott, "One of America's Longest Serving Mayors Steps Down," NPR, January 9, 2016.

18. Email with Brian Hicks, July 6, 2020.

19. "Remembering the 1955 Cannon Street All-Star Team," February 11, 2016.

20. Interview with Gus Holt, September 16, 2014.

21. Interview with Gus Holt, September 16, 2014.

22. Interview with Gus Holt, July 10, 2014.

23. Interview with Gus Holt, September 16, 2014.

24. Interviews with Gus Holt, July 10, 2014, and September 16, 2014.

25. Interview with Gus Holt, March 3, 2018.

26. Interview with Gus Holt, September 16, 2014.

27. Interview with Gus Holt, March 3, 2018.

28. Interview with Gus Holt, September 16, 2014.

29. Interview with Gus Holt, September 16, 2014.

30. Interview with Gus Holt, March 3, 2018.

31. Interview with Gus Holt, March 3, 2018.

32. Interview with Gus Holt, March 3, 2018. Holt was stationed at Fort Hood when Martin Luther King Jr. was assassinated.

33. Interview with Gus Holt, March 3, 2018. The Little Red Book, or *Quotations from Chairman Mao Zedong*, included about 270 aphorisms from the Communist Chinese leader.

34. Interview with Lamar Holt, May 28, 2020.

35. "Lenevar" is Ravenel spelled backward.

36. Interview with Gus Holt, July 10, 2014.

37. Interview with Gus Holt, March 3, 2018.

38. "America in Black and White," *Nightline*, ABC, transcript, August 11, 2005.

39. Interview with Gus Holt, March 3, 2018.

40. Interview with Vermort Brown, June 2, 2018.

41. Sapakoff, "Little League's Civil War in '55," *Sports Illustrated*, October 30, 1995.

42. Interview with Gus Holt, March 3, 2018.

43. Interview with Gus Holt, March 3, 2018.

44. Minutes of the Charleston City Council, March 8, 1994, Augustus Holt Papers, Avery Research Center; interview with Gus Holt, March 3, 2018.

45. Minutes of the Charleston City Council, March 8, 1994.

46. Minutes of the Charleston City Council, March 8, 1994.

47. Jones, "Holt Starts Second Baseball League," *Charleston Post and Courier*, April 14, 1994.

48. Minutes of the Charleston City Council, March 8, 1994.

49. Minutes of the Charleston City Council, March 8, 1994.

50. Interview with Gus Holt, March 3, 2018.

51. Patricia B. Jones and Deidre May, "Little League Baseball Is Flexing Its Muscles," *Charleston Post and Courier*, January 5, 1995, Augustus Holt Papers, Avery Research Center.

52. "Little League Welcomed to Charleston," *Coastal Times*, October 21, 1994, Augustus Holt Papers, Avery Research Center.

53. Augustus Holt, "They Just Wanted to Play Ball," *Charleston Post and Courier*, February 23, 1995, Augustus Holt Papers, Avery Research Center.

54. Patricia B. Jones, "YMCA Little League to Mark 40th Anniversary," *Charleston News and Courier*, February 23, 1995, Augustus Holt Papers, Avery Research Center.

55. Augustus Holt Papers, Avery Research Center.

56. "Charleston Little League to Meet on '95 Season," *Charleston Post and Courier*, February 9, 1995.

57. Elsa McDowell, "A Man Who Went to Bat for His Community," *Charleston Post and Courier*, November 15, 1994.

58. Interview with Gus Holt, July 28, 2014.

59. McDowell, "A Man Who Went to Bat for His Community," *Charleston Post and Courier*, November 15, 1994.

60. McDowell, "A Man Who Went to Bat for His Community," *Charleston Post and Courier*, November 15, 1994.

61. Emily Abedon, "Baseball Was the Start of a Close Relationship Between Lawrence Holt and His Father," *Charleston Post and Courier*, June 12, 1998.

62. Abedon, "Baseball Was the Start," *Charleston Post and Courier*, June 12, 1998.

63. Abedon, "Baseball Was the Start," *Charleston Post and Courier*, June 12, 1998.

64. Abedon, "Baseball Was the Start," *Charleston Post and Courier*, June 12, 1998.

65. Jonathan Sanchez, "Founder Devoted to Baseball," *Charleston Post and Courier*, January 16, 1997, Augustus Holt File, Charleston County Public Library.

66. Rico Reed, "Lenevar Baseball Field Named for Lawrence Holt," *Charleston Post and Courier*, July 29, 1999, Augustus Holt File, Charleston County Public Library.

67. Mike Mooneyham, "Holt's Legacy Honored by Plaque," *Charleston Post and Courier*, January 3, 2008, Augustus Holt Papers, Avery Research Center.

68. Interview with Gus Holt, September 25, 2019.

69. Interview with Lamar Holt, May 28, 2020; email correspondence with Steve Hoffius, July 29, 2020.

20. Return to Williamsport

1. "Banned Team Finally Gets Its Day in the Sun," *Pittsburgh Post-Gazette*, October 17, 2002.

2. Grossfeld, "Justice Delayed," *Boston Globe*, August 20, 2002.

3. "Little League Honors Cannon Street Team," *Greenwood (SC) Index-Journal*, August 11, 2002; interview with Leroy Major, June 2, 2020.

4. Grossfeld, "Justice Delayed," *Boston Globe*, August 20, 2002.

5. Interview with Leroy Major, June 2, 2020.

6. "A Big Day for Little League—and the Cannon Street All-Stars," BaseballRoundTable.com, August 16, 2013, http://www.baseballroundtable.com/a-big-day-for-little-league-and-the-cannon-street-ymca-all-stars/; Douglas E. Abrams, "Youth Sports Heroes of the Month: 1955 Cannon Street YMCA All-Stars Baseball Team," August 1, 2012, MomsTeam.com, https://www.momsteam.com/cannon-street-ymca-all-stars/youth-sports-heroes-month-1955-cannon-street-ymca-all-stars-baseball-te.

7. "Little League Honors Cannon Street Team," *Greenwood (SC) Index-Journal*, August 11, 2002.

8. Interview with Vermort Brown, June 2, 2018.

9. Interview with John Rivers, April 20, 2020.

10. Sapakoff, "Little League's Civil War in '55," *Sports Illustrated*, October 30, 1995.

11. Sapakoff, "Little League's Civil War in '55," *Sports Illustrated*, October 30, 1995.

12. "Israel, Jordan Match Up Signals an End of an Era," *Wilkes-Barre (PA) Times-Leader*, August 23, 1994.

13. Sapakoff, "Little League's Civil War in '55," *Sports Illustrated*, October 30, 1995.

14. Sapakoff, "Little League's Civil War in '55," *Sports Illustrated*, October 30, 1995.

15. Sapakoff, "Little League's Civil War in '55," *Sports Illustrated*, October 30, 1995.

16. *World News Tonight*, ABC, transcript, August 13, 2005.

17. Andrew Carter, "After 50 Years, S.C. Team Hears Cheers Again," *Baltimore Sun*, August 27, 2005.

18. Interview with Lance Van Auken, June 30, 2018.

19. Sapakoff, "Cannon Street All-Stars Get to Smile," *Charleston Post and Courier*, August 6, 2000.

20. Sapakoff, "Never Too Late," *Charleston Post and Courier*, August 5, 2000.

21. *Talk of the Nation*, NPR, transcript, August 22, 2005.

22. Jackson, "Sacrifices and Errors," 116.

23. Obley, "Segregation Holds Back Cannon Street All-Stars," *The State*, July 15, 2007.

24. Gene Sapakoff, "Crowd Roars for Cannon Street All-Stars," *Charleston Post and Courier*, August 20, 2005.

25. Carter, "After 50 Years, S.C. Team Hears Cheers Again," *Baltimore Sun*, August 27, 2005.

26. Sapakoff, "Crowd Roars for Cannon Street All-Stars," *Charleston Post and Courier*, August 20, 2005.

27. Obley, "Segregation Holds Back Cannon Street All-Stars," *The State*, July 15, 2007.

28. "America in Black and White," *Nightline*, ABC, transcript, August 11, 2005.

29. "America in Black and White," *Nightline*, ABC, transcript, August 11, 2005.

30. *World News Tonight*, ABC, transcript, August 13, 2005.

31. Gene Sapakoff, "All-Stars off to D.C.: 1955 Team from Cannon Street Y Seeks Recognition," *Charleston Post and Courier*, August 15, 2011.

32. Raven, *Let Them Play*.

33. George Will, "Cannon Street All Stars Reminding America How Far We've Come," *Washington Post*, January 12, 2012, https://www.washingtonpost.com/opinions/cannon-street-all-stars-reminding-america-how-far-weve-come/2012/01/10/gIQA6rlwrP_story.html.

34. "A Big Day for Little League and the Cannon Street All-Stars," BaseballRoundTable.com, August 16, 2013.

21. No City Owes Its Success More

1. Felicia R. Lee, "Bench of Memory at Slavery's Gateway," *New York Times*, July 28, 2008.

2. Toni Morrison, *Beloved*.

3. Bruce Scott, "A Mother's Desperate Act: 'Margaret Garner,'" NPR, November 19, 2010.

4. Monica Rohr, "Discovery of African-American Graves in Texas Highlights 'Moment of Reckoning,'" *USA Today*, December 27, 2018, https://www.usatoday.com/story/news/2018/12/27/graves-95-african-americans-forced-into-labor-after-slavery-convict-leasing-system-texas/2364201002/.

5. Lee, "Bench of Memory at Slavery's Gateway," *New York Times*, July 28, 2008.

6. Jason Silverstein, "The Persistence of Whitewashing," *New Republic*, May 31, 2018.

7. Stodghill, "In Charleston, Coming to Terms with the Past," *New York Times*, November 15, 2016.

8. "Talk of Reparations for Slavery Moves to State Capitols," PEW, October 3, 2019.

9. See Ta-Nehisi Coates, "The Case for Reparations," *Atlantic*, June 15, 2014.

10. Kriston McIntosh, Emily Moss, Ryan Nunn, and Jay Shambaugh, "Examining the Black-White Wealth Gap," Brookings Institute, February 27, 2020.

11. Jung Hyan Choi, "Breaking Down the Black-White Home Ownership Gap," Urban Institute, February 21, 2020, https://www.urban.org/urban-wire/breaking -down-black-white-homeownership-gap.

12. Emily Tate, "Graduation Rates and Race," *Inside Higher Ed*, April 26, 2017.

13. "Economic Drivers: Tourism," Charleston Regional Development Alliance, accessed March 2, 2020, https://www.crda.org/doing-business-here/economic-drivers /tourism/.

14. Evening Post Publishing, https://eveningpostnewspaperjobs.com/?page_id=44.

15. "Home on Charleston's Battery Brings Record $7.7. Million," *Bluffton Today*, August 20, 2015.

16. Traci Magnus, "Captivating History of Rainbow Row," Charleston.com, September 28, 2017.

17. Ritu Prasad, "The Awkward Questions about Slavery from Tourists in US South," BBC News, October 2, 2019.

18. "Barry Unsworth on the Middle Passage," PBS, https://www.pbs.org/wgbh /aia/part1/1i3068.html.

19. Bob Herbert, "In America; Of Flags and Slurs," *New York Times*, January 20, 2000.

20. Will Moredock, "End of a Dynasty: The Ravenels Were Victims of a Changing Culture," *Charleston City Paper*, June 18, 2008.

21. Schuyler Kropf, "Ravenel Sentenced on Federal Drug Charges," *Charleston Post and Courier*, March 14, 2008.

22. Will Moredock, "The Ravenels Were Victims of a Changing Culture," *Charleston City Paper*, June 18, 2008.

23. "Former Southern Charm Star Thomas Ravenel Pleads Guilty to Assault and Battery Charge," *Deadline*, September 11, 2019.

24. Joelle Goldstein, "Thomas Ravenel Puts His $3.9 Million South Carolina Plantation on the Market Amid Ongoing Legal Issues," *People*, June 26, 2019.

25. Meredith Nardino, "Southern Charm's Kathryn Dennis Apologizes After Sending Racially Insensitive Message," *US*, May 11, 1920. MAGA refers to "Make America Great Again," the campaign slogan of Donald Trump when he ran for president in 2016.

26. Foster, *Legendary Locals of Charleston*, 60.

27. Jenna Schiferl, "College of Charleston Black Alumni, Students Push for Systematic Reform," *Charleston Post and Courier*, June 28, 2020.

28. "A Brief History of the College," College of Charleston, https://www.cofc.edu /about/historyandtraditions/briefhistory.php.

29. Talia Avakian, "Take a Tour of America's Most Beautiful College Campus," *Travel and Leisure*, July 21, 2017.

30. Morrison, *A History of the College of Charleston*, 43–44; Schiferl, "College of Charleston Black Alumni, Students Push for Systematic Reform," *Charleston Post and Courier*, June 28, 2020.

31. The author of this book was a professor of communication at the College of Charleston from 1997 to 2012.

32. Ry Rivard, "Charleston Divided," *Inside Higher Ed*, March 26, 2014; Diane Knich, "McConnell's Support for Rebel Banner Raises Flag," *Charleston Post and Courier*, December 12, 2013.

33. Melissa Block, "150 Years Later, America's Civil War Still Divides," NPR, April 8, 2011.

34. Block, "150 Years Later, America's Civil War Still Divides."

35. Rivard, "Charleston Divided," *Inside Higher Ed*, March 26, 2014; Knich, "McConnell's Support for Rebel Banner," *Charleston Post and Courier*, December 12, 2013.

36. Rebecca R. Ruiz, "Baltimore Officers Will Face No Federal Charges in Death of Freddie Gray," *New York Times*, September 12, 2017.

37. "Student in Freddie Gray Halloween Costume Faces Heat from C of C's Black Student Union," *Charleston City Paper*, October 31, 2017; Joe Marusak, "College of Charleston Investigates Racially Derogatory Halloween Costume Photo," *Charlotte Observer*, October 30, 2017.

38. "College of Charleston Is Investigating Another Racist Social Media Post," *Charleston City Paper*, March 7, 2019.

39. Mark Berry, "C of C's New President is Top Flight," *College of Charleston Magazine*, July 2, 2019.

40. "C of C Day: A Moment for Celebration and Reflection," *The College Today*, January 30, 2020.

41. "President Hsu Vows to Address Racial Inequalities at CofC," *The College Today*, June 11, 2020.

42. Melissa Gomez, "Charleston Apologizes for City's Role in Slave Trade," *New York Times*, June 19, 2018.

43. Melissa Block, "150 Years Later, America's Civil War Still Divides," NPR, April 8, 2011.

44. Ted Mellnick, "The Remarkable History of Charleston's Racial Divide, as Told by the City's Silent Statues," *Washington Post*, June 24, 2015, https://www.washingtonpost.com/news/wonk/wp/2015/06/24/the-remarkable-history-of-charlestons-racial-divide-as-told-by-the-citys-silent-statues/.

45. Denmark Vesey House, https://www.scpictureproject.org/charleston-county/denmark-vesey-house.html.

46. Kinsey Gidick, "Damaged Kress Plaque Honoring Lunch Counter Sit-Ins Could Be Reinstalled Before End of Year," *Charleston City Paper*, August 15, 2007, https://www.charlestoncitypaper.com/story/damaged-kress-plaque-honoring-lunch-counter-sit-in-could-be-reinstalled-before-end-of-year.

47. International African American Museum, https://iaamuseum.org/.

48. "Robert F. Morrison," *Charleston News and Courier*, April 24, 1970, Robert Morrison Papers, Charleston County Public Library.

49. Patrick Obley, "Coach Touched All the Bases: Civil Rights Era Legend."

22. The "Emanuel Nine"

1. Glenn Smith, Jennifer Berry Hawes, Abigail Darlington, "Graphic Crime Scene Photos at Dylann Roof's Trial Show Carnage inside Emanuel AME Church," *Charleston Post and Courier*, December 8, 2016; Richard Perez-Pina, "Sentenced to Death: A Look at Dylan Roof's Rampage and Aftermath," *New York Times*, January 10, 2017, https://www.nytimes.com/2017/01/10/us/dylann-roof-trial-sentencing-verdict.html; Frazier, Powers, and Wentworth, *We Are Charleston*, 2.

2. "Slain Pastor Was an Icon," *Anniston (AL) Star*, June 19, 2015.

3. "Water Scott Shooting: Michael Slater, Ex-Officer, Sentenced to 20 Years in Prison," NBC News, December 9, 2017, https://www.nbcnews.com/storyline/walter-scott-shooting/walter-scott-shooting-michael-slager-ex-officer-sentenced-20-years-n825006.

4. "Slain Pastor Was an Icon," *Anniston (AL) Star*, June 19, 2015.

5. "Black Lives Upended by Policing: The Raw Videos Sparking Outrage," *New York Times*, August 19, 2017 (updated August 19, 2018), https://www.nytimes.com/interactive/2017/08/19/us/police-videos-race.html.

6. Perez-Pina, "Sentenced to Death," *New York Times*, January 10, 2017.

7. Mark 4:14–20, English Standard Version; Frazier, Powers, and Marjorie Wentworth, *We Are Charleston*, 2.

8. Frazier, Powers, and Wentworth, *We Are Charleston*, 3.

9. Frazier, Powers, and Wentworth, *We Are Charleston*, 14–15.

10. Smith et al., "Graphic Crime Scene Photos," *Charleston Post and Courier*, December 8, 2016.

11. Smith et al., "Graphic Crime Scene Photos," *Charleston Post and Courier*, December 8, 2016.

12. Smith et al., "Graphic Crime Scene Photos," *Charleston Post and Courier*, December 8, 2016.

13. Smith et al., "Graphic Crime Scene Photos," *Charleston Post and Courier*, December 8, 2016.

14. Jelani Cobb, "Inside the Trial of Dylann Roof," *New Yorker*, January 30, 2017; Rebecca Hersher, "Dylann Roof Sentence to Death," NPR, January 10, 2017.

15. Perez-Pina, "Sentenced to Death," *New York Times*, January 10, 2017.

16. Jamelle Bouie, "Brothers in White Resentment," *Slate*, December 15, 2016.

17. Joseph Tanfani, Timothy B. Phelps, and Richard A. Serrano, "Online Manifesto Linked to Charleston Suspect Dylann Roof Shows Evolving Views on Race," *Los Angeles Times*, June 20, 2015.

18. Bouie, "Brothers in White Resentment," *Slate*, December 15, 2016.

19. Rosalind Bentley, "After Dylann Roof, What's the Fate of the Confederate Flag," *Atlanta Journal-Constitution*, January 9, 2017; Francis Robles, "Dylann Roof Photos and a Manifesto Are Post on Website," *New York Times*, June 21, 2015.

20. Elizabeth Chuck and Jon Schuppe, "Crowd Cheers as Confederate Flag Removed from South Carolina Capitol," NBC News, July 10, 2015.

21. Jesse Byrnes, "Lindsey Graham Defends Confederate Flag," *The Hill*, June 19, 2015.

22. Frances Robles, Richard Fausset, and Michael Barbaro, "Nikki Haley, South Carolina Governor, Calls for Removal of Confederate Battle Flag," *New York Times*, June 22, 2015.

23. Daniel Strauss, "Lindsey Graham Shifts on Confederate Flag," *Politico*, June 22, 2015.

24. Alan Blinder and Richard Fausett, "South Carolina House Votes to Remove Confederate Flag," *New York Times*, July 10, 2015, https://www.nytimes.com/2015/07/10/us/confederate-flag-south-carolina.html.

25. Aimee Ortiz, "Nikki Haley's Confederate Flag Comments Spark Backlash," *New York Times*, December 7, 2019.

26. Interview with Lamar Holt, May 20, 2020.

27. "Skepticism of 'New South' Slow to Give Ground," *Detroit News*, June 28, 2015.

28. "The State of Racial Disparities in Charleston County, South Carolina, 2000–2015," report commissioned by the College of Charleston Race and Social Justice Initiative, 5, 73, 75, https://rsji.cofc.edu/wp-content/uploads/2017/01/The-State-of-Racial-Disparities-in-Charleston-County-SC-Rev.-11-14.pdf.

29. Lena V. Groeger, Annie Waldman, and David Eads, "Miseducation: Is There Racial Inequalities at Your School?" *ProPublica*, October 16, 2018.

30. Brentin Mock, "How Slavery Built Charleston," *Bloomberg CityLab*, July 20, 2015, https://www.bloomberg.com/news/articles/2015-07-20/how-confederate-monuments-obscure-the-economic-history-of-slavery-in-charleston.

31. Juliana Menasch Horowitz, Anna Brown, and Kiana Cox, *Race in America 2019*, Pew Research Center, April 9, 2019, https://www.pewsocialtrends.org/2019/04/09/race-in-america-2019/.

32. Michael Barbaro, "Donald Trump Clung to 'Birther' Lie for Years, and Still Isn't Apologetic," *New York Times*, September 17, 2016.

33. "Donald Trump Announces Presidential Run With Eccentric Speech," *The Guardian*, June 16, 2015, https://www.theguardian.com/us-news/2015/jun/16/donald-trump-announces-run-president.

34. Bouie, "Brothers in White Resentment," *Slate*, December 15, 2016.

35. Yoni Applebaum "I Alone Can Fix it," *The Atlantic*, July 21, 2016.

36. Deana Pan and Jennifer Berry Hawes, "In 1944, George Stinney Was Young, Black and Sentenced to Die," *Charleston Post and Courier*, March 25, 2018, https://www.postandcourier.com/news/special_reports/in-1944-george-stinney-was-young-black-and-sentenced-to-die/article_a87181dc-2924-11e8-b4e0-4f958aa5ba1c.html.

37. Interview with Brian Hicks, May 30, 2018.

38. Interview with Ron Menchaca, June 19, 2020.

39. Interview with Brian Hicks, May 30, 2018.

40. "Public Service," Pulitzer Prizes, accessed July 1, 2020, https://www.pulitzer
.org/prize-winners-by-category/204; "Breaking News Reporting," Pulitzer Prizes,
accessed June 29, 2020, https://www.pulitzer.org/prize-winners-by-category/205.

41. "Breaking News Reporting."

42. "Feature Photography," Pulitzer Prizes, accessed June 29, 2020, https://www
.pulitzer.org/prize-winners-by-category/217.

23. John Rivers's Dream

1. Derrek Asberry, "Gus Holt, Longtime Advocate for Charleston's Cannon Street
Team, Has Died," *Charleston Post and Courier*, April 17, 2020.

2. Interview with Lamar Holt, May 28, 2020; Patricia Silva, "Black Women Far
More Likely Than Other Americans to Develop Sarcoidosis, AOA Reports," *Sarcoidosis News*, June 7, 2017.

3. Asberry, "Gus Holt," *Charleston Post and Courier*, April 17, 2020.

4. Interview with Lamar Holt, May 28, 2020.

5. Interview with Lamar Holt, May 28, 2020.

6. Interview with Lamar Holt, May 28, 2020.

7. Interview with Steve Hoffius, May 1, 2020.

8. Email with Steve Hoffius, May 4, 2020.

9. Interview with John Rivers, April 20, 2020.

10. Interview with John Rivers, April 20, 2020.

11. Interview with Leroy Major, June 2, 2020.

12. Alex Altman, "Why the Killing of George Floyd Sparked an American Outrage," *Time*, June 4, 2020; Evan Hill, Ainara Tiefenthäler, Christiaan Triebert, Drew
Jordan, Haley Willis, and Robin Stein, "How George Floyd Was Killed in Police
Custody," *New York Times*, May 31, 2020, https://www.nytimes.com/2020/05/31/us
/george-floyd-investigation.html.

13. Altman, "Why the Killing of George Floyd Sparked an American Outrage,"
Time, June 4, 2020; Hill et al., "How George Hill Was Killed in Police Custody," *New
York Times*, May 31, 2020.

14. Email correspondence with Brian Hicks, July 6, 2020.

15. Interview with John Rivers, April 20, 2020.

16. Interview with John Rivers, April 20, 2020.

17. Interview with John Rivers, April 20, 2020.

18. Interview with John Rivers, April 20, 2020.

19. Email correspondence with John Rivers, December 1, 2020.

20. Sapakoff, "Little League's Civil War in '55," *Sports Illustrated*, October 30, 1995.

BIBLIOGRAPHY

Archives and Manuscript Materials

Avery Research Center, Charleston SC.
>Augustus Holt Papers.
>Esau Jenkins File.
>Lee Drago Papers.
>Robert Morrison File.

Charleston County Public Library, Charleston SC.
>Augustus Holt File.
>Danny Jones File.
>J. Waties Waring File.
>Robert Morrison Papers.

South Carolina Historical Society, Addlestone Library, College of Charleston, Charleston SC.
>Charleston YMCA Collection.
>Thomas R. Waring Jr. Papers.

Published Works

Abrams, Douglas E. "The Little League Champions Benched by Jim Crow in 1995: Resistance and Reform after *Brown v. Board of Education.*" *Journal of Supreme Court History* 38, no. 1 (2013): 51–62.

Aptheker, Herbert, ed. *A Documentary History of the Negro People in the United States.* Vols. 3–5. New York: Citadel, 1973, 1974, 1993.

Ball, Edward. *Slaves in the Family.* New York: Farrar, Straus, and Giroux, 1998.

Bass, Jack. *The Orangeburg Massacre.* Macon GA: Mercer University Press, 1996.

Bass, Jack, and Marilyn Thompson. *Ol' Strom: An Unauthorized Biography of Strom Thurmond.* Marietta GA: Longstreet Press, 1998.

Bass, Jack, and W. Scott Poole. *The Palmetto State: The Making of Modern South Carolina.* Columbia: University of South Carolina Press, 2012.

Bedingfield, Sid. *Newspaper Wars: Civil Rights and White Resistance in South Carolina, 1935–1965.* Urbana: University of Illinois Press, 2017.

Berlin, Ira. "American Slavery in History and Memory and the Search for Social Justice." *Journal of American History* 90, no. 4 (March 2004): 1251–68.

Biddle, Daniel R., and Murray Dubin. *Tasting Freedom: Octavius Catto and the Battle for Equality in Civil War America.* Philadelphia: Temple University Press, 2010.

Branch, Taylor. *Parting the Waters: America in the King Years, 1954–1963*. New York: Simon and Schuster, 1988.

Brinson, Claudia Smith. *Stories of Struggle: The Clash Over Civil Rights in South Carolina*. Columbia: University of South Carolina Press, 2019.

Brown, Millicent. "Civil Rights Activism in Charleston, South Carolina, 1940–1970." PhD diss., Florida State University, 1997.

Budiansky, Stephen. *The Bloody Shirt: Terror After Appomattox*. New York: Viking Press, 2008.

Burns, Ken. *Baseball*. Public Broadcasting Service, 2010. https://www.pbs.org/show/baseball/.

Capers, Gerald M. *John C. Calhoun: Opportunist: A Reappraisal*. Gainesville: University of Florida Press, 1960.

Carriere, Michael. "'A Diamond Is a Boy's Best Friend': The Rise of Little League Baseball, 1939–1964." *Journal of Sport History* 32, no. 3 (Fall 2005): 351–78.

Cash, W. J. *The Mind of the South*. New York: Knopf, 1941.

Cherron, Katherine Mellen. *Freedom's Teacher: The Life of Septima Clark*. Chapel Hill: University of North Carolina Press, 2012.

Conroy, Pat. *The Lords of Discipline*. New York: Dial, 1980.

Davis, William C., ed. *A Fire-Eater Remembers: The Confederate Memoir of Robert Barnwell Rhett*. Columbia: University of South Carolina Press, 2000.

D'Orso, Michael. *Like Judgment Day: The Ruin and Redemption of a Town Called Rosewood*. New York: Putnam, 1996.

Drago, Edmund Lee. *Charleston's Avery Center: From Education and Civil Rights to Preserving the African-American Experience*. Charleston SC: History Press, 1990.

———. *Hurrah for Hampton: Black Red Shirts in South Carolina during Reconstruction*. Fayetteville: University of Arkansas Press, 1998.

Dray, Philip. *At the Hands of Persons Unknown: The Lynching of Black America*. New York: Modern Library, 2002.

Duberman, Martin Bauml. *Paul Robeson*. London: Pan Books, 1991.

Edgar, Walter. *South Carolina: A History*. Columbia: University of South Carolina, 1998.

Egerton, Douglas R. *The Wars of Reconstruction: The Brief, Violent History of America's Most Progressive Era*. New York: Bloomsbury Press, 2014.

Egerton, John. *Speak Now Against the Day*. Chapel Hill: University of North Carolina Press, 1994.

Eig, Jonathan. *Opening Day: The Story of Jackie Robinson's First Season*. New York: Simon and Schuster, 2007.

Ellison, Ralph. *Invisible Man*. New York: Random House, 1952.

Faucett, Gary. *A Team to Remember*. Bloomington IN: Xlibris, 2011.

Fine, Gary. *With the Boys: Little League Baseball and Preadolescent Culture*. Chicago: University of Chicago Press, 1987.

Foster, Mary Preston. *Legendary Locals of Charleston*. Charleston SC: Arcadia Publishing, 2013.

Franklin, John Hope. *From Slavery to Freedom: A History of African-Americans.* New York: Knopf, 1994.

Frazier, Herb, Bernard Edward Powers, and Marjory Wentworth. *We Are Charleston: Tragedy and Triumph at Mother Emanuel.* Nashville TN: W. Publishing Group, 2016.

Fredrickson, Kari. *Dixiecrat Revolt and the End of the Solid South, 1932–1968.* Chapel Hill: University of North Carolina Press, 2001.

Frommer, Harvey. *Growing Up at Bat: Fifty Years of Little League Baseball.* New York: Pharos, 1989.

Gathers, Barbara. *From Back da Green: Stories from the Heart.* Denver CO: Outskirts, 2015.

Gergel, Richard. *Unexampled Courage: The Blinding of Sgt. Isaac Woodard and the Awakening of President Harry S. Truman and Judge J. Waties Waring.* New York: Sarah Crichton Books, 2019.

Godfrey, Buck. *The Team Nobody Would Play.* Pittsburgh PA: Dorrance, 2008.

Gravely, William B. *They Stole Him Out of Jail: Willie Earle, South Carolina's Last Lynching Victim.* Columbia: University of South Carolina Press, 2019.

Hawes, Jennifer Berry. *Grace Will Lead Us Home: The Charleston Church Massacre and the Hard, Inspiring Journey to Forgiveness.* New York: St. Martin's Press, 2019.

Hicks, Brian. *In Darkest South Carolina: J. Waties Waring and the Secret Plan That Sparked a Civil Rights Movement.* Charleston SC: Evening Post Books, 2018.

———. *The Mayor: Joe Riley and the Rise of Charleston.* Charleston SC: Evening Post Books, 2015.

Jackson, Ramon. "Sacrifices and Errors: The Story of the Cannon Street YMCA All-Stars." Master's thesis, College of Charleston and The Citadel, 2007.

Kantrowitz, Stephen. *Ben Tillman and the Reconstruction of White Supremacy.* Chapel Hill: University of North Carolina Press, 2000.

Kelly, Joseph. *America's Longest Siege: Charleston, Slavery, and the Slow March Toward the Civil War.* New York: Overlook Press, 2013.

Kirsch, George. *Baseball in Blue and Gray.* Princeton NJ: Princeton University Press, 2003.

Kluger, Richard. *Simple Justice: The History of Brown v. Board of Education, the Epochal Supreme Court Decision that Outlawed Segregation, and of Black America's Century-Long Struggle for Equality Under Law.* New York: Vintage, 1975.

Kytle, Ethan J., and Blain Roberts. *Denmark Vesey's Garden: Slavery and Memory in the Cradle of the Confederacy.* New York: New Press, 2018.

Lacy, Sam, and Moses Newton. *Fighting for Fairness: The Life Story of Hall of Fame Sportswriter, Sam Lacy.* Centreville MD: Tidewater Publisher, 1998.

Lamb, Chris. *Blackout: The Untold Story of Jackie Robinson's First Spring Training.* Lincoln: University of Nebraska Press, 2004.

———. *Conspiracy of Silence: Sportswriters and the Long Campaign to Desegregate Baseball.* Lincoln: University of Nebraska Press, 2012.

————, ed. *From Jack Johnson to LeBron James: Sports, Media, and the Color Line*. Lincoln: University of Nebraska Press, 2016.

Lewis, David Levering. *W. E. B. Du Bois: The Fight for Equality and the American Century, 1919–1963*. New York: Henry Holt, 2000.

Martin, Charles H. "Integrating New Year's Day: The Racial Politics of College Bowl Games in the American South." In *From Jack Johnson to LeBron James: Sports, Media, and the Color Line*, edited by Chris Lamb. Lincoln: University of Nebraska Press, 2016.

McCullough, David. *Truman*. New York: Simon and Schuster, 1991.

McWhirter, Cameron. *Red Summer: The Summer of 1919 and the Awakening of Black America*. New York: St. Martin's, 2011.

Mellinger, Gwyneth. "Saving the Republic: An Editor's Crusade Against Integration." *Journalism History* 42, no. 4 (Winter 2017): 212–24.

Mjagkij, Nina. *Light in the Darkness: African Americans and the YMCA, 1852–1946*. Lexington: University of Kentucky Press, 2003.

Moredock, Will. *Banana Republic: A Year in the Heart of Myrtle Beach*. Charleston SC: Frontline Press, 2003.

Morrison, Nan. *A History of the College of Charleston*. Columbia: University of South Carolina Press, 2011.

Morrison, Toni. *Beloved*. New York: Vintage Books, 1987.

Myrdal, Gunnar. *An American Dilemma: The Negro Problem and American Democracy*. New York: Harper and Row, 1962.

O'Neill, Stephen. "From the Shadows of Slavery: The Civil Rights Years in Charleston." PhD diss., University of Virginia, 1994.

Rampersad, Arnold. *Jackie Robinson*. New York: Knopf, 1997.

Raven, Margot Theis. Let Them Play. Ann Arbor MI: Sleeping Bear Press, 2005.

Reisler, James. *Black Writers/Black Baseball: An Anthology of Articles from Black Sportswriters Who Covered the Negro Leagues*. Jefferson NC: McFarland, 1994.

Ribowsky, Mark. *A Complete History of the Negro Leagues 1998–1955*. New York: Birch Lane Press, 1995.

Robbins, Becci. *Modjeska Monteith Simkins: A South Carolina Revolutionary*. Columbia: South Carolina Progressive Network, 2014.

Roberts, Gene, and Hank Klibanoff. *The Race Beat: The Press, the Civil Rights Struggle, and the Awakening of a Nation*. New York: Vintage, 2006.

Roberts, Randy. *Papa Jack: Jack Johnson and the Era of White Hopes*. London: Macmillan, 1983.

Robinson, Jackie. *I Never Had It Made*. Hopewell NJ: Ecco Press, 1995.

Sass, Herbert Ravenel. *Outspoken: 150 Years of the News and Courier*. Columbia: University of South Carolina Press, 1958.

Simkins, Francis Butler. *Pitchfork Ben Tillman, South Carolinian*. Baton Rouge: Louisiana State University, 2002.

Smith, Adam I. P. *The American Civil War*. New York: Palgrave Macmillan, 2007.

Stotz, Carl, and Kenneth D. Loss. *A Promise Kept: The Story of the Founding of Little League Baseball*. Jersey Shore PA: Zebrowski Historical Services, 1992.

Swanson, Ryan A. *When Baseball Went White: Reconstruction, Reconciliation, and Dreams of a National Pastime*. Lincoln: University of Nebraska Press, 2014.

Taeuber, Karl E., and Alma F. Taeuber. *Negroes in Cities: Residential Segregation and Neighborhood Change*. New York: Atheneum Press, 1965.

Timothy Tyson. *The Blood of Emmett Till*. New York: Simon and Schuster, 2017.

Tygiel, Jules. *Baseball's Great Experiment: Jackie Robinson and His Legacy*. New York: Oxford University Press, 1997.

Ulloa, Luis. "The Perfect Game." Graduate paper, Indiana University–Purdue University at Indianapolis, November 15, 2016.

Van Auken, Lance, and Robin Van Auken. *Play Ball! The Story of Little League Baseball*. University Park PA: Penn State University, 2001.

Wallenfeldt, Jeff. *Africa to America: From the Middle Passage through the 1930s*. New York: Rosen Publishing, 2010.

Wallis, Jim. *America's Original Sin: Racism, White Privilege, and the Bridge to a New America*. Ada MI: Brazos Press, 2017.

Washburn, Patrick, and Chris Lamb. *Sports Journalism: A History of Glory, Fame, and Technology*. Lincoln: University of Nebraska Press, 2020.

Whitehead, Colson. *The Nickel Boys*. New York: Random House, 2019.

Wiggins, David, and Patrick Miller. *The Unlevel Playing Field: A Documentary History of the African American Experience in Sport*. Urbana: University of Illinois Press, 2003.

Wilkerson, Isabel. *The Warmth of Other Suns: The Epic Story of America's Great Migration*. New York: Vintage, 2011.

Williams, Chad, Kidada Williams, and Keisha N. Blain, eds. *Charleston Syllabus: Readings on Race, Racism, and Racial Violence*. Athens: University of Georgia Press, 2016.

Williams, Juan. *Eyes on the Prize: America's Civil Rights Years, 1954–1965*. New York: Penguin Books, 1987.

——. *Thurgood Marshall: American Revolutionary*. New York: Times Books, 1998.

Williams, Kidada E. "Slavery, Survival, and Community Building." In *Charleston Syllabus: Readings on Race, Racism, and Racial Violence*, edited by Chad Williams, Kidada Williams, and Keisha N. Blaine. Athens: University of Georgia Press, 2016.

Williams, Susan Miller, and Stephen G. Hoffius. *Upheaval in Charleston: Earthquake and Murder on the Eve of Jim Crow*. Athens: University of Georgia Press, 2011.

Wood, Peter. *Black Majority: Negroes in Colonial South Carolina from 1670 through the Stono Rebellion*. New York: W. W. Norton, 1996.

Woodward, C. Vann. *The Strange Career of Jim Crow*. New York: Oxford University Press, 1974.

Yarborough, Tinsley E. *A Passion for Justice: J. Waties Waring and Civil Rights*. New York: Oxford University Press, 1987.

INDEX

Charleston SC (*cont.*)
recreational facilities in, 98–99; residents leaving, 16–17, 130; slavery in, 2–3, 11–14, 20, 248–50, 258–59; tourist economy in, 3, 222, 248, 249, 251–53; YMCA starting in, 104–5
Charleston Sunday News, 28
Charleston Welfare Council, 111
Chauvin, Derek, 274
Cheney, James, 208
Chicago Defender, 66, 172, 191, 202
Cincinnati Enquirer, 124
Cincinnati Red Stockings, 31
Citadel Green, 17, 18, 21, 23–24, 28, 51, 98
The Citadel Military Academy, 17, 23, 157, 217–21, 248
Citizens' Councils, 129–30, 134, 171, 172
City Island Ballpark (Jackie Robinson Ballpark), 160
Civil Rights Act (1964), 215, 255
civil rights movement, 1, 71, 196, 205, 206, 208, 213–14, 215–16, 221–22
Civil War, 3, 21, 24, 29, 34, 38, 75, 221
Clarendon County SC, 80–81, 84–85, 131
Clark, Mark, 218, 248
Clark, Septima Poinsette, 46, 47, 52, 54, 57–58, 59, 75, 209–10, 215, 218
Clark, Tom, 69
Cleaver, Eldridge, 230
Cleaver, Kathleen, 230
Clement, Arthur J. H., Jr., 52, 103, 209–10
Clement, Arthur J. H., Sr., 105
Clemson University, 40, 217
Clyburn, James, 221–22
coaches as positive influence, 106, 109, 189, 231, 232, 260
Coleman-Singleton, Sharonda, 265
Colhoun, John E., 17
College of Charleston, 55, 57, 217–18, 255–56, 257–58, 268
College Park (Charleston SC), 36, 120–21, 227
Columbia SC, 17, 40, 55
Columbia State, 73
Columbia TN, 64–65
Cominski, Mrs., 184
Cominski, Rich, 184
"Committee of 52," 133–34

communism, 94–95, 132, 134–35, 205
Compromise of 1850, 18
Confair Bottling, 91
Confederacy, 21, 28, 254
Confederate Defenders of Charleston memorial, 248
Confederate flag: on Dixie Youth uniforms, 10, 198, 225–26, 227, 271; Heritage Act protecting, 221, 223; and Little Boys League, 197; protests against, 222–23, 232–34; removal of, 234, 274; symbolic power of, 221–22, 256, 257, 266–67
Congressional Record, 204, 209, 245
Conroy, Pat: *The Lords of Discipline*, 219–20
Considine, Bob, 174
Constitution, 59, 78, 123–24, 125, 172
constitutional amendments, 21, 30, 37, 77, 85, 123–24
Cook, Bob, 166–67
Cooper, John Sherman, 210
Cooper River Parks and Playgrounds Commission, 99, 101, 138–39
cotton industry, 20, 108
Covid-19, 274
Cowart, Jerry, 161
Cox, Benjamin, 53
The Crisis, 45
Crow, E. R., 84

Dailey, Cleveland, 155–56, 161, 162, 164
Danny Jones Sportsmanship Award, 197
Darby, Joseph, 256, 267
Davis, J. Rolfe, 163
Davis, Lonnie, 159
Daytona Beach FL, 159–60
Debnam, W. E.: *Weep No More My Lady*, 132
DeCosta, Frank, Jr., 103
DeLaine, Joseph, 81, 84, 130
Delany, Martin R., 22
Delaware County Daily Times, 152
Delaware Township (NJ) team, 166–67, 176, 177, 183–84, 239
Democratic Party: and Blacks, 24, 38, 52; civil rights platform of, 71; after Civil War, 37; and elections, 39, 40, 55, 77–78, 117, 208; and Franklin D. Roosevelt, 83; segregationists leaving, 207

183–84; and racial discrimination, 1, 2; significance of, 245–46

Little League World Series (1957), 186

Little League World Series (1958), 186

Little League World Series (2002), 10, 239–41

Little League World Series (2005), 244

Little Red Book (Mao), 230–31

Little Rock Central High School, and "Little Rock Nine," 206

Livingston, Tesa, 100, 102, 144

Locke, Hugh, 142–43

Loeb, William, 207

Long, Eliot, 62

Long, Kenny, 64

Long Time Coming (documentary), 155, 156

Looby, Alexander, 65

Look, 193

The Lords of Discipline (Conroy), 219–20

Los Angeles Angels, 186

Los Angeles Times, 199

"Lost Cause" movement, 37–38, 254

Louis, Joe, 68, 117

Louisiana, 39

Lubelsky, Max, 44

Lundquist, Carl, 184

Lundy, Jack, 90

Lundy Construction, 89

Lundy Lumber Company, 88, 89, 90

Lycoming College, 169, 178, 180

Lycoming Dairy Farms, 89

lynchings, 39–40, 41, 42, 44–45, 50, 54, 68, 70–71, 157–58, 191–92

Macias, Angel, 186

Mack, Connie, 92

Mack, John, 173

Maiz, José "Pepe," 186

Major, Leroy: in adult life, 232, 276; as baseball player, 119; and district tournament, 145; height of, 138; and Little League World Series, 141, 173, 179, 180–81, 183, 239–40, 243–44; racial awareness of, 113, 115, 273; recognition for, 242

Major Leagues, 31, 92, 118–19, 121, 174, 175, 195, 227

Malcom, Dorothy, 67

Malcom, Roger, 67

Manchester Union-Leader, 207

Manifesto of Southern Rights, 133–34

Manigault family, 251, 270

mansions, 248, 250, 251

Mao, Chairman: Little Red Book, 230–31

Marianna FL, 158–59, 162

marriage, interracial, 131, 142–43, 202–3

Marshall, George C., 174

Marshall, Thurgood, 55, 65, 76–77, 81–82, 84–85

Martin, Charles H., 142

Martin, J. Robert, Jr., 216

Martin, Nathaniel M., 105

Martin, Trayvon, 160

Masthead, 201

Maybank, Burnet, 76, 125

Mays, Willie, 119

McCain, Cindy, 209

McCain, Franklin, 211

McCain, John, 209

McCarthy, Joseph, 95

McConnell, Glenn, 222–23, 248, 256–58

McCray, John, 52, 54–55, 57, 66, 83–84

McCullough, David, 70

McDougald, Gil, 195

McDowell, Elsa, 235–36

McFadden, Sam, 159

McFall, John, 54, 55, 103

McGovern, Peter: circumstances surrounding, 143, 144, 147; in conflict with associates, 94, 149, 198–99; criticism of, 150, 152–53, 154; decisions of, 5–6, 8, 145, 148, 162, 169, 242–43; on Little League Baseball, 97, 196; at Little League World Series, 180

McKaine, Osceola F., 54

McKinley, William, 41–42

McLeod Plantation, 251–52

McNair, Robert, 215, 216

McNeil, Joseph, 211

Medical College Hospital, 216

Medical University of South Carolina Hospital, 236

Memorial Park (Philadelphia PA), 88, 89, 91

memorials: to African American culture, 247; to Confederacy, 155, 248, 252, 267; laws about, 221, 223; personal, 237; and slavery, 248; to Wade Hampton III, 254; to white supremacy, 18. *See also* Calhoun Memorial

114–16; in schools, challenged, 6–7, 42, 52, 81–82, 85, 123–24, 130–31, 132; in schools, maintained, 85, 131, 212, 218–19, 268; support for, 3–4, 128–30, 134–35, 142–43, 146, 196–97, 201–5, 207, 209; as threat to South, 1; in transportation, 9, 42–43, 194

segregationists, 5, 54, 110, 128–29, 131, 142–43, 207, 210

Senterfitt, Donald T., 163

"separate but equal" concept, 42, 53, 60, 82, 101, 107–8, 123–24, 125–26

sexual assault, 12, 19–20

Shea, Frank, 96

Shelton, Ike, 172

Shepherd, Polly, 265

Shull, Lynwood, 62–63, 67, 69–70, 72, 73

Silverstein, Howard, 226–27, 233

Simkins, Modjeska Monteith, 54, 57

Simmons, Daniel L., Sr., 265

Simple Justice (Kluger), 80, 124

Singleton, Ben, 137, 170, 173, 177–78, 184, 232, 234

Singleton, Maurice, 170, 173, 182, 184, 188, 234, 242

sit-down strikes, 211–12, 213–14, 215

Sitton, Claude, 212

Slager, Michael, 263, 266

slave code, 14, 15, 22

slavery: abolition of, 21–22, 24, 37; acknowledgment of, 247–49; defenders of, 18–19; domestic labor compared to, 113; economics of, 13, 20, 249, 250, 258–59; in Exodus, 115; legacy of, 268; opposition to, 16. *See also* Blacks; enslaved people

Slimm, Bill, 167

Smalls, Robert, 21, 22

Smith, Ellison D. "Cotton Ed," 41, 76

Smith, Lamar, 172, 194

Smith, Wendell, 160

Smith v. Allwright, 77

South: civil rights actions in, 211–13; economic concerns of, 17–18, 19, 20; post–Civil War politics in, 38–39; segregation in, 6, 112–13, 134–35, 142–43, 165, 197, 201–4, 242–43; self-protective attitude of, 1–2, 124, 125, 206; white supremacy in, 108, 129; William F. Buckley defending, 207

South Carolina: Black population of, 20; Blacks in legislature of, 37; Confederate symbols in, 222, 266–67, 274; desegregation in schools of, 216–17; elections in, 39, 71, 208–9; extradition orders from, 130; hangings in, 44; in Isaac Woodard case, 67, 69–70; laws of, 17, 58, 59, 77–78, 128, 141, 263; racist legacy of, 40–41, 133–34; reputation of, 12, 80; secession of, 20–21; segregation in, 6, 56, 98, 110; slavery in, 13–14, 16, 20; violence in, 37–38; voting rights in, 40, 59; women's safety in, 270

South Carolina Military Academy, 218

South Carolina Recreation Society, 145–46

South Carolina State University, 52, 56

Southern Charm (television show), 254

Southern Christian Leadership Council, 215

Southern League, 31

Southern Manifesto, 206

Southern Strategy, 207

Southwest DeKalb High School, 188–89

Spalding (company), 93

Spalding, Albert G., 28, 34

Speak Now Against the Day (J. Egerton), 68

Spink, J. G. Taylor, 175

Sporting News, 31, 175

sports, benefits of playing, 53, 100, 106, 109, 246

Sports Illustrated, 241–42, 273

Stanford, Nicholas. *See* Briggs, John W.

states' rights, 208

States' Rights Democrats (Dixiecrats), 71, 208

statues, 18, 30, 40, 51, 154, 155, 259, 274. *See also* Calhoun Memorial; memorials

Steele, Michael, 267

Sterling, Tommy, 163

Stevenson, Gladys, 64

Stevenson, James, 64

Stinney, George, Jr., 80–81, 265, 270

Stodghill, Ron, 3

Stoney, Paul, 103–4, 109

Stono Rebellion, 14, 259

Stotz, Carl: background of, 87; in conflict with associates, 93–94, 198–99; and Cy Young, 92, 174; ideas of, 88, 90; Little League developed by, 88–90, 91–93, 101; work of, 88, 90

228; on "separate but equal" concept, 125; threats against, 17, 75, 79–80; and voting rights cases, 78–79

Waring, Thomas (Tom Waring's father), 75, 127

Waring, Tom: on *Brown*, 125, 128–29; character of, 209–10, 269–70; on Emmett Till murder, 192–93; influences on, 127–28; on J. Waties Waring, 126; legacy of, 217; and Little League Baseball, 6, 143–44, 148–49, 151; on NAACP, 146–47, 192–93; as newspaper editor, 116–17; as segregationist, 3, 5, 7, 85, 131–34, 202–7; and White Citizens' Councils, 129–30; as white supremacist, 3, 127, 129; work history of, 127

Warren, Earl, 123

The Wars of Reconstruction (D. Egerton), 37

Washington, Booker T., 50, 53

Washington, Kenny, 117

Washington, Maurice, 227

Washington, Nathaniel, 106

Washington Chronicle, 30

Washington Cornet Band, 23, 27

Washington DC, 29, 104

Washington Nationals, 174, 245

Washington Olympics, 29

Washington Post, 124–25

Washington Senators, 174, 175

Washington Tribune, 175

We Are Charleston (Frazier, Powers, and Wentworth), 265

Weaver, Maurice, 65

Weeks, A. O., 132

Weep No More My Lady (Debnam), 132

Welles, Orson, 66–67, 68, 70

Wells, A. H. "Cappy," 95

Wells-Barnett, Ida B., 45

Wentworth, Marjory: *We Are Charleston*, 265

Werner, Ludlow, 66, 118

"What Happens to a Dream Deferred?" (Hughes), 235

White, Arnold, 162

White, Walter, 54, 66, 68, 69, 83, 160

White Citizens' Councils, 129–30, 134, 171, 172

Whitehead, Colson: *The Nickel Boys*, 159

White House Boys, 159

whites: and accommodationists, 59; advantages for, 107–9, 111–15, 155–56, 161, 250, 268, 274; Americanism defined by, 33; anti-slavery, 16–17; Black reality invisible to, 116, 157; and Blacks in church, 14–15; as civil rights activists, 77; jobs for, 46; in justice system, 81, 193–94; on J. Waties Waring, 79; in law enforcement, 62, 63–65, 156, 263–64; in military, 230; political control by, 267; and press, 25–26, 117–18; Reconstruction resisted by, 37–38, 40–41; in response to protests, 212; and school system, 55–58, 81, 84–85, 131; self-delusion by, 207, 269; as slave owners, 13; social expectations for, 43; violence by, 38, 41–42, 44–45, 46–47, 67–68, 70–71, 78, 157–59, 172; voter suppression by, 30

whites, in baseball environment: Black players scouted by, 141–42; with Blacks, 28–29, 97–98, 159–60, 164–65, 166–68, 176; Blacks exploited by, 36; in Charleston riot, 25–27; compared to Blacks, 35; parental influence on, 151–54; press on, 148–49; separate from Blacks, 29–30, 98, 145–47, 174–75, 176–77, 189–90, 275–76; and supremacist symbols, 228–30

white supremacy: in Charleston SC, 3; education influenced by, 217–18; and judicial opinions, 126; memorials celebrating, 18; in politics, 40, 77–78; resistance to, 213, 230, 254; supporters of, 83, 127, 129, 192, 203–4, 269; symbols of, 221–22, 225, 267; and violence, 191–92, 260

Wiedenhafer, Jim, 183

Wilkes' Spirit of the Times, 26

Wilkins, Roger, 118

Wilkins, Roy, 117–18, 191–92

Wilkinson, Francis L., 49

Wilkinson, J. Harvie, III, 124

Will, George, 245

William "Buck" Godfrey Stadium, 189

Williams, Bob, 149

Williams, Juan, 65

Williams, Ted, 121

Williams, Walter, 249

Williamsport Grays (baseball team), 87, 91